Militant Around the Clock?

Protest, Culture and Society

General editors:
Kathrin Fahlenbrach, Institute for Media and Communication, University of Hamburg
Martin Klimke, New York University Abu Dhabi
Joachim Scharloth, Technische Universität Dresden, Germany

Protest movements have been recognized as significant contributors to processes of political participation and transformations of culture and value systems, as well as to the development of both a national and transnational civil society.

This series brings together the various innovative approaches to phenomena of social change, protest and dissent which have emerged in recent years, from an interdisciplinary perspective. It contextualizes social protest and cultures of dissent in larger political processes and socio-cultural transformations by examining the influence of historical trajectories and the response of various segments of society, political and legal institutions on a national and international level. In doing so, the series offers a more comprehensive and multi-dimensional view of historical and cultural change in the twentieth and twenty-first century.

Militant Around the Clock?

Left-Wing Youth Politics, Leisure, and Sexuality in Post-Dictatorship Greece, 1974–1981

By

Nikolaos Papadogiannis

berghahn

NEW YORK · OXFORD

www.berghahnbooks.com

First published in 2015 by
Berghahn Books
www.berghahnbooks.com

Library of Congress Cataloging-in-Publication Data
Papadogiannis, Nikolaos.
   Militant around the clock? left-wing youth politics, leisure, and sexuality in
post-dictatorship Greece, 1974-1981 / by Nikolaos Papadogiannis.
      pages cm
   Includes bibliographical references.
   ISBN 978-1-78238-644-5 (hbk)—ISBN 978-1-78920-074-4 (pbk)—ISBN
978-1-78238-645-2 (ebook)
   1. Youth—Political activity—Greece—History—20th century. 2. New Left—
Greece—History—20th century. 3. Political activists—Greece—History—20th
century. 4. Youth—Greece—Social conditions—20th century. 5. Youth—Sexual behavior—Greece—History—20th century. 6. Leisure—Political aspects—
Greece—History—20th century. 7. Political culture—Greece—History—20th
century. 8. Social change—Greece—History—20th century. 9. Greece—Politics and government—1974- 10. Greece—Social conditions—20th century.
I. Title.
   HQ799.G9P365 2015
   320.40835—dc23
                                                                    2014033558

British Library Cataloguing in Publication Data

A catalogue record for this book is available from the British Library

ISBN: 978-1-78238-644-5 hardback
ISBN: 978-1-78920-074-4 paperback
ISBN: 978-1-78238-645-2 ebook

Contents

Figures and Tables

Figures

Tables

Acknowledgments

I owe an enormous intellectual debt to Adam Tooze, Christopher Clark, Efi Avdela, Mark Mazower, Philip Carabott, and Frank Trentmann, who have read earlier versions of this monograph and have repeatedly tolerated my interruptions to their own work. I am really fortunate and honored to have received their detailed and thoughtful evaluation.

I would also like to thank the publisher, Marion Berghahn, as well as the editors of the book series *Protest, Culture and Society*—Martin Klimke, Kathrin Fahlenbrach, and Joachim Scharloth—for their interest in my research and their relentless and multifaceted support throughout the process of the preparation of this monograph. Their feedback, along with the remarks of the three anonymous reviewers, has been invaluable.

It would certainly be an omission not to extend my gratitude to a number of scholars who have commented impeccably on parts of the book and/ or have discussed ideas of mine that have seen print in this monograph. I would like to thank Thomas Mergel, who hosted me in 2012–2013 at the Humboldt-University of Berlin as an Alexander von Humboldt Foundation Postdoctoral Fellow, as well as Belinda Davis, Victoria de Grazia, Mary Nolan, and Neni Panourgia, whom I met, while being a Visiting Fellow at Columbia University in New York, hosted by Mark Mazower. Moreover, I have particularly benefited from the detailed comments and the encouragement I have received from Giorgos Agelopoulos, Eirini Avramopoulou, Alexandra Bakalaki, Maude Bracke, Timothy Brown, Anna Davin, Anta Dialla, Richard Evans, Dora Giannaki, Sebastian Gehrig, Vasilis Gounaris, Hannes Grandits, Pothiti Hantzaroula, Loukis Hassiotis, Jasper Heinzen, David Holton, Gerd-Rainer Horn, Leonidas Karakatsanis, Kostis Kornetis, Eirini Kotsovili, Pantelis Lekkas, Antonis Liakos, Peter Mandler, Pavlos Pantazis, Dimitris Papanikolaou, Paris Papamichos-Chronakis, Evthymios Papataxiarchis, Miltos Pechlivanos, Nikos Rotzokos, Detlef Siegfried, Eleonora Skouteri, Giannis Stavrakakis, Ruža Fotuadis, Riki van Boeschoten, Polymeris Voglis, Giannis Voulgaris, Bernd Weisbrod, Nassia Yakovaki, Kostas Yannakopoulos, Giannis Yannitsiotis and Panagiotis Zestanakis. I am indebted to all of them. I would certainly like to thank my students at the University of Cambridge, Humboldt University of Berlin, and Free University of Berlin for their inspiring questions.

I would like to offer my appreciation to library and archival staff, especially to Vangelis Karamanolakis of the ASKI Archives, Christos Mais of the archive of the KKE(m-l) and Fanis Paris of the Library of the Communist Party of Greece in Athens. I am also grateful to Areti Anastasiadou, Dimitris Aravantinos, Dimitris Dimitriadis, Giannis Kallipolitis, Aimilia Karali, Giorgos Karoubis, Sifis Kotsantis, Kostas Livieratos, Aris Marakopoulos, Maria Repousi, Nikos Samanidis, Donald Sassoon, Roura Sifnaiou, and Niki Simou for having offered me access to their private collections. I would like to thank Christos Bistis, Dimitris Chatzisokratis, Giorgos Karabelias, Dimitris Psarras, and Grigoris Vallianatos for having granted me permission to reproduce images of the period. Moreover, I am grateful to Damian Mac Con Uladh and Mollie Firestone for having carefully edited and proofread my book. It would be an omission not to thank IKY, the Greek State Scholarship Foundation, for funding my research in the period from 2006 to 2009. Without their financial support, the completion of this work would have not been possible.

I would also like to mention that previous, substantially different versions of the section "Avid cinephiles" as well as of "'Healthy' Sex, 'Unhealthy Sex'" of chapter 3 have been published in Papadogiannis, "Between Angelopoulos and *The Battleship Potemkin*: Cinema and the Making of Young Communists in Greece in the Initial Post-dictatorship Period (1974-1981)." *European History Quarterly* (Sage Publications) 42, no. 2 (2012): pp. 286–308 and Nikolaos Papadogiannis, "Confronting 'Imperialism' and 'Loneliness: Sexual and Gender Relations Among Young Communists in Greece, 1974–1981." *Journal of Modern Greek Studies* (The Johns Hopkins University Press) 29, no. 2 (2011): pp. 219–50, respectively. Moreover, substantially different versions of the first two sections of chapter 6 have been published in Nikolaos Papadogiannis, "Greek Communist Youth Identities and Rock Music in the late 1970s." In *Between the Avant Garde and the Everyday: Subversive Politics in Europe from 1957 to the Present,* ed. Timothy Brown and Lorena Anton, pp. 77–91. New York, Berghahn Books 2011; Nikolaos Papadogiannis, "Red and Purple? Feminism and young Greek Eurocommunists in the 1970s." *European Review of History—Revue européenne d'histoire* (Routledge: Taylor and Francis Group) 22, no.1 (2015):pp. 16–40; and Papadogiannis, "Confronting 'Imperialism' and 'Loneliness,'" pp. 219–50.

Finally, I would like to express my gratitude toward Koula Adaloglou, Elma Charalampidou, and Giannis Papadogiannis, who have rendered this journey far less daunting through their endless affection and enduring support. This book is dedicated to them.

Abbreviations

AAEPS	Aristera Antisynainetika Enotika Psifodeltia, Left Anti-Compromise Unity Lists
AASPE	Antifasistiki Antiimperialistiki Spoudastiki Parataxi Elladas, Antifascist Anti-imperialist Student Movement in Greece
AEPS	Aristera Enotika Psifodeltia, Left Unity Lists
ASF-S	Aristeres Syspeiroseis Foititon-Spoudaston, Left Convergence of University and Higher Technical School Students
DAP-NDFK	Dimokratiki Ananeotiki Protoporia-Nea Dimokratiki Foititiki Kinisi, Democratic Renewal Vanguard-New Democratic Student Movement
DIMAK	Dimokratiki Mathitiki Kinisi, Democratic Pupils' Movement
DKN	Dimokratikes Kiniseis Neon, Democratic Youth Movements
DNL	Dimokratiki Neolaia Lambraki, Democratic Youth Lambrakis
EAM	Ethniko Apeleytherotiko Metopo, National Liberation Front
EDA	Eniaia Dimokratiki Aristera, United Democratic Left
EEC	European Economic Community
EFEE	Ethniki Foititiki Enosi Ellados, National Student Union of Greece
EOT	Ellinikos Organismos Tourismou, Greek Tourist Organization
EPON	Eniaia Panelladiki Organosi Neon, United Panhellenic Organization of Youth
KKE	Kommounistiko Komma Elladas, Communist Party of Greece
KKE Es	Kommounistiko Komma Elladas Esoterikou, Communist Party of the Interior

KKE (m–l)	Kommounistiko Komma Elladas (marxistiko-leninistiko), Communist Party of Greece (Marxist-Leninist)
KNE	Kommounistiki Neolaia Elladas, Communist Youth of Greece
MODNE	Mathitiki Organosi Dimokratikis Neolaias Elladas, Pupils' Organization of the Democratic Youth in Greece
NEK	Neos Ellinikos Kinimatografos, New Greek Cinema
OKNE	Omospondia Kommounistikon Neolaion Elladas, Federation of Communist Youths in Greece
ONNED	Organosi Neon Neas Dimokratias, New Democracy Youth Organization
OPA	Organosi gia mia Proletariaki Aristera, Organization for a Proletarian Left
PAK	Panellinio Apeleytherotiko Kinima, Panhellenic Liberation Movement
PAPOK	Panellinia Politistiki Kinisi, Panhellenic Cultural Movement
PASOK	Panellinio Sosialistiko Kinima, Panhellenic Socialist Movement
PASP	Panellinia Agonistiki Spoudastiki Parataxi, Panhellenic Militant Student Organization
PCE	Partido Comunista de España, Communist Party of Spain
PCI	Partito Comunista Italiano, Italian Communist Party
PKS	Proodeytikes Kiniseis Synergasias, Progressive Allied Movements
PMSP	Proodeytiki Mathitiki Syndikalistiki Parataxi, Progressive Pupils' Unionist Movement
PPSP	Proodeytiki Panspoudastiki Syndikalistiki Parataxi, Progressive All-Students' Unionist Movement
PSK	Panspoudastiki Syndikalistiki Kinisi, All-Students' Unionist Movement
RF	Rigas Feraios

Transliteration

Greek Latin

Greek	Latin
α	a
β	v
γ	g
δ	d
ε	e
ζ	z
η	i
θ	th
ι	i
κ	k
λ	l
μ	m
ν	n
ξ	x
ο	o
π	p
ρ	r
σ	s
τ	t
υ	y
φ	f
χ	ch or h
ψ	ps
ω	o
αυ	av or ay, depending on pronunciation

Introduction

The Post-Dictatorship Years From the Perspective of Leisure and Sexuality

Shortly after the collapse of Greece's dictatorial regime in July 1974, a significant segment of the Greek youth experienced a political fever. Intense debates in student assemblies and Party[1] congresses as well as the distribution of flyers at factory gates and university amphitheaters were integral pieces of this puzzle. Youth politics, however, did not revolve solely around manifestos and speeches at that point. According to H.Z., who was a university student in Salonica and affiliated with a Communist youth organization in the aftermath of the dictatorship, leisure featured prominently and served as a means of demarcating left-wingers. He transparently narrated that "watching progressive, high quality films, reading classics, these were among the three or four habits that distinguished [left-wing] people," adding that "we sang a lot, even with our friends in the streets" (H.Z., Interview). In general, the left-wingers under study did not construe "politics" in the narrow sense, namely confined to elections and protest, but formulated diverse ways in which they linked these with the behavior patterns they endorsed.[2]

Assigning weight to leisure was not specific to young Greek left-wingers in the 1970s, however. Several social and political actors in the "West," at least since the Industrial Revolution, have construed leisure as a realm where "the dominant values" of a particular society are "opposed or reinforced."[3] Relevant activities, such as visiting spas, lying on the seaside, or patronizing an opera house have functioned as a testing ground for a wide array of norms, which encompass sexual patterns, gender and class relations, as well as national identities.[4] The spread of mass consumption and the growing internationalization of leisure through developments in the media, communications, and transport in post–World War II Western Europe have further fuelled reflection on leisure and its potential impact on cultural norms.[5] Left-wingers of all stripes have been involved in relevant debates, endorsing, however, differing viewpoints. Some revisionist members of the British Labor Party, such as Tony Crosland and Roy Jenkins, championed the "expansion of consumption" in post–World War II Britain and placed a premium on the spread of styles of living grounded on affluence.[6] From the late 1950s onward in West Germany, the Social Democratic Party of Germany joined its political opponent, the Christian Democratic Union, in promoting a "liberal consensus" centering on "free consumer choice," which also included a tolerant attitude toward cultural imports that reshaped the leisure landscape of the Federal Republic at that point.[7] Communists in Western Europe, such as in Italy, also began to wrestle with the challenge that the spread of mass consumption and its impact on youth leisure posed to their cultural politics. However, according to historian Stephen Gundle, the members of the main Italian Communist Party, despite the "flexibility" that they demonstrated, "never really grasped the appeal of either mass culture or the consumer society."[8]

The growing internationalization of leisure, which had also reached Greece in the 1960s, attracted extensive attention by the Greek Left as well already during that decade in the framework of its cultural politics. The establishment of the authoritarian regime, which ruled from 1967 to 1974, brought such left-wing initiatives to an abrupt end. However, youth involvement in left-wing politics, on the rise since the final years of the dictatorship, escalated after the collapse of the authoritarian regime. This study investigates the relationship between leisure and left-wing youth politics in the first post-dictatorship years, namely until the formation of the government in 1981. Since young left-wingers in the 1950s and 1960s construed leisure as interconnected with sexuality, it also surveys whether and the extent to which the Socialist and Communist youth linked both with politics in the mid-to-late 1970s. Moreover, it examines how the interaction of youth leisure and sexuality with the intensifying youth politicization was mediated by the conceptualizations of the "Greek nation" that were espoused by young Communists and Socialists; it considers whether and how the concepts of "tradition," "modernity," "Western," "European," and "American" were employed by left-wing youth organizations, in their pursuit of constructing a normative framework regulating the politicization of leisure and sexuality.[9] The volume probes continuities and ruptures between the 1960s and the 1970s, scrutinizing two levels: the cultural politics of the left-wing youth organizations in Greece in that period as well the leisure and sexual practices of their cadres, members, and sympathizers, analyzing the extent to which the latter were in accordance with official guidelines, set down by the Party leaderships. In dealing with those issues, it seeks to provide a nuanced understanding of the first era of postauthoritarian transformation in Greece and how this period was tracked, but, also, to an extent shaped by left-wing youth and cultural politics.

In order to illuminate such endeavors, this volume critically interrogates approaches that define leisure negatively as "non-obligated" time, namely as an escape from work as well as other categories of experience, such as work, education, and politics.[10] Similarly, it does not fully endorse the argument of historian Peter Borsay that leisure "can embrace any experience which is 'other' than that conceived of as normal" and the "real world."[11] By contrast, it seems more promising as a point of departure to probe the issue of whether and the extent to which those domains are interrelated in the rhetoric and practice in the modern world. Actually, advocates of the Left in contemporary Greece have openly and consistently striven to discern leisure patterns that would be conducive to ideological engagement. Their attitude resembled what historian Raphael Samuel mentioned in his account of the "Lost World of British Communism," namely that "what we called Marxism … claimed jurisdiction over every dimension of experience, every department of social life."[12] Rather than being treated as synonymous with "freedom" from routine and time apart, its interconnections with politics, sexuality, and gender, as appeared in the rhetoric and practice of those militants,[13] need to be taken seriously into account.

My research centers on the main Socialist and Communist youth organizations in Greece in the period from 1974 to 1981, since, as especially chapter two of this book shows, right-wing youth groups did not actively engage in the shaping of leisure activities of their members in that country at that point. Moreover, while other groups, such as the scouts, sought to influence the behavior of youngsters in Greece and while it is certainly worthwhile to examine whether these groups regarded this as a political act, the case of the Left is distinct due to the fact that it aimed to stir certain forms of mass mobilization, namely various types of protest, also by encouraging specific attitudes towards leisure and sexuality. Communist organizations became legal in 1974 after twenty-seven years of clandestinity. Two very influential ones were the Communist Youth of Greece (KNE) and Rigas Feraios (RF).[14] The former, established in 1968, was affiliated with the Communist Party of Greece (KKE), whereas the latter, also created in 1968, was affiliated with the Communist Party of the Interior (KKE Es.); the KKE and KKE Es. had split in the same year.[15] The orientation of the KNE was pro-Soviet, while RF was Eurocommunist.[16] Especially since the Soviet invasion of Czechoslovakia in 1968, but mostly in the mid–1970s, a number of Communist parties in Western Europe, such as the Spanish and the Italian, but also in other continents, as the case of the Australian Communist Party shows, became less and less influenced by the Soviet regime and embraced the doctrine of Eurocommunism. The student groups, whose members were aligned with or leaning toward the KNE and RF were the PSK (Panspoudastiki Syndikalistiki Kinisi, All-Students' Unionist Movement) and the DA-DE (Dimokratikos Agonas-Dimokratiki Enotita, Democratic Union-Democratic Struggle), respectively; the high-school groups were called the MODNE (Mathitiki Organosi Dimokratikis Neolaias Elladas, Pupils' Organization of the Democratic Youth in Greece) and the DIMAK (Dimokratiki Mathitiki Kinisi, Democratic Pupils' Movement), respectively.

Less popular, but still ideologically influential, were the Maoist organizations. The main Maoist (or Marxist-Leninist, as they described themselves) student and pupil groups were the PPSP (Proodeytiki Panspoudastiki Syndikalistiki Parataxi, Progressive All-Students' Unionist Movement) and the PMSP (Proodeytiki Mathitiki Syndikalistiki Parataxi, Progressive Pupils' Unionist Movement), which were aligned with the OMLE (Organosi Marxiston-Leniniston Elladas, Organization of Marxist-Leninists of Greece), as well as the AASPE (Antifasistiki Antiimperialistiki Spoudastiki Parataxi Elladas, Anti-fascist Anti-imperialist Student Movement of Greece) and the AAMPE (Antifasistiki Antiimperialistiki Mathitiki Parataxi Elladas, Anti-fascist Anti-imperialist Pupils' Movement of Greece), which were affiliated with the EKKE (Epanastatiko Kommounistiko Kinima Elladas, Revolutionary Communist Movement of Greece). The EKKE had been created in March 1970 by a group of Greek students based in West Berlin and appeared in Greece in 1972. Communists who endorsed China as a role model after the Chinese-Soviet split in the early 1960s founded the OMLE in the mid–1960s in Greece; similarly, PPSP was established in 1966. Their student groups were visible in student assemblies and garnered a significant percentage of votes in student elections in the mid–1970s, but fell into disarray, as did their Parties, in the late 1970s, mainly due to escalating internal strife over developments in post-Mao China. The EKKE, in tune with the party line of the Communist Party of China, chastised the Cultural Revolution. However, its biggest segment disagreed with its leadership and gradually abandoned it, accusing it of having become a "mouthpiece" of a Party that no longer represented Marxist-Leninist values. Meanwhile, the OMLE split in 1976 into the KKE(m-l) and M-L KKE. The former denounced the new leadership of the Communist Party of China as a "revisionist clique," as terrorism studies expert George Kassimeris mentions, while the latter continued to view the Chinese regime favorably.[17] Trotskyite Parties also operated in the 1970s Greece. The main ones were the EDE (Ergatiki Diethnistiki Enosi, Workers' Internationalist Union) and the OKDE (Organosi Kommouniston Diethniston Elladas, Communist Organization of Greek Internationalists). However, they failed to gain significant support from Greek youngsters.

Beyond the Communist Left, the Youth of PASOK (Panellinio Sosialistiko Kinima, Panhellenic Socialist Movement), established alongside PASOK in 1974, was also quite influential. PASOK and its Youth attracted many members of the PAK (Panellinio Apeleytherotiko Kinima, Panhellenic Liberation Movement), founded in 1968, which rallied centrist and radical left-wing militants. The members of the Youth of PASOK were entitled to participate simultaneously in the activities of the Party. Its student organization, established in 1975, was the PASP (Panellinia Agonistiki Spoudastiki Parataxi, Panhellenic Militant Student Organization), while its high-school group was the PAMK (Panellinia Agonistiki Mathitiki Kinisi, Panhellenic Militant Pupils' Movement). The PASP has been designated to function autonomously from the Youth of PASOK. The members of the former were allowed, but not obliged, to be aligned with PASOK and its Youth. Socialist groups endorsed dependency theories that juxtaposed the industrialized "North" with the dependent "South," situating Greece in the latter, as analyzed in more detail in chapter two.

After 1978, all left-wing youth organizations suffered from a series of splinters, which resulted in the formation of a fluid network of autonomous left-wingers, mainly students, who named themselves Choros (Space).[18] Besides B Panelladiki, which split from RF in 1978, another constituent of Choros was the radical left-wing OPA (Organosi gia mia Proletariaki Aristera, Organization for a Proletarian Left). In addition, ex-members of the Maoist groups, the KNE, and the Youth of PASOK also joined. Most, though not all of them, described themselves as Communists. Choros never acquired a clear organizational structure, but the common points of the people who participated in it were the loud critique of centralized Party structures—which were blamed for fostering bureaucratic relations—the rejection of the *entatikopoiisi* (intensification) of university studies, as well as the challenging of dominant social norms, especially in the domain of sexuality.[19]

At the opposite end of the political spectrum, Center-Right or right-wing youth organizations failed to gain momentum. ONNED (Organosi Neon Neas Dimokratias, New Democracy Youth Organization), the youth group of the governing Center-Right Party, did not attract substantial support at that point, at least in comparison with the Party it was aligned with. The same was true of Centre-Right student groups, which merged in 1976 and created DAP-NDFK (Dimokratiki Ananeotiki Protoporia-Nea Dimokratiki Foititiki Kinisi, Democratic Renewal Vanguard-New Democratic Student Movement). Moreover, its activity in student assemblies and cultural societies during those years was rather limited, as shown in chapter two in more detail. It became influential, mainly among university students, only after the election of PASOK to power in 1981.[20] In addition, extreme rightist and fascist youth groups remained marginal during those years.

A Social-Cultural History of the Left-Wing Youth

In wrestling with the leisure pursuits and sexual practices of young left-wingers, this book offers a social/cultural history of politics, premised on the concept of "culture." Echoing novelist and academic Raymond Williams, I treat "culture" as "ordinary," connected with lived experience. The book also draws upon an issue that arises in Williams's work, namely the relationship between "culture" as a "whole way of life" and forms of signification, such as films, theatre plays and songs.[21] As a swelling chorus of scholars, such as historian Thomas Mergel and anthropologist David Kertzer, has aptly remarked, symbols and rituals are not merely "accessories," but played a preponderant role in the formation of political subjects.[22]

Drawing on the historiography of emotions, the social/cultural history of politics embraced in this work aims to call into question one factor that has been depicted as distinguishing the "Old," "New," and "Far Left" in the case of Greece in the 1970s:[23] British historian, playwright, and journalist David Caute argues that, in general, membership of the so-called "Old Left" was "dull," confined to "occasional demos, [and] sending small cheques to good causes."[24] However, young Greek left-wingers of all directions construed their political activity as an intensely emotional experience. They came into dialogue with diffuse descriptions of these emotions in Greek society and in the broader European context.

In approaching emotions, this work draws particularly on the argument put forth by historians Peter and Carol Stearns, who claim that researchers should differentiate between "the attitudes or standards that a society, or a definable group within a society, maintains toward basic emotions and their appropriate expression," which they call "emotionology," and the actual emotions of the subjects they study. They aptly remark, however, that "emotionology" and "emotions" interact: the former create emotional standards, which affect the latter.[25] Similarly, the official texts of Greek left-wing youth groups often contained comments on the emotions that activism was expected to instill in their members, statements which tracked and helped shape the actual emotions of young Communists and Socialists in Greece. Either "disciplined" or "spontaneous," militancy won hearts and minds.

In addition, this study indicates internal variations and underlines the interaction between the groups under examination. A recent book that has particularly propelled the heterogeneity of Communist organizations into the limelight is entitled *Le Siècle des Communismes*. This book was a response to the *Livre noire du Communisme,* which linked this ideology in a one-dimensional fashion to coercion and violence.[26] By contrast, *Le Siècle des Communismes* offers a significantly more nuanced understanding of communism. Its authors portray communism as a "plural" phenomenon: it is argued that people joined a Communist organization for a wide range of reasons and experienced their membership in diverse ways, depending on factors such as social class and gender.[27] This is certainly true for Greek left-wingers of all stripes in the 1970s.

Defining "Youth": Moving Beyond "Generation"

Not only left-wing militancy, but also "youth" is a culturally provincial category, according to historian Oded Heilbronner. Heilbronner argues that it is based on particular symbols and practices and does not remain static over time and in different social and cultural contexts. Prior to the nineteenth century, "'youth' was distinguished by its rites and rituals. In the modern era, … it was distinguished mainly by leisure, but also by secondary education and adolescent norms and behaviour."[28]

The twentieth century witnessed the emergence of what numerous historians and sociologists have labeled "youth culture."[29] According to historians Axel Schildt and Detlef Siegfried, it was "primarily defined by the young age of its proponents and by their particular tastes in music, fashion, hairstyles, political practices etc."[30] Impelling the momentum for its appearance was the increasing capacity of the youth to purchase consumer goods, which rendered them key players in the dawning era of mass consumption.[31] Concomitantly, a consumer market grew, which particularly targeted the youth. The creation of the miniskirt by the British fashion icon Mary Quant, in 1964, is perhaps one of the most striking success stories of that market that addressed the youth. Siegfried and Schildt claim that youth culture appeared in the post–World War II period, albeit not simultaneously throughout Western Europe: it first emerged in Scandinavian countries as well as in Western European countries, such as France and West Germany. Other European countries, such as Italy, Portugal, and Ireland, followed the path later, due to "poorer material and social conditions, lower educational status, as well as more restrictive religious and family bonds." However, they argue that youth culture had spread throughout Western Europe by the end of the 1970s.[32] Its emergence in the postwar decades coincided with two more developments: demographic changes, mainly in the case of France and, beyond Europe, in the United States, usually dubbed as the "baby-boom";[33] and the vast expansion of the number of university students.[34]

The concept of "youth culture" has drawn substantial criticism from scholars. Proponents of cultural studies, such as Stuart Hall, John Clarke, Tony Jefferson, and Brian Roberts, reject the term, which had become "most common in popular and journalistic usage" in post–World War II Britain, as obscuring class differences; they put forward that of "youth subcultures" instead. Based on the work of Antonio Gramsci, they explore "youth subcultures" as a subset of "class cultures," but also in relation to the "dominant culture."[35] Schildt and Siegfried actually offer a nuanced conceptualization of "youth culture," which echoes some of those concerns: they stress that researchers should be mindful of two issues: its heterogeneity, especially with regard to gender and class differences, but also its diverse links with the "larger society" through institutions, such as the educational ones.[36] This study aims to further problematize the concept of "youth culture": at least in the case of the left-wing youth in the 1970s, their lifestyles[37] were not necessarily predicated on age-specific leisure activities; their distinctive element was sociality, namely the formation of peer groups, comprised solely or mostly of young people. The book examines the interplay among diverse types of the social relationships that those young left-wingers maintained, ranging from the peer group to the political youth organizations, surveying the specific ways in which they experienced and framed leisure activities and sexual practices. It echoes anthropologists Nicholas Long and Henrietta Moore, who suggest complex ways of analyzing sociality, and especially their argument that "the most productive way forward is not to focus on those 'ties' in isolation, but rather to examine the dynamic matrix in which they are continually made, sustained or dissolved."[38]

Although "generation" need not necessarily be young, youth cultures in post–World War II Europe have extensively been approached through the use of this conceptual tool. Diverse specialists maintain that the first post–World War II decades witnessed the formation of a "generation," often called the "68ers" or the "baby-boomers," born after the end of World War II. Relevant scholarship has mostly relied on the definition offered by sociologist Karl Mannheim: according to him, "generation" is an age group "with a common location in the historical dimension of the social process," limiting its members "to a specific range of potential experience, predisposing them for a certain characteristic mode of thought and experience, and a characteristic type of historically relevant action."[39] A number of historians, such as Ronald Fraser and Ingrid Gilcher-Holtey, have scrutinized the "generation of 68ers" in Italy, West Germany, France, and Northern Ireland.[40] They argue that this generation was radicalized, due to the eruption of the anti–Vietnam War movement and the growing influence of anti-hierarchical ideological trends,[41] stemming from the increasing dissatisfaction with either the Social Democrats or the pro-Soviet Communists.[42] Historian Konstantinos Kornetis employed another version of the concept of "generation" in the case of Greece. He delineated two age cohorts of left-wing students during the dictatorship years: people born between 1944 and 1949 and those born after 1949 until 1954. He claims that the latter, in stark contrast to the former, were influenced by protests that occurred elsewhere in the late 1960s, at least in their lifestyle, developing, for instance, an informal clothing style.[43]

Nevertheless, what historian Belinda Davis argues about the "generation of 68ers," namely that it is a concept which "must be used with great circumspection," seems appropriate for the young Socialists and Communists in

Greece in 1974–1981 as well.[44] In general, young activists in Greece did not depict their collective action in the mid-to-late 1970s in terms of generation, but, rather, in terms of affiliation to a particular political group. The label of generation, however, appeared sometimes in the publications of the young left-wingers in Greece, albeit as a claim for authority: as is mentioned in the following chapters, the actors that utilized it aimed to ascribe particular characteristics to the youth of Greece.[45]

Apart from the emergence of distinct youth lifestyles, the twentieth century also witnessed protracted discussions about representations of the "youth." As historians Luisa Passerini, Efi Avdela, and Richard Jobs convincingly argue, "youth" served as a metaphor for social change in twentieth-century Europe, such as the "economic miracle" in the postwar period, decolonization, the Cold War, the spread of mass consumption patterns, as well as urbanization.[46] Avdela and Jobs add that "youth" as a metaphor encapsulated the hopes and fears that those transformations generated in the broader society. Diverse actors, such as the educational institutions, the Church, the media, the cultural industry, and the political Parties were involved in discussions about what the "youth" represents. Even though "youth" as a metaphor did not only address "young" people, but, sometimes, entire societies, its use certainly shaped expectations about the behavioral patterns of the former. Nevertheless, young people were hardly passive recipients of such representations. In that respect, Heilbronner has argued that the twentieth century has witnessed a veritable earthquake, namely a transition "from a culture *for* youth to a culture *of* youth." Heilbronner maintains that there was a shift from "a culture initiated by a 'parent culture' (that of mothers and fathers, the establishment, state authorities, entrepreneurs and producers of mass culture) to a culture largely invented, initiated and inspired (with a little help from the parents) by young people."[47]

Defining the "youth" was certainly a major battleground in the initial post-dictatorship period in Greece. This era is important for the history of youth in Greece, since, as the book will show, the Left did not repeat some of the worries that it had raised about the comportment of the Greek youth in the preceding decades—for instance in relation to rock music, as mentioned in detail in chapters four and five. However, the post-authoritarian years did not exactly serve, either, as an era, during which the Greek society in general "no longer construed youth as a source of concern, but purely as a factor that helped bring progress and creative renovation to the political, social and cultural life of the country," as historian Kostas Katsapis argues.[48] In particular, left-wing Parties and youth organizations elaborated extensively on the Greek youth, since it embodied both their hopes and concerns, which derived from the transition to democracy as well as their fears of mass consumption, which had been spreading in Greece since the 1960s. Meanwhile, young Greek left-wingers were particularly innovative during those years in developing conceptualizations not only of "youth," but also of politics and culture in general, since the initiatives, in which they participated, did not solely address issues of the youth.[49] Those Communist and Socialist youngsters sometimes challenged and even affected the relevant views endorsed by their "parent cultures." They did not initiate, however, a transition from a culture for youth to a culture of youth. What actually emerged in Greece in terms of left-wing youth politics, as the 1970s progressed, was a process of diversification of the politicized youth vis-à-vis parent cultures. The meddling of political Parties was increasingly contested, albeit only by a segment of the left-wing youth in the late 1970s.

"Americanization" and Its Limits

The history of "youth" in Western Europe since the end of World War II is connected with the impact of the spread of American cultural patterns—coined the issue of "Americanization." This paradigm deals with practices, objects, and symbols which emanated from the United States and which are presented as having deeply transformed attitudes in other parts of the globe. It correctly stresses that since the interwar period the United States has exported technologies that help increase productivity, such as Taylorism, as well as spread consumption, such as full-service advertising agencies. These patterns and objects mainly appeared in Western Europe in the post–World War II years. The same period witnessed the widespread popularity of American popular cultural products in Europe, such as jazz, rock 'n' roll music, "western" movies, and pulp fiction, particularly appreciated by young people in Western Europe. The influence of American popular culture in postwar Europe was so exponential that it caused widespread reflection. Quite notably, the character Robert (Hanns Zischler), from Wim Wenders's seminal 1976 film *Kings of the Road,* maintained that "[t]he Yanks have colonized our subconscious." Was that true, however?

Up to the end of the Cold War and even into the early 1990s, the concept of "Americanization" usually tended to be defined in a highly polarized and normative way. One approach, that of cultural imperialism, described the active imposition of a "false consciousness" of mass consumption on a global scale by American monopolies, assisted by local "reactionary" elements.[50] The other powerful story, which structured the history of "Americanization," equated it to "economic modernization" and "political and cultural democratization."[51] Despite these seemingly conflicting arguments, there was a point in common: it was usually taken for granted that the receiving end was a passive actor, shaped by American products.[52] The 1990s witnessed the emergence of a different approach, which has sought to problematize the form of transfer of goods and symbols from the United States to other countries. The common aspect of this paradigm is the emphasis on the selective character of reception. American studies expert Rob Kroes has asserted that the potential freedom to "dissect patterns of traditional and organic cohesion" and to "rearrange the components" into "new wholes" has been a major element of the cultural life in the United States, which has also spread in Europe. Following a similar approach, anthropologist Kaspar Maase has gone even further to express his cautiousness toward the very concept of "Americanization"; in the late 1990s he used it in the form of "grassroots Americanization," claiming that social groups in West Germany picked some of the "offers, which were presented with great economic and media power;" in other words, those which suited their expectations. In the 2000s, he revised his position to discard the concept and to substitute it with "cultural democratization," which he used to describe the emerging youth identities in West Germany since the late 1950s and their impact on the "flattening of cultural hierarchies."[53]

The "selective reception" approach has focused heavily on the making of youth identities and gender relations in Western Europe since the mid–1950s. The young are argued to have distinguished themselves through specific symbols and activities, which have a key aspect in common: they stemmed from American popular culture, which served as a "major vehicle" for protest against parents. Moreover, in West Germany, Austria, and Italy, these patterns helped in the formation of postfascist identities among young people, who aimed at distancing themselves from the recent history of their country and perhaps their very family and its potential fascist past. An influential cultural product was that of rock 'n' roll music, especially the singer Elvis Presley.[54] The first group to appropriate elements of his way of dancing and his outer appearance was a mainly working-class masculine subculture, which appeared in numerous different national contexts and was labeled in a variety of ways: *Halbstarken* in West and East Germany, *Teppisti* in Italy, *Teddy-boys* in Britain, *tentimpoides* in Greece, and *Hooligans* in Austria, to name just a few.[55]

The impact of Hollywood movies appears to have been the same, according to relevant research. In the case of Britain, cultural studies expert Jackie Stacey argues that their consumption served as a means of making of an "American" feminine identity, which was "exciting, sexual, pleasurable and in some ways transgressive." Female Hollywood actors, such as Marilyn Monroe, were a major source of inspiration for young West German women. Monroe, according to historian Karin Schmidlechner, was a role model for

Austrian girls as well, functioning as a symbol of overcoming the "ascetic morality," which lambasted sexual relations before marriage and stigmatized behaviors and clothing styles, which did not conceal feminine sexuality.[56]

Still, Schildt and Siegfried have raised the concern whether it was not solely American cultural products that shaped youth cultures in Western Europe in the 1960s–1980s.[57] In what follows I argue that "Americanization," even if conceptualized as "selective reception," hardly furnishes a complete explanatory package for the examination of youth cultures in 1970s Western Europe. For sure, the appropriation of American cultural products played a key role in the construction of youth identities in Western Europe in the 1970s, including Greece. Still, the variety of flows within Europe, as well as the non-Western transfers that shaped the young left-wingers under study, may require us to avoid defining them simply as "Americanized." The leisure patterns of a significant segment of the post-dictatorship Greek left-wing youth was predicated on representations of the USSR as a role model society, a phenomenon I would like to name "Sovietism." The latter gained momentum from 1974 onwards, due to the intensification of contacts between Greek political groups and Soviet institutions in several domains, such as youth travel, as analyzed in chapter three. The Sovietism that a segment of the Greek left-wing youth developed in the 1970s was largely a grassroots and, to an extent, selective trend: not even the young pro-Soviet Communists in Greece received uncritically the prerogatives of the cultural politics of the Eastern European and the Soviet regime. Cultural patterns from Western Europe, especially in cinema, were also an important ingredient of left-wing youth cultures in Greece in the 1970s. In addition, similar to what happened in other European countries, such as Sweden,[58] the "invention of tradition" was a key aspect of the tastes of young left-wingers in Greece since the 1960s and certainly in the early and mid–1970s, particularly in the domain of music.[59] Still, performances of what young Socialists and Communists in Greece construed as quintessentially "authentic Greek culture" sometimes involved the appropriation and resignification of cultural imports stemming from other regions of the globe. The term "glocal," especially as employed by sociologist Robert Robertson, according to whom "homogenizing and heterogenizing tendencies [manifest in transnational flows] are mutually implicative," is particularly appropriate to describe the latter tendency.[60]

Rebels With a Sexual Cause?

Regardless whether they can be labeled "Americanization," significant cultural transformations occurred in postwar Europe. Historian Arthur Marwick, focusing on Britain, France, Italy, and the United States, has discerned a process of "cultural revolution," which unfolded during an epoch he dubs "the Long Sixties." He sets out a linear development of this "revolution" from the late 1950s (c. 1958) until the early 1970s (c. 1974). He insists, however, that many of the transformations have continued to the present. Marwick points to "multiculturalism," "individualism," and "permissiveness" as key elements in this progressive subversion of conservative modes of thinking and acting. He defines this permissiveness as "a new frankness, openness and indeed honesty in personal relations and modes of expression," the first signs of which arose in the late 1950s and which emerged in full force in the late 1960s, an era when "there was more sex, in more variations and, crucially, there was less guilt, less fear and less furtiveness." However, he goes on to argue that "more frequent intimate contact with men created in some women a very strong reaction against unrestricted male licentiousness in its predatory, arrogant and inconsiderate aspects"; as a result, the Feminist[61] movement of the 1970s appeared, which helped to establish divorce, abortion, and contraception, which again Marwick regards as "elements in the liberalization projects of the sixties."[62] Historian Konrad Jarausch reached a similar conclusion in his work on "recivilizing Germans": he claimed that, although the late 1960s youth revolt in West Germany petered out rapidly, it helped unleash a liberalization of "social values," including "greater tolerance for unconventional lifestyles" and a "veritable 'sexual revolution,'" which lasted throughout the 1970s.[63]

A dawning "sexual openness," sometimes labeled as "sexual revolution," has been the leitmotiv of many historical and sociological works about the United States and Western and Eastern Europe since the 1960s.[64] The growing disconnection of sexuality from procreation through primarily the contraceptive and secondarily the "morning after pill," the legitimization of premarital flirting, especially through the close body contact of young men and women in wild rock dance or during holidays, as well as the "saturation" of the visual landscape with "nude and semi-nude images," including sexually explicit advertisements and the introduction of the miniskirt, have been outlined as factors leading to "sexual emancipation."[65] The rise of actors, such as the "New Left" in the late 1960s, who addressed sexuality as an explicitly political issue, was yet another facet of this openness. The "Make Love Not War" slogan is testament to the belief shared by its advocates that "sexual liberation" was "politically significant."[66] However, an increasing number of scholars maintain that changes in sexual behavior from the 1960s onward were far less "sweeping" than has been hitherto acknowledged.[67] Historian Dagmar Herzog claims that a "sexual revolution" occurred in West Germany in the late 1960s and the early 1970s. Nevertheless, she is quite steadfast in denying that the first six decades of the twentieth century were marked by an uninterrupted hegemony of conservative sexual norms. By contrast, she has put forth the compelling argument that the National Socialist regime, while denigrating "Jewish" sex, tolerated premarital sex for its supporters more than the Adenauer government and the Churches did in West Germany during the 1950s.[68] In addition, the "sexual revolution" or "liberalization" argument, in the case of Marwick, has been criticized for one more reason: it often presents the sexual patterns of young people from the 1960s onward in an undifferentiated manner—the abovementioned work of historians Josie McLellan and Dagmar Herzog is a notable exception. Numerous scholars argue that individuals of differing gender in Western Europe appear to have experienced transformations in sexual norms and practices since the interwar period in diverse ways and certainly not always as emancipatory.[69]

Indeed, "sexual revolution" may become a catch-all concept, lacking analytical utility, unless one probes the precise changes to sexual patterns that occurred in a particular context and era, the actors that spearheaded them, and the diverse ways in which individuals of differing backgrounds experienced them. What transpired in Greece was no copycat of sexual transformations that occurred elsewhere in Western Europe and North America at that point: quite tellingly, the use of the contraceptive pill never gained momentum in Greece. More importantly, this process was neither a story of steady liberalization, initiated by the Left, nor a process that can be conceptualized in a triumphalist and uniform manner as a "cultural" or "sexual revolution"; rather, it contained multiple and contradictory sexual transformations, dependent not only on gender, but a wide array of factors, such as ideological differences, geographical origin, and class.[70]

The Party's Over?

The Sixties have not only been described as the beginning of an era of substantial cultural transformations, but also one of intense political activity. Toward the end of the decade, protests erupted in various areas around the world. Militants, comprising students, but also workers, acted in close contact with each other, a phenomenon that has been described as "global Sixties" or "1968 as a global or transnational phenomenon."[71] However, various scholars argue that the left-wing political fever that was related to "1968" vanished in the mid–1970s, giving way to "individualistic" tendencies and the emergence of "neoliberalism." Historian Gerd-Rainer Horn best exemplifies this argument. He treats "1968" not as a moment, but as a period lasting ten years, from 1966 to 1976. This era was largely followed by the "decline of participatory democracy" and the "deradicalization" of "personal/political itineraries."[72] Historian Gerd Koenen, who was an activist in the 1970s, draws almost the same boundaries, discerning a "red decade" in West Germany, lasting from 1967 to 1977.[73] What followed in the late 1970s, according to political scientist Claus Leggewie, was the prevalence of neo-liberalism; the "New Right" has substituted the struggle of the "New Left" against the "authoritarian" state, heralding a period of "depoliticized individualization."[74]

Some other scholars working on Western Europe take a similar though not identical approach. Their point is that individualization and privatization need not necessarily lead away from radical politics. Such an argument is repeated in the historiography of the cultural politics of the Communist Parties in postwar Western Europe, especially in the work by Gundle about the PCI (Partito Comunista Italiano, Italian Communist Party). Gundle claims that the attempt by the PCI and its youth organization, the FGCI (Federazione Giovanile Comunista Italiana, Italian Communist Youth Federation), to establish "a new pattern of hegemony founded on frugality and collective solidarity" in postwar Italy had little if any prospect of success in the context of the triumph of mass consumption. On the contrary, youth cultures that combined "postcollective individualism with a rejection of pre-existing political mediations," such as the naturists and alternative medicine centers, proved much more influential during the 1970s.[75]

By contrast, an absolutely fundamental contention of this volume is that the left-wing collective action that intensified after the collapse of the dictatorship in Greece in 1974 endured not only until the late 1970s, but until the early-to-mid 1980s. The issue whether this perpetuation of collective action beyond the late 1970s is a Greek exception needs further scrutiny, but the case study of Greece shows that narratives that depict that point as the beginning of an era of depoliticization in Western Europe should be approached with caution. In any case, left-wing Parties and their youth organizations featured prominently in mass mobilization in Greece during those years. The case study of Greece shows that Eurocommunist and pro-Soviet groups were among the most popular ones in the Greek youth. Their influence, however, is no Greek exception: Communism in Western Europe in the 1970s was a palette that featured various shades of red, some of which did not fade during that decade. While the relatively well-researched "Far Left" largely withered away toward the end of the 1970s in Western Europe, this is not necessarily true of pro-Soviet and Eurocommunist Parties and youth organizations in the same region in general. Their significant and enduring support during this decade is manifest in the case of the pro-Soviet Communist Party and its youth wing in the aftermath of dictatorship in Portugal.[76] David Gouard also demonstrates that in the period from 1974 to 1978 the reluctantly Eurocommunist French Communist Party (PCF) continued to be very strong in a number of working-class districts in Paris, which was also coined as the "Red Belt," until the mid–1980s.[77] With regard to Italy, the membership of the youth organization of the Italian Communist Party, the FGCI, had plummeted in the 1960s: from 240,000 in 1961 to 66,451 in 1970.[78] However, by 1976 it had risen rapidly to 142,790 with 47,641 new members joining in 1975–1976; by 1978 it had fallen to 113,505, but still the figure was almost double in comparison with that of 1970.[79] Meanwhile, the Eurocommunist youth groups, either by themselves or together with the Communist Parties with which they were aligned, organized festivals and established cultural societies in various northern or southern European countries, such as Spain, Italy, Greece, and France in this period. Such evidence suggests something of a *Eurocommunist moment,* at least in the mid–1970s. Similar to left-wing radicals of other stripes, the advocates of the Eurocommunist and the pro-Soviet Communist Left were conveyors of ideas and cultural patterns that transgressed national borders. Transnational links among them were quite strong. Pro-Soviet Communists in Greece and Portugal were in close contact with their role-model regime in the USSR. In the same way, an aspect of the Eurocommunist moment of the 1970s was the close contact among Eurocommunist groups, mainly the Italian, Greek, and Spanish Eurocommunists.

In arguing that left-wing Parties played a preponderant role in youth politics in Greece, this book resonates to an extent with a main argument of Greek political scientists, such as Giannis Voulgaris, Ilias Nikolakopoulos and Christos Lyrintzis, who have conducted research on the post-dictatorship period.[80] Those scholars also argue that mass mobilization in post-dictatorship Greece in general was controlled—or, as Voulgaris puts it, "colonized"—by political Parties.[81] Nevertheless, while this volume acknowledges the dominant role that political Parties played in the political life of Greece at that point, it simultaneously demonstrates that their prevalence was not uncontested: subjects of protest emerged in the late 1970s in Greece, as shown in detail in chapters five and six, which were not linked with any Parties, including left-wing ones, and which loudly criticized the ways in which those Parties operated. Thus, radical mobilization in post–1974 Greece should not necessarily be linked with the activities of left-wing Parties and youth organizations. Moreover, the left-wing Parties and their youth organizations were malleable entities, which became to a lesser or greater extent involved in experimentations concerning the relationship between the "individual" and political collectivities that occurred in Greece in the late 1970s. Such reformulations were particularly manifest in the domain of leisure: Communist and Socialist youth groups began to praise or at least tolerate the heterogeneity in the leisure pursuits of their members at the end of the decade. This was the first time this happened at the level of cultural politics in the history of the Greek Left.

Again, such experimentation was no Greek exception: For instance, through their cultural politics, the Italian Eurocommunists growingly accepted and made an effort to cater to a broad range of youth lifestyles.[82] Eurocommunist Parties in general also tried, albeit often cautiously, to bring substantial changes to their apparatus, allowing some initiatives developed by their members to function with a degree of autonomy from Party structures. In doing so, they responded to the spread of dual militancy during those years, namely simultaneous participation in a left-wing Party, but also in novel protest groups, such as Feminist initiatives, which did not follow the line of that Party. This condition was not atypical for some female members of RF in Greece, but also of the French Communist Party in the mid-to-late 1970s.[83] Mass mobilization may have been an actual condition or an unrealized goal of diverse subjects of protest in the late–1970s in Western Europe. Nevertheless, one way or another, the experimentation on patterns of collective action, in which broad segments of the Left in Western Europe engaged in the 1970s, is underestimated by approaches that view the 1970s as the beginning of an era characterized by a "retreat into the private" or, in a teleological fashion, as a preliminary stage of "depoliticized individualization" that emerged in full force in the subsequent decades. The energy that left-wingers expended on formulating novel relationships between the "individual" and the "collective" should be seriously considered in its own right. Even if such initiatives failed to become hegemonic, they were not marginal phenomena either: they mobilized numerous activists in various Western European countries, often in collaboration with one another.

Notes

1. When the term Party refers to any political organization, it will henceforth appear with a capital P; when indicating a gathering of people for the purposes of socializing, I will use a small p.
2. About the idea that researchers should not conceptualize politics in such a "narrow sense," but, rather, explore the exact way in which the subjects under study construe this term, see, for instance: Jenny Edkins, *Poststructuralism and International Relations. Bringing the Political Back In* (London, 1999), p. 2.
3. See, for instance: Joffre Dumazedier, "Leisure," in *International Encyclopedia of the Social Sciences,* D.L. Sills, ed., vol. 9 (New York, 1979), p. 251.
4. About leisure in relation to class and gender norms, see, for instance: John K. Walton, "Consuming the Beach: Seaside Resorts and Cultures of Tourism in England and Spain from the 1840s to the 1930s," in *Being Elsewhere: Tourism, Consumer Cul-*

ture, and Identity in Modern Europe and North America, ed. Shelley Baranowski and Ellen Furlough (Ann Arbor, MI, 2004), pp. 272–98; Douglas P. Mackaman, "The Tactics of Retreat: Spa Vacations and Bourgeois Identity in Nineteenth-Century France," in Baranowski and Furlough, *Being Elsewhere,* pp. 35–62.

5. Peter Borsay, *A History of Leisure* (Houndmills, UK, 2006), p. 16. Borsay refers to an "internationalization" of leisure that has occurred from this point onward. I have added "growing," since such transnational cultural transfers had existed already in the preceding decades, albeit not in such intensity.

6. Frank C. Mort, "Competing Domains: Democratic Subjects and Consuming Subjects in Britain and the United States since 1945," in *The Making of the Consumer: Knowledge, Power and Identity in the Modern World,* ed. F. Trentmann (Oxford, 2006), p. 236.

7. Uta Poiger, *Jazz, Rock, and Rebels, Cold War and American Culture in a Divided Germany* (Berkeley, CA, 2000), pp. 111–14.

8. Stephen Gundle, *Between Hollywood and Moscow: The Italian Communists and the Challenge of Mass Culture, 1943–1991* (Durham, NC, 2000), p. 9.

9. This study focuses on the activity of Greek left-wing organizations in Greece. It outlines some main aspects of their activity among Greek migrants who resided elsewhere in Western Europe during those years, especially when these affected the political landscape in Greece. However, a detailed exploration of Greek left-wing migrants would also require an extensive analysis of the political condition of the countries where those migrants lived, for which just a single monograph would not suffice.

10. For instance: Dumazedier, "Leisure," p. 250.

11. Borsay, *A History of Leisure,* pp. 1–8.

12. Raphael Samuel, "The Lost World of British Communism," *New Left Review* I, no. 154 (1985): p. 40.

13. I employ the term "militant" in my work to refer to ideologically engaged and vigorously active youngsters. I would like to make clear that I do not mean that they were involved in violent acts, as the term may also imply. I use the terms "militant" and "activist" interchangeably, referring to the same people.

14. RF was created as PAOS RF (Panellinia Antidiktatoriki Organosi Foititon, Panhellenic Antidictatorial Student Organization). Its name changed in 1974 to PON RF (Panelladiki Organosi Neolaias Rigas Feraios, Panhellenic Youth Organization Rigas Feraios) and in 1976 to EKON RF (Elliniki Kommounistiki Neolaia Rigas Feraios, Greek Communist Youth Rigas Feraios). What was made clear in 1976 was the Communist orientation of the organization, on the one hand, and its distance from the Soviet Bloc on the other, as the precedence of the nation ("Greek") over "Communist" revealed. The latter was common pattern for Western European Communist Parties that were critical of the USSR. In fact, the name of the Italian Communist Party functioned as a model.

15. RF leaned toward KKE Es. from 1968 onward, while in 1974 it proclaimed itself the youth organization of the latter.

16. Eurocommunism, according to Tony Judt, was given official currency by the secretary-general of the Spanish Communists, Santiago Carillo, in his 1977 essay *Eurocommunism and the State.* For relevant bibliography, see Annie Kriegel, *Eurocommu-*

nism: A New Kind of Communism? (Stanford, CA, 1978); Stephen Hellman, *Italian Communism in Transition: The Rise and Fall of the Historic Compromise in Turin, 1975–1980* (Oxford, 1988); Gundle, *Between Hollywood and Moscow;* Tony Judt, *Postwar: A History of Europe since 1945* (London, 2007), pp. 495–96, 550; Donald Sassoon, *One Hundred Years of Socialism: The West European Left in the Twentieth Century* (London, 1997), pp. 572–93.

17. George Kassimeris, "Junta by Another Name? The 1974 *Metapolitefsi* and the Greek Extra-parliamentary Left," *Journal of Contemporary History* 40, no. 4 (2005): pp. 752–55.

18. I choose to refer to Choros "participants" instead of "members" in order to indicate the difference between the loose structures of Choros in comparison to those of the youth orgainzations of left-wing parties. Choros participants are also mentioned as "autonomous young left-wingers."

19. See, for instance, a flyer produced by autonomous young left-wingers in the Department of Mathematics in the University of Salonica in the late 1980s. The flyer was titled "Schedio apofasis tis sygkentrosis tou G Mathimatikou" and was signed by the "Kakoi Foitites tou G Mathimatikou." I have found this document in the personal collection of Nikos Samanidis.

20. Kassimeris, "Junta by Another Name?," pp. 745–62; Giannis Voulgaris, *I Ellada tis Metapolitefsis, 1974–1990: Statheri Dimokratia Simademeni apo ti Metapolemiki Istoria* (Athens, 2002), pp. 25–141.

21. Raymond Williams, "Culture is Ordinary," in *Conviction*, ed. Norman McKenzie (London, 1958), pp. 74–92. An outline of the approach of the Birmingham School of Cultural Studies toward "culture" can be found in: Hugh Mackay, introduction to *Consumption and Everyday Life,* ed. Hugh Mackay (Milton Keynes, UK, 1997), p. 7. However, in contrast to what Williams argues, I do not wish to examine whether popular culture was "bad" or not and whether it "degraded" the "actual lives" of the subjects under study. Anthropologist Evelyn Payne Hatcher also deals with the relationship between forms of signification and lived experience and suggests that art is treated as "culture," namely situated in its cultural context. In this vein, she encourages scholars to probe questions, such as "where the art was made . . . what its use was . . . and what it meant to the people who made use of it." See Evelyn Payne Hatcher, *Art as Culture: An Introduction to the Anthropology of Art* (Westport, CT, 1999), pp. 1–20.

22. Thomas Mergel, "Überlegungen zu einer Kulturgeschichte der Politik," *Geschichte und Gesellschaft* 28 (2002), pp. 574–606; David I. Kertzer, *Politics and Symbols: The Italian Communist Party and the Fall of Communism* (New Haven, CT, 1996).

23. I believe that the terms "New" and "Old Left" are rather normative, signifying what a number of activists and some scholars view as "novel" and "parochial" protest patterns, respectively. Although I acknowledge that there were marked differences in the rhetoric and practice of those left-wing actors, I wish to avoid such negative and positive associations and, thus, put those terms in quotation marks.

24. David Caute, *The Year of the Barricades* (New York, 1988), p. 22.

25. Peter N. Stearns and Carol Z. Stearns, "Emotionology: Clarifying the History of Emotions and Emotional Standards," *The American Historical Review* 90, no. 4 (1985): pp. 813–36.

26. Stephane Courtois et al., *Le Livre noir du communisme: Crimes, terreur, répression* (Paris, 1997).

27. Bernard Pudal et al., introduction to *Le Siècle des Communismes*, ed. Bernard Pudal et al. (Paris, 2000).

28. Oded Heilbronner, "From a Culture *for* Youth to a Culture *of* Youth: Recent Trends in the Historiography of Western Youth Cultures," *Contemporary European History* 17, no. 4 (2008): p. 577. Two other illuminating reviews of the state-of-the-art in the scholarly analysis of youth cultures are: Paolo Capuzzo, "Youth Cultures and Consumption in Contemporary Europe," *Contemporary European History* 10 (2001): pp. 155–70; Nikos Demertzis and Giannis Stavrakakis, "I erevna gia ti neolaia- synoptiki anadromi," in *Neolaia, o astathmitos paragontas*, ed. Nikos Demertzis et al. (Athens, 2008), pp. 15–29.

29. A comprehensive presentation of the sociology of youth cultures is offered in: Mike Brake, *The Sociology of Youth Culture and Youth Subcultures: Sex and Drugs and Rock 'n' Roll?* (London, 1985).

30. Axel Schildt and Detlef Siegfried, "Introduction: Youth, Consumption, and Politics in the Age of Radical Change," in *Between Marx and Coca-Cola: Youth Culture in Changing European Societies, 1960–1980*, ed. Axel Schildt and Detlef Siegfried (New York, 2007), p. 5.

31. Schildt and Siegfried, *Between Marx and Coca-Cola*; Richard I Jobs, *Riding the New Wave: Youth and the Rejuvenation of France after the Second World War* (Stanford, CA, 2007).

32. Schildt and Siegfried, "Introduction: Youth, Consumption," p. 6.

33. Ibid., p. 18. See also: Arthur Marwick, *The Sixties: Cultural Revolution in Britain, France, Italy, and the United States, c.1958–c.1974* (Oxford, 1998), p. 42, 45, 256. For the "baby-boom" and the generation of "baby-boomers" in France, see Jean-François Sirinelli, "La France des *sixties* revisitée," *Vingtième Siècle: Revue d'histoire* 69 (2004), pp. 111–24. However, Schildt and Siegfried point out that the "baby boom" did not appear throughout Western Europe: as they note, the 15- to 29-year-olds' demographic share increased until the years 1970–71 and then declined again until the years 1979–80 in Sweden and Denmark; exactly the opposite development occurred in West Germany. The number of newborn babies did not boom in post-war Greece, either. In fact, the fertility rate fell from 2.6 children in 1950 to 2.3 in 1975. See Schildt and Siegfried, "Introduction. Youth, Consumption," p. 18. David H. Close, *Greece since 1945: Politics, Economy and Society* (London, 2002), p. 59.

34. Schildt and Siegfried, "Introduction: Youth, Consumption," pp. 17–20.

35. For instance, John Clarke et al. "Subcultures, Cultures and Class" in *Resistance Through Rituals: Youth Subcultures in Post-War Britain*, ed. Stuart Hall and Tony Jefferson (London, 2006), pp 3–59

36. Schildt and Siegfried, "Introduction: Youth, Consumption," p. 5.

37. This term, when employed in Greek, often denotes only poshy lifestyles. I wish to clarify that I do not endorse such a link in my work.

38. Nicholas J. Long and Henrietta L. Moore, "Introduction: Sociality's New Directions," in *Sociality: New Directions*, ed. Nicholas J. Long and Henrietta L. Moore (New York, 2012), pp. 4, 7.

39. See Karl Mannheim, "The Problem of Generations," in *Essays on the Sociology of Knowledge,* by Karl Mannheim (New York, 1952), pp. 290–91.
40. Ronald Fraser et al., *1968: A Student Generation in Revolt* (London, 1988); Ingrid Gilcher-Holtey, *Die 68er Bewegung: Deutschland-Westeuropa-USA* (Munich, 2001).
41. In referring to such trends, Gilcher-Holtey mentions the contributors to the *New Left Review* in the UK, *Socialisme ou Barbarie* in France, *Das Argument* in West Germany, and *Quaderni Rossi* in Italy. See Gilcher-Holtey, *Die 68er Bewegung,* pp. 11–14.
42. Gerd-Rainer Horn, *The Spirit of '68: Rebellion in Western Europe and North America, 1956–1976* (Oxford, 2007), pp. 136–42.
43. Kostis Kornetis, *Children of the Dictatorship. Student Resistance, Cultural Politics, and the "Long 1960s" in Greece* (New York, 2013).
44. Belinda Davis, "Violence and Memory of the Nazi past in 1960s-70s West German Protest," in *Coping with the Nazi Past: West German Debates on Nazism and Generational Conflict, 1955–1975,* ed. Philipp Gassert and Alan E. Steinweis (Oxford, 2006), pp. 210–37. For one more critical interrogation of the concept of "generation" with regard to protests that erupted in the late 1960s, see Maud Anne Bracke, "One-dimensional Conflict? Recent Scholarship on 1968 and the Limitations of the Generation Concept," *Journal of Contemporary History* 47, no. 3 (2012): pp. 638–46.
45. Since the young Socialists and Communists in Greece did not utilize the term "generation," in order to define their political identity at that point, it would not be fruitful to approach them by employing even a nuanced understanding of that term, as historian Anna von der Goltz did with regard to the "1968ers," namely as "diverse, nevertheless entangled generations." See Anna von der Goltz, "Generational Belonging and the '68ers' in Europe," in *"Talkin' 'bout my generation": Conflicts of generation building and Europe's "1968,"* ed. Anna von der Goltz (Göttingen, 2011), p. 79.
46. Luisa Passerini, "Youth as a Metaphor for Social Change: Fascist Italy and America in the 1950s," in *A History of Young People in the West,* ed. Giovanni Levi and Jean-Claude Schmitt, vol. 2 (Cambridge, MA, 1997), pp. 281–340; Efi Avdela, "'Corrupting and Uncontrollable Activities': Moral Panic about Youth in Post-Civil-War Greece," *Journal of Contemporary History* 43, no. 1 (2008): pp. 25–44; Jobs, *Riding the New Wave.*
47. Heilbronner, "From a Culture *for* Youth," p. 577.
48. He argues this in the following very important work: Kostas Katsapis, *To "provlima neolaia." Monternoi Neoi, paradosi kai amfisvitisi sti Metapolemiki Ellada, 1964-1974* (Athens, 2013), p. 585.
49. Actually, in addressing the activity of the subjects in question, the most accurate way to conceptualise it would be through the term "left-wing (youth) politics." The parenthesis demonstrates that their interests were linked with, but not necessarily confined to the youth. While taking this point seriously into account, I avoided the use of the parenthesis in the title of the book in order to make it more succinct.
50. For example, see Lewis H. Gann and Peter Duignan, *The Rebirth of the West: The Americanization of the Democratic World, 1945–1958* (Cambridge, MA, 1992).
51. For example, Jeremy Tunstall, *The Media are American* (London, 1977).

52. However, it would be very schematic to argue that until the 1990s all historians of Americanization treated Europeans as passive recipients of American patterns. For example, Volker Berghahn did not portray this process as a slavish adherence to American models. He mentions, for instance, that some West German businessmen dismissed managerial training and the very term "manager." See Volker R. Berghahn, *The Americanization of West German Industry, 1945–1973* (Leamington Spa, 1986).

53. About works exploring the selective reception of the American popular culture by youngsters in Western Europe, see, for instance: Rob Kroes, "American Mass Culture and European Youth Culture," in Schildt and Siegfried, *Between Marx and Coca Cola*, pp. 82–105; Kaspar Maase, "Establishing Cultural Democracy: Youth, 'Americanization' and the Irresistible Rise of Popular Culture," in *The Miracle Years: A Cultural History of West Germany, 1949–68*, ed. Hanna Schissler (Princeton, NJ, 2001), pp. 428–50; Kaspar Maase, *BRAVO Amerika. Erkundungen zur Jugendkultur der Bundesrepublik in den fünfzigen Jahren* (Hamburg, 1992); Poiger, *Jazz, Rock and Rebels*; Mike-Frank G. Epitropoulos and Victor Roudometof, "Youth Culture and Lifestyle in Modern Greece," in *American Culture in Europe: Interdisciplinary Perspectives*, ed. Mike-Frank G. Epitropoulos and Victor Roudometof (Westport, CT, 1998), pp. 119–44.

54. See Maase, "Establishing Cultural Democracy," pp. 428–50. Poiger, *Jazz, Rock and Rebels*.

55. Maase, "Establishing Cultural Democracy," pp. 428–50. Other works dealing with that phenomenon are: Clarke et al., "Subcultures"; Simonetta Piccone Stella, "'Rebels Without a Cause': Male Youth in Italy around 1960," *History Workshop Journal* 38, no. 1 (1994): pp. 157–78.

56. Jackie Stacey, *Star Gazing: Hollywood Cinema and Female Spectatorship* (London, 1994), p. 204; Karin M. Schmidlechner, "Austrian Youth in the 1950s," in *Power and the People: A Social History of Central European Politics, 1945–56*, ed. Eleonore Breuning, Jill Lewis, and Gareth Pritchard (Manchester, 2005), pp. 182–99.

57. Schildt and Siegfried, "Introduction: Youth, Consumption," p. 28.

58. Thomas E. Jørgensen, *Transformations and Crises: The Left and the Nation in Denmark and Sweden 1956–1980* (Oxford, New York, 2008), pp. 138–45.

59. In analyzing the practice of left-leaning students in the early 1970s, Kornetis has appropriated the concept of "invented traditions" introduced by Hobsbawm and Ranger. For its original use, see Eric Hobsbawm and Terence Ranger, eds., *The Invention of Tradition* (Cambridge, 1992). For its use by Kornetis, see *Children of the Dictatorship*, pp. 196–99.

60. Roland Robertson, "Glocalization: Time-Space and Homogeneity-Heterogeneity" in *Global Modernities*, ed. Mike Featherstone, Scott Lash, and Roland Robertson (London, 1995), pp. 25–44. "Local" has been construed in diverse ways in scholarly works based on the concept of glocalization. It has been equated with the "national" or the "regional" level or even linked with particular cities. I focus on the contextualization of transnationally circulating flows in the urban settings of Athens and Salonica and how these transfers are often embedded in a left-wing patriotic narrative.

61. As historians Efi Avdela and Angelika Psarra have also remarked, that movement was not a uniform one, including the one that appeared in Greece. Thus, with regard to

the women's liberation movement of the 1970s, I try to outline its varying tendencies as far as possible below. See Efi Avdela and Angelika Psarra, "Xanagrafontas to parelthon: Synchrones diadromes tis istorias ton gynaikon," in *Siopires Istories: Gynaikes kai Fylo stin istoriki afigisi,* ed. Efi Avdela and Angelika Psarra (Athens, 1997), p. 81.

62. Marwick, *The Sixties,* pp. 16–20, 680–82. Marwick did not confine the scope of these changes to the "youth," but he argued that they also influenced older in age people as well.

63. Konrad Jarausch, *After Hitler: Recivilizing Germans, 1945–1995* (Oxford, 2008), p. 180.

64. For the case of Eastern Europe, see Josie McLellan, *Love in the Time of Communism: Intimacy and Sexuality in the GDR* (Cambridge, 2011).

65. Peter N. Stearns, *Sexuality in World History* (Abingdon, UK, 2009), pp. 133–64; Lorenz Durrer, "Born to be Wild: Rockmusik und Protestkultur in der 1960er Jahren," in *Handbuch 1968 zur Kultur- und Mediengeschichte der Studentenbewegung,* ed. Martin Klimke and Joachim Scharloth (Stuttgart, 2007); Dagmar Herzog, "Between Coitus and Commodification: Young West German Women and the Impact of the Pill," in Schildt and Siegfried, *Between Marx and Coca Cola,* p. 261.

66. Dagmar Herzog, *Sexuality in Europe: A Twentieth-Century History* (Cambridge, 2011), p. 146.

67. Stearns, *Sexuality*; Simon Szreter and Kate Fisher, *Sex Before the Sexual Revolution: Intimate Life in England 1918–1963* (Cambridge, 2010).

68. Herzog, "Between Coitus," p. 263.

69. Scott Gunther, *The Elastic Closet: A History of Homosexuality in France: 1942–present* (London, 2009); Matt Houlbrook, *Queer London: Perils and Pleasures in the Sexual Metropolis, 1918–1957* (Chicago, 2005); Julia Paulus, Eva-Maria Silies, and Kerstin Wolff, eds., *Zeitgeschichte als Geschlechtergeschichte: Neue Perspektiven auf die Bundesrepublik* (Frankfurt/M., 2012).

70. This is true not only of Greece, but of Europe in the 1970s in general. A detailed presentation of the politicization of sexuality in diverse contexts across Europe during the 1970s, which shows that this decade was not necessarily marked by a growing spread of sexual freedom, may be found in the special issue entitled "'The Personal is Political': Sexuality, Gender, and the Left in Europe during the 1970s," which is co-edited by Nikolaos Papadogiannis and Sebastian Gehrig and was published in the *European Review of History—Revue européenne d'histoire* 22, no. 1 (2015).

71. Caroline Fink, Philipp Gassert, and Detlef Junker, introduction to *1968: The World Transformed,* ed. Caroline Fink, Philipp Gassert, and Detlef Junker (Washington DC, 1998), pp. 1–27; Martin Klimke, *The Other Alliance: Student Protest in West Germany and the United States in the Global Sixties* (Princeton, NJ, 2011); Hans Righart, "Moderate Versions of the 'Global Sixties': A Comparison of Great Britain and the Netherlands," *Journal of Area Studies* 13 (1998): pp. 82–96.

72. Horn, *The Spirit,* pp. 232–34.

73. Gerd Koenen, *Das rote Jahrzehnt: Unsere kleine deutsche Kulturrevolution 1967–1977* (Frankfurt/M., 2002). For a counter-argument, depicting the 1970s in West Germany as a "Social Democratic Decade," see Bernd Faulenbach, "Die Siebziger-

jahre—ein sozialdemokratisches Jahrzehnt?," *Archiv für Sozialgeschichte* 44 (2004): pp. 1–37.

74. Claus Leggewie, "A Laboratory of Postindustrial Society: Reassessing the 1960s in Germany," in Fink, Gassert, and Junker, *1968*, pp. 277–94. Similarly, Kristin Ross, an expert in comparative literature, has argued that several former radical left-wingers in France in the late 1970s "refashioned" the protests of the late 1960s as a "purely spiritual . . . revolution." Such a representation functioned as "the harbinger of the 1980s, an era marked by "the return to the individual" and the "triumph of market democracies." This is a trend which Ross maintains that has accommodated the prevalence of a narrative that she calls "the long march of democratic individualism." See Kristin Ross, *May '68 and its Afterlives* (London, 2002).

75. Gundle, *Between Hollywood and Moscow*, pp. 157, 163.

76. A valuable primary source is the partly digitalized archive of the Portuguese Communist newspaper *O Militante*. Researchers can access online volumes for the years 1974 and 1975. See http://www.pcp.pt/publica/militant/ (last accessed 15 August 2012).

77. David Gouard, "La 'Banlieue Rouge' face au renouvellement des générations. Une sociologie politique des cites Maurice Thorez et Youri Gagarine à Ivry-sur-Seine" (PhD diss., University of Montpellier 1, 2011).

78. These figures appear in Horn, *The Spirit*, p. 142.

79. Massimo Ilardi and Aris Accornero, *Il Partito Comunista Italiano, Struttura e storia dell'organizzazione 1921/1979* (Milan, 1982), p. 255; Roberto Guerzoni, "La Presenza del PCI e della FGCI: ampiezza, limiti e problem," in *La Crisi della societa italiana e gli ornamenti delle nuove generazioni. Atti del Convegno tenuto a Roma il 7–9 ottobre 1977*, pp. 179–80, Personal Collection of Donald Sassoon.

80. Dimitris A. Sotiropoulos, Ilias Nikolakopoulos, Christos Lyrintzis, "'Eisagogi: I poiotita kai I leitourgia tis Tritis Ellinikis Dimokratias," in *Koinonia kai Politiki. Opseis tis G' Ellinikis Dimokratias, 1974–1994*, ed. Christos Lyrintzis, Ilias Nikolakopoulos, Dimitris A. Sotiropoulos (Athens, 1996), pp. 19–42.

81. Voulgaris, *I Ellada tis Metapolitefsis*, p. 215. A much more simplistic and normative version of this argument gained traction in public debates that occurred after Greece received a bailout from the European Union, the European Central Bank, and the International Monetary Fund in 2010. Those discussions often revolved around the issue whether developments in postauthoritarian Greece were to blame for the crisis ensuing in that country. Diverse actors, such as right-wing liberals, asserted that those transformations heralded a surge of Party politics revolving around "clientelism," which brought Greece to this critical condition. For a liberal critique of the postauthoritarian transformations in Greece, see http://e-drasis.blogspot.gr/ (last accessed 18 December 2013). Nevertheless, such claims did not reign unchallenged. Socialist and Communist subjects rejected them, asserting that, in the environment of the crisis, democracy's achievements since the collapse of the dictatorial regime in 1974 were called into question. See "I politiki katastasi stin Ellada," Central Committee Document, First Congress of SYRIZA, 2012.

82. Gundle, *Between Hollywood and Moscow*, pp. 156–57.

83. Jane Jenson, "The French Communist Party and Feminism," *The Socialist Register* 17 (1980): pp. 121–47.

Part I

Prelude

Chapter 1

Cold War Consumers

Cultural and Social Transformations in the 1960s and the Early 1970s

Crucial social and cultural transformations occurred in postwar Greece. Rural areas were increasingly deserted, due to migration and urbanization. Alongside this, mass consumption spread its appeal in the urban centers. One of its manifestations was new leisure venues frequented by the youth, which appeared from the late 1950s onward in Athens and Salonica. Mass consumption and youth leisure, however, became contested fields, in which diverse social and political actors flexed their muscles. The Left initially decried new youth leisure patterns as conducive to inappropriate for the standards of the Left sexual behavior, even "crime." Aiming to challenge the accusations of the staunchly anti-communist Right that it did not represent "national interests," left-wing organizations were seriously involved in constructing and spreading a Greek "progressive" culture. Such "progressive" culture was also expected to act as a bulwark against "corruptive" for the youth cultural products. Nevertheless, the freedom of expression of left-wingers was limited in Greece during the 1950s and 1960s. Their condition deteriorated from 1967 to 1974, when they lived under the grip of the dictatorship. The early 1970s, however, were marked by the revival of left-wing youth radicalism, especially among university students. Those dissidents transgressed in their practice the cultural taxonomies that the Left had set in the preceding decades. I argue that this period was the hotbed of contradictions in the leisure activities and the sexual patterns of the left-wing youth, which emerged in full force in the mid-to-late 1970s, after the restoration of democracy.

Social and Cultural Transformations in a Financially Developing Greece

Post–World War II Greek society witnessed a number of profound changes. Two prominent ones were the growing urbanization from the late 1940s onward and the spread of mass consumption patterns due to the convergence of consuming styles of different social strata since the 1960s. As Campbell shows, the population of the city of Greater Athens rose from 1,378,686 in 1951 to 2,530,209 in 1971.[1] In total, the population of the urban centers, including Greater Athens and Greater Salonica, increased from 3,628,000 in 1961 to 5,659,000 in 1981, while that of the rural areas decreased in the same period from 3,675,000 to 2,956,000.[2] Middle-class people in the urban centers functioned as the prime proponent of change within society, displaying a "diminishing toleration of material deprivation," as Vassilis Karapostolis convincingly argues; this trend gradually filtered down the social ladder in the urban centers during the 1960s and 1970s.[3]

The diffusion of mass consumption was certainly connected with the effects of rapid economic development.[4] The Gross Domestic Product (GDP) growth rate in the period from 1960 to 1972, prior to the financial crisis that started in 1973, was 7.4 percent on average.[5] The motor of development, on the one hand, was the secondary sector. While in 1960 only 20 percent of the GDP was produced in the secondary sector, this figure rose to 34.7 percent in 1973.[6] Its growth can be attributed mainly to building construction projects, involving the erection of hotels in the tourist resorts and blocks of flats in the urban cities for the masses of people who migrated there from the rural areas. On the other hand, the contribution of the tertiary sector, and, especially, of tourism, to financial development, should not be underestimated. From the 1960s onward, Greece was visited by an increasing number of non-Greek tourists.[7] It is remarkable that Greece attracted only 37,464 foreign tourists in 1950. Nevertheless, this figure rose to 572,303 in 1962, 1,500,577 in 1970, 3,037,373 in 1973 and 4,247,233 in 1976.[8] In general, official data indicate that, from 1965 to 1973, the increase in the average real wage was significant every year, ranging from 9.5 percent in 1968 to 1.5 percent in 1973.[9]

This prosperity was certainly uneven, as a number of researchers demonstrate. According to Karapostolis and Nicos Mouzelis, income disparities were enduring throughout the period 1960–1975.[10] Still, the lower and lower-middle strata could afford to spend by relying on diverse sources of income, which included salaries and land rents, a situation that has been described by sociologist Konstantinos Tsoukalas as *polystheneia*.[11] For instance, their income was certainly complemented by the emigrants' remittances. From the late 1940s until the early 1970s a significant number of Greeks seeking a job emigrated to Australia and Canada, and from the 1960s to West Germany. The net emigration from 1946 to 1974 was 666,355; further 200,000 temporary emigrants, who returned in these years, should be added to that figure.[12]

The dawning era of mass consumption brought sweeping changes in leisure activities. It was tracked and, to an extent, shaped by the proliferation of Greek popular cinema movies in the period between the 1950s and early 1970s. Diverse films, ranging from comedies to melodramas, helped construct a fantasy of material abundance. Meanwhile, television arrived in Greece with a delay in comparison to the other Western European countries. A single state channel started operating in 1966 on a strict experimental level and was turned into a real television station with two channels in 1968. In 1968, its transmission was limited to Athens and its viewers were estimated to be around 60,000.[13] Nevertheless, TV audiences increased rapidly during the dictatorship years, especially due to the electrification of rural areas, which was actively supported by the regime. This development was at the detriment of Greek popular cinema, which had reached its apogee in the late 1960s and early 1970s. In 1970 the most successful film *Lieutenant Colonel Natasha* (1970) sold a record 751,117 tickets.[14] However, soon the audience shifted from the cinemas to television. The result was a disaster for Greek film production companies, such as Finos Films, which faced dwindling revenues, and many of them even closed.[15]

In addition, the expanding market that emerged in the environment of such financial development proved a fertile ground for the making of youth identities. Youth venues multiplied from the mid–1960s.[16] These were found either in the center of Athens and Salonica or in the squares of the lower-middle and working-class districts of these cities. Cafeterias and boîtes began to appear from the 1960s at the center of Athens. Cafeterias should not be confused with old-style *cafés*, existing both in villages and in the cities: the latter, as anthropological research has shown, attracted solely men, who would play cards, settle financial issues, or discuss politics.[17] On the contrary, women could frequent cafeterias as well, without being subjected to pejorative comments about their moral standards. The drink served was no longer merely the Turkish coffee, but also Nescafé (instant coffee), alongside alcoholic drinks, such as whiskey and cognac. Cafeterias usually remained open until late in the evening. Boîtes were small, often semi-underground spaces, where young people gathered to listen to live music. They were "imported" from France in the early 1960s and existed until the late 1970s. Another type of youth space that emerged in Greece in the 1960s was the discotheque.[18] They first appeared in the late 1960s, again mainly in the center of Athens and Salonica. Boîtes and discotheques proliferated in Plaka, an area in Athens, which was the hottest nightlife spot throughout Greece at that point and a prime tourist attraction, according to sociologist Michalis Nikolakakis.[19]

The significance of the youth spaces as well as mass media should be considered in relation to the shifts in sexual and gender norms that they accommodated. Unfortunately, there has hitherto been a remarkable scarcity in the examination of sexuality in Greece in the twentieth century, especially in historiography. However, research conducted by anthropologists provides important insights in this respect. In particular, British anthropologist John Campbell examined the nomadic community of *Sarakatsanoi* in the 1950s, premised on the conceptual framework of symbolic anthropology. He argued that the individual *timi* (honor) was inextricably linked with the family one. Both female and male Sarakatsanoi were assigned honor: in the case of the former, it was linked with *dropi* (shame): A woman had to conceal her sexuality or channel it to marriage and procreation. Her male kin were expected to guard her chastity. If she developed premarital sexual relations, they had to react violently against both her and her lover.[20] John Campbell, alongside Julian Pitt-Rivers and John Peristiany, went further and introduced the "Mediterranean paradigm," arguing that honor and shame were the core values in the entire "Mediterranean society," both in rural and in urban settings.[21]

One way or another, this conjugal model regulated gender and sexual relations in Greece in the 1950s and 1960s. Female sexuality was regarded as legitimate only after marriage.[22] The male kin settled the marriage of young women, providing the bride with the dowry of either an amount of money or some valuable objects.[23] The juvenile justice system also reinforced limitations on sex before marriage for women: regardless of the crime in which female minors were accused of being involved, they were subjected to chastity tests, which the state treated as a yardstick of moral integrity. By contrast, the juvenile justice system classified premarital sexual relationships of male heterosexuals as "normal." Male masturbation was similarly tolerated, unless accompanied by "excesses," such as voyeurism.[24] However, the prescriptive level did not necessarily reflect the actual sexual relationships in these societies, which were far more complicated. As anthropologist Michael Herzfeld has demonstrated, in the mountain villages of western Crete in the early 1980s women were demanded to be virgin until they got married. However, it was not atypical for men to find "complaisant young women" who were "willing to engage in sexual relationships with them—sometimes, though not always successfully, as a means of trapping them into marriage." There were even circumstances where young men had sexual relationships with two sisters on successive occasions. Still, as Herzfeld underlines, premarital sex had to be kept covert.[25]

Nevertheless, shifts in gender representations appeared in popular films, albeit in a contradictory manner, as sociologist Yvonne Cosma and historian Achilleas Hadjikyriacou show.[26] Unless they abided by the principle of marriage, women were presented as "superficial," ending up living a "lonely" life. Such representations of femininity featured prominently in the Greek dramas of that period. On the other hand, in 1960s comedies dynamic female figures often appeared and it was regarded as legitimate for them to demand that they progress toward the higher ranks in state institutions as well as in enterprises. In this vein, they were expected to choose their partner themselves, in a process based on "love" beyond "financial interests." Both "matchmaking" and the institution of "dowry" were vehemently criticized as parochial, coterminous with provincial life. However, despite the growing consensus among a variety of social and political actors, who concurred in condemning dowry, it still remains to be examined to what extent there were changes in practice.

In addition, popular Greek films and magazines demanded the substitution of a patriarchal family model, based upon the violent imposition of patriarchal authority, with a "modern" one, based on the mutual understanding of all members. Again, according to Cosma, men were expected to have the final say in the family decision-making. However, physical or psychological violence against women was lambasted in popular films—and not only there:[27] As Avdela has argued, in stark contrast to the 1950s, crimes stemming from the settlement of stigmatization of a girl's and her family's honor were no longer tolerated in the courts and in the press from the following decade.[28] To borrow a term introduced by Stearns and Stearns, it was a significant shift in the "emotionology," namely the standards of a society toward emotions—in this case, the emotion of "honor" in relation to anger and love within families.

So far, I have outlined some trends that appeared in popular culture in the wake of dissemination of mass consumption in Greece. However, different social and political actors received these in diverse ways. As historian Frank Trentmann argues convincingly, "historians now need to contextualize the different forms and functions of consumption, and the affiliated social visions and political systems competing with each other at the same time."[29] In this vein, the definition of "youth," "masculinity," and "femininity" were inextricably linked with competing conceptualizations of social relations that fought it out in the context of postwar Greece.

Left-Wing Youth Identities: Detachment or Intermixing?

Greece was mired in violence throughout the 1940s. Following an invasion by the forces of the Axis during World War II, the country experienced a Tripartite Occupation in 1941–1944 by Germany, Italy (until 1943), and

Bulgaria. In the meantime, a bloody Civil War raged, which, according to a number of scholars, had started in 1943; it pitted resistance against collaborationist groups as well as left-wing against non-left-wing resistance forces.[30] The Civil War in Greece terminated in 1949 with the crushing defeat of the Left. Greece was certainly no exception: as historian Claudio Pavone has aptly remarked, World War II was in general a "civil war," one which, as historian Mark Mazower underlines, was identified in various ways, be it class, ethnicity, or "rival factions fighting it out in the name of a bankrupt state" and which occurred in numerous contexts across Europe—Italy and France, to name some of them.[31] While, however, other Western European countries, such as West Germany and the United Kingdom, experienced a postwar period of political consensus, the Civil War left a clear imprint on postwar Greece.[32] Anti-communism became the official ideology of the Greek State and left-wingers were excluded from the higher ranks of the public administration. The state closely monitored the political beliefs of all citizens, recording these in the notorious *pistopoiitika koinonikon fronimaton* (certificates of social conviction) files. Conservative parties governed the country until 1967 apart from short intervals of centrist administration in 1950–1952 and 1963–1965; the Left, however, was totally excluded from government. Although some rules of parliamentary democracy, such as the holding of elections, were followed, the royal court and the armed forces played a major role in decision-making. In addition, a set of decrees that were introduced during the Civil War was used extensively to persecute left-wingers until 1974; Nikos Alivizatos, specialist in law, has named this legislation "parasyntagma,"[33] claiming that it functioned as a complement to the constitution.[34] The Communist Party was outlawed in 1947. The only option for political engagement open to its members was to join an umbrella group, called EDA (United Democratic Left).[35] Actually, from 1958 the KKE did not function at all as a separate entity. It reassembled itself as a clandestine organization in 1965; however, all its members were also affiliated with the EDA throughout the 1950s and the early-to-mid 1960s. As many political scientists have claimed, the post–Civil War era was characterized by a "weak" (*kachektiki*) or "disciplined" (*peitharchimeni*) democracy, which was followed from 1967 until 1974 by the imposition of a dictatorial regime.[36]

Nevertheless, the late 1950s witnessed a significant strengthening of the Left in Greece. The EDA emerged as the second strongest Party in the 1958 elections, when it garnered 24.43 percent of the vote. The youth groups affiliated with EDA were the N.EDA (Neolaia EDA, United Democratic Left Youth) until 1964, and later the DNL (Dimokratiki Neolaia Lambraki, Democratic Youth Lambrakis). N.EDA merged with DKNGL (Dimokratiki Kinisi Neon Grigoris Lambrakis, Democratic Youth Movement Grigoris Lambrakis), a group affiliated with, but not guided by EDA, as was the N.EDA, in 1964. The merger led to the creation of the DNL. N.EDA, DKNGL, and DNL were all legal groups.

For left-wing youth groups, the year 1962 represented a watershed: up to that point, N.EDA was very cautious about recruiting new members, fearing infiltration by the security forces. However, since 1962 the organization benefited from its interaction with the emerging youth protest movements. Groups of young left-wingers rallied against the violation of university asylum by the police in 1962. They broadened their aims, claiming to be engaged in the struggle for the protection of democracy, as the article 114 of the constitution demanded all Greek citizens to do. They called themselves the "movement of 114." In addition, left-wing university students complained about the meager state funding of the educational institutions—this stood at only 6.8 percent of the GDP in the early 1960s. Those students demanded that this figure be increased to 15 percent. The early 1960s also witnessed the emergence of peace activists, rallying around Syndesmos Neon dia ton Pyrinikon Afoplismon Bertrand Russell (Youth League for the Nuclear Disarmament Bertrand Russell), which organized since 1963 peace marches from Marathon, a village close to Athens, to the capital city of Greece. Young people taking part in these movements sooner or later joined the N.EDA or DNL, or at least participated in the activities spearheaded by these groups. In fact, in April 1965, according to political scientist Christoforos Vernardakis as well as political scientist and economist Yiannis Mavris, the DNL had 37,000 members and could mobilize up to 100,000.[37]

Both the EDA and its affiliated youth groups struggled to combat the official rhetoric of anti-communism, which labeled the Left as having betrayed "national interests" to Slav "enemies." The EDA by contrast represented itself as the genuine expression of the Greek nation, in juxtaposition with the Conservative political forces, which it described as "serving the imperialist centers," mainly the United States and secondarily Britain. Throughout the period extending from the mid–1940s to 1974 and despite its cultural anti-Americanism, the Greek Right was staunchly pro-United States in the foreign affairs domain. One important exception, however, concerned the Cyprus issue, over which there were disagreements between Greek right-wing policymakers and U.S. officials, as historian Ioannis Stefanidis has stressed.[38] On the contrary, in the 1950s and the 1960s, the Left was both politically and culturally anti-American. The issues that it usually raised were the deployment of U.S. troops in American military bases in Greece; the fact that American citizens in Greece were subject not to Greek, but U.S. law, the so-called *eterodikia* status; and the Cyprus issue, where its critique was leveled against both the United States and the United Kingdom. The EDA rallied its supporters around the "anti-colonial" struggle of the Greek-Cypriots against the British administration in the period from 1955 to 1959 and accused the Conservative government of Konstantinos Karamanlis of siding with the forces of "imperialism." Such a combination of patriotism/nationalism[39] and anti-Americanism was predominant in the language of the Left throughout the 1950s and 1960s and from the mid–1960s it was the common ground between the Left and what political scientist Andreas Pantazopoulos calls the "center-left" wing of the then-governing liberal Center Union Party. Andreas Papandreou informally led this wing and its supporters rallied in favor of what they labeled as "progressive nationalism." Their central aim was to achieve the "financial independence" of Greece from foreign capital and to promote national economic development through "rapid industrialization" and the "development" of agriculture.[40]

The left-wing patriotic narrative extended to the domain of leisure, revolving around "Greek popular tradition." For the Greek Left, "tradition" was in fact traced to a recent period, notably the nineteenth-century War of Independence, and not in patterns dating back to ancient Greek History. The way left-wingers conceptualized it could be aptly described with the Janus-faced metaphor introduced by political theorist Tom Nairn: the gaze of the left-wing patriotic discourse extended both to "modernity" as well as to the legacy of "tradition."[41] Actually, it did not treat "tradition" as a set of practices that belonged to a distant past, but as a timeless concept running through contemporary cultural products as well as stimulating cultural production in the future. However, the Left did not necessarily laud the actual cultural tastes of the contemporary lower-middle and working-class people. Already in the interwar years as well as in the subsequent decades, it had espoused an idealized version of the "Greek people," which sociologist and political scientist Panayis Panagiotopoulos names "deon laiko" (ideal popular).[42] The "Greek people" was represented as a "victim" of "fascist" or "imperialist exploitation"; simultaneously, as Akis Gavriilidis, philosophy expert and translator, correctly points out, it was designated as "inherently resistant."[43] This representation revolved around the archetype of the "uncompromising" militant rooted in the lower classes, who struggled indefatigably against the "exploitation" or "enslavement" (sklavia) of Greece. The "imperialist" intrusion was perceived as having entered through cultural products as well. The "resistant" spirit of the people was not enough to face this challenge, however, and required the guidance of the Left. From the late 1950s, leisure patterns that were associated with the youth were a cause of serious concern for the Greek Left. The so-called "American way of life," which it associated mainly with rock 'n' roll, porn, and "gangster"[44] movies as well as sfairistiria (halls with flipper games), was dismissed on the grounds that it bred unstable sexual relationships, individualism and, ultimately, "crime."[45] Such a reaction toward new youth leisure patterns was not, however, confined to the Left. In what both Avdela and Katsapis describe as "moral panic,"[46] the Left, the Center, and the Right alongside the Church of Greece depicted the fans of rock 'n' roll in the late 1950s as "tentimpoides" (teddy-boys).[47] "Teddy-boyism" was a reference to both a specific subculture, whose members used to provoke through various practices, such as by throwing yogurt and harassing women, as well as to reconfigurations of sexual norms in new forms of social interaction of young people, such as parties. A palpable result of that panic was the voting of law 4000/1958 by all the parliamentary parties, including EDA.[48]

In order to counter the "detrimental effects" of the "American way of life" and to challenge the monopolization of national symbols by the Right, the Left supported cultural projects introduced from the early 1960s by left-wing intellectuals, many of whom were young. These intellectuals, acting in dialogue with the EDA, regarded the possibility of linking "high" with "popular" culture as a tangible project. In this vein, the 1960s witnessed the emergence of a politically engaged cinematic genre, known as "New Greek Cinema" (NEK, Neos Ellinikos Kinimatografos). In stark contrast to the plummeting popularity of Greek popular cinema from the early 1970s onward, NEK outlived the 1960s. Its title was meant to differentiate it from the former or "Old Greek Cinema" (PEK, Palaios Ellinikos Kinimatografos), which was criticized for lacking any direct political references.[49] The advocates of NEK also chastised PEK's "simplistic" plots, opting for experimental forms, including photomontage. To the melodrama of popular movies, they counterposed an unsentimental approach. In fact, many NEK filmmakers, such as the directors Dimos Theos and Fotos Labrinos, were actively involved in politics, especially in the EDA.[50] NEK movies featured prominently in what began in 1960 as the "Greek Cinema Week" and was renamed in 1966 as the "Greek Film Festival." The latter took place annually in Salonica and was under the aegis of the ministry of industry, as the state-regarded cinema in financial terms as a motor of economic development. Nevertheless, the content of many Greek film productions was starkly at variance with the ideological orientation of the governments of the 1960s and 1970s.[51]

Apart from NEK, *entehno laiko* (artistic popular) music was another hobbyhorse of the Greek Left.[52] It was spearheaded by the president of the DNL, Mikis Theodorakis. A core component of *entehno laiko* was *melopoiimeni poiisi,* namely setting poetry into "Greek popular music." It was conceptualized as an effort to render poetry accessible "to the people."[53] The strategy was soon met with enthusiasm within the Left. *Epitheorisi Technis,* an influential magazine among left-wingers, welcomed it.[54] Theodorakis actually presented the first recording of this genre in the early 1960s. It was *Epitaphios,* which comprised songs based on the poetic eponymous collection by Giannis Ritsos, himself a member of the KKE and the EDA.[55] In this recording, *bouzouki,* a Greek popular instrument, featured prominently and songs were sung by Grigoris Bithikotsis, a veteran of the working-class district of Kokkinia in Athens. Mikis Theodorakis was preoccupied with *rebetiko* music sounds. In doing so, he continued, to an extent, the effort already made in the 1950s by another renowned Greek composer, Manos Hadjidakis, to employ *rebetiko* in order to compose songs that fall simultaneously into the category of "popular" and "high culture" or capture, as the expert in cultural and gender studies Papanikolaou put it, the space of the "high-popular." Hadjidakis, however, differed from Theodorakis in refusing to situate his music within a political project. Although he leaned to the Right, he did not construe his work as part of right-wing cultural politics. Rather, he sought in a somewhat escapist manner to construct a "personal space of dreams."[56]

In fact, the *entehno laiko* project marked the beginning of a process of rehabilitation of the Greek popular music genre of *rebetiko* among Greek leftwingers. *Rebetiko* had flourished in Greece in the interwar period, especially among an underclass comprising a segment of refugees from Asia Minor.[57] Initially, the Greek Left approached *rebetiko* from the prism of the "mystique of marginality": "Figures of the underworld were perceived as spontaneous representatives of social subversion."[58] However, the KKE soon associated it with the consumption of drugs, especially hashish. In his research about *rebetiko* in the concentration and deportation camps where members of the Communist Party were held, Panagiotopoulos explains that the genre was repudiated by the Party in order to avoid the left-wing "political detainees" being identified with the "penal detainees."[59] Nevertheless, Theodorakis employed *rebetiko* sounds in a "refined" popular music form combined with poetry. This was a move which, according to Papanikolaou, prompted a widespread debate within the Left, which gradually accepted *rebetiko* as the continuity of Greek folk music.[60]

The magazine *Epitheorisi Technis,* another major left-wing cultural project, was published from 1956 to 1967, mainly by intellectuals that had been born in the 1920s, such as Titos Patrikios and Tassos Leivaditis. It published reviews on literature, but also contained coverage about other arts, such as music. The magazine was supervised, but not necessarily controlled by the EDA. According to Aimilia Karali, specialist in modern Greek literature, even though the majority of the members of its first editorial board were affiliated with the KKE and EDA, the magazine was not launched following a decision of the apparatus of these organizations.[61] Throughout its existence, *Epitheorisi Technis* strove for autonomy from the EDA and the KKE line. Its endeavors were helped by the fact that the KKE decided in 1958 to cease the activities of its basis organizations in Greece and to merge them with those of the EDA. This move gave rise to reflection among some KKE members in Greece, who opted for more polyphony in the activities of the Left in Greece and, concomitantly, for less restrictive organizational structures. Similarly, the iconoclastic 20th Congress of the Communist Party of the Soviet Union in 1956 also sparked the interest of the contributors to *Epitheorisi Technis* to challenge left-wing intellectual orthodoxies of the preceding decades. The magazine raised many contentious issues, including its critique of social-ist realism.[62,63] From the mid–1930s, socialist realism had been pervasive in the literature produced by Communist authors, including the Greek ones, while reviewers in Communist magazines and newspapers demanded that genuinely revolutionary authors conform to its principles. However, socialist realism was growingly challenged in Greece in the twenty years from 1947 to 1967.[64] *Epitheorisi Technis* drew on and simultaneously reinforced this tendency. Some of the major contributors to the magazine, such as Kostas Kouloufakos and Dimitris Raftopoulos, claimed that left-wing intellectu-als should not be instructed by the Party apparatus to advocate a particu-lar dogma (including socialist realism). Nevertheless, the re-establishment of the basis organizations of the KKE in Greece in 1965 and the concomitant drive for more rigid approaches to Marxism-Leninism affected the domain of "culture." High-ranking KKE cadres sought ways to curtail the circula-tion of *Epitheorisi Technis*. This would soon happen, but was not due to the KKE's efforts, but to the establishment of the dictatorship in 1967 and the subsequent ban on all sorts of left-wing publications.[65]

The organized left-wing youth in this period not only played a pivotal role in the inception of some of those projects, but also actively participated in the circulation of all of them. *Epitheorisi Technis* was often advertised in the publications of the youth aligned with or leaning toward EDA, such as in the student magazine *Panspoudastiki*.[66] Similarly, the left-wing youth organi-zation DNL actively supported the spread of "artistic popular" music as well as NEK cinema through the numerous cultural associations it founded, the so-called clubs. These were venues where the theatrical or musical groups re-lated to the DNL gathered and where a library usually existed as well. Apart from the bigger urban centers, DNL clubs could be found in smaller towns in rural areas, even in villages.[67]

As the 1960s progressed, however, the relationship of young left-wingers to new leisure patterns became far more complex. Social interaction among young left-wingers did not occur solely in events fostered by the DNL, but also in commercial venues. As B.N.-C.,[68] a female, student and member of the N.EDA in the early 1960s, narrated in an interview: "After the protests, my friends and I gathered in a cafeteria close to Syntagma Square. We were all young people, boys and girls, chatting and singing until late at night, until 2–3 am" (B.N.-C., Interview).

In the mid–1960s, Greek left-wing organizations began to endorse American protest songs associated with the Civil Rights Movement, especially those of Bob Dylan and Joan Baez from the mid–1960s. More notably, rock 'n' roll increasingly penetrated the leisure pursuits of DNL members, with rock parties being held even in their clubs.[69] Although the official language of the group continued to lambast the "American way of life" and the fans of rock 'n' roll music as "ye-yedes," the DNL began, not without hesitation, to invite rock 'n' roll bands to its events. Katsapis confirms this trend, showing that the DNL asked one such Greek band, *Cinquetti*,[70] to participate in an anti–Vietnam War concert in March 1967, shortly prior to the establishment of the dictatorship.[71]

One way or another, social interaction among young male and female left-wingers intensified in the mid–1960s. A landmark was certainly the massive protests against the unconstitutional sacking of the centrist government headed by Georgios Papandreou by king Constantine in July 1965, in which thousands of young protesters participated. Although data to support this argument is scarce, a number of interviews conducted by Kornetis indicate that these encounters were "liberal outbreaks" and facilitated premarital sexual relationships.[72] Still, while not banning sexual relationships among their members, as the left-wing partisans had done during the Civil War, the Left clearly endorsed marriage in the event that unmarried people had come into sexual contact. Young female left-wingers involved in sex before marriage were pressured by EDA cadres, as well as by their families, to get married, as T.T., male, cadre of N.EDA and, subsequently, of the DNL, narrates (T.T., Interview).[73] In general, affiliation to the youth organizations of the EDA both provided new opportunities and set limits to the socialization and the leisure pursuits of youngsters.

The Condition of Politics in Greece During the Dictatorship Years

The mid-to-late 1960s in Greece were marked by continuing turmoil, which affected both the Left and the condition of democracy in the country. The KKE suffered a serious setback following its split in 1968 into the pro-Soviet KKE, headed first by Kostas Koligiannis and then, after 1972, by Charilaos Florakis, and the KKE Es., led by Babis Drakopoulos. The KKE Es. gradually developed the demand for greater autonomy from Moscow. This split was precipitated by internal tensions that were simmering throughout the period from 1964 to 1968. The issue of whether the members of the then-illegal KKE should demand the legalization of the Party or whether that would be premature, as argued by many of those who joined the KKE Es., caused rancorous debates. Following the split, the pro-Soviet Communists, backed by the Soviet Union, as their correspondence with the Soviet Embassy in Athens indicates, regarded themselves as the only legitimate Communist Party, denouncing the KKE Es. either as the "Revisionist Group" or simply "Es." The KKE Es., for its part, criticized the "dogmatism" of the KKE and its claim to represent the sole genuine Communist Party.[74]

In the meantime, the centrist government, which was formed in 1963, collapsed in 1965 following a wave of defections, encouraged by King Constantine. Subsequently, it proved very difficult for any Party to command a parliamentary majority. In the streets the DNL organized massive protests against the meddling of the king.[75] In order to forestall what they described as the "imminent danger of Greece becoming a Communist country," a number of army officers staged a coup d'état on 21 April 1967. The dictatorship that was soon established was led by colonels Georgios Papadopoulos and Nikolaos Makarezos as well as by the brigadier Stylianos Pattakos. All political parties and youth organizations were declared illegal. As political scientist Nancy Bermeo notes, the Greek junta is "unique," compared to the Latin American dictatorial regimes that were established in the same period, in its treatment of the parliamentary Right. As she maintains, it was just in the Greek case that leaders of right-wing parties were "immediately rounded up and jailed."[76] However, a constitution was introduced in 1968. Initially the regime was declared to be a "constitutional monarchy." Nevertheless, the relationships of the military regime with the royal court deteriorated: after a failed coup attempt by royalist officers in December 1967, the king fled the country. Subsequently, lieutenant general Georgios Zoitakis was sworn in as regent. He held this post until 21 March 1972, when Georgios Papadopoulos assumed the regency for one year, until the monarchy was officially abolished. In July 1973, Greece was proclaimed a "presidential republic," still under the grip of the dictators.[77]

In the so-called "presidential" phase of the dictatorial regime in 1973, the restrictions on political parties of all directions and multi-Party elections continued. Nevertheless, the dictatorship tried to forge an alliance with the most Conservative forces to the point where it formed a government with a rightist politician, Spyridon Markezinis, as prime minister, which lasted from 8 October to 25 November 1973. The presidential regime of Papadopoulos, however, was only short-lived; a junta headed by brigadier Dimitrios Ioannidis, the head of the ESA or Greek Military Police, soon overthrew him. Colonel Gkizikis was sworn in as president and retained the position until December 1974, overseeing the transition to democracy.

The 1967–1974 dictatorship, according to sociologist and philosopher Nikos Poulantzas, was not a fascist regime. It never created a mass Party or mass organizations, such as the Hitler Jugend (Hitler Youth).[78,79] Historian Thanos Veremis also argues that it lacked a coherent ideology.[80] However, it certainly endorsed some strands of social conservatism and anti-communism. It cloaked itself in the slogan of "Fatherland, Religion and Family." To enforce "decent mores," it banned miniskirts and imposed mandatory maximum hair lengths for men. [81] Nevertheless, it tolerated Greek popular movies that were produced during those years, such as *Epicheirisi Apollon* (Operation Apollo, 1968), which showed young Greek women wearing miniskirts—even two-piece swimsuits.Moreover, the Greek Orthodox character of the Greek nation was proclaimed as a bulwark against the "intrusion of communism." To describe its anti-communist orientation, the dictatorship employed a discourse that teemed with medical metaphors: The country was represented as needing a "bandage," so that it might recover from the threat of the "Communist danger."

The regime managed to gain relative consensus, as Kornetis argues compellingly, among some segments of the Greek population: although active support for it was limited, a number of social groups apparently tolerated the dictatorship. Democracy had largely been discredited in the mid–1960s, not least due to the "continuous alteration of short-lived governments." Meanwhile, segments of the population benefitted from the regime: for instance, several rural residents witnessed infrastructure projects in the areas where they lived, including road construction and the introduction of electricity.[82]

Rebels With Many Causes

Despite such relative consensus, the dictatorship did not reign unchallenged. Its first years, 1967–1969, witnessed the most extensive activity of groups endorsing political violence against the junta; still, their influence was limited to merely a segment of the "few thousand" citizens that historian Polymeris Voglis estimates that joined clandestine organizations in this period.[83] He aptly remarks that the lack of mass mobilization against the dictatorship during those years is vindicated by the relatively few citizens who were tried by military tribunals from April 1967 to August 1971 for subverting the regime. Voglis draws on data presented by historian Giorgos Mitrofanis, according to whom 3,363 citizens were tried by military tribunals in this period and

2,045 were charged. The situation changed to an extent in the early 1970s, the period of the so-called "controlled liberalization." The dictatorship, with the aim of broadening its social base and of silencing criticism abroad, opted for the softening of censorship alongside the removal of martial law in most regions of the country. These policies lasted until the eruption of student uprisings in 1973, which provoked a belated return to the iron fist. According to Kornetis, the "controlled liberalization" brought results which certainly did not meet the expectations of the regime: it created "room for the student body to maneuver," allowing opposition groups to voice their critique and gather support.[84] The opposition attracted segments of Greek youth and especially the students, who underwent a progressive radicalization.[85] It is noteworthy that, at that point, similar to what occurred in Western Europe in general, the number of university students in Greece was growing significantly. In fact, from less than 30,000 in 1960 they amounted to 70,161 in 1971–1972 and to 87,476 in 1981–1982.[86]

The youth groups that emerged out of the split in the KKE commanded some support among radical students, although their membership was very low. Estimates by the left-wing youth groups about their membership during the dictatorship, corroborated by sociologist Argyris Yfantopoulos in the case of RF, indicate that they attracted barely more than a few hundred in each case.[87] However, these figures are not a good guide to the breadth of the opposition. Left-leaning dissident students were usually not affiliated with a particular Party during those years. The disavowal of the dictatorship was the glue that kept them together. In this period, although some young people who opposed the regime positioned themselves in the Center or even at the Right of the political spectrum, dissent was dominated by left-leaning young people, who, as the early 1970s progressed, increasingly couched their disenchantment with the regime in a language more or less influenced by Marxism.[88] Rather than Party membership, the narratives of affiliated left-wing students in the early 1970s are premised on membership in a common "generational experience," that of the "anti-dictatorial movement" of 1970–1974. This is evident in numerous testimonies, such as that of N.T., male, student, and high-ranking cadre of RF since the early 1970s, and of A.H., male, student, and member of the KNE since the early 1970s.

Regarding their organizational structures, students rallied around the FEA (Foititikes Epitropes Agona, Student Committees of Struggle), created in December 1971 by students of left-wing inclination who had no strict political affiliation. The FEA began as peer groups of students who shared an anti-regime spirit and soon spread to all Faculties. Besides the FEA, left-leaning dissident students socialized through regional student groups, such as the student societies for those originating from Crete or Istanbul. Anti-regime students did not get involved in the official administrative councils of their university departments, because they were controlled by the dictatorship appointees.[89]

Student radicalization culminated in 1973 with something akin to a mass movement: February witnessed protests in the Law School in Athens, which was briefly occupied on 14 February. Simultaneously, Kornetis claims that around 3,000 opposition students gathered outside the School of Physics and Mathematics in Salonica.[90] The most massive protest, however, occurred in the Polytechnic School of Athens from 14 to 17 November 1973.[91] A broad range of opposition students joined: many were not aligned with a specific group. But the crowd also included members of the student group affiliated with the KNE, which was called Anti-EFEE (Ethniki Foititiki Enosi Ellados, National Student Union of Greece), alongside RF, PAK, Trotskyites, and Maoists.[92] The KNE and RF endorsed a more moderate line: the former wished the demands to be limited to student issues, while RF argued in favor of the formation of a "national unity" government. Radical demands were confined to the Trotskyites and the Maoists who used slogans such as a "Workers' and Peasants' Government." In addition, it was these groups that supported the occupation from the beginning to the end.[93] Soon, a coordinating committee was established in the occupied school. Although most left-leaning protestors continued to be unaffiliated, the coordination of the protest was provided by the bickering left-wing youth organizations. The protests soon spread to other cities: left-leaning dissident students occupied university departments in Salonica, Patras, and Ioannina. However, they were all finally suppressed by the regime, which now adopted a tougher approach toward dissidents that would last until its collapse in July 1974. In particular, by February 1974 the main operational figures of A-EFEE and the Maoist EKKE were arrested, while left-wingers of all directions were persecuted. Michalis Sabatakakis and Vera Damofli explained to Kornetis how they lived on the run during this period to escape arrest.[94]

Although they could claim a major role in the leadership of the protests, the impact of left-wing youth organizations on the life of left-leaning dissident students was not substantial. Youth politicization can be described as rather fluid, since the Parties could not control much of their lives. Consequently, the militants found themselves caught up in a range of ideological and lifestyle influences. This fluid condition served to highlight the heterogeneity and a number of ambiguities both in their everyday life and in their ideological background.

The conceptual framework shared by the left-leaning dissident students was a far cry from theoretical homogeneity. In fact, the left-leaning youth were intimately linked with the production and circulation of translated texts, which blossomed particularly in the early 1970s. According to translation studies expert Dimitris Asimakoulas, left-wing publishers suffered from severe restrictions on their activity on the eve of the dictatorship; however, they soon bounced back.[95] Since 1968, small left-wing publishing houses emerged, such as Skaravaios Publications, created mainly by young entrepreneurs. Those houses published translations of the works of diverse authors, such as Karl Marx, Friedrich Engels, Vladimir Ilyich Lenin, Louis Althusser, Mao Zedong, figures from the Frankfurt School, Eugène Ionesco, and Bertolt Brecht. Left-leaning students were avid readers, especially of those translated works. In the early 1970s, they gathered in bookshops, such as the one owned by the Kaiti Saketa in Salonica, to read and exchange views. Though intellectually heterogeneous, left-leaning students did not regard such readings as incompatible. In this vein, the appeal of books, published by the Trotskyite editions "Neoi Stochoi," which drew on the thinking of the Frankfurt School—especially Herbert Marcuse—extended far beyond the Trotskyites. It was not at all unusual for a person leaning toward the pro-Soviet KNE to be open to the ideas of the so-called "New Left" in Western Europe.[96] As Asimakoulas maintains, translated texts helped those young dissidents "experience and manage connectedness and alterity as they make sense of the world around them," especially of the ideological orientation of contemporary protest movements; thus, the ramifications of "translation" were far broader than plainly "textual and cultural production."[97]

More notably, the conflicting tendencies concerning the leisure pursuits of young left-wingers that had appeared already in the 1960s were perpetuated and, actually, became even starker. In the last years of the dictatorship, what arose were symbols and practices that kept together young left-leaning dissidents. Those dissidents were certainly not indifferent to the mapping of Greek history. In this vein, "tradition" was invoked by the Left to dispute the monopolizing of patriotism by the regime. This effort certainly resonated with the rationale behind the cultural politics of the Left since the 1950s, namely to designate itself as the "genuine expression of the Greek nation." Cultural products that these students appreciated as "traditional" were connected to a great extent with music. One such genre was the *rizitika*, Cretan folk songs, which were rediscovered by the composer Giannis Markopoulos. They were usually sung by Nikos Xylouris, Cretan singer and lyra-player, who was adored by left-leaning students. One *rizitiko* song, "Pote tha kamei xasteria" (When will the skies clear) accompanied student protesting against the regime, marking their longing for its collapse. Opposition students also sang the *klephtika* of the Ottoman period, the ballads of the brigands.[98] They were enamored of *rebetika* songs as well: the genre, already rehabilitated among left-wingers since the 1960s, functioned as a signifier of subversion and resistance. In general, this phenomenon, as Kornetis argues convincingly, was a resignification and recontextualization of cultural patterns in order to express disavowal of the dictatorship.

The second important axis in those symbols and practices of the left-leaning students was the self-designation of left-leaning dissident students as the heirs of the "anti-fascist, anti-imperialist struggle" since the 1930s. This discourse functioned as a counterweight to the official anti-communist propaganda. The dictatorial regime lambasted the activities of left-wing forces under the Occupation in the early 1940s: it belittled their activity against the fascist rulers and maintained that they forged alliances with "enemies of the nation," such as Bulgaria, while persecuting the "genuine resisting forces."[99] The military junta appropriated the doctrine of national continuity and consistency. It portrayed the Civil War as part of a sequence dating back from the Trojan War as well as more proof that Greeks would struggle against those purportedly posing a threat to their existence. The state-sponsored annual festival, which was entitled "Celebration of the Martial Virtue of the Greeks" (*Eorti polemikis aretis ton Ellinon*), and publications referring to this event, were undergirded by this idea.[100] Moreover, the dictatorship promoted movies, such as *Grammos Vitsi* (1971), where left-wing partisans in the Civil War were portrayed as blood-thirsty instruments of the USSR. Despite the fact that this assumption was a staple of the official ideology in Greece throughout the 1950s and the early-to-mid 1960s, Greek popular movies at that point, aiming to instill national unity, contained no reference to those partisans as perpetrators of violence against their compatriots.[101] It was not prior to 1967 that images of the "Red Terror" spread in the Greek cinema. By contrast, the anti-fascist discourse of left-leaning dissidents revolved around the left-wing resistance against the Tripartite Occupation of 1941–1944. A book titled *Les Kapetanios* (Paris, 1970), written by the French author Dominique Eudes, which glorified partisans, became a bestseller among left-leaning dissident students.[102] Old partisan songs also began to reemerge in this period. The memory of left-wing resistance against the Tripartite Occupation of Greece (1941–1944) would affect their outer appearance as well. Affiliated left-wingers or left-leaning students started growing beards in order to resemble the partisans. The same trend had a significant impact on both the production and the reception of Greek cinema in this period. The early 1970s witnessed the increasing production of politically engaged Greek movies. Despite the fact that Greece was under the grip of a military junta, these films usually made their debut in the state-sponsored film festival. The softening of censorship since 1970 and the rise of youth radicalism facilitated this trend. The politically charged Greek cinema made its initial efforts to construct a counter to the official anti-communist commemoration of

Greek history. One of the first examples was Theodoros Angelopoulos's film *Meres tou '36* (Days of '36), first shown in 1972. This movie was the first of Angelopoulos's so-called history trilogy, which continued after the collapse of the dictatorship. Its first part focused on the decline of the parliamentary democracy in the 1930s in Greece and the establishment of the dictatorial regime of Ioannis Metaxas.[103] Left-leaning dissident students, as Kornetis and Kokkali describe, proved to be a responsive audience to this project.[104]

The works of Mikis Theodorakis, an artist who was immensely popular among left-leaning dissident students and significantly helped them shape their collective memory, were banned by the regime. Theodorakis himself had been persecuted by the regime until 1970, when he exiled himself from Greece for four years, until the collapse of the dictatorship, becoming a symbol of resistance. As in the case of "traditional" cultural products, left-leaning dissidents sought to distil political messages from his work, such as "Tha simanoun I kabanes" (The Bells Will Ring), from the album *Romiossini* (1966), based on the poetry of Giannis Ritsos as well as *Ta Tragoudia tou Agona* (Songs of Struggle), which was first recorded in 1971. The references those songs made to imprisonment and torture, but also to the enduring struggle of left-wingers from the 1930s until the dictatorship years, struck a chord with the young left-leaning dissidents. They met at homes and listened to his music on cassettes, which circulated hand to hand. More notably, as Kornetis describes, Theodorakis's songs were played throughout the occupation of the Polytechnic School in Athens.[105]

The left-wing patriotic discourse was also pervasive in theatre performances in the early 1970s. During the first years of the dictatorial regime, theatre activities suffocated, since the regime ruled with an iron fist. The junta banned a number of classical dramas by Aeschylus, Sophocles, and Euripides, as well as comedies by Aristophanes, which the regime suspected that could help cultivate subversive ideas.[106] A telling example is Sophocles' *Antigone,* in which Antigone self-consciously defies the authority of Creon, the ruler of Thebes. She finds his orders as contradicting "divine law," which she regards as superior and which she follows until her bitter end. As a result, she is severely punished by Creon and she finally hangs herself. Such acts of disobedience, the dictatorship feared, could spark political upheaval in contemporary Greece. However, the softening of censorship in the early 1970s affected theatre as well, which began to blossom once again. According to Kornetis, "by 1972 a great number of directors, playwrights, actors and actresses had devoted themselves to a theatre that would reach the people and would communicate political messages."[107] The theme of "dependence" of Greece in the nineteenth and twentieth century on foreign actors featured prominently in these initiatives.

However, the young left-leaning dissidents of the late 1960s did not draw solely on the "Greek tradition" or contemporary Greek history. They also developed a sense of identification with youth protest in Western Europe and the hippie counterculture in the United States. In the case of the latter, its influence expanded beyond the left-leaning dissident students. The "hippies" were an object both of fascination and of criticism for large segments of Greek society in the early 1970s.[108] The perception that they were prone to drug consumption raised eyebrows, not only among left-leaning dissident students, but also in popular Greek films, such as *Marijuana Stop* (1971).[109] On the other hand, newspapers and popular magazines teemed with images of "hippy-style" clothes: dressing formally was portrayed as out of tune with "the spirit of our times." Correspondence from New York and Rome in Greek fashion magazines and newspapers reported that the hippies "had conquered fashion" and publicized colorful shirts and large belts as stylish items. The same publications were particularly dismissive of "grey suits."[110]

Left-leaning dissident students became familiar with youth protest in Western Europe and the United States mainly through films, such as *Woodstock* (1970) and *The Strawberry Statement* (1970), as well as by books, such as *Counterculture*, which referred to them.[111] Displaying this self-fashioning, L.M., male and high-school pupil in this period, narrated: "We had watched *Woodstock* and *The Strawberry Statement*. In my mind, there was an image of youth as a force that would change the world" (L.M., Interview).[112] N.E., a female who graduated high school in 1973 and studied in Paris, also argued: "We were very close to the generation of '68, we saw *The Strawberry Statement* and *Woodstock. Woodstock* was a landmark for us" (N.E., Interview). Cinema served to "transmit experiences" that Greek students lacked.[113] As Angeliki Xydi narrated to Kornetis, watching *Woodstock* helped her to understand "what incredible things were taking place outside Greece."[114] Various young people, who disavowed the regime, ranging from left-leaning students to non-politicized rockers, were inspired by these movies to voice their opposition to it. As a result, those screenings were often followed by spontaneous demonstrations. The dictatorship responded by banning such films shortly after release.[115]

In turn, the narrower circle of the affiliated students alongside the larger group of unaffiliated students that shared disenchantment with the dictatorial regime invested their cultural tastes with representations of "1968" and "Woodstock." This connection is evident in the story that a then left-wing student Antonis Davanelos narrated to Kornetis: "The message that was coming from abroad, mainly from abroad, was the following: the wind of freedom that was unleashed after May '68. Since in Greece there was no political discussion, it was banned by the Junta, it's strange but I think, without being sure, these are at least my memories, that the message came mainly from the States and mainly through music. Woodstock, the music, Dylan, Crosby, Stills, Nash & Young and so on."[116]

The important shift that occurred in the early 1970s lay in the fact that the interaction of young left-leaning dissidents with rock music, which had begun in the mid–1960s, intensified. Clubs where rock music was played, like *Kyttaro* in Athens, or record shops where rock was available, such as *Pop 11* in Athens, were among the favorite venues of the left-leaning dissident students. The latter would be usually enamored of rock music from the mid–1960s until the mid–1970s in the United Kingdom and the United States: the Beatles and the Rolling Stones, but also psychedelic rock artists, like Jimi Hendrix, and progressive rock, such as the music of the Pink Floyd. However, rock music did not necessarily signify left-wing politicization: Whether militant or not, numerous young people enjoyed the music in clubs and at house parties.

By the 1970s, the influence of "Woodstock" and "May 1968" among left-leaning dissident students was also evident in their clothing style. In the 1960s, male members of the DNL wore suits and ties in their public appearances, even at rallies and open-air concerts. From the early 1970s, however, suits would be replaced by blue jeans: the latter clothing style served as a means of identification of left-leaning dissident students with the youth protest in Western Europe and the United States of the late 1960s. It would be appropriated and reinvested with meaning to signify opposition to the dictatorial regime. One way or another, a globally circulating product simultaneously acquired "localized" connotations, to employ a term used by Daniel Miller, expert in material culture.[117] Blue jeans remained popular throughout the 1970s among young Communists and Socialists, although from 1974 onward this clothing style would no longer be linked with "1968."

In addition, the connection of youth tourism with "Woodstock" was an important ingredient for the making of a number of peer groups in the early 1970s among pupils who attended private high schools in Athens, such as the Athens College, and belonged to the upper middle class.[118] Athens College was founded in 1925 on the model of the British "public school." It educated prominent businessmen as well as well-known right-wing politicians, such as Miltiadis Evert, Antonis Samaras, and Stephanos Manos.[119] However, the College, alongside other private schools, also produced peer groups of pupils who leaned to the Left. Many of them subsequently attended famous French and British universities, such as the Sorbonne and the London School of Economics, where they came into contact with semiotics and second-wave Feminism. Some of those pupils joined RF, when they became university students in the early 1970s.[120] Until that point, they were not affiliated with any Party. They identified in a vague sense with youth protest in Western Europe and the United States, not only to express their opposition to the dictatorship, but also as a means of challenging the image of "respectable" children through the display of lack of discipline toward their upper-class family. Tourism featured prominently in this process, as a rite of passage to personal autonomy from parents. It entailed destinations in Western Europe, such as Amsterdam, Spain, and even the United States. N.E., female and a private high school pupil, recalls: "I traveled to New York in 1971.... I thought that it was very revolutionary to cross the Village, to visit the Bronx and Harlem by myself. I wanted to smoke hashish. We had to differ from our parents, we had to differ from the bourgeois class" (N.E., interview). However, the most usual element of their vacations was travels to Greek islands. As N.E. also narrates, referring to her experiences as a high school pupil until 1972 and, subsequently, as a university student in France: "[W]e stayed in some miserable hotels, in camping sites. We had to travel to the least popular tourist attractions, the less expensive destinations. It was part of the framework of our emancipation" (N.E., interview).

Interviews with members of these peer groups described the lack of luxury coupled with the display of their bodies through nudism as subversive "hippy" acts (N.E., interview). These excursions were certainly a very important moment of transgression that these former pupils shared and which has frozen in their memories as a site of affective investment. In their oral testimonies, all of these former elite high school pupils could narrate in detail the itineraries of these excursions as well as when and with whom they traveled there. The experience and the shared memory of it appear to have consolidated an enduring friendship that has actually outlived their membership of RF.[121] To borrow the phrase of oral historian and social anthropologist Riki van Boeschoten, it is a part of "collective memory (that) remains unchanged."[122]

In fact, tourism was not a privilege of upper class pupils and students in the early 1970s. An increasing number of Greek holidaymakers set off for the Greek beaches during the summer vacation especially from the 1960s and the 1970s onward. The rise in the number of Greeks going on vacation was apparently accommodated by rising living standards; it was also facilitated by relevant legislation. In particular, in 1945 a law foresaw that employees who were aged eighteen and older and who had worked for at least twelve months for the same employer, were entitled to twelve days of paid vacation.[123] Unfortunately, the hitherto examination of youth travel patterns in postwar Greece has been limited. Thus, it is necessary to speculate about some relevant trends.[124] It could be assumed that, at least since the 1960s, there must have been a limited number of peer groups, comprising usually middle-class left-wing students, male and female, who went on vacation, on the condition that a male relative would act as a chaperone; B.N.-C. remembers that, during her student years, in the early 1960s, she would go on vacation with both male and female comrades two or three times a year. Nevertheless, her usual mode of vacation would be with her family at her grandfather's home in Spetses, a small island close to Athens (B.N.-C., Interview). From the 1970s onward, however, an apparently growing number of young Greeks, especially but not solely university students, went on holidays with their young friends instead of their parents.

One way or another, left-leaning dissident students appreciated diverse cultural patterns, connected with "Greek tradition" and the "Global Sixties." As a result, Papanikolaou suggests that a type of identity lacking a stable point of reference became predominant in the cultural and political endeavors of the Greek youth after 1967, which he describes, based on Hall's ideas, as a "subject in motion"[125]: a subject that does not seek stable foundations in a clearly articulated narrative, but who is self-consciously hybrid and ambiguous. According to Papanikolaou, the composer and singer Dionysis Savvopoulos, whom the left-leaning dissident students of that period regarded as a key symbol alongside Mikis Theodorakis, largely tracked and shaped this trend: Savvopoulos did not intend to distil "authenticity" from the "popular," but, rather, he construed the latter as "mimicry, performance, paid entertainment, and popular satisfaction."[126] He mixed Greek folk music with psychedelic rock, as in the case of the song "Black Sea." His song "Zeibekiko" contained in the album *Vromiko Psomi* (1972) also combined *rebetiko* with rock sounds. This subversion by Savvopoulos had broader implications in the making of left-wing youth identities in the early 1970s. The artist challenged the very foundation of the cultural politics of the Left, namely the taxonomy in "Greek traditional" and "imported/American" cultural products, with the former purportedly conveying "values" that facilitate commitment to struggle. On the contrary, Savvopoulos formulated a different relation of politics to culture, whereby the intellectual would cease to serve as the "instructor."[127] Papanikolaou convincingly argues that Savvopoulos sought to "confuse the personal" by mixing cultural products that transgressed the dominant classifications in the Left.[128] However, left-leaning dissident students in the last years of the dictatorship seem to have pendulated between being "in motion" and seeking stable foundations by reconceptualizing contemporary Greek history, without following decisively one direction or another. It was perhaps not until the late 1970s that a significant segment of young left-wingers threw themselves solely and self-consciously into the project of acting out "subjectivity in motion"—not surprisingly, drawing again heavily on the work of Savvopoulos.

In any case, the fluid character of left-leaning dissident student politicization had one more repercussion: as already shown in the case of rock music, the limits between the leisure pursuits of left-leaning dissident and non–left-wing or apathetic young people were blurred and easily traversed. In the case of the first, practices such as watching NEK movies would be complemented by activities that had no political significance at all. Parties at homes was such a case, which were very common since the 1960s, both among politicized and non-politicized students and, in fewer cases, high school pupils, usually in Athens and Salonica, but also in smaller urban centers, such as Veroia and Rethymno; even when left-leaning students participated, however, parties did not become a politicized leisure activity (T.L., Interview; A.A., G.K., Interview). They attracted both young men and women and usually took place at the house of a person living without his/her parents or whose parents would agree to be absent during the gathering. A common venue was actually an apartment belonging to a student who came from a rural area and who had moved to Athens or Salonica without his/her parents—quite a common product of the geographic and social mobility that had occurred in Greece since the 1960s, as newspapers began to notice at the time.[129] The people who gathered drank fizzy drinks or vermouth. Parties usually began with the playing of records of French and Italian pop artists, such as by Salvatore Adamo, Johnny Hallyday, and Adriano Celentano, who were highly popular among the Greek youth, politicized or not. Sixties rock, usually Beatles and the Rolling Stones, as well as blues, followed. In some cases, patrons also sang folk ballads by Joan Baez and Bob Dylan, led by a person who played the guitar. The essential element of these parties was dancing in couples, a fertile ground for closer contact that began with a kiss and could sometimes lead to having sex. The narration by T.L., male, a school pupil in Athens until 1975 and later a high-ranking cadre of the KNE and at the point of the interview member of the left-wing Party NAR,[130] is telling: "We organized parties very often. We danced to the Beatles, but mostly, blues music. We turned down the lights and danced as couples, dancing closely together. Hardly a party ended without a new couple being formed" (T.L., Interview). Nevertheless, in smaller cities, such as in Corfu, and especially in the case of female pupils, things did not work so smoothly. As G.K., male, student and member of KNE since 1974 remembers about his high school years: "[A]fter the parties there were some cases where the parents punished their daughters, they did not allow them to leave the house for days!" (A.A., G.K., Interview). Apparently, young male and female students mingled very often. Was that enough, however, to help bring growing sexual openness?

In general, the late 1960s and the early 1970s witnessed contradictory developments in the field of sexual relations. The dictatorship promoted a normative discourse, which praised sexual restraint and marriage. However, by 1972–1973, according to Kornetis, women had become about one third of all students.[131] They mingled with young men not only within the premises of the university, but also in youth leisure spaces, such as in discotheques, which had been emerging from the preceding decade. This interaction, as Kornetis argues and some of the interviews I have conducted show, apparently encouraged open flirting, which often—though not always—entailed premarital sexual relationships in heterosexual couples.[132] Those youth spaces apparently served as "transformational contexts," in the words of Loizos and Papataxiarchis: "[There] women defend[ed] versions of their personhood that are total, i.e. that include their sexuality as an independent variable instead of concealing it or merging it with procreation."[133] Young unmarried women felt less constrained to keep their sexual activity covert. Meanwhile, the echo of 1968 and the hippie counterculture reached Greece. Their major connotation, not only for radical university students, but also for broader segments of the Greek society, was "sexual liberation": Such an understanding is manifest in several popular Greek films, which were screened in the early 1970s, such as *Ti 30, ti 40, ti 50* (30s, 40s, 50s: It makes no difference) produced in 1972. In that film, the hippies were often evoked as conveying the "spirit of contemporary times," connected with the transgression of some dominant sexual norms in Greece.[134] In fact, the movie included many scenes of courtship between people, whose age differed significantly. Still, these relations would end up in marriage: not all institutions would be subject to subversion. The same association between the hippie counterculture and sexual openness also appeared in popular women's magazines, such as *Fantasio,* in the early and mid–1970s.[135]

Nevertheless, the issue of whether trends of sexual liberalization were limited to students and were far less prevalent in rural areas and in working-class districts during those years is not clear. As anthropologist Renée Hirschon argues of the working-class area of Kokkinia in the 1970s, premarital sexual relationships were still considered to be a stigma not only for the woman, but also for her entire family.[136] Women were pressured by their family to get married soon after they graduated from high school, still a common practice in these areas. Their marriage was settled by their family and was hardly conceivable without dowry. Sex before marriage was not criticized in the case of men. Nevertheless, an unduly prolonged bachelorhood could earn them the reputation of "frivolity."[137] By contrast, Avdela claims that sex before marriage was becoming increasingly common and legitimate in the

1970s, even prior to the collapse of the dictatorship, among youngsters in the urban centers, who were not university students.[138] The topic certainly awaits further examination.

In any case, the relaxation of family control in the socialization of young people did not lead to a marriage crisis during the 1970s. The number of divorces per 100 marriages increased from 4.23 (1960) to 8.92 (1981). The percentage of men ever married rose from 42.8 percent (1961) to 53.9 percent (1981) for men aged between 25 and 29 years; from 34.9 (1961) to 52.9 (1981) percent for women aged between 25 and 29 years old; from 93.7 (1961) to 95 (1981) percent for men aged between 45 and 49 years old; and slightly decreased from 94.2 (1961) to 93.9 (1981) for women aged between 45 and 49 years old.[139] It is also telling that the average age at first marriage actually fell from 29.97(1960) to 28.15(1980) years for men and from 25.22(1960) to 23.46(1980) for women.[140]

Left-leaning students partook in those sexual transformations. One case in point was that of the peer groups of upper-middle class pupils, who became affiliated with RF in the early or mid–1970s. Those young left-wingers construed "emancipation" as the freedom of both young men and women to develop not just premarital relations, but actually unstable ones (N.E., Interview). Students affiliated with the KNE at that point were also influenced. A.H., a male student commented that "in the universities, there was sexual freedom. Having watched *Woodstock*, you no longer thought of yourself as a weirdo if you sought sex before marriage" (A.H., Interview).

Still, while enjoying a period of unstable relationships, most of them eventually got married, as is shown in the following chapter. In addition, homosexuality was by and large a taboo topic for them. In any case, it is unclear whether such a form of sexual transformation gained momentum among young left-wingers in Greece during the early 1970s for the first time or if already existing trends in the 1960s emerged in full force. Although left-wing Parties and youth groups endorsed a moralistic language in the 1960s, there has been scant research on the actual sexual patterns of the left-wing youth during this period. Actually, such a normative approach to sexuality in the official texts of left-wing youth groups hardly changed in the early 1970s. In contrast to what Herzog and Eitler mention about what they describe as the "New Left" in West Germany, namely the framing of "sexual emancipation" as an anti-fascist imperative, "sexual liberation" was hardly articulated as a demand by radical students in Greece during those years.[141] As both Aris Maragkopoulos and Kornetis claim, the conceptual framework of the dominant left-wing ideology was not put into doubt in this period.[142]

In general, left-leaning students in the early 1970s were ambivalent toward stable cultural foundations. Nevertheless, the collapse of the dictatorship and the prevalence of Party politics in the domain of youth militancy ushered in a period where those ambiguities were sooner or later experienced by young left-wingers as mutually incompatible and produced varying left-wing cultural politics.

Notes

1. John K. Campbell, "Traditional Values and Continuities in Greek Society," in *Greece in the 1980s,* ed. Richard Clogg (London, 1983), p. 184.
2. Laura Maratou-Alipranti, "Demographic Trends," in *Recent Social Trends in Greece 1960–2000,* ed. Dimitris Charalambis, Laura Maratou-Alipranti, and Andromachi Hadjiyanni (Quebec, 2004), pp. 25–34.
3. Vassilis Karapostolis, *Katanalotiki Symperifora sti Neoelliniki Koinonia, 1960–1975* (Athens, 1983), p. 332.
4. With the exception of a few sociological and anthropological works, the examination for consumption in Greece has largely been neglected. As a result, it is not possible to provide a more detailed explanatory model, shedding light onto the potential reasons for the expansion of mass consumption: for instance whether it was linked to new patterns of circulation of goods, such as the supermarkets, whose role Victoria de Grazia stresses with regard to the spread of novel cultures of consumption in Western Europe in the second half of the twentieth century. See Victoria de Grazia, *Irresistible Empire: America's Advance through 20th-Century Europe* (Cambridge, MA, 2005), pp. 376–415.
5. Panos Kazakos, *Anamesa se Kratos kai Agora: Oikonomia kai oikonomiki politiki sti metapolemiki Ellada, 1944–2000* (Athens, 2001), pp. 268–69.
6. Giannis Voulgaris, *I Ellada apo ti Metapolitefsi stin Pagkosmiopoiisi* (Athens, 2008), pp. 123–24.
7. Paris Tsartas, *Koinonikes kai Oikonomikes Epiptoseis tis Touristikis Anaptyxis* (Athens, 1989); Richard Clogg, *A Concise History of Greece* (Cambridge, 1992), p. 149.
8. "Oi afixeis ton xenon touriston ypervainoun kata poly tis anachoriseis Ellinon", *To Vima,* 23 June 1977, p. 8.
9. Figures published by the Ministry of Finance and reproduced in Kazakos, *Anamesa se Kratos,* p. 277.
10. Karapostolis, *Katanalotiki Symperifora,* pp. 295–302. According to Mouzelis, in the early 1970s 40 percent of the lowest income groups received after taxation and social benefits 9.5 percent of the national income, while 17 percent of the highest income groups received 58 percent of the national income. See Nicos Mouzelis, *Modern Greece: Facets of Underdevelopment* (London, 1978), pp. 122–23.
11. Konstantinos Tsoukalas, *Kratos, koinonia, ergasia sti metapolemiki Ellada* (Athens, 1986), pp. 145, 171, 300.
12. Close, *Greece since 1945,* pp. 62–64.

13. Giannis Bakogiannopoulos, "Ena syntomo istoriko," in *Opseis tou Neou Ellinikou Kinimatografou*, ed. Diamantis Leventakos (Athens, 2002), p. 13. For an analysis of the programs screened on Greek television, see Franklin Hess, "Singular Visions, Multiple Futures: Culture, Politics, and American Mass Media in Modern Greece" (PhD diss., University of Iowa, 1999).

14. *Ta Theamata*, 20 September 1975, p. 47.

15. Konstantinos Gasparinatos, Ioannis Ioannidis, and Konstantinos Tsakiris, *I katastasi tou systimatos dianomis stin Ellada* (Athens, 2000), pp. 22–25. Recent scholarly approaches to the Greek popular cinema include: Stassinopoulou, "Creating Distraction after Destruction," pp. 37–52; Gianna Athanasatou, "Ellinikos Kinimatografos (1950–1967): Laiki Mnimi kai Ideologia" (PhD diss., University of Athens, 1998); Maria Paradeisi, "I politiki os simptoma stis komodies tou ellinikou theatrou kai kinimatografou," *To Vima ton Koinonikon Epistimon* 5, no. 17 (1995): pp. 163–74; Maria Komninou, *Apo tin Agora sto Theama* (Athens, 2001); Lydia Papadimitriou, *The Greek Film Musical: A Critical and Cultural History* (Jefferson, NC, 2006).

16. According to Rojek, the establishment of a social space allocated mostly to the youth is a necessary prerequisite for the emergence of youth cultures. Chris Rojek, "Leisure Time and Leisure Space," in *Leisure for leisure: Critical Essays*, ed. Chris Rojek (New York, 1989), pp. 191–204.

17. For example, see the research by Papataxiarchis on the old-style *cafés* in the island of Lesvos: Evthymios Papataxiarchis, "O kosmos tou kafeneiou. Tavtotita kai antallagi ston andriko symposiasmo," in *Tavtotites kai Fylo sti Synchroni Ellada*, ed. Evthymios Papataxiarchis and Theodoros Paradellis (Athens, 1992), pp. 209–50.

18. Michalis Nikolakakis, "Tourismos kai elliniki koinonia tin period 1945–1974" (PhD diss., University of Crete, 2013), p. 363.

19. Ibid., p. 408.

20. John K. Campbell, *Honour, Family and Patronage: A Study of Institutions and Moral Values in a Greek Mountain Community* (Oxford, 1964). This is also more or less the image that historian Thomas Gallant provides about nineteenth-century Greece, when describing knife fights among men as a means of settling issues of honor. See Thomas W. Gallant, "Honor, Masculinity, and Ritual Knife Fighting in Nineteenth-Century Greece," *The American Historical Review* 105, no. 2 (2000), pp. 359–82.

21. John G. Peristiany, ed., *Honour and Shame: The Values of Mediterranean Society* (London, 1965). American anthropologist Ernestine Friedl also conducted research on honor and gender in Vassilika, a village in Boeotia, a region in Central Greece, in the 1960s. In contrast with Campbell, she did not claim that the findings of her research were applicable to the countries around the Mediterranean in general. In Vassilika, she argued, male honor was associated mainly with the capacity of men to provide sufficient material goods to their wives and daughters and secondarily with the guarding of their sexuality. See Ernestine Friedl, *Vassilika: A Village in Modern Greece* (New York, 1962). Friedl is also well known for putting forth the distinction of the nominal from the real power of men over women, stressing the important role that women played in the decision-making of families with regard to the nurturing of their children. See Ernestine Friedl, *Women and Men: An Anthropologist's View* (New York, 1975).

22. Peter Loizos and Evthymios Papataxiarchis, "Gender, Sexuality, and the Person in Greek Culture," in *Contested Identities: Gender and Kinship in Modern Greece,* ed. Peter Loizos and Evthymios Papataxiarchis (Princeton, NJ, 1991), p. 223.

23. For instance, in those communities, in which the married couple resides in the vicinity of the wife's parents, the dowry was usually houses built close to their natal homes. See Peter Loizos and Evthymios Papataxiarchis, "Gender and Kinship in Marriage and Alternative Contexts," in Loizos and Papataxiarchis, *Contested Identities,* p. 9.

24. About the gender and sexual norms reproduced by the juvenile justice system in Greece during the 1960s, see Efi Avdela, *"'Neoi en kindyno'": Epitirisi, anamorfosi kai dikaiosyni anilikon meta ton polemo* (Athens, 2013), pp. 325–41.

25. Michael Herzfeld, "Semantic Slippage and Moral Fall: The Rhetoric of Chastity in Rural Greek Society," *Journal of Modern Greek Studies* 1, no. 1 (1983): pp. 161–72.

26. Yvonne Cosma, "Eikones gia to fylo mesa apo ton elliniko kinimatografo stin dekaetia tou '60: fylo kai sexoualikotita sto eidos tis aisthimatikis komenti (1959–1967)" (PhD diss., University of Athens, 2007); Achilleas Hadjikyriacou, "Studying Men: A Comparative Approach to Contemporary Greek Masculinity" (PhD diss., European University Institute, Florence 2010).

27. Cosma, "Eikones," pp. 230–36.

28. Avdela, *Dia Logous timis: Via, Synaisthimata kai Axies sti metemfyliaki Ellada* (Athens, 2002), pp. 235–36.

29. Frank Trentmann, "Beyond Consumerism: New Historical Perspectives on Consumption," *Journal of Contemporary History* 39, no. 3 (2004): pp. 373–401.

30. Stathis N. Kalyvas, "Emfylios Polemos (1943–1949): To telos ton mython kai I strofi pros to maziko epipedo," *Epistimi kai Koinonia* 11 (2003): pp. 37–70. Similarly, van Boeschoten argues that, apart from some exceptions, such as the region of Grevena, the Civil War broke out in 1943–44. See Riki van Boeschoten, *Anapoda chronia: Syllogiki Mnimi kai Istoria sto Ziaka Grevenon (1900–1950)* (Athens, 1997): p. 147.

31. Claudio Pavone, "The General Problem of the Continuity of the State and the Legacy of Fascism," in *After the War: Violence, Justice, Continuity and Renewal in Italian Society,* ed. Jonathan Dunnage (Hull, 1999), pp. 5–21; Mark Mazower, "Changing Trends in the Historiography of Postwar Europe, East and West," *International Labor and Working-Class History* 58 (2000), pp. 275–82.

32. Scholarly publications on the Civil War have significantly increased in number from the 1980s onward. In that decade, they were mainly preoccupied with political structures and the social stratification in Greece in the late 1940s. See, for example: John O. Iatrides, *Greece in the 1940s: A Nation in Crisis* (Hannover, NH, 1981). From the late 1990s onward, research has expanded on other facets of the Civil War, such as gender relations, constructions of childhood, national/ethnic minorities, and political prisoners. See, for example: van Boeschoten, *Anapoda chronia;* Polymeris Voglis, *Becoming a Subject: Political Prisoners During the Greek Civil War* (New York, 2002); Bea Lewkowicz, "After the War We Were All Together: Jewish Memories of Postwar Thessaloniki," in *After the War Was Over: Reconstructing the Family, Nation, and State in Greece, 1943–1960,* ed. Mark Mazower (Princeton, NJ, 2000), pp. 247–72.

33. It could be translated as "parallel Constitution."

34. Nikos Alivizatos, *Oi Politikoi Thesmoi se Krisi, 1922–1974: Opseis tis ellinikis empeirias,* 3rd ed. (Athens, 1995), p. 641.

35. For the examination of the EDA and its youth organizations, see Katerina Saint-Marten, *Lamprakides: Istoria mias genias* (Athens, 1983); Ioanna Papathanasiou et al., *I Neolaia Lambraki ti dekaetia tou '60: Archeiakes tekmirioseis kai avtoviografikes katatheseis* (Athens, 2008); Efi Avdela, "'Corrupting and Uncontrollable Activities': Moral Panic about Youth in Post-Civil-War Greece," *Journal of Contemporary History* 43, no. 1 (2008): pp. 25–44; Kostas Katsapis, *Ichoi kai apoichoi: Koinoniki istoria tou rock 'n' roll phenomenou stin Ellada, 1956–1967* (Athens, 2007).

36. Ilias Nikolakopoulos, *I kachektiki dimokratia: kommata kai ekloges, 1946–67* (Athens, 1995); Alivizatos, *Oi Politikoi Thesmoi.* About the persecution of left-wingers by the Greek state in the period 1950–67, see also: Neni Panourgia, *Dangerous Citizens: The Greek Left and the Terror of the State* (New York, 2009), pp. 117–23.

37. Christoforos Vernardakis and Yiannis Mavris, *Kommata kai koinonikes symmachies stin prodiktatoriki Ellada: Oi proypotheseis tis Metapolitefsis* (Athens, 1991), p. 102.

38. Ioannis Stefanidis, *Stirring the Greek Nation: Political Culture, Irredentism and Anti-Americanism in Post-War Greece, 1945–1967* (Hampshire, UK, 2007).

39. I use both "nationalism" and "patriotism" alternatively. Resonating with sociologist Pantelis Lekkas, I do not approach the former as an ideology based merely on exclusion, but also as one fostering strong bonds of solidarity among those who feel that they belong to the same nation. For more about the approach of Lekkas, see Pantelis Lekkas, "O ypertaxikos charaktiras tou ethnikistikou logou," *Mnimon* 16 (1994): pp. 95–106; Pantelis Lekkas, *To paichnidi me ton chrono: Ethnikismos kai neoterikotita* (Athens, 2001).

40. Andreas Pantazopoulos, *"Gia to Lao kai to Ethnos": I stigmi Andrea Papandreou, 1965–1989* (Athens, 2001), pp. 108–26.

41. Tom Nairn, *Faces of Nationalism: Janus Revisited* (London, 1997), pp. 67–72.

42. Panayis Panagiotopoulos, "Oi egkleistoi kommounistes kai to rebetiko tragoudi: mia askisi eleytherias," in *Rebetes kai rebetiko tragoudi,* ed. Nikos Kotaridis (Athens, 2007), p. 299; Akis Gavriilidis, *I atherapevti nekrofilia tou rizospastikou patriotismou* (Athens, 2006), p. 216; Aimilia Karali, *Mia imitelis Anoixi … : ideologia, politiki kai logotechnia sto periodiko Epitheorisi Technis* (Athens, 2005), pp. 46, 51.

43. This viewpoint has been endorsed by several Marxists in Greece from the 1940s onward, including historian Nikos Svoronos and Nikos Zachariadis, the general secretary of the KKE from 1931 to 1956. See: Gavriilidis, *I atherapevti,* p. 146.

44. These included Western films as well as crime movies, such as the James Bond films.

45. Avdela, "'Corrupting and Uncontrollable Activities,'" pp. 25–44; Katsapis, *Ichoi kai apoichoi,* pp. 276–328.

46. The concept of "moral panic" was introduced by Stanley Cohen, who referred to a double process, during which something that is defined by the mass media and a wide spectrum of social and political agents as a "threat for the social values and interests" simultaneously serves as a role model for those who cannot identify with the dominant social role models. For more, see Stanley Cohen, *Folk Devils and Moral Panics: The Creation of Mods and Rockers* (Oxford, 1987).

47. Avdela, "'Corrupting and Uncontrollable Activities,'" p. 31; Katsapis, *Ichoi kai apoichoi,* pp. 12, 243–360.

48. Katsapis, *Ichoi kai apoichoi,* p. 344, 352.

49. The issue of whether Greek popular cinema movies contained political messages is controversial in relevant scholarship. While Maria Komninou, sociologist and specialist in film theory, argues that they were devoid of any overt political comment, modern Greek studies expert Maria Stassinopoulou claims that they included subtle political messages. See Maria Komninou, *Apo tin Agora sto Theama: Meleti gia ti sygkrotisi tis dimosias sfairas kai tou kinimatografou sti Synchroni Ellada, 1950–2000* (Athens, 2001), p. 101. By contrast, Stassinopoulou argues that Greek popular cinema films contained political messages, which, however, were subtle. See Maria A. Stassinopoulou, "Creating Distraction after Destruction: Representations of the Military in the Greek Film," *Journal of Modern Greek Studies* 18, no. 1 (2000): pp. 37–52.

50. Lisianna Delveroudi, "Kinimata Neolaias kai kinimatografos stin Ellada tis dekaetias tou 1960," in *I elliniki neolaia ston 20o aiona: Politikes diadromes, koinonikes praktikes kai politistikes ekfraseis,* ed. Vangelis Karamanolakis, Evi Olympitou, and Ioanna Papathanasiou (Athens, 2010), pp. 309–17.

51. See Nikolaos Papadogiannis, "Between Angelopoulos and *The Battleship Potemkin*: Cinema and the Making of Young Communists in Greece in the Initial Post-Dictatorship Period (1974–1981)," *European History Quarterly* 42, no. 2 (2012): pp. 289–90.

52. For a relevant analysis, see Dimitris Papanikolaou, "Schimatizontas ti neolaia: O Theodorakis, o Savvopoulos kai 'tou '60 oi ekdromeis,'" unpublished article, and Dimitris Papanikolaou, *Singing Poets: Popular Music and Literature in France and Greece* (Oxford, 2007).

53. Papanikolaou, *Singing Poets,* p. 88.

54. According to Papanikolaou, an editorial in the magazine stated in 1966 that Theodorakis managed to "transfuse the high meaning of a great poetry." Papanikolaou, *Singing Poets,* p. 89.

55. Soon afterward, another work of "artistic popular" emerged: it was *Axion Esti* (Worthy it Is), written by Odysseas Elytis in 1959 and set into music by Theodorakis until 1964, when it appeared in public.

56. Papanikolaou, *Singing Poets,* p. 8. Hadjidakis has also been described, albeit retrospectively, as an *entehno laiko* composer.

57. See, for example: Yiannis Zaimakis, "'Bawdy Songs and Virtuous Politics': Ambivalence and Controversy in the Discourse of the Greek Left on *rebetiko*," *History and Anthropology* 20, no. 1 (2009): p. 17.

58. Ibid.

59. Panagiotopoulos, "Oi egkleistoi kommounistes," pp. 259–301.

60. Papanikolaou, *Singing Poets,* p. 63.

61. Karali, *Mia imitelis,* p. 70.

62. According to the 1934 Congress of the Communist Party of the Soviet Union, artistic production had to comply with this style. The latter was premised on four principles: realism in the representational sense, precluding any imaginary or metaphysical element; scenes of everyday life of the people; the demonstration of revolu-

tionary proletarians as "role models"; and a clear narrative, easily understandable by the working class.

63. Karali, *Mia imitelis*, p. 50.
64. Miltos Pechlivanos, *Apo ti Leschi stis Akyvernites Politeies: I stixi tis anagnosis* (Athens, 2008), p. 193.
65. Karali, *Mia imitelis*, pp. 267–75. Even though the contributors to *Epitheorisi Technis* challenged the hegemony of socialist realism, they evinced, according to Karali, no interest in experimentations in literary styles; the ultimate criterion in their reviews was the degree to which literary texts conveyed effectively the political concerns raised by left-wing circles. Thus, their cautious iconoclastic approach stirred a dialogue, which unfolded in full force only after the collapse of the dictatorship in 1974. As she maintains, the circulation of the magazine only brought an "unfinished spring" in the cultural life of the Greek Left. Raftopoulos, however, himself one of the magazine's contributors, published a book in response, in which he maintains that Karali underrates the subversive spirit of the *Epitheorisi Technis* and he wishes to demonstrate the "anti-dogmatic" and "heterodox" character of the magazine. One way or another, the magazine was a bastion neither of intellectual "dogmatism" nor of "renewal," as Giannis Papatheodorou, an expert in Modern Greek Literature, has stressed. See Dimitris Raftopoulos, *Anatheorisi Technis: I Epitheorisi Technis kai oi anthropoi tis* (Athens, 2006); Giannis Papatheodorou, "To dianoitiko kai to politiko klima mias epochis," *Vivliothiki* (attached to *Eleytherotypia*), 13 April 2007, pp. 14–15.
66. See, for example: *Panspoudastiki*, issue 27, 27 March 1961, p. 14; *Panspoudastiki*, issue 43–44, January–February 1963, p. 24. The left-wing student magazine *Panspoudastiki*, which was published in the period extending from 1956 to 1967, should not be confused with the student newspaper of the KNE after the dictatorship, which bore the same name.
67. Saint-Marten, *Lamprakides*, pp. 96–97.
68. I use initials that do not correspond to the real names of the interviewees. Quotations followed by the interviewee's initials in parentheses refer to interviews which I have conducted and which will not be referenced by an endnote. Interviewees were aware from the beginning that our discussion was recorded and any restrictions set by the interviewees have been respected. Quotes have been translated as accurately as possible. Passages in English cited from Greek interviews and other primary sources are my own translations unless otherwise indicated. Complete interviews are kept at my personal archive.
69. Manolis Daloukas, *Elliniko Rok: Istoria tis neanikis koultouras apo ti genia tou Chaous mexri to thanato tou Pavlou Sidiropoulou, 1945–1990* (Athens, 2006), p. 215.
70. It is not totally clear from the existing primary sources whether *Cinquetti* regarded themselves as a "pop" or a "rock 'n' roll" band. However, mass media used those terms often interchangeably at that point. I would like to thank Kostas Katsapis for raising this point.
71. Katsapis, *Ichoi kai apoichoi*, p. 348.
72. Kornetis, *Children of the Dictatorship*, p. 207.
73. Concerning the sexual norms of left-wing partisans during the Civil War, see Tasoula Vervenioti, "Left-Wing Women between Politics and Family," in Mazower,

After the War Was Over, pp. 105–21; Katherine Stefatos, "*Engendering the Nation*: Women, State Oppression and Political Violence in Post-War Greece (1946–1974)," (PhD diss., Goldsmiths College, University of London, 2012), pp. 68–110; Nikos Marantzidis, *Dimokratikos Stratos Elladas, 1946–1949* (Athens, 2010), pp. 147–48.

74. For this correspondence, see Basil G. Afinian et al., eds., *Oi scheseis KK kai KK Sovietikis Enosis sto diastima 1953–1977* (Salonica, 1999), pp. 217–49. A collection of documents edited by Panos Dimitriou may also provide important insights into the split of the KKE in 1968. For more, see Panos Dimitriou, *I diaspasi tou KKE*, vol. 1–2 (Athens, 1978).

75. Saint-Marten, *Lamprakides,* pp. 136–42.

76. Nancy Bermeo, "Classification and Consolidation: Some Lessons from the Greek Dictatorship," *Political Science Quarterly* 110, no. 3 (1995): pp. 435–52.

77. Alivizatos, *Oi Politikoi Thesmoi*, pp. 300–301.

78. The youth organization of the National Socialist German Workers' Party in Germany.

79. See Nikos Poulantzas, *La Crise des Dictatures: Portugal, Grèce, Espagne* (Paris, 1975). About his definition of fascism, see Nikos Poulantzas, *Fasismos kai Dimokratia* (Athens, 1975).

80. Thanos Veremis, *The Military in Greek Politics: From Independence to Democracy* (New York, 1997), p. 153.

81. Thomas W. Gallant, *Modern Greece* (London, 2001), p. 199.

82. Kornetis, *Children of the Dictatorship*, pp. 45–46.

83. Giorgos Mitrofanis, "Politikoi kratoumenoi: Metemfyliako kratos, diktatoria," in *Istoria tou Neou Ellinismou, 1770–2000*, vol. 9 (Athens, 2003), p. 131; Polymeris Voglis, "'The Junta Came to Power by the Force of Arms, and Will Only Go by Force of Arms': Political Violence and the Voice of the Opposition to the Military Dictatorship in Greece, 1967–74," *Cultural and Social History* 8, no. 4 (2011): pp. 551–68.

84. Kornetis, *Children of the Dictatorship*, p. 116.

85. Nevertheless, it was not only left-wing or left-leaning dissidents that opposed the dictatorship. Centrists and a segment of the Right did not advocate it, either. For instance, royalist officers also organized a mutiny within the Navy in May 1973, which, however, also failed to topple the regime.

86. Kornetis, *Children of the Dictatorship*, p. 205. Hara Stratoudaki, "General Education," in *Recent Social Trends in Greece 1960–2000*, ed. Dimitris Charalambis, Laura Maratou-Alipranti, and Andromachi Hadjiyanni (Quebec, 2004), pp. 574–88.

87. Argyris Yfantopoulos, "I organotiki anaptyxi tou Riga Feraiou sta prota metadiktatorika chronia: I periptosi ton synoikiakon organoseon ths Athinas," in Karamanolakis, Olympitou, and Papathanasiou, *I elliniki neolaia ston 20o aiona*, pp. 94–99.

88. Since the limits among them were not acute, both students organized in a particular left-wing organization and the broader masses of unaffiliated students whose common element was to a lesser or greater extent opposition to the dictatorship, will be referred to as "left-leaning dissident" in this subchapter. Many of the latter, though certainly not all, described themselves as "left-wing" at that point.

89. Kornetis, *Children of the Dictatorship*, pp. 116–18, 123–24, 129.

90. Ibid., pp. 230–41.
91. Many of the protagonists of these anti-dictatorial protests have written articles or books about them. One of them, Olympios Dafermos, has authored a PhD dissertation on that topic: *Foitites kai Diktatoria: To antidiktatoriko foititiko kinima 1972–1973* (Athens, 1999). Other interesting accounts of those protests, written by their protagonists, are: Dimitris Chatzisokratis, "I syntonistiki epitropi," in *Polytecnheio '73: Reportaz me tin istoria,* ed. G. Gatos (Athens, 2003), pp 214–19; Giorgos A. Vernikos, *Otan thelame na allaxoume tin Ellada: To antidiktatoriko foititiko kinima; I EKIN kai oi katalipseis tis Nomikis* (Athens, 2003).
92. Kornetis also notes the participation of a limited number of anarchists, who were targeted as "agents provocateurs," especially by the members of Anti-EFEE. Kornetis, *Children of the Dictatorship*, pp. 253–280.
93. Ibid.
94. Ibid., p. 289
95. Dimitris Asimakoulas, "Translating 'Self' and 'Others': Waves of Protest Under the Greek Junta," *The Sixties* 2, no. 1 (2009): pp. 25–47.
96. U.L., Interview. U.L. is male and was a university student in the early and mid-1970s as well as aligned with KNE from the early 1970s. See also: Kornetis, "Student resistance," pp. 209–11.
97. Asimakoulas, "Translating 'Self,'" p. 26.
98. Kornetis, *Children of the Dictatorship*, pp. 200, 202.
99. *Ekthesis tis polemikis istorias ton Ellinon,* vol. 2, pp. 612–34.
100. Gonda van Steen, "Joining our Grand Circus," *Journal of Modern Greek Studies* 25, no. 2 (2007): p. 302.
101. Giorgos Andritsos, *I Katochi kai I Antistasi ston Elliniko Kinimatografo, 1945–1966* (Athens, 2004), p. 83.
102. Kornetis, *Children of the Dictatorship*, p. 167.
103. Papadogiannis, "Between Angelopoulos," p. 291.
104. Kornetis, *Children of the Dictatorship*, p. 170. Angeliki Kokkali, "Ellinikos Kinimatografos kai Antidiktatoriko Foititiko Kinima," *Epitheorisi Koinonikon Erevnon* 92–93 (1997): p. 145.
105. Kornetis, *Children of the Dictatorship*, pp. 189–91, 276.
106. Ibid., pp. 181–82.
107. Ibid., p. 45.
108. For the case of the reaction of Cretans toward the hippy community in Matala in southern Crete, see Thanasis C. Theodorou, "Viografikes rixeis kai ithikos panikos: I koinotita ton hippies sta Matala, 1965–1975" (MA diss., University of Crete, Rethymno, 2007).
109. Kornetis, *Children of the Dictatorship*, pp. 176–77.
110. See "Oi taseis stin andriki moda," *Tachydromos,* 22 October 1969, p. 4.
111. Kornetis, *Children of the Dictatorship*, pp. 177–78.
112. L.M. leaned toward *Synaspismos,* the Coalition of the Left, of Movements and Ecology, at the point of the interview.
113. Kornetis, *Children of the Dictatorship*, p. 175.
114. Ibid.

115. Leonidas F. Kallivretakis, "Provlimata istorikopoiisis tou Rock fainomenou: Empeiries kai stochasmoi," *Ta Istorika* 20 (1994): pp. 157–74; Nikos Bozinis, *Rock pagkosmiotita kai elliniki topikotita: I koinoniki istoria tou rock stis chores katagogis tou kai stin Ellada* (Athens, 2007), pp. 342–43.

116. Kornetis, *Children of the Dictatorship*, p. 190.

117. See Daniel Miller, "Consumption and Its Consequences," in *Consumption and Everyday Life*, ed. Hugh Mackay (London, 1997), pp. 13–50.

118. Interviews have proved to be valuable to the illumination of those peer groups; as Alan Johnson has argued, "relationships, both personal and political, can escape the documented record." See Alan Johnson, "'Beyond the Smallness of Self': Oral History and British Trotskyism," *Oral History* 24, no. 1 (1996): pp. 39–48.

119. John Koliopoulos and Thanos Veremis, *Greece: The Modern Sequel: From 1831 to the Present* (London, 2002), p. 199.

120. They certainly did not constitute the majority of those aligned with the organization, which attracted many members from lower-middle strata as well, but, as will be indicated below in detail, their voice was very influential in the Eurocommunist youth publications.

121. People involved in these peer groups have often maintained friendly relations to the present, in spite of their diverging political orientation nowadays.

122. van Boeschoten, *Anapoda chronia*, p. 213.

123. One of the first governments to establish paid vacations as a right of citizenship was that of the Popular Front government in France in the interwar period. Various governments across all of Western Europe implemented this measure in the postwar years. Ellen Furlough, "Making Mass Vacations: Tourism and Consumer Culture in France, 1930s to 1970s," *Comparative Studies in Society and History* 40, no. 2 (1998): pp. 250–51.

124. Actually, figures concerning the number of young Greeks going on vacation are not available for the 1960s or the 1970s, but only for the early 1980s. In particular, a National Center of Social Studies in Greece (EKKE) survey, carried out from July 1983 until February 1984, indicated that 33 percent of young men and women aged 20–24, as well as 33 percent of young women aged 15–19 and 25 percent of young men aged 20–24, went on vacation frequently. By contrast, the figure of young men and women not going on vacation at all was very low: 10.5 percent in the case of young men aged 15–19. For more, see Christos Kelperis et al., "Neoi: Diathesi Chronou, Diaprosopikes Scheseis," *Epitheorisi Koinonikon Erevnon* 57 (1985): p. 98.

125. Papanikolaou, "Schimatizontas ti neolaia," pp. 10–11. Papanikolaou refers to a "subject in motion", drawing on Hall's work. See particularly: Stuart Hall, "The Meaning of New Times," in *New Times: The Changing Face of Politics in the 1990s*, ed. Stuart Hall and Martin Jacques (London, 1989), pp. 116–34.

126. Papanikolaou, *Singing Poets*, p. 126.

127. Kornetis, *Children of the Dictatorship*, p. 193.

128. Papanikolaou, *Singing Poets*, p. 128.

129. See, for example, the left-wing student magazine *Panspoudastiki* in the early 1960s: "Omorfine to domatio sou," *Panspoudastiki*, 25 January 1962, p. 14.

130. The NAR (Neo Aristero Reyma, New Left Current) split from the KNE in 1989, ushering in a period of massive defection mainly from the KNE, but also from the KKE. It still exists, albeit with a very low level of support. The NAR members decried the fact that the KKE participated in a coalition government with the Center-Right New Democracy Party, which is analyzed below in detail. They also accused the KKE of having tried to force them to accept this decision and of trying to silence dissent.

131. Kornetis, *Children of the Dictatorship*, p. 204.

132. N.E., Interview; A.H., Interview; Konstantinos Kornetis, "Student Resistance," pp. 255–57.

133. Loizos and Papataxiarchis, "Gender, Sexuality and the Person in Greek Culture," p. 231. Although the authors argue that such contexts appeared after 1974, they seem to have existed already in the preceding years.

134. Nikolaos Papadogiannis, "Confronting 'Imperialism' and 'Loneliness': Sexual and Gender Relations Among Young Communists in Greece, 1974–1981." *Journal of Modern Greek Studies* 29, no. 2 (2011): pp. 225–26.

135. "Interview with Vicky Vanita," *Fantasio*, 2 September 1975, pp. 42–45.

136. Renée Hirschon, *Heirs of the Greek Catastrophe: The Social Life of Asia Minor Refugees in Piraeus* (New York, 1998), pp. 106–33.

137. Ibid.

138. Avdela, *"Neoi en kindyno,"* p. 472.

139. Data published by the ESYE and reproduced in: Laura Maratou-Alipranti, "Matrimonial Models," in *Recent Social Trends in Greece 1960–2000,* ed. Dimitris Charalambis, Laura Maratou-Alipranti, and Andromachi Hadjiyanni (Quebec, 2004), pp. 128–39.

140. Ibid. See also Papadogiannis, "Confronting 'Imperialism,'" p. 224.

141. Pascal Eitler, "Die 'sexuelle Revolution'—Körperpolitik um 1968," in *1968. Ein Handbuch zur Kultur- und Mediengeschichte der Studentenbewegung,* ed. Martin Klimke and Joachim Scharloth (Stuttgart, 2007), pp. 235–46; Herzog, "Between Coitus," pp. 261–86; Kornetis, "Student Resistance," pp. 280–81.

142. A. Marangkopoulos, "Paidia tou Marx kai tis Coca-Cola," *O Politis* 99 (April 2002): p. 22; Kornetis, *Children of the Dictatorship*, pp. 148–49.

Part II

The Mid–1970s

Chapter 2

The Left Gains Momentum

The Turkish invasion of Cyprus in 1974 led to the collapse of the dictatorship. After an abrupt transition, democracy was stabilized. Anti-communism, the official ideology in Greece since the Civil War, was delegitimized
and Communist organizations became legal for the first time since 1947.
In this environment, Socialist and Communist youth groups became massive. More or less, they all sought to cultivate a "progressive" way of life
among their members and their followers. In this vein, from 1974 onward
the left-wing youth was really active in establishing cultural associations at
the university as well as in the districts of Athens and Salonica. In terms of
the cultural politics of Socialist and Communist youth groups, 1974 was a
semi-rupture: young left-wingers largely reproduced the cultural taxonomies
that the Left had espoused prior to the establishment of the dictatorship.
Still, their leisure pursuits also tracked and shaped novelties in the political
condition of post-dictatorship Greece: a prominent example was their increasing and unprecedented freedom to express their viewpoint, as manifest
in the "explosion" of memory of "anti-fascist struggle," centering on left-
wing partisan struggle in the early-to-mid 1940s. Such a memory figured
prominently in cultural events held by young Socialists and Communists in
the aftermath of the dictatorship.

The Transition to Democracy

The year 1974 would signal dramatic developments in Greece. In the aftermath of the seizure of power by the Ioannidis regime, the Greek government
interfered actively in the Cypriot crisis. Cyprus had been torn by ethnic
conflict between the Greek and the Turkish Cypriots since the 1950s. Actually, in the early part of the century, there was no deep-rooted hostility between these two main communities in the island.[1] Intermarriages as well as
linguistic and religious transfers were especially common in the rural areas,
but also occurred in urban areas. However, the elites in both cases gradually
developed nationalist beliefs that brought them closer to Turkey and Greece
and allowed no place for a common Cypriot identity.[2] Such an orientation
spread to the rural masses, mainly through the educational institutions.[3]

The end of the British rule in 1960 could be followed by two possible solutions: the partition of the island into a Greek and a Turkish-Cypriot sector and their subsequent annexation by Greece and Turkey, the so-called *dipli enosi* (double union) solution; or the establishment of an independent Republic of Cyprus. The United States, as historian Sotiris Rizas has shown, aiming at defusing the enmity between two NATO member-states, oscillated between these two paths.[4] On the contrary, the archbishop and president of Cyprus (1960–1974, 1974–1977), Makarios III, initially favored the union of the island with Greece. Nevertheless, diplomatic material that has been brought to the fore by historian Konstantinos Svolopoulos shows that he consented to the independence option, which was decided by Greece, Turkey, and the United Kingdom in the London and Zurich agreements of 1959 and 1960.[5] In Zurich, the Treaty of Guarantee was also signed by the United Kingdom, Greece, and Turkey and foresaw that "in so far as common or concerted action may prove impossible, each of the three guaranteeing Powers reserves the right to take action with the sole aim of reestablishing the state of affairs established by the present Treaty." The Zurich and London agreements regulated power sharing regarding the presidency, the house of representatives, the high court of justice, and the armed forces between the Greek and the Turkish Cypriot community. Britain retained two military bases, in Dhekelia and Akrotiri.

The agreements did not prove viable, though. The following years proved turbulent. In the early 1960s, the Turkish Cypriots abandoned all their positions in government. Meanwhile, paramilitary forces from both communities were often involved in violent clashes. The crisis culminated in 1974, when the Greek dictatorship, led by Ioannidis, supported the toppling of Makarios by a junta headed by Nikos Sampson. The Greek dictatorship apparently sought to bolster its popularity by achieving the union of Cyprus with Greece—a staunch advocate of which was Sampson himself. Fearing such a move and mindful of Greece's intervention, Turkey claimed that under the Treaty of Guarantee, it was legitimate for it to act against Sampson's regime. Thus, Turkish forces landed in Cyprus in July 1974 and soon occupied 37 percent of the island. This attack resulted in the formation of two nationally homogenous entities, since many Greek Cypriots moved to the South and numerous Turkish Cypriots to the North.

The role of the United States in the crisis of 1974 has been a contentious issue in scholarship. A number of scholars have also evinced interest in it: especially the activity of the American Secretary of State, Henry Kissinger, has been put into question. One approach, shared by Brendan O'Malley and Ian Craig, presents Kissinger as displaying cynicism and even conspiring, actively supporting or at least approving the Sampson regime as well as the

Turkish invasion.[6] A number of recent works embrace another viewpoint, however: they argue that the dominant aspect of the American stance was actually indifference, as the Watergate scandal consumed all the energies of Nixon administration.[7] Does that mean, however, that the United States was not to blame at all? Alexis Heraclides, an expert in International Relations, following the latter body of research, puts forth the nuanced argument that the lack of decisiveness on the part of a superpower that could have prevented a conflict should certainly be criticized.[8]

The Greek government reacted to those developments by bracing for war. However, the Greek armed forces turned out to be in poor condition and military commanders refused to attack Turkey. Soon afterward, high-ranking military officials gathered and, in consultation with senior members of the old political establishment, invited the right-wing leader Konstantinos Karamanlis, who had been into self-imposed exile to Paris after his electoral defeat in 1963, to oversee the transition to democracy. The military dictatorship came to an inglorious end.

The transition to democracy was abrupt, but velvet, according to Voulgaris, and eventually occurred on 24 July 1974.[9] Common forces of political liberalization were at work in other southern European countries in this period. In 1974, a group of junior army officers toppled the dictatorial regime in Portugal, which was initially established by Salazar. In Spain, democracy was restored in 1976 in a less abrupt fashion thanks to the active efforts of the conservative elites. The analysis of the transition from dictatorship to democracy in these countries has attracted scholarly interest. Adopting a structuralist Marxist approach, Poulantzas offered an explanation in his work *I krisi ton diktatorion: Portogalia-Ispania-Ellada* (The Crisis of Dictatorships: Portugal-Spain-Greece), soon after the collapse of the dictatorial regimes in Portugal and Greece. He placed a premium on internal factors of the societies in question, arguing that class relations were the major determinants of the demise of authoritarianism. Divisions within the bourgeois class were refracted in the higher ranks of the army, which also faced pressure from the popular movement. Being inherently unable to reform themselves, in order to neutralize these tensions, the dictatorial regimes introduced a process of liberalization, which, however, proved uncontrollable and led to their toppling.[10] More recent analyses, such as that by sociologist Robert Fishman, have downscaled the significance of class relations. Fishman concentrates on the nature of the political structures of the dictatorships, without connecting them with class struggles, as Poulantzas did. He distinguishes the regime from the state. According to him, a regime is "the formal and informal organization of the center of political power, and of its relations with the broader society." The state, on the contrary, is a "(normally) more permanent structure of domination and coordination including a coercive apparatus and the means to administer a society and extract resources from it."[11] Fishman maintains that, in the case of Greece, the military hierarchy, acting as a state institution and not as a mechanism of the regime, transferred power from the dictatorship to civilian leaders.

Both the moment of the transition and the postauthoritarian years are usually defined in public history as well as in political science as the *Metapolitefsi* or the "democratic transformation."[12] What emerged in the aftermath of the dictatorship in Greece was a stable democratic regime. With the exception of a failed coup d'état in 1975, the armed forces submitted to civilian authorities. The new regime was a presidential republic rather than a constitutional monarchy. In a referendum organized in 1974 by the government, the vast majority of the Greek people voted against the restoration of the monarchy: 3,245,111 (69.18 percent) people supported the abolition of monarchy, while 1,445,875 (30.32 percent) opposed it.[13] In contrast with post-authoritarian Spain, the royal court played no role in decision-making. The interventions of both the court and the armed forces, in order to ensure the monopoly of the Right over power, as had happened in Greece in the preceding decades, were brought to an end. Nevertheless, the judiciary and police force remained a bastion of conservatism, harassing left-wingers and preventing commemorations of the left-wing Resistance in the early 1940s, or disrupting concerts organized by left-wingers.[14] Still, the stabilization of democracy was vindicated by the smooth government change in 1981: the Socialist PASOK, after a landslide victory in the elections, as shown in table 2.1 below, succeeded the Center-Right government and formed the first left-wing government in postwar Greece. A few scaremongers in the right-wing press claimed that Greece was on the verge of becoming a "people's republic." But that did not suffice to mobilize any military officers. However, as political scientists Christos Lyrintzis and Dimitris Sotiropoulos as well as sociologist Ilias Nikolakopoulos argue, describing this process with a totalizing concept, such as "democratization" in general, may elude its subtleties and fail to account for the varying levels in the democratization of particular state institutions.[15] A major concern they raise is connected with the over-mighty executive power, in contrast with the relatively weak legislative. Historian David Close's analysis confirms this point, by quoting data that show the percentage of legislation initiated by opposition parties and passed by parliament in the period from December 1974 to June 1987: In Italy, it was 30.7 percent, in Portugal 60.2 percent, in Spain 10.5 percent, and in Greece less than 0.1 percent.[16]

The inability of the dictatorship to prevent the Turkish military victory in Cyprus put a main pillar of the post–Civil War hegemonic ideology into question: the doctrine of *ethnikofrosyni,* namely the self-representation of the

Right as the sole guardian of the national interest in contrast with the Left and, to an extent, the Center forces. The anticommunist critique was increasingly delegitimized and was toned down even in the language of New Democracy, the governing Center-Right party. According to Close, this was the outcome of the cooperation between left-wing and some right-wing forces against the dictatorial regime and of the persecution of even Conservative politicians by the dictatorship, which implemented anti-communist measures that the latter had once supported.[17] From 1974 onward, many prominent Center-Right politicians preferred to position themselves as moderates and to avoid as far as possible the designation as "rightist": a prominent member of the New Democracy, Panayis Papaligouras even went so far as to describe the Party he belonged to as aligned with the "socialist, social-democratic and other democratic forces in Europe."[18] Similarly, none of the founding texts of the New Democracy contained the terms "right-wing" or "Conservative" as elements of its ideological profile; rather the Party described itself as "radical liberal." Under this banner, the Center-Right stressed that it subscribed to political as well as a moderate version of economic liberalism, namely a market economy combined with a degree of government regulation.[19] Above all, the Center-Right Party tried to reinvent itself as a force championing "modernization," which it connected with the establishment of parliamentary democracy and the entry into the EEC (European Economic Community).[20] In this vein, New Democracy participated in the government of national unity, which legalized all Communist Parties and youth organizations in September 1974 and did not reverse this decision after its victory in the parliamentary elections in November 1974. Prominent Communists started to return from exile, in order to help establish the apparatus of their party. The EEC was anticipated by the New Democracy as serving as an alternative "Western" role model, which would counterbalance and even substitute the American influence on which they had relied since 1947. It does not come as a surprise that the image of the United States as the "bastion of the Free World," which in the wake of the Civil War had been endorsed as the official ideology of the Greek State, lost much ground. Increasingly, a growing segment of Greek society associated the United States, especially the hated figure of Henry Kissinger, as well as the CIA, with the prevalence of the Turkish forces in Cyprus.[21] Concomitantly, in order to express the discomfort at the failure of the U.S. administration to exercise restraint over Turkey regarding the Cyprus Issue, the Prime Minister Konstantinos Karamanlis decided, in 1974, to withdraw Greece from the military (albeit not the political) wing of NATO, a status that remained until 1980.

In this environment, student resistance against the dictatorship was credited even by Center-Right forces. It is not a coincidence that the first elections

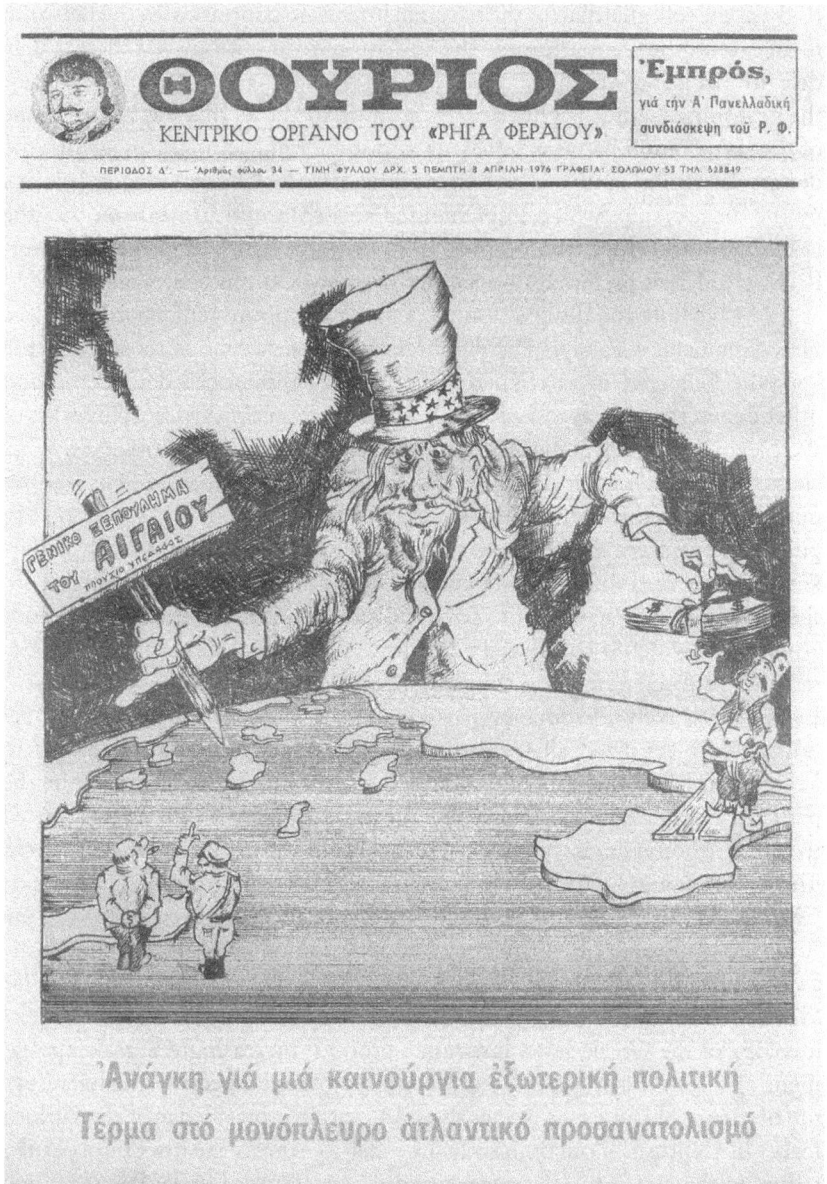

Figure 2.1. Cover page of *Thourios*, the newspaper of RF, displaying Uncle Sam as financing and encouraging the "Turkish occupiers" of Cyprus to set claims in the Aegean Sea as well. *Source: Thourios,* 8 April 1976, cover page. Used with permission from Dimitris Chatzisokratis.

in the *Metapolitefsi* took place on the first anniversary of the Polytechnic Uprising, on 17 November 1974. The memory of the Polytechnic Uprising certainly figured prominently among left-wingers. Even though it was mainly students who had taken part and although organized resistance against the regime was limited, especially during the first three years of its rule, it served as a symbol of the "culmination" of what they dubbed "universal popular resistance against the dictatorship."[22] Such an approach was embraced by the high-ranking cadre of the KKE, Grigoris Farakos, as well as of the prominent left-winger Manolis Glezos in the article "Aristera, Theseis kai antitheseis," published in *ANTI* just after the collapse of the dictatorship. Manolis Glezos has been a very well-known and highly respected figure in the Greek Left. He gained reputation by tearing down together with Manolis Santas the Nazi swastika flag from the Acropolis in Athens on 31 May 1941.

Despite the obvious ruptures, it is not totally accurate to depict this condition as a "shift from anticommunism to antifascism" as a source of legitimacy in the post–1974 political scene, as Voulgaris does.[23] The Center-Right government continued to avoid any references to the Resistance to the Occupation in the period from 1941 to 1944, which was officially recognized in 1982 by the government of PASOK. Still, having abandoned the project of imposing ideological conformity on all Greek institutions, the post-dictatorial state witnessed what Voulgaris depicts as a "duality of power." He appropriates a term used by Vladimir Lenin to describe tensions between the Provisional Government and the Soviets from February until October 1917.[24] In the case of Greece, the Center-Right formed the government. It implemented its choices in the foreign relations of Greece and ensured its entry into the EEC, which was detested by the vast majority of the Communists and the Socialists at that point. At the same time, in some state institutions and across much of civil society, the anti-fascist, anti-imperialist language of the Left became predominant. Intellectual circles and student unions were two notable cases in point. During the dictatorial regime, pro-regime students had been appointed in the official student unions; however, its collapse meant that positions in the latter were up for grabs. On the contrary, the Center-Right found it difficult to legitimize itself among university students. Its advocates limited themselves to taking part in student elections, obtaining a relatively meager share of the vote until the mid–1980s, in comparison with the overall influence of the Center-Right in Greek society. Similarly, after the collapse of the dictatorship, prominent left-wing intellectuals, who had either lived on the run or had fled to other countries, such as Mikis Theodorakis, could express themselves freely and, actually, dominated in the cultural landscape. It should also be noted that in contrast with the early-to-mid 1960s, the performance of centrist Parties in parliamentary elections steadily declined from 1974 onwards. While Enosis Kentrou-Nees Dynameis (Center Union-New Forces) harvested around 20 percent of the vote in 1974, EDIK (Enosi Dimokratikou Kentrou, Union of Democratic Center), which was established in 1976 through the merger of the Center Union-New Forces with the smaller Dimokratiki Enosi Kentrou (Democratic Center Union), received around 12 percent in 1977 and less than 1 percent in 1981. Many centrist politicians joined either PASOK or New Democracy in the late 1970s. Centrist forces did not gain momentum in university student elections at that point, either.

Another core element of the *Metapolitefsi* was the key role played by formal political Parties of all stripes. In pre-dictatorship Greece, although ideological polarization existed, citizens did not necessarily join a Party that they felt best expressed their viewpoint. During that period it was only the Left that had created mass parties.[25] However, from 1974 onward, according to Voulgaris, Parties across the political spectrum began to organize on large scale, establishing local branches all over the country. This fact is manifest, first of all, in the membership of all parliamentary Parties, which in the case of PASOK rose from 25,000–30,000 in 1977–1978 to 110,000 in 1981; in the case of KKE from 25,000 in 1977–1978 to 46,000 in 1981; and in the case of KKE Es. from 6,000 in 1977–1978 to 7,000 in 1981. The members of New Democracy also increased from 20,000 in 1977–1978 to 130,000 in 1981.[26] The Parties of the Center and the Right for the first time developed

Table 2.1. Parliamentary election results and turnout, 1974–1981 (in percentages).

	1974	1977	1981
New Democracy	54.37	41.84	35.87
Center	20.42 (as Enosis Kentrou-Nees Dynameis)	11.95 (as EDIK)	0.4 (as EDIK)
PASOK	13.58	25.34	48.07
KKE	9.47 (together with KKE Es.)	9.36	10.93
KKE Es.		2.72 (in alliance with smaller Parties called Symmachia)	1.34
Turnout	79.5	81.1	81.9

Note: The table contains the percentage of the Parties that harvested most votes. Table prepared by the author, based on data found in: Richard Clogg, *Parties and Elections in Greece: The Search for Legitimacy* (London, 1987).

formal organizations, no longer functioning as more or less fluid associations revolving around a particular leader (*prosopopagi kommata*). The transition was not complete. Strong personal leadership did not disappear, as Lyrintzis, Nikolakopoulos and Sotiropoulos argue; internal democracy was often weak in the new organizations.[27] But the shift was nevertheless undeniable.

The postauthoritarian years were not marked merely by the transition to democracy, however, but also by the "diminishing toleration of material deprivation" that had appeared in the 1960s and continued. This trend is evident in some figures indicating the percentages of families possessing a number of consumer goods: in the urban areas, 43 percent owned a fridge in 1974 and 77 percent in 1980; 54 percent owned a cooking appliance in 1974, with this number rising to 87 percent in 1980. Moreover, in 1976–1977, 12.5 percent of the residents of the urban centers owned a TV set, compared to 20.8 percent in Italy and 11.8 percent in Portugal in the same period.[28] Meanwhile, the spending patterns of various social groups changed. As sociologist Nikos Souliotis shows, the amount of money spent on leisure by different social strata, such as scientists, high-ranking executives, office clerks, merchants, and workers, tended to converge from 1974 to 1981.[29] It was against the backdrop of those political and social transformations that the Greek Left designed its cultural politics in the post-dictatorship years.

Left-Wing Youth Politics on an Upward Trajectory

The membership and the appeal of all left-wing youth groups also rose in the aftermath of the dictatorship. Since left-wing groups have largely been secretive about their membership, it is difficult to estimate the exact magnitude of their following. The most detailed data are available for the case of RF. While 1,003 people were affiliated with RF in September 1974, this figure rose to 4,079 by spring 1976. In 1978, the total number of RF members was estimated at 3,500, a figure which excluded people in the periphery of the organization. The documents of the RF central council furnish some evidence about the number of people who attended the pre-festival activities of the organization in 1978, which, at 10,000, was not at all meager.[30] The Maoist student group PPSP declared in August 1977 that several hundreds of university students had joined since 1974, while in January 1967 its members were no more than a "few dozen."[31] Unfortunately, the archival material concerning the membership statistics of the KNE in the period 1974–1981 is kept mainly by the Communist Party of Greece, which does not permit access to historians. Documents of the East German regime include estimates, according to which the KNE cadres and members were more than

40,000 in 1979; it is not clear whether those figures should be taken at face value, since it is not possible to cross-check them.[32] Some further evidence, however, about the influence of the KNE is provided by *Odigitis*, its newspaper, and has to do with the number of people who attended the first(1975), second(1976), and fifth(1979) festival of KNE-Odigitis.[33] The newspaper estimated them to be 150,000, 800,000, and 1,000,000, respectively, which are quite impressive numbers; however, the reliability of this figure is limited, since it cannot be corroborated by independent sources. Similarly, the Youth of PASOK, whose membership figures are also not available, claimed that 700,000 people visited its festival events in Athens in 1977.[34] Even if this figure is inflated, the appeal of the organization was certainly broader than that of PAK, which, according to Kornetis, "had limited representation among young people."[35] This increase is also indicated by the votes harvested by the PASP in the university student elections, as shown below.

Socialist and Communist university student groups witnessed an enduring strength throughout the period extending from 1974 to 1981, as manifest in the results of the annual student elections of those years, whose turnout was significant (see table 2.2). Given that the total number of university students in Greece was 70,161 in 1971–1972 and 87,476 in 1981–1982, as already shown, more than half of them voted in the university student elections. Similarly, left-wing organizations dominated in the mid-to-late 1970s the societies of Greek migrant students in Western Europe, such as in West Germany, Italy, the United Kingdom, and France.[36] This was no negligible tendency, since the figure of Greek university students abroad also increased remarkably from 9,985 in 1970 to 41,086 in 1981.[37]

With regard to their appeal in the lower-middle and working-class districts of Athens and Salonica, it varied. Yfantopoulos argues convincingly that the membership and the influence of RF were limited.[38] By contrast, the KNE obtained some influence: reports from local RF branches offer estimations on the popularity of the KNE in these areas. These sources are certainly not the most accurate, since members of RF may have attempted to minimize the influence of their political opponents. However, they mention that in a number of such districts, namely in Keratsini and Kokkinia, the young pro-USSR Communists had a significant following, in marked contrast with RF.[39] The members of the local branches of left-wing youth groups in those districts were not necessarily young workers; many were working and lower-middle class university students.

Helping to establish the apparatus of mass political organizations, particularly those aimed at youth, was a new realm of activity for many young left-wingers in the aftermath of the dictatorship. T.L., male, member of the KNE and onetime high-ranking cadre, narrated that "from 1975, we had to

Table 2.2. The results of university student elections in Greece, 1974–1981.

	1974	1975	1976	1977	1978	1979	1980	1981
PASP (affiliated to the Youth of PASOK)	24.6	26.2	25.9	21.6	27.6	26.7	26.8	25.2
PSK (affiliated to KNE)	20	23.2	27.4	27.3	30.6	31.2	31.3	32.3
DA-DE (affiliated to RF) and collaborating groups	19.8	17.3	18.1	21.2	16.7	7.5	8.9	10.1
DA-APK and/or groups linked with Choros						7.2	11.3	8.4
Student groups linked with New Democracy (DAP-NDFK since 1976)	16.2	17.05	11.1	13.4	12.1	10.9	10.3	11.4
AASPE (affiliated to the EKKE)	3.8	3.7	5	4	3.2	1.9	n/a	n/a
PPSP (affiliated to the KKE(m-l))	2.7	4.5	5.6	4.9	5.4	5.6	5.6	2.1
Turnout (in number of voters)	23,863	45,460	39,383	47,743	49,656	50,513	50,690	47,916

Note: Percentage of votes received by each of the student groups mentioned and voter turnout in the student elections. Table based on data from: Dimitris Aravantinos, "To Metapoliteytiko foititiko kai syndikalistiko kinima," in *75 chronia: To panepistimio tis Thessalonikis stin avgi tou neou aiona,* ed. Ioannis K. Hassiotis and Dimitris Aravantinos (Salonica, 2002), pp. 465–560. I have cross-checked, as far as possible, the figures he provides with those that appear in left-wing youth publications of that period.

work hard for the KNE; we were hyper-active" (T.L., Interview). The condition was the same in RF: S.L. depicted himself as a "Stakhanovite," "who forced members to attend the assemblies" of the local branch of RF in the area where he lived, the lower-middle and working-class district of Kokkinia in Athens (S.L., Interview). As S.K., male, narrated to Kornetis: "After '74 I got organized in AASPE together with Mavrogenis; alright, Mavrogenis had been "tainted" from before ... I think that this happened quite soon, because everyone was entering something then, one organization. You couldn't avoid it. It was a period of a great politicization. ... Our conflict, from one point onward as AASPE, was mainly with the official parties of the Left, because this was where the game was played."[40]

Cadres spent many hours per day working in the headquarters of their organization. Planning and participating in discussions, distributing flyers and posters, and writing announcements were part of their everyday roster of activities. And many ordinary members shared in the fever of activity. And although this time economy was certainly prescribed in the official texts, especially of the KNE, it was far from being simply imposed from the top down. Many former members of Socialist and Communist youth groups have described this demanding program in a positive way. The emotional vocabulary that has been employed in the testimonies I have elicited varies: phrases such as "our life had a purpose" and "we served principles" are very common. N.E., female, student and high-ranking cadre of RF in the mid–1970s, claimed: "[W]e had the feeling that we had a timetable. We were self-disciplined; this aspect was not imposed on us, we liked this condition" (N.E., Interview). This enthusiasm is confirmed in interviews with other young left-wingers of different directions. A.A., female, pupil and member of the KNE in Salonica in the mid–1970s, narrates: "It was something that came from the way you lived, as though revolution would occur tomorrow" (A.A., G.K., Interview). A.A. is no longer a member of KKE. Her party had joined forces with other left-wing organizations in 1989 to form the Coalition of the Left and Progress. In 1991, the KKE split from the Coalition. A.A. was among those who remained affiliated with the Coalition, even at the point of the interview she no longer supported the Coalition. 1991 marked for her as well a "biographical turning point," to follow sociologist and psychologist Gabriele Rosenthal's conceptual framework.[41] Her testimony is based in general on the argument that KNE wanted to produce "soldiers" by imposing the opinion of the high-ranking cadres to the members. Nevertheless, her narration also includes moments that show that she did not experience her membership as (or only as) "imposition," but also through the lens of grassroots commitment. In his work, Horn makes the interesting point that "the frequent get-togethers at Party branch headquarters, the typing of leaflets, the distribution of newspapers at school or factory gates was experienced as a great communal effort and uplifting of spirits."[42] He limits his comments to the "Far Left," but in the case of Greece at least, it certainly seems applicable to members of all left-wing youth organizations.

But amid this activity were also disappointments. A segment of the militants who had been active in the anti-dictatorial struggle appears to have nurtured the hope that along with the dictatorship, capitalism would be overthrown as well. This expectation seems to have been particularly pronounced among those on the Left not associated with the formal party organizations. For them, the post-1974 period was an era of frustration.[43] However, it would be erroneous to draw sharp dividing lines along "generations": many students who had been active in the struggle against the dictatorial regime, like Nikitas Lionarakis and Michalis Sabatakakis, were protagonists in the post-1974 era.

Did, however, this feeling of pride on membership of left-wing groups herald a period of fractionalism in the Greek Left? In the aftermath of the dictatorship, the various Communist and Socialist organizations, often dubbed each other "progressive" and "democratic" forces.[44] "Progressive" individuals, regardless of their specific political orientation, agreed that the prospect for democratization and economic development depended on gaining "full national independence." Put simply, this meant that U.S. bases should be removed from Greek soil, Greece should withdraw from both the military and the political wing of NATO, and American and Western European companies should stop "plundering" Greek resources.[45] In addition, they all lambasted what they viewed as the domination of "monopolies" in the Greek market.[46] They also concurred in demanding that pro-dictatorship officials should be purged (the so-called process of *apochountopoiisi,* namely de-juntification). De-juntification featured prominently in the activities of Communist and Socialist organizations in the first three years after the collapse of the dictatorial regime. They did not allow students that they regarded as advocates and/or collaborators of the dictatorship to be members of the student associations and to participate in student assemblies. Moreover, left-wing students tried to have members of academic staff at the universities, whom they accused of having supported and benefited from the dictatorial regime, removed.[47] One way or another, this feeling of affinity among young left-wingers is evident in articles about student elections: *Agonistis,* the newspaper of the Youth of PASOK, distinguished the "democratic" and "progressive" forces from the right-wing students.[48] The KNE also claimed in *Odigitis* that its aim was the increase in "the strength of the progressive forces in the university."[49] In the case of both KNE and, mainly, of RF, the "democratic" forces included the "progressive" ones, namely the Communists, the Socialists, and the Center, but extended to pro-democracy right-wingers as well, as is analyzed below. This common identity was not limited to the universities, however. It was also manifest, for instance, in the municipal elections. PASOK, KKE, KKE Es., and smaller left-wing and centrist parties often fielded common candidates. If they did not do so in the first round, they would certainly support the "progressive" candidate in the second round.[50]

Nevertheless, the most important aspect of the identity of young left-wingers in the mid–1970s was the membership of a particular Communist or Socialist youth group. Despite common reference points, divisions among the many groups on the Left were bitter. As a repercussion, peer groups split along affiliation, even in the case of the people who had been bound by the common struggle against the dictatorship in the early 1970s. The narrative of C.L., male, student and high-ranking cadre of RF since the early 1970s, is telling: "After 1974 I no longer met with old friends who joined the KNE. I could not stand them: they became morons" (C.L., Interview). The transition to organization-specific peer groups was apparently more complex for other young left-wingers, as indicated in the form of the testimony of N.T., male, also high-ranking cadre of RF and university student since the early 1970s. Whenever he referred to the early 1970s, he regarded himself as member of the "generation of anti-dictatorial struggle," without distinguishing young left-wingers of other ideological directions. When speaking of the mid–1970s, he would counterpose the "open-minded" members of RF to the "soldiers" of the KNE. But when asked how he viewed the comrades of the "generation of the anti-dictatorial struggle," who after 1974 joined the KNE, his narrative became ambiguous. He admitted that though "they were trained to be soldiers ... they often defied the regulations in practice." N.T. found it more difficult than C.L. to speak in a pejorative way about pro-USSR young left-wingers, with whom he claimed that he had shared a "very important struggle for democracy." However, again his account of the period 1974–1981 revolved around the identity of RF membership and no longer of "generation": "my life was centered on RF, I spent almost all day at the headquarters and, when I went to have lunch or dinner, I would always be with members of the organization" (N.T., Interview). Despite autobiographical accounts that were published in the subsequent decades, in which the authors, who had been active in a left-wing youth group during the 1970s, referred to the "generation of the *Metapolitefsi*," the latter was hardly employed by the activists under study in the mid–1970s as a means of identifying themselves.[51]

Members of different left-wing organizations flexed their muscles in long-lasting discussions. These occurred in student assemblies, which sometimes lasted for days, in cultural societies, even in an informal fashion, in the so-called *pigadakia* within the premises of the universities, in cinemas and in tavernas. Throughout the period from 1974 to 1981, universities were the main locus of youth politicization. Left-wing youth activity in high schools, lower-middle and working-class districts and factories was not negligible, but certainly not of the same intensity despite the fact that some notable strikes in Greece occurred in 1974–1981, such as in the factories PITSOS (1975–1976), MADEM-LAKKO (1977), and LARKO (1977).[52] In general, the first post-dictatorship years were marked by employees' protests: the rate of employees on strike per 1,000 employees was high in 1979 and 1980; the intensity of strikes (number of strikes per 100,000 employees) was also high in 1976 and 1980 and the length of strikes in days was significant in 1976 and 1980.[53] The employees on strike, including the workers, usually demanded higher wages, better working conditions and the freedom to participate in trade unions. Nevertheless, despite the intentions of left-wing students, there was no simultaneous eruption of protracted strikes and student protest actions throughout the period lasting from 1974 to 1981.[54]

Proposed strategies of transition were a first and foremost point of contention among young left-wingers. In Greece, the KKE Es. and RF distinguished themselves from the KKE and KNE by naming their strategy the "democratic path to socialism," which did not call for the abolition of parliamentary democracy and which allowed political pluralism, as opposed to the "non-democratic" Soviet Socialist system. A major pillar of the "democratic path," as endorsed by the KKE Es. and RF, were the *diarthrotikes metarrythmiseis* (structural reforms): the gradual Socialist transformation of Greece through radical changes in state institutions. This strategy was much argued over the KNE, but also within RF, alongside the tactics of EADE (Ethniki Antidiktatoriki Dimokratiki Enotita, National Antidictatorial Democratic Union). The KKE Es. and the majority in the Central Council of RF in the period from 1974 to 1981 endorsed the "broadest possible" unity of "democratic forces," which they defined as extending from the radical Left to the moderate Right, including a part of the governing Party, New Democracy. Haunted by Greece's political regression in the 1960s and early 1970s, their aim was to forge a broad alliance that would act as the bulwark of democratic legality, preventing the staging of a new coup d'état.[55] The strategies endorsed by the KKE and KNE in the post-dictatorship years, coined the "anti-imperialist convergence" and "cooperation and common action of democratic forces," did not preclude an alliance with "pro-democracy" right-wingers, either. While the pro-Soviet Communist Party and its youth organization portrayed themselves as the vanguard of popular struggle, on no account did they view this as mutually exclusive with the aim to collaborate with political subjects that did not belong to the Communist Left. However, the KNE accused RF of toning down its "anti-imperialist" demands, in order to build such a front.[56] The strategy of a broad democratic alliance was also vehemently criticized by a sizeable contingent within RF as well. Soon after the restoration of democracy, RF suffered a period of protracted internal strife between the majority of the central council and the minority (in the central council). The latter was coined "left-wing opposition" by its sympathizers and "fraction" by its opponents. Actually, RF did not officially allow the existence of organized sub-groups, but it did not ban the expression of diverging opinions in the pages of *Thourios,* its leading newspaper. The RF "opposition" argued that the major issue at stake since 1974 was not the stabilization of democracy, but the terms of *bourgeois modernization:* In its view the threat of dictatorship was not real any longer. The entire Greek bourgeois class had burned all bridges with pro-dictatorship elements in favor of the "introduction of reforms that would render Greece a modern, European state." Thus, an alliance with the "democratic" elements of the Right was misplaced in their view. Similarly, they argued that the "structural reforms" could be easily co-opted by the reinvented Right, unless RF paved the way for the moment of "rupture" that would signal the "revolution against capitalism."[57] Another contentious issue within RF revolved around the concept of "integration," derived by the opposition wing from the writings of one of its members, Antonis Maounis. The latter, drawing on the structuralist Marxist concept of the ideological state apparatus, introduced the concept of *michanismoi entaxis* (integration mechanisms): in this vein, he viewed the education system as a means of incorporating youth into "bourgeois society" and thus as a key site of struggle.[58] This conception was vehemently criticized by prominent members of the majority of the central council, like Kostas Karis and Christos Lazos. In a number of articles they penned in *Thourios* in 1978, they responded by maintaining that "integration" was no real peril for workers in Western European countries; they claimed that, under democratic regimes, like Italy and France, the working class "proved capable of struggling for the socialist transformation of institutions."[59]

In addition, the resurgent left-wing Parties and youth groups were zealously involved in debates on how to define the "avant-garde Party." One way or another, they all aimed at "guiding" the masses of "progressive" or "democratic" students or the "youth movement," as they called it. An extract from the "Black Book," published by AASPE, manifests an approach that was not atypical in the language of the other left-wing youth organizations in this period. It stated that the Maoist group offered a "progressive" program that could mobilize "all democratic students" and link their struggle with that of the "working class" and the "Greek people."[60] The KNE underwent what Voulgaris coins a *remarx-leninization,* in that it attempted to invent itself as a "disciplined" organization, which followed Marxism-Leninism rigorously.[61] The cadres of the KKE and KNE blamed the establishment of the dictatorship in 1967 on the fact that the main Communist Party in Greece had ceased to function autonomously and was substituted by the loose left-wing alliance of EDA, which because of its "vague ideological profile" had been incapable of "guiding the masses." Thus, in order to repel another coup d'état and to ensure Greece's socialist transformation, they argued that a strong Communist Party was required. In this vein, the pro-USSR group favored a centralized model, regarding the "avant-garde Party and its youth organization" as necessary in order to guide social movements. The primary task of its members was to ensure that the line of the KNE became predominant in the decision-making of the latter. They thus came inevitably into conflict with the KKE Es. and RF who also portrayed themselves as avant-garde forces, but in a more complex way. For the KKE Es. and RF, another pillar of the "democratic path" was the principle of the "autonomy" of "popular movements." In its first conference in 1976, RF declared that the decisions on the activities of protest movements, but also of a broad range of actors, including cultural associations, had to be taken by their own structures and not by an outside Party apparatus. The KKE Es. and RF positioned themselves as nothing more than coordinators of the "common popular struggle."[62]

In developing its line as well as its organization structure, PASOK, including its Youth, deviated to an extent from the conventions of the Communist Left. PASOK assigned much importance to the leader in the group's decision-making, which consequently resulted in the atrophy of party structures. The leader was conceived of communicating directly and, thus, genuinely representing the masses. Moreover, PASOK (and its Youth) attracted a wider array of members and supporters than the Communist ones. People aligned with or sympathizing with it ranged, at least during the first years of its existence, from the radical Left to the Centre. What they had in common was their opposition to the practice of right-wing forces in Greece since the end of the Civil War, which Voulgaris coins *antidexismo* (anti-rightism).[63] Similarly, it employed broader categories than the Communist Left, concerning the social groups, whose interests it professed to represent: in its class analysis, in contrast with the Communist organizations, PASOK and its youth wing progressively and, particularly since 1976, did not single out the "working class" as the vanguard in socialist transformation. It claimed to represent the "people" or the "underprivileged," terms that included workers, peasants, and the lower-middle class without assigning a particular valorization to each of them.[64] Members of the PASP who demanded a more rigidly Marxist, class-based analysis were purged in 1976. Due to those characteristics, PASOK and its Youth have been described as "populist," albeit not only by some of their left-wing adversaries, but also by political scientists, such as Andreas Pantazopoulos.[65] Other political scientists, though, such as Yiannis Voulgaris, are more skeptical toward the depiction of PASOK as merely "populist": he argues that PASOK's profile was fluid throughout the post-dictatorship years until at least 1990. As such, it does not fall squarely into the category of "populism," but can simultaneously be described as "centrist" and "radical socialist": this is, as Voulgaris has aptly described it, the "PASOK enigma."[66] In any case, the term "populism," highly normative and carrying negative connotations, is certainly controversial and not employed by PASOK itself.

The aftermath of the dictatorship also heralded a period when left-wing terrorist groups emerged.[67] They included mainly the ELA (Epanastatikos Laikos Agonas, Revolutionary Popular Struggle), the EO 17N (Epanastatiki Organosi 17 Noemvri, Revolutionary Organization 17 November), and the Group June 1978.[68] Their favorite targets were either U.S. military and business facilities or prominent officials of the dictatorship, who they argued had not faced proper justice. Two such attacks were the assassination of Evangelos Mallios by EO 17N in 1976 and of Petros Bambalis by Group June 1978 in June 1978. Mallios had been accused of being a torturer during the dictatorship and was put on trial after its collapse. He had been convicted in November 1975 and sentenced to ten months' imprisonment, a decision which provoked outrage among the entire Left and the Center for being too lenient. Bambalis had also been accused of acting as a torturer during the dictatorial regime. He was put on trial together with Mallios, but finally the charges against him were dropped. In stark contrast to the case of the Italian Autonomia Operaia, the Greek Left was not divided over the issue of their stance toward left-wing terrorism. In Italy, as historian Robert Lumley notes, the *autonomisti* were divided into the "creative" wing (whose ideas came from artistic avant-garde and the women's movement) and the "organized/ armed" one, which was sympathetic to the Brigate Rosse (Red Brigades).[69] By contrast, the overwhelming majority of the Greek Left, including Choros and the Maoists, opposed both terrorist violence and the counter-terrorist legislation, which was introduced by the Center-Right government in 1978. As journalist George Kassimeris aptly remarked, with the exception of ELA and EO 17N, the extra-parliamentary Left realized that "guerilla struggle would lead them nowhere" after 1974 and criticized EO 17N, arguing that their activity was counter-productive and could lead to more coercive state policies. The terrorist group rejected such accusations as a "classic revisionist argument."[70]

The models of socialist transformation that left-wing youth organizations put forth were linked with the way they positioned themselves in the international Communist and Socialist movement. In the case of the KNE, the pro-Soviet socialist countries of Eastern Europe and, especially, the USSR, served as a signifier of the desirable form of modernity.[71] The *present* of the socialist societies was represented as the future for Greek society: according to the KNE, the "flourishing" "anti-imperialist" movements worldwide were a clear proof that socialism, which had already been established in the "one third of the globe," would further expand, including Greece.[72] Socialist modernity was portrayed as displaying technological advancement and an egalitarian distribution of income, in sharp contrast to the capitalist world, where the majority was depicted to be suffering from poverty and unemployment. Various articles in *Odigitis* claimed that people in the USSR, Czechoslovakia, Bulgaria, the German Democratic Republic, and other socialist countries profited from a system that made sure that every citizen was entitled to free education, free medical treatment, and the right to enjoy vacations in comfortable settings at a low cost.[73] The state was described as very well-organized, providing patronage to "culture," sustaining numerous museums, libraries, concert halls, and other spaces where people could familiarize themselves with various genres of art.[74] All these were elements of the "full development of the human personality," according to the KNE. According to those publications, the consequent satisfaction of the citizens led to minimal levels of criminality, in contrast with what happened in the "capitalist world."[75] Photos of smiling workers or students standing next to sophisticated equipment were a staple in the pages of *Odigitis*. By contrast, the images from the United States and Western Europe had nothing to display but desperate people, especially drug addicts.[76] Nevertheless, the bonds of the KNE and KKE with the Soviet Communists were not confined to literary inspiration. Material that has been recently declassified in the archives of the USSR has revealed that the Soviet Union the latter provided significant financial aid to the KNE and KKE. A relevant document records the discussion of the Soviet ambassador to Athens, I. Unalchov, with Charilaos Florakis, the secretary general of the KKE. The latter intervened successfully to ensure that the government of the USSR signed a deal with the company VET, managed by his nephew, John Florakis. As the document shows, the KKE was to profit significantly from the contract.[77]

By contrast, members of RF were rather critical of the Soviet Union and its allied regimes, which in their view suffered from lack of democracy. Their favorite texts, in contrast to those consumed by the members of the KNE, stressed not discipline, but two other concepts: autonomy and pluralism. "Autonomy" was the relationship that Eurocommunist parties hoped to develop with protest movements, as already mentioned. The term also denoted the demand that the Communist Party of Soviet Union does not interfere with the decision-making of other Communist Parties, which would adapt Communist doctrines to the specificities of the societies, in which they were active. In addition, in advocating the "democratic path" to socialism, as mentioned above, RF and the KKE Es. distinguished the vision of the path to socialism espoused by the Italian Communist Party and the Communist Party of Spain from the Soviet model. These Western European Communist Parties embraced a version of socialism, which would not preclude "democracy and freedom" or "pluralism," namely the existence of a multi-party democracy. By contrast, members of RF were quite cautious toward the PCF (French Communist Party). The PCF, although briefly experimenting itself with Eurocommunism in the mid–1970s, recognized the KKE as the sole legitimate political expression of communism in Greece.[78] Thus, RF blamed the PCF for trying to impose the line of the USSR and, consequently, violating the principle of autonomy of the Communist movement in Greece.[79]

The Maoist organizations drew inspiration from the Communist Party of China until the mid–1970s. The death of Mao Zedong sparked rancorous debates among them, with a segment of the Maoists, especially those affiliated with the KKE(m-l) and the PPSP, distancing itself from China and portraying the Albanian regime as its role model. In addition, a major cause of friction throughout the 1970s both within and among Maoist groups was Mao Zedong's "Three Worlds Theory." According to the "Three Worlds Theory," the First World consists of the main "imperialist" forces, namely the United States and the USSR; the Second World comprises secondary "imperialist" countries, such as France and Japan; and the Third World includes the exploited countries as well as the socialist ones, who are their allies. EKKE and M-L KKE, in contrast with KKE(m-l), endorsed this theory. As a result, they developed differing friend/foe patterns: even though both the EKKE and the KKE(m-l) detested what they viewed as U.S. "imperialism" and Soviet "Social-imperialism," the KKE(m-l) claimed that U.S. imperialism posed a greater danger than the Soviet regime for the "genuine socialist" cause worldwide, while the EKKE treated them as equally perilous.

Beyond the Communist youth organizations, the Youth wing of PASOK distinguished itself above all through its *tiersmondisme* (Third-Worldism). They conceptualized a division of the world along the lines of dependency theories, into the "industrialized, imperialist North" or the *center* and the "dependent South," or *periphery* or "Third World," in which they included Greece.[80] Andreas Papandreou, the PASOK founder and leader as well as a prominent economist, was influenced by dependency theories, especially those of Paul Baran and Paul Sweezy, whose impact is evident in his work *Paternalist Capitalism*.[81] The USSR and the socialist countries in Europe were not described as "imperialist," but were lambasted for coercing workers, preventing them from freely expressing their will. On the other hand, although they were in contact with the Socialist Party in France, PASOK and its Youth criticized most Social Democratic parties in Western Europe and, especially, the SPD (*Sozialdemokratische Partei Deutschlands,* Social Democratic Party of Germany) in West Germany, for actually upholding "capitalism."[82] On the contrary, they advocated alliances with Socialist parties from developing countries, especially from the Middle East.[83] PASOK established strong bonds with the PLO (Palestine Liberation Organization) as well as the Baath parties of Syria and Iraq.[84] Loudly criticizing both NATO and the EEC (a famous slogan of theirs was "EOK kai NATO to idio syndikato," namely "EEC and NATO, the same syndicate"), they favored the Non-Aligned Movement.[85]

Regardless of their particular role models and the path to socialism that they envisioned, all the left-wing groups of Greek youth in the mid–1970s espoused a language saturated with the collective memory of contemporary Greek history and the "Greek popular tradition." As both of them served as a bridge that connected politics with culture in Communist and Socialist publications, it is necessary to examine their various conceptualizations in depth.

Travelers on History's Great Pier

The collapse of the dictatorship signaled the gradual decline of the post–Civil War status quo, which was characterized by the systematic marginalization and persecution of left-wing citizens, as analyzed in the previous section.[86] This shift caused reflection on collective memory issues across the political spectrum. The Center-Right was also affected: it reinvented and distanced itself from the discourse of right-wing political forces of the pre-dictatorship years. *Ethnikofrosyni* no longer stood at the epicenter of the analyses of New Democracy and its youth and student groups. DAP-NDFK and ONNED stressed their firm support for "democracy" as opposed to "tyranny," which was linked not only with the dictatorship, albeit also with the Soviet regime, which they accused of stifling dissent. Quite often the Center-Right youth approached "anti-fascism" from the perspective of "anti-totalitarianism," since both communism and fascism were described as equally perilous to "democracy" and "freedom." Similarly, it tried to envision new possibilities in remembering the recent past in Greece—an attempt, however, marked by ambiguities. In tune with the effort of New Democracy to operate as a moderate force, ONNED and DAP-NDFK aimed to develop a critical attitude toward right-wing anti-communism of the 1949–1974 era. One DAP-NDFK leaflet, which was supposed to be distributed in all university schools, refrained from reproducing a core component of postwar right-wing anti-communism: the violent confrontation in the period 1946–1949 was not referred to as a war against "bandits," but as one among "siblings."[87] The latter term had sometimes appeared in the dominant collective memory in the preceding decades, such as in the propagandistic film *Grammos Vitsi* (1971). However, the left-wing "sibling" was portrayed as the only one manipulated by "foreign" forces and was represented as much more blood-thirsty and cunning than the other one. By contrast, the leaflet of DAP-NDFK in 1976 reconceptualized this family metaphor: it treated both leftists and rightists as "victims" and members of the Greek nation. Obviously, this was an effort to water down the (post–)Civil war argument that the Right was the sole guardian of the national interest. However, the reconfiguration of the discourse of Center-Right youth organizations was only partial in the post-dictatorship period. Apparently, differing tendencies coexisted within DAP-NDFK and ONNED. The DAP-NDFK magazine at the Department of Mathematics at the University of Athens reiterated the argument about the "threat from the North," namely that the Communists want to cede territories in Northern Greece to Yugoslavia and/or Bulgaria, oft-repeated from the late 1940s until 1974.[88] In any case, throughout the period from 1974 to 1981 this "anti-totalitarian" discourse was hardly visible at the university schools, where the left-wing versions of "anti-fascism" were overwhelmingly predominant.

Meanwhile, a large part of society, previously excluded from the higher ranks of the state, developed a deep collective reflection of Greek society and its history—a process which, in the case of left-wing students had begun as we have seen already in the last years of the dictatorship. Venetia Apostolidou illustrates very well how such discussions unraveled in *ANTI, Avgi,* and the popular center-left newspaper *Ta Nea.*[89] ANTI was a left-wing magazine, which served as a forum of exchange of views among young left-wingers of different directions.[90] A number of prominent Marxist historians as well as left-wing authors reflected on the period that extended broadly from the 1930s to the 1970s. At least until the late 1970s, they focused on the Resistance against the Tripartite Occupation. Their intellectual endeavor sometimes extended beyond these limits, however, to include what was defined in each case as "Modern Greek History" in general.

Music and cinema also served as a means of bringing into the fore the very recent history of Greece from the vantage point of the Left. The Theodorakis albums that had been composed during the dictatorship years, such as *18 Songs for the Bitter Fatherland* (based on the poetry of Giannis Ritsos), *Epiphania Averoff* (based on the poetry of Giorgos Seferis),[91] and the soundtrack for the movie *Z* directed by Costa Gavras, were solid points of reference for all young left-wingers. Theodorakis himself, who had returned from exile after the collapse of the dictatorial regime, organized huge concerts which were indeed a landmark:[92] He gathered young singers, such as Antonis Kalogiannis, Maria Faradouri, and Giorgos Dalaras. They appeared in sport stadiums, such as the Kaytantzoglio in Salonica or the Karaiskaki in

Athens, attracting tens of thousands of people, as contemporary newspapers reported. A very famous massive concert by Theodorakis took place in Athens on 13 August 1975. According to the newspaper *Kathimerini,* more than 50,000 people attended.[93] A film shot by Nikos Koundouros, entitled *Tragoudia tis Fotias* (Song of Fire), which was released in 1974 and is accessible on YouTube, gives insight into the atmosphere in these concerts: songs referring to the oppression of dissidents during the dictatorial regime dominated the program, making extensive references to torture.[94] "Sfageio" (Slaughterhouse) from the *Songs of Andreas* is a telling example. The song mentions the way political prisoners communicated, namely by knocking on the wall that separated their cells, in order to gain courage and face torture: "They torture Andreas at night on the roof, I am counting the knocks. I feel the pain, behind the wall we will be together again. You will knock, I will knock, which means in this silent language that I keep my faith, I am strong."

These concerts were a rite de passage: by depicting suffering and struggle under the dictatorial regime, they evoked the trope of "universal popular resistance against the dictatorship," but, more importantly, they galvanized militancy in the post-dictatorship years as well. In one of those concerts, Faradouri, referring to the Polytechnic Uprising, sang "it was 17 November" instead of "it was 18 November," as the verses of the song "On the Eighteenth Day of November" mentioned.[95] In another video from a massive concert organized by Theodorakis in this period, Kalogiannis sings "Ena to chelidoni" (One the swallow) from *Axion Esti*; the audience appears to be chanting the slogan "give the junta to the people (to punish it)" as well as to be clapping hands rhythmically throughout the song.[96] As H.Z., male, university student, and mid-ranking cadre of KNE in the mid–1970s, insisted: "We were not passive in these concerts: all of us actively participated. We sang most songs from beginning to end" (H.Z., Interview).

Theodorakis was not an isolated case: Many other singer-song writers turned to what was called "political song" in the post-dictatorship era. Reflection on recent history was predominant in this Greek music genre, although references to contemporary protests were extensive. Christos Leontis produced the album *Kapnismeno Tsoukali* (Blackened Clay Pot, 1975), setting Giannis Ritsos's poem of the same name to music. It was written in 1949, when Ritsos was kept in a detention camp in Kontopouli, on the island of Limnos. The imprisonment and torturing of left-wing political prisoners featured prominently in the poem. Manos Loizos set verses by Fondas Ladis to music in his album *Ta tragoudia mas* (Our songs, 1976), with vocals by Giorgos Dalaras. One of the album's best-known songs, "Pagose i tsiminiera" (The chimney froze), described striking workers who would prefer to emigrate rather than surrender to the demands of their employers. Two other prominent political song albums of that period were *Metanastes* (Immigrants, 1974) by Giannis Markopoulos, which appeared just after the collapse of the dictatorship, as well as *Politika Tragoudia* (Political songs, 1975) by Thanos Mikroutsikos, based on poems by Wolf Biermann and Nazim Hikmet. Quite telling of this atmosphere is an interview with the young singer and composer Loukianos Kilaidonis, who in 1975 recorded the album *Apla Mathimata Politikis Oikonomias* (Simple Lessons in Political Economy]. Kilaidonis argued that his previous work, *Mikroastika* (Of the Petty Bourgeoisie), was not "clear enough" regarding the political message it sought to transmit, an issue that he wished to rectify in his new album.[97] The political current affected rock musicians, some of whom would reinvent themselves by participating in political song albums: Vlasis Bonatsos, the singer of the rock band Peloma Bokiou, provided vocals for the album *Ekeini ti nychta* (That Night, 1974), which refers to oppression during the dictatorship years.

Similarly, the politically engaged films of the so-called "New Greek Cinema" also gained momentum, both in terms of production and reception. They were among those that topped the list of box-office hits. In the mid–1970s, the somewhat older film *Z* (1969) by Costa Gavras was screened and became immensely popular: it sold 454,855 tickets from autumn 1974 to December 1975 in Athens and Piraeus. It implicitly addressed the assassination of the left-wing MP Grigoris Lambrakis in 1963—whose name, however, was not mentioned in the movie—and the slipping into dictatorship in the following years. Another notable case in point is the second and the third part of the *Trilogy of History* by Theo Angelopoulos, *Thiassos* (The Travelling Players, 1975) and *Kynigoi* (The Hunters, 1977) respectively. The former contained two levels of narration: the personal stories of the members of an actor's colony in Greece from 1939 to 1952, who travel around Greece and wish to stage the folk play *Golfo the Shepherdess*; and the broader historical context, including the eruption of World War II, the Tripartite Occupation of Greece, the Civil War, and the Greek legislative election in 1952, which resulted in the victory of the Right. Still, according to film historian Eleftheria Rania Kosmidou, Angelopoulos offered a "melancholic" view of history, since "no solutions or answers" are given in the movie; "despite the empathy we are meant to feel for the left-wing resisters . . . nothing changes in the end."[98] *Thiassos* was very popular and sold 189,620 tickets in 1975–1976 in Athens and Piraeus, according to the magazine *Ta Theamata*.[99] *Kynigoi* narrated the discovery of the corpse of a dead partisan of the 1940s by bourgeois hunters in the mid–1970s and their subsequent attempt to hide the body. However, they suffered from nightmares, in which the partisan came back to life. The film symbolized their desire to repress the memory of popular struggle. This film also proved to be rather popular and sold 104,290 tickets from its release in late 1977 to 2 April 1978 in Athens and Piraeus.[100] One more film that touched upon contemporary Greek history was *Happy Day* (1976) by Pantelis Voulgaris, which sold 61,503 tickets in 1976–1977 in Athens and Piraeus, according to *Ta Theamata*.[101] This film made an implicit reference to the detention center on Makronisos Island, which was constructed during the Civil War. All the above mentioned films of the New Greek Cinema approached the Civil War and the post–Civil War era from the perspective of the victimization of the Left, focusing on the impact of the defeat in the Civil War on its advocates.

Communist and Socialist youth organizations were actively involved in this reflection on recent history. The official memories they endorsed replicated the anthropomorphic representation of the Greek nation as both "suffering" and "militant," which was evident already in the language of the Left prior to the dictatorship. This narrative differed from the anti-communist strand of nationalism mainly in two ways. The concept of "people" was given not only a national, but also a class meaning: it signified a category juxtaposed with the "ruling," "dependent bourgeois class." Moreover, Socialists and Communists placed no emphasis on the "Christian Orthodox" character of "Greekness," which had been a cornerstone of anti-communism. The left-wing conceptualization of the "Greek people" was secular.[102] In particular, the anti-fascist, anti-imperialist patriotism/nationalism resignified one "moment" that was very important for the anti-communist nationalist narrative, namely the War of Independence in 1821. This is not really surprising. As Pantelis Lekkas has argued, a broad range of discourses appropriate the same national symbols.[103] The main "moment" that the anti-fascist, anti-imperialist patriotism revolved around, however, was the Resistance of the EAM (Ethniko Apeleytherotiko Metopo, National Liberation Front) and its military wing, ELAS (Ethnikos Laikos Apeleytherotikos Stratos, National People's Liberation Army) against the Tripartite Occupation in the period from 1941 to 1944 and the representation of the Left as the only challenge to "dependence" from either "fascist" or "imperialist" rule. EAM/ELAS, in which KKE participated, were the most massive organizations that fought against the Occupation forces. Left-wingers could freely and loudly criticize the anti-communist publications of the 1949–1974 period, which had either silenced the activity of the EAM or portrayed the latter as a "treacherous" organization, which confronted forces that resisted the Occupation troops. In general, the initial post-dictatorship period witnessed a widespread reflection on the early 1940s. Numerous memoirs were published, a lot of associations of resistance fighters were founded, and relevant commemorations took place frequently. However, the focus was on the years from 1941 to 1944.

As the memory of the left-wing partisans was brought back to life in the post-dictatorship period there was a relative silence on the Left about the Civil War as historians Antonis Liakos and Vangelis Karamanolakis argue.[104] Violent clashes among Greeks during the World War II were sidelined in this narrative: those opposing the left-wing partisans were lambasted as "collaborators" of the Occupation forces. The Greek Left in the 1970s spoke merely of a "patriotic" war in the early 1940s and on no account of a "civil" one. As regards the Civil War of the late 1940s, the version of history that appeared in left-wing publications in the 1970s could be described as the unfinished struggle for national independence: the fight of mass left-wing organizations against the Tripartite Occupation was portrayed as having aroused the hostility of the "imperialists" in the aftermath of World War II, since they purportedly wished to keep Greece "dependent" on them. Thus, the nationalist and conservative parties in Greece, according to the Left, cooperated with former Nazi collaborators, who were promoted to the higher ranks of the state administration; by contrast, left-wingers, "who had shed their blood for national liberation," were purged. The late 1940s would thus see a new period in which Greece was forced into military and financial dependence on the emerging "imperialist" centers of the post–1945 period. This was largely the trope that the Left had employed to describe the outcome of the War of Independence in 1821, claiming that despite the defeat of the Ottoman Empire, Greece was soon subordinated to the rule of the Great Powers. It is not coincidental that key figures of "1821," such as Makrygiannis,[105] featured prominently in the publications of the Left in postwar Greece. But the Civil War of the late 1940s itself was hardly discussed. The "glorious fight" of the partisans in the early 1940s found no equivalent in the narrative of the Left about the years from 1946 to 1949, having been replaced by a language of self-victimization. References were limited to detention camps, such as Makronisos, trials, and the executions of left-wingers.[106] According to Karamanolakis, this "silence" should be attributed to the rejection of armed struggle as a means to assume power by the Left in the aftermath of the dictatorship. Historian Ioanna Papathanasiou has also remarked that it was not until 1981 that the bipolar model of "us" versus "them," which depicted the Left as a patriotic force confronting "imperialists and their Greek stooges," would be abandoned in favor of an introspective reflection on the mistakes of the Left throughout the 1940s.[107] Nevertheless, there was one exception in this relevant silence: the publications of both major Maoist youth organizations. PPSP for instance, defined the activity of the left-wing Democratic Army of Greece, namely the army founded by the Communist Party of Greece in the latest phase of the Civil War, from 1946 to 1949, as the struggle against "Anglo-American imperialists" or the "second partisan uprising" (*deytero antartiko*), portraying it as linked with the struggle against the Occupation forces in the early 1940s. In any case, the Maoists refrained from depicting it as a "civil war." Various publications of the AASPE and the PPSP as well as of the Parties that those groups were affiliated with glorified the Democratic Army of Greece throughout the 1970s.[108]

The silence about civil wars was not a peculiarity of the Greek Left in the 1970s: According to the political scientist and sociologist Paloma Aguilar, what prevailed in Spain during the years of the *Transición,* the transition from the Francoist regime to democracy (1975–1982), was a consensual memory of the past, which largely avoided references to the Spanish Civil War (1936–1939). The most influential organizations of the Spanish Left, PSOE (Partido Socialista Obrero Español, Spanish Socialist Workers' Party) and the PCE (Partido Comunista de España, Communist Party of Spain), adopted this stance as well. In contrast with the Greek Left, however, they did not seek to reconstruct a narrative vindicating their "patriotic" character and a concomitant "submissive" attitude of the Right. Rather, they oriented themselves toward a present and future based on compromise with their political opponents.[109]

The left-wing narrative of the "antifascist, anti-imperialist struggle" was not confined to struggle in Greece. The Greek Left associated its "struggle for national liberation" with three other prominent cases of the "anti-imperialist combat" worldwide: the establishment of the Socialist government of Salvador Allende in Chile; the victory of the Marxist-Leninist MPLA (Movimento Popular de Libertação de Angola, Popular Movement for the Liberation of Angola) in 1975; and the victory of the Communists in the Vietnam War, which was completed in the same year. Not surprisingly, left-wing newspapers regarded Vietnam as the most decisive defeat of U.S. "imperialism" and a cause that "spreads optimism."

The anti-fascist, anti-imperialist collective memory was evident in the publications of left-wing youth organizations. All major Socialist and Communist Parties and youth groups in this period tried to legitimize themselves by designating their particular organization as the inheritor of the tradition of left-wing struggle in Greece since the 1930s, and, especially, during the Occupation years in the early 1940s. Their newspapers included extensive references of the activity of three groups: first of all, the OKNE (Omospondia Kommounistikon Neolaion Elladas, Federation of Communist Youths in Greece), which existed from 1922 until 1943 and was aligned with the then–newly founded KKE. Moreover, the EPON (Eniaia Panelladiki Organosi Neon, United Panhellenic Organization of Youth), the youth branch of the EAM, which was the main Resistance organization against the Tripartite Occupation, featured prominently. The DNL also appeared in this narrative.

In this vein, all of the left-wing youth media published accounts of the "torture" that the "martyrs and heroes" of their purported precursors faced at the hands of the Nazis or the dictatorship of 1967–1974. Militancy appeared as something "sacred," but metaphorically: it was invested with the attachment to *mission,* in the sense that young left-wingers would dedicate themselves to their political organization, in order to affect the course of history and pave the way toward the socialist transformation of Greece. *Odigitis* presented the life-stories of militants of left-wing youth groups since the interwar years, either cadres, like Christos Maltezos, general secretary of the OKNE, or ordinary members; these were model autobiographies that offered the vision of a "life with meaning" concluded heroically by a "death with meaning."[110] In those archetypical biographies, the heroes always emerged from working-class or lower-middle class families and usually had a distinguished school record.[111] This trope would valorize commitment and discipline, which was followed, especially in the case of the members of the EPON, by torture and death a martyrdom that resulted from the young Communists refusing to renounce their ideology or disclose secrets of the organization to which they belonged. In one such text, a young member of the EPON, Tsaprazis Taxiarchis, is described as being forced by the Nazis to dig his own grave, which he did without losing faith.[112] In a sense, this was a reverberation of the attitude that the Greek Left had developed already in the late 1940s, assigning important weight to "sacrifice." As Voglis claims: "Under the specter of death, commemoration, as the imaginary unity between the collectivity of those who live (political prisoners) and the collectivity of those who have died heroically ('people's heroes'), had the purpose of diluting the fear of dying, or justifying and attaching meaning to death."[113] Nevertheless, in the context of post-dictatorship Greece, the KKE and the KNE did not aim to convince their members to put their lives in danger by engaging in clandestine activity, but, simply, to deepen their commitment to the aims those organizations subscribed to.

Such narratives signified the valorization of suffering, which is also reflected in the testimonies of many KNE cadres since the early 1970s, especially those who are currently KKE cadres. A.S., male and, at the time, a young worker, KNE cadre in the early 1970s and KKE cadre nowadays, commented to me during an interview: "Excursions? The only excursions we know are the ones where the junta sent us on to prison and to the torture chamber" (A.S., Interview). A.S. did not mention at all parties at homes during the dictatorship years, either. In his narrative, the early 1970s was just a grim era. In their present-day narratives, what was valorized was suffering masculinities and femininities, connected with imprisonment and torture in the period from 1967 to 1974, which were transformed into "determined militancy" in the post-dictatorship period. These interviewees apparently guarded vigilantly their testimony, so as not to appear to deviate from the "official script" of the 1970s. As historian John Saville has warned, the activist is a "special kind of person" who, when interviewed, may speak "exactly as he speaks at a public meeting" delivering a worked out and potentially rehearsed "line."[114] These KNE cadres in the early 1970s and currently KKE cadres would accentuate these claims by usually employing the first person plural, in order to show that the experience of Communist membership was uniform and their case a typical one. This trope, very common in the life-stories of British Communists as well, is an aspect of a "self-abnegating political culture," expressed through the "habit of seeing [the] self [as] less important than the movement."[115] By contrast, youth leisure during the dictatorship was mentioned extensively by KNE members and cadres in the early and mid–1970s, who nowadays either belong to the other left-wing groups or are not actively engaged in politics. Thus, this divergence might not necessarily be attributed to different experiences, but to a varying signification of similar experiences due to differing political affiliation nowadays.

The glorification of the EPON also appeared in *Thourios*. The latter newspaper, for example, published a short novel by Dido Sotiriou, called *Oi 14 neolaioi, prodromoi ths EPON* (The 14 Young People, Precursors of the EPON). The story revolves around a young woman that delivered milk to EAM members, who suffered from serious diseases and were hospitalized in Athens. The girl joined EPON and, as a consequence, was imprisoned for fifteen years after the end of World War II. In the two last paragraphs, the particular heroes of that novel appeared as a metonymy for the entire EPON. An extract is telling: "Who would save Greece from genocide? That accomplishment should be attributed to the EAM, EPON, ELAS, and nobody can efface their history from our Nation's memory ... Later on, during the years of the imprisonment, we were thinking that the collaborators, the bourgeois vagabonds and the fascists that were serving the Americans sent our bravest patriots into exile on Makronisos or executed them. How did that happen? How?"[116]

Nevertheless, once again the collective memory of left-wing militancy in contemporary Greece differed in the Maoist texts. EKKE, AASPE, KKE(m-l), and the PPSP approached the post-Civil War activities of the KKE by situating them in the broader context of the international Communist Movement after the Twentieth Congress of the Communist Party of the Soviet Union, in which the personality cult of Joseph Stalin was denounced. The Maoists defended the legacy of Stalin and maintained that, after the aforementioned Congress, a "new bourgeois class" had gained control of the regime and steered its course in a "reactionary," "revisionist" direction. As a repercussion, the new leadership of the Communist Party of the Soviet Union interfered with the KKE, purged its leadership and installed its "puppets" in the higher ranks of the Party hierarchy, rendering the KKE a satellite of the "revisionist" and "social-imperialist" Soviet regime from that point onward. The new KKE leaders, according to the Maoists, were cadres that had subverted the "second partisan uprising" in the late 1940s and also liquidated the basis organizations of the KKE as well as EPON in 1958, because they could not easily control them, and they actively supported that their activity be superseded by that of EDA. Therefore, the main Maoist Parties and their student groups voiced a vehement critique of the KNE's effort to portray itself as a continuation of the struggle of EPON.[117]

No matter the version of collective memory that they endorsed, all Communist and Socialist youth organizations concurred in establishing a culture of commemoration of "antifascist, anti-imperialist struggle."[118] As David Kertzer argues for the Italian Communist Party, a "key to the ritualization of history was the taming of time."[119] In the case of the young Greek Communists and Socialists, two were the main anniversaries: the Polytechnic Uprising (17 November 1973), as representing the "culmination of the universal anti-dictatorial popular resistance," as well as the inception of the EPON (23 February 1943), whose anniversary was accompanied by the demand, regardless of the left-wing force that organized it, for the official recognition of the left-wing resistance in the early 1940s by the State. The latter would have to wait, however, until the electoral victory of PASOK. The commemoration of both events was the common property of all left-wing youth groups as well as the EFEE, the National Student Union of Greece. These consisted of lengthy speeches by high-ranking cadres of left-wing Parties and youth groups, followed by live concerts with bands playing Theodorakis music or partisan songs of the early 1940s. With regard to the Polytechnic Uprising, its first anniversary, a three-day celebration that started on 22 November 1974, was arranged by an organizing committee, in which diverse left-wing Parties figured prominently. As 17 November did not become designated as an official holiday until PASOK assumed power, it was not atypical for left-wing high school pupils to abstain from classes, in order to participate in commemorative events. In general, the commemoration of the Polytechnic Uprising can be construed as an enactment of continuity: the organizers and the participants employed some of the very songs that had been sung by the radical students in 1973, such as "Pote tha kamei xasteria." Similarly, the crescendo of the commemoration, the march which in Athens passed in front of the Polytechnic School as well as the American Embassy, was led in 1974 by the father of Diomidis Komninos, a 17-year-old pupil who had participated in the Polytechnic Uprising and was killed by pro-junta elements.[120] Such continuity was made clear in one of the slogans chanted by the activists who took part in the commemoration: "To Polytechneio Zei," which could be interpreted as, "The (spirit of the) Polytechnic Uprising is still alive." The latter was a recurring theme in various Socialist and Communist publications at that point, which concurred that the message of the Uprising was timely. Quite tellingly, in the case of the pro-Soviet Communist Party, Grigoris Farakos, one of its high-ranking cadres, claimed that the moment of the transition to democracy was a compromise, but not a static one: although the Polytechnic Uprising did not itself topple the dictatorial regime, it set a precedent of struggle that would eventually lead to the socialist transformation of Greece.[121]

The Multiple Heirs of "Tradition"

No longer banned, and actually witnessing a spectacular increase in their influence, left-wing Parties and youth organizations embarked again after a pause of seven years on their effort to "purify" "Greek tradition" from "foreign imports." The delegitimization of the doctrine of *ethnikofrosyni,* alongside a flourishing anti-Americanism, proved to be a fertile ground for Socialist and Communist groups to postulate themselves as the "genuine patriots," in contrast with the Right. In this vein, producing taxonomies of "traditional" and "American" cultural products was inextricably linked with their effort to inculcate a militant spirit in their members, by regulating how their members should comport themselves. For groups that portrayed themselves as constituting the "vanguard" in the "popular struggle," this issue was certainly of paramount importance. In this vein, to a lesser or greater extent, they combined recreation with indoctrination in a mixture that resembles "serious fun," as construed by historian Anne Gorsuch.[122]

All groups employed the term "culture" in a highly normative manner, as is manifest in the announcements of the central councils of the KNE and RF, in the publications of the Youth of PASOK as well as from the Decision of the First Post-Dictatorship Congress of the Maoist PPSP.[123] Resonating with the taxonomy that the Greek Left had adopted since the 1950s, they distinguished "progressive culture [*politismos*]," which they described as one of "high quality,"[124] from the "American way of life," depicted as a "pseudoculture," capable of generating only "sub-products."[125] In the case of the Youth of PASOK, it can also be found as the "democratic tradition" in *Agonistis,* its newspaper, when references were made to the recent past, counterposed to "cultural imperialism," the equivalent of the "American way of life": reproducing its *tiermondiste* viewpoint, the Socialist youth organization argued that "imperialists" aimed at eliminating "national traditional cultures" in the "Third World" and substituting them with cultural products that carry their "values."[126] To make this distinction more palpable, the KNE and the Maoist groups in particular employed a broad range of metaphors to describe the "foreign cultural products." Some of them were biological, such as "ailing" and "rotten," which, however, as shall be shown below, did not imply racial superiority. "Dirt" also featured prominently in the way they described what they viewed as the "American way of life."[127] To appropriate the conceptual framework introduced by anthropologist Mary Douglas, this appears to be another case of a very common practice that can be found in different regions and eras, namely a group defining itself by excluding what it designates as "dirty."[128]

Still, while PPSP and the KKE(m-l) embraced the dichotomy of "progressive culture" as opposed to the "American way of life," they did not pursue systematic cultural politics: although references to cultural issues were touched upon in their publications, none of the PPSP or KKE(m-l) newspapers published a column about such topics on a regular basis until 1978. In contrast with other left-wing organizations, the high-ranking cadres of those Maoist groups did not regard getting an excellent grasp of "progressive culture" as one of their tasks. V.S., male, high-ranking cadre of OMLE and, subsequently, of the KKE(m-l) argued that this should be attributed to the size of the KKE(m-l) and the PPSP. "We were not many and we had to deal with a lot of issues. [We could not deal effectively with culture and this was] an issue of insufficient strength." (V.S., Interview). V.S. himself felt much more comfortable during the interview to discuss issues of "high politics" that mattered among Maoists in the 1970s, adding: "I cannot say much about culture." The KKE(m-l) and PPSP seem to have implicitly construed this field as of secondary importance in shaping political consciousness. By contrast—and once again vindicating the multiple dimensions of Maoism—the AASPE and EKKE imputed more attention to "culture," which stemmed from the fact that some of its members and cadres were artists. A prominent case is Christos Bistis, affiliated with the EKKE since the dictatorship years, who was a director and had studied at the Berliner Ensemble.[129]

Similarly, while *Agonistis* was replete with analyses about music, theatre, cinema, and literature, high-ranking cadres of the Socialist youth did not derive prestige from developing and demonstrating sophisticated analyses of art. S.M., male, university student, and a high-ranking cadre of the Youth of PASOK in the mid-to-late 1970s mentioned during his interview with me, while referring to the movies of Theodoros Angelopoulos: "I did not reject them, I regard them as the first serious effort to analyze the condition of post-Civil War Greece. But their slow pace was somewhat tiring for me"

(S.M., Interview). Even though he is still a prominent figure in politics, he did not feel that such a statement would tarnish his image. Similar to the case of other former cadres and members of the Youth of PASOK, he aimed at showing that he was knowledgeable, but not an expert in such topics.

Actually, the KNE offered the most systematic classification of cultural patterns, including those it associated with the "American way of life."[130] The latter, as defined in the publications of the pro-Soviet Communist youth group, encapsulated fears about the impact of aspects of social transformation, mainly linked with the spread of mass consumption, on Greek youth. It was depicted as eroding social bonds and triggering "individualism" and "careerism."[131] However, the pro-Soviet young Communists were not the only ones who engaged themselves in defining this term: Both the KNE and RF claimed that these were the "pseudo-values" that capitalism bred due to its "nature" as a system that was based on exploitation and antagonism between individuals. They also argued that the "imperialist centers" and the "dependent bourgeois class in Greece" deliberately sought to foster such behavioral patterns among Greek youth, in order to render it "passive" and counter the further strengthening of the Left. Resolutions by the KNE and RF in the immediate post-dictatorship period proclaimed that "the bourgeois class fills the free time of the youth with activities that lead in a reactionary direction."[132] Drawing heavily on the language that the EDA and DNL used in the 1960s, a decision of the Panhellenic gathering of RF cadres in 1975 declared that "acculturation [*ekpolitismos*] and leisure [*psychagogia*] have become totally separated."[133] Similarly, *Mathitiki Genia*, the newspaper of the pupils who were aligned with the PPSP, proclaimed that the "ruling class" tries to "corrupt" and "disorient" the Greek youth by spreading a "foreign" and "fake" pop music. In a confident manner, though, the newspaper underlined that "tens of thousands" of young people participated in the march on 17 November 1974, commemorating the Polytechnic Uprising that had occurred two years ago. Those youngsters, according to the same article, turned their back on such imported culture and the "ideals" it contains.[134]

In contrast, the KNE went further and linked the "American way of life" to drug consumption. The moral concern over the impact of drugs on the Greek youth was neither a novelty of the postauthoritarian years nor confined to the KNE: the first relevant references, according to Nikolakakis, had already appeared in the Greek popular press already in the final years of the dictatorship.[135] Still, especially from 1976 onward, the KNE repeatedly raised this issue, portraying it as both an indirect and a direct repercussion of capitalism. Its publications argued that the grave social problems that arose due to this mode of production spread frustration among young people. To prevent them from transforming this emotion of dissatisfaction into "organized struggle," the CIA, the Greek Right, and the Greek "bourgeois class" were encouraging them to "escape" to the "fake Eden of drugs," by tolerating the circulation or even the promotion of drugs.[136] Such assumptions, however, earned the young pro-Soviet Communists the critical comments of the AASPE, which accused them of exaggerating a problem of "some upper-class children."[137]

In general, numerous cultural products associated with the "American way" of life in the official texts of left-wing youth groups in the mid–1970s were largely the same as those which the DNL had denounced in the 1960s: Spaces that arose in the 1960s, namely "nightclubs," and cinemas screening "gangster," "karate," and "porn" movies, featured prominently.[138] New purported threats included cinemas where "horror" films were shown. The formulation of this concept was far less systematic in RF and the Youth of PASOK publications: rarely were particular titles of movies, or music albums described as "American" or "foreign" in their newspapers and magazines.

In any case, the term "American way of life" did not necessarily refer to customs and patterns existing in the United States. It was a rather broad, and to an extent a free-floating signifier, thus lending support to the argument by historians Ioanna Laliotou and Luisa Passerini that "America" is often "deterritorialized" in the sense that its presence "is traced in areas beyond the specific geographical reference."[139] Its meaning sometimes had to do with the United States: *Odigitis* in particular maintained that the U.S. troops, usually of the United States Sixth Fleet, gathered in "nightclubs" where they got drunk, became violent to passersby, harassed heterosexual women, or were engaged in homosexual acts. This perception had been dear to the EDA and DNL in the 1950s and the 1960s. A number of areas in or near Athens, namely Elefsina,[140] Glyfada,[141] and the Plaka,[142] were described as having been "plagued" by the "American way of life" due to the presence of the Sixth American Fleet.[143] However, although some famous porn films, such as *Emmanuelle,* were French, they were also described as elements of the "American way of life." Furthermore, in the case of the KNE and KKE as well as the Maoists, the "American way of life" functioned as a *prism* for the representations of the youth of the countries of the European Economic Community. Greece had signed an agreement, under which it would join the EEC in 1984—it finally did in 1981. As the day of the entry came closer, the reflection on its impact on the life of the Greek youth increased, not only in *Odigitis,* but in the entire Greek press. The EEC countries were portrayed in *Odigitis* as being steeped in the "American way of life." Above all their young people were represented as having been thoroughly "Americanized" since the end of World War II.[144] Concomitantly, the KNE claimed that the government, in pursuing the goal of Greek membership of the EEC, or to serve the "European Ideal," had only contributed to the increase in the influence of the "American way of life."[145] In stark contrast, both the RF and the KKE Es. were the sole left-wing organizations in the 1970s that favored Greece's entry into the EEC. RF members claimed that the EEC could be transformed into "Worker's Europe," which might serve as a bulwark against both American and Soviet influence and, as such, it would constitute an area where Eurocommunism could achieve the "democratic path" to socialism.[146] Still, despite their affirmative stance toward the EEC, the young Eurocommunists never identified a particularly "European" culture as a set of already existing cultural products or as an ideal to be accomplished within the EEC.

The activity of the left-wing youth groups was extroverted and aimed at indoctrinating not only their members, but the entirety of Greek youth. The "values" that "progressive culture" would help disseminate were linked with the representations of the "ideal popular hero," well-established in the language of the Left since the interwar period, as shown in chapter 1. The pro-Soviet KNE was, once again, the organization that elaborated most extensively on the definition of "progressive culture" and the particular cultural products that were purportedly associated with it. While this group turned mainly to "Greek popular tradition" as a source of inspiration for the "real Communist," the content of the meaning was defined mainly by extracts from Lenin's works or by articles of Soviet politicians, such as Konstantin Chernenko, member of the Central Committee of the Communist Party of the Soviet Union at that point and a cadre dealing extensively with ideological Party work.[147] The "real Communist" had to be educated as an "uncompromising militant."[148] His/her main quality would be discipline and active participation in the "organized struggle," meant as membership of the KNE and KKE. The elaboration of these definitions by the pro-USSR organization occurred throughout the period from 1974 to 1977. Numerous prescriptive texts were published in *Rizospastis* and *Odigitis.* The issue of "culture" and "leisure" was always addressed in the speeches of the general secretaries of the KNE and KKE to the annual festivals of KNE-Odigitis.[149] These guidelines were clarified and discussed extensively in a series of booklets published by the KNE up to 1977;[150] the best-known one included two relevant texts of its central council alongside an extract of a book by Grigoris Farakos, a high-ranking KKE cadre in charge of guiding the KNE.[151] This booklet, usually referred to by friends and foes of the pro-Soviet youth organization as the "Farakos Guidelines," gave rise to a protracted dialogue, especially between the KNE and RF, throughout the late 1970s, as is shown below. By contrast, the young Eurocommunists, counterposing themselves to the KNE, refrained from offering a rigid description of what a "real Communist" was. Maintaining that they did not monopolize Communist ideology, they did not state a singular definition of how an ideal Communist should behave in everyday life.

In the case of the KNE, the fight against the purported erosion of social bonds due to the "American way of life" that this group aimed at spearheading entailed the regulation of the behavior of its members mainly in three domains: sexuality, family and education. Sexuality lay at the forefront of the biopolitics[152] of the pro-Soviet Communist youth group and was taxonomized in its official language into "good"/"healthy"/"normal" and "bad"/"unhealthy"/"perverted." To a great extent, this classification resembled what cultural anthropologist Gayle Rubin has coined a general system of the sexual value system in modern Western societies: "According to this system," as she argues, "sexuality that is 'good,' 'normal,' and 'natural' should ideally be heterosexual, marital, monogamous, reproductive, and non-commercial. It should be coupled, relational, within the same generation, and occur at home. It should not involve pornography."[153] The KNE described the so-called "American" products as breeding unstable sexual relationships. In general, it was usually young women who were portrayed as the "victims" of "corruption," which mainly spread through popular women's magazines and purportedly demoted them to the status of "frivolous" persons, caring solely for their outer appearance in order to sexually attract men.[154] The guidelines offered by the KNE contrasted these relations with stable heterosexual relationships that would lead to marriage. A number of articles in *Odigitis* featured couples whose "genuine love" and happy marriage had begun in the comradely relations of the KNE. This in turn was juxtaposed not only with "oversexualization," but also with marriage regulated by the family through *proxenio* (match-making), and the institution of dowry.[155]

In fact, the group reversed an accusation, central to the official anticommunist ideology in the period from 1949 to 1974, which had stigmatized female left-wing partisans as "sexually corrupted." According to Tasoula Vervenioti, the title *synagonistria* (fellow-combatant), which left-wing partisans during the Resistance in the early 1940s employed as an honorary term of address, was assigned a different meaning by the dominant ideology in post–Civil War Greece and denoted "disreputable women."[156] Perpetuating an argument that had already been put forth by the Greek Left in the 1950s and the 1960s, the KNE and KKE asserted that the right-wing forces, by disseminating American "pseudo-cultural" patterns, were truly synonymous with sexual corruption.

Intergenerational tensions were not exempt from the scope of these guidelines. The KNE claimed that often the moral code and the political preferences of the two sides differed, creating tensions. However, the Party demanded that young people show "restraint," even if their parents detested their Communist militancy. Parents, the KNE insisted, had "worked hard" for the welfare of their children, an effort that the latter should respect and take as their example in the struggle against "imperialism and the monopolies."[157] It denounced theoretical analyses, such as those by Herbert Marcuse, which, according to the pro-Soviet Communist youth group, aimed at substituting class conflict with generational conflict.[158] According to the KNE, youth was a special category, but its struggle was represented as "inseparable" from that of the "people" in general, including that of older people. In this vein, the KNE regarded its role as supplementary to that of the KKE, providing the latter with "real revolutionaries" as its members graduated from the youth group to the adult Party. This perception is also manifest in the fact that the high-ranking cadres of the KNE were also members of the KKE and was best encapsulated in the slogan of the KNE "Timimeno KKE me fytorio tin KNE" (Glorious KKE, with the KNE as its nursery).[159] The ideal relationship between the Party and its youth organization was perhaps better illustrated by the anthropomorphic metaphor used by the secretary general of the KKE, Florakis: "youth and experience in one body for the most beautiful ideal."[160]

Moreover, the KNE and the KKE expected young people to regulate their behavior in the domain of education. Pupils and students had to excel, to be "first in the classroom and first in the struggle."[161] To vindicate its views, the pro-USSR youth organization resorted to a quote by Lenin, namely "Learn, learn and learn."[162] The eventual target of the KNE was that its members persuade their parents to shift political allegiance and join the KKE through their political behavior.[163] A segment of the Maoists endorsed a similar approach, albeit somewhat less demanding: In particular, the PMSP did not ask "progressive" pupils to achieve top performances in class. However, it argued that pupils should "act responsibly" and not ignore their "school tasks," even if the curricula reproduced the dominant ideology. "Progressive" pupils, according to the organization, had to finish with their studies quickly and to stop relying financially on their parents. Its newspaper, *Mathitika Neiata* (Pupil Youth), maintained that: "A progressive pupil knows how to fulfill his/her school responsibilities on the one hand, without reproducing what s/he is taught in courses such as religious education, on the other."[164] However, divergence on that issue existed among the Maoist organizations, lending support to the argument by Felix Wemheuer, an expert in Chinese studies, that scholars should deal with the diverse manifestations of Maoism, which he calls "Maoisms," across Europe.[165] Flexing their muscles against the relevant campaign of the KNE, AASPE members reversed the argument of the pro-USSR Communists to claim that the insistence of the latter on pupils making a strenuous effort to be "first in the classroom" actually reinforced the very behavioral patterns that the KNE purportedly rejected, namely "careerism" and "individualism."[166]

Whatever their ideal militant, all Communist and Socialist youth groups linked him/her with what they called "progressive art." For all left-wing youth organizations, its dominant aspect was the "militant popular tradition of the Greek people." Most references under the rubric of "tradition" were to music and, particularly, the following genres: *"folk [dimotiko]*—especially *klephtiko,* namely the ballads of the brigands in the Ottoman Empire, *rebetiko and the songs of the Resistance"* [antartiko, usually referring to the EAM, the National Liberation Front].[167] Again, the KNE offered the most detailed definition of the content and the limits of "progressive art." In an anthropomorphic fashion, official texts of the pro-USSR group argued that the activity of its members should follow both the "mind" and the "heart": It defined two emotions as congenial to the "Greek people": "suffering" due to "exploitation" and a spirit of "spontaneous resistance," as already analyzed. However, this expression of "suffering," unless channeled into "organized struggle," could generate a feeling of impasse, which, according to *Odigitis,* was evident in many folk songs. The "popular" cultural production would reach its consummation only by becoming "progressive," namely containing easily graspable political messages that transformed "spontaneous" into "organized" resistance, since only the latter was effective, as the group maintained. It was the cooperation between the KNE/KKE and "progressive artists," which would, on the one hand, "elevate" the production of the latter and would construct committed young Communists on the other. Thus, the "spontaneous" did not have to be eliminated, but be subsumed under the guidance of the "rational." "Discipline" was not contradictory, but complementary to "popular psyche."

However, it was not only the KNE that formulated such definitions. Various articles in left-wing youth official publications discussed how young Communists and Socialists should approach the "Greek traditional" music genres. For instance, *Mathitiki Poreia,* the newspaper of high-school pupils aligned with or leaning toward RF, published an article about the "proper presentation of the militant spirit embodied in *klephtiko* songs." This appeared in its special issue to coincide with the high-school commemorations of the 1821 War of Independence held annually on 25 March. The Greek folk songs were presented in the same article as evidence of the "unbroken continuity in the poetic production of our nation."[168] *Agonistis* designated Greek folk songs as the expression of the militant spirit of the Greek people.[169] Similarly, the PMSP urged pupils to assign weight to "our rich popular tradition," such as the Greek folk songs, especially those developed from 1940 to 1949.[170]

In demarcating the "progressive" culture, all Socialist and Communist groups relied more on less on the same vocabulary. Certainly, they were loudly critical of those Greek popular artists who chose to play in "very expensive night clubs." *Odigitis,* the newspaper of the KNE, argued that their songs were frivolous, referring to love and its disappointment in such a way that did not illuminate the class origins of the suffering of the lower strata. The newspaper went on further to argue that the bourgeois class and the cultural industry it controlled had, since the 1950s, systematically co-opted a number of Greek popular artists, who produced these *arhontorebetiko*[171] songs. As a result, their work has been "rigged." They cited Manolis Chiotis, a famous composer of Greek popular music, as a prominent such case.[172] Similarly, *Mathitiki Poreia* described those songs as *emetika* (repulsive), distinguishing them from the "old" and "genuine" *rebetiko* songs, which were produced until the 1950s.[173] This search for the "authentic" *rebetiko* music was not a peculiarity of young left-wingers, however. As ethnomusicologist Dafni Tragaki notes, by the end of the 1960s and in the early 1970s, a growing number of journalists and folklorists sought what they described as genuine expressions of this music genre. This was what she labels as the "first *rebetiko* revival." During those years, the popularity of the first generation of *rebetiko* musicians, who had appeared in the interwar period, skyrocketed.[174]

In addition, publications of the Socialist and the Communist youth organizations during this period had to grapple with the fact that Greek folk songs were dear to the dictatorship. Actually, the dictatorial regime had promoted this genre, from radio programs to performances in high schools. In reclaiming the nation and its "tradition," however, left-wing youth groups largely silenced this. By contrast, they maintained that the dictatorship fostered "foreign" cultural products and supported Greek contemporary cultural products, which were not "genuinely popular," but "rigged." The pro-USSR young Communists also turned against the "Festival of Greek Song." The latter began in 1959 and took place annually in Salonica from 1962. *Odigitis* glossed it as the equivalent of the Italian Festival of Sanremo and of the Eurovision; the newspaper argued that the contested songs were either pop that could be barely described as "Greek" or "rigged" popular music, adding that no "progressive" artists bothered to participate. To make things worse, these festivals had been backed by the dictatorship, which also established the "Olympiad of Music," promoting relevant "low-level" genres.[175]

The promotion of Greek "progressive" music had repercussions beyond the left-wing youth. A prominent case is the popular women's magazine *Pantheon.* In the aftermath of the dictatorship, *Pantheon* no longer advertised pop music in its pages; by contrast, it adopted the left-wing categorization of cultural products into "progressive" and "reactionary." It provided extensive coverage of the boîtes springing up across Greek cities and stressed that both *rebetiko* and partisan songs were venerable and belonged to the progressive genres. Under a headline announcing that "the Resistance songs have never been forgotten by the people!," an article in *Pantheon* argued that the Athens district of Plaka was in the process of transformation in the aftermath of the dictatorship, from an area full of discotheques to one full of venues, where *rebetiko* and partisan songs were played.[176]

Left-wing youth organizations did not limit, however, "progressive art" to "popular Greek tradition." While the former may have emanated from national settings different from the Greek one, it was acceptable provided that it helped disseminate the "resentment of exploitation" and, optimally, the "optimism for the victory of the oppressed against the oppressors." All in all, the cultural politics of all strands of the Left aimed at promoting "internationalism" and "solidarity among peoples." The KNE presented Bulgarian and Georgian folk music in *Odigitis* and in its cultural activities. RF also praised Romanian "traditional culture" and its "preservation" by the Ceausescu regime. The latter could not be easily conceived of as a case of democratic socialism. However, the KKE Es. and RF were positive toward it, due to the fact that it confronted the USSR and aimed at a "national path to socialism." The Youth of PASOK lauded the Chilean author Pablo Neruda.[177] Gavriilidis is correct to an extent when he points out that this solidarity was based on the assumption that it occurred among groups with deeply entrenched national identities, precluding hybridization.[178] Thus, he described all versions of left-wing patriotism in the 1970s as falling squarely into the category of "differentialist racism."[179] Although by no means groundless, I find this accusation exaggerated. There were two cases of non-Greek cultural products, which were acceptable to young left-wingers in Greece, without being assigned to a particular "national culture": classical music and jazz.[180] The latter attracted a modest level of popularity in the late 1970s in Greece, when a few jazz bars, as well as the Greek jazz band, Sphinx, appeared.[181] All left-wing youth groups welcomed the genre; still the approach of the KNE was remarkable. While the KNE initially construed jazz as the product of the "oppressed Black people of the USA," it gradually shifted and designated it as an "international language of protest," which was also cultivated in Eastern European countries, such as Czechoslovakia and Poland.[182]

The "Progressive Cultural Movement"

In elaborating on "Greek popular tradition" as the foundation of the enduring "Greek progressive culture," Greek left-wing organizations were not limited to writing relevant texts; they also established spaces and associations, where such culture would circulate and would help foster committed militants. Their invention of tradition was a matter of practice, akin to the definition provided by Hobsbawm and Ranger: "'Invented tradition' is taken to mean a set of practices, normally governed by overtly or tacitly accepted rules and of a ritual or symbolic nature, which seek to inculcate certain values and norms of behavior by repetition, which automatically implies continuity with the past."[183] Those spaces and associations were coined by all left-wing groups as the "progressive cultural movement" (*proodevtiko politistiko kinima*).[184] Similar moves dated back to the 1960s and restarted with the reinstitution of democracy with the initiative of various left-wing groups, especially KNE, RF, and the Youth of PASOK. They all aimed at creating links among left-wing intellectuals, amateur and professional music bands, and theatrical groups.

It should be underlined that these intellectuals did not necessarily belong to or support a particular Party. Many of them, such as Nikos Xylouris, appeared at the cultural events organized by various left-wing organizations. What also transpired was that some "progressive" intellectuals did not get along well with a left-wing Party that lauded their work. Perhaps the most notable such divergence had to do with the strained relations between the KNE/KKE with Theodorakis. His work was venerated by the pro-USSR Communists, who regarded his music as one of the most important products of "Greek progressive culture." However, Theodorakis did not reciprocate, at least in the mid–1970s. He even dubbed the KNE an "enemy of culture [*politismos*]," describing its members as a "totalitarian force" that endangered the freedom of expression.[185] Members of the pro-Soviet organization responded by accusing him of "playing the game of the bourgeoisie" by attacking the group. The composer, however, was rehabilitated in 1978 and he was the candidate of KKE for the mayoralty of Athens.

The two main pillars of the "progressive cultural movement" for all left-wing youth groups were cultural societies/clubs and youth festivals (apart from the Maoists, as mentioned below in more detail, who did not hold such festivals). Cultural associations spread after the collapse of the dictatorship in the lower-middle and working class districts as well as in the universities. In contrast with the cultural politics of the dominant left-wing youth organization in the 1960s, namely the DNL, the appeal of the "progressive cultural movement" in the rural areas in the 1970s was minimal. Those associations acquired two forms: they were either established by a specific youth organization or by members of various left-wing or center-left Parties and youth groups collectively. One way or another, they were battlegrounds for control among young Communists and Socialists of different direction, who both aimed to recruit new members. ONNED members were totally outgunned in this domain, failing either to intervene in the existing societies or to establish alternatives.

Cultural societies quickly spread in the districts of Athens and Salonica from late 1974 until 1977, when they entered a brief period of decline before reemerging from 1978. These societies usually gathered amateur music bands and theatre groups comprising young people and organized screenings of cinema movies.[186]

In the domain of the university, the most well-known cultural society was the *Theatriko Tmima Panepistimiou Athinon* (Theatre Section of the University of Athens). The Section was created in 1969, but its activity was limited until the collapse of the dictatorship. In its aftermath, it cooperated with various municipalities and toured around Greece to present its work. The content of its activities was defined through a charter of principles, which boiled down to the "production of anti-fascist, anti-imperialist culture." It was controlled by the KNE in the aftermath of the dictatorship. The Section presented theatrical plays, at least once annually. However, its activity was not confined to theatre: it included an orchestra, a choir, and a cine club, as well as literature and visual arts sub-groups.[187] Besides the Section, there were more cultural societies at universities, such as those in the Polytechnic School of Athens, ASOEE,[188] and *Panteios*[189] School.[190]

The operation of the cultural societies was sucked into the force field of Party political competition over the question of how to create a central body that would coordinate their activity. The KNE and KKE strove for the creation of an organization, called the PAPOK (Panellinia Politistiki Kinisi, Panhellenic Cultural Movement). This group was envisaged as one that would rigidly define which cultural products were "progressive" as well as promote them in cooperation with local government and cultural societies. The PAPOK was founded in late 1976 and published a magazine, initially

Table 2.3. The main cultural societies in the districts of Salonica and Athens in the mid–1970s.

Name/social background of the district	Translation in English	Details on the affiliation of the participants
Exoraistikos Syllogos Sykeon/ working-class, lower-middle class	Embellishing Society of Sykies	
Proodeytikos Morfotikos Syllogos Kokkinias/ working-class	Progressive Educational Association in Kokkinia	Controlled by the OMLE/PPSP.

Morfotiki Lecshi Palaiou Falirou/middle-class	Educational Club of Palaio Faliro	RF, Youth of PASOK, PPSP. Re-established in 1977 as *Politistikos Syllogos Palaiou Falirou* (Cultural Society of Paleo Faliro), which was controlled by KNE, even though members of RF also participated.
PEK in Keratsini/working-class		Initially controlled by the KNE and later by RF.
Morfotikos Exoraistikos Ekpolitistikos Syllogos Petralonon/lower-middle-class	Society for Culture, Education and Embellishment in Petralona	
POMNE in Holargos/ middle-class, working-class		Created in 1976. Controlled by RF until 1979; subsequently controlled by the KNE. Members of the Youth of PASOK also participated.
ESYN in Brahami/ working-class		Youth of PASOK, RF.
Dimokratiki Protovoulia Kifissias/upper- middle-class	Democratic Initiative in Kifissia	
Morfotikos Touristikos Psyhagogikos Syllogos Ilioupolis/middle-class	Educational Tourist Recreational Society of Ilioupoli	
Pneymatiki Estia Terpsitheas-Glyfadas/ lower-middle-class	Intellectual Center of Terspithea-Glyfada	
Politistiko Kentro Peiraia/ middle-class, working-class	Cultural Center of Piraeus	
Morfotiki Leschi Neon Menidiou/working-class, lower-middle-class	Youth Educational Club in Menidi	
Ekpolitistikos Epimorfotikos Syllogos Korydallou/ working-class	Cultural and Educational Association in Korydallos	
Morfotiki Leschi Agion Anargiron/working-class	Educational Club in Agioi Anargyroi	Controlled by the KNE.

called *Deltio tis PAPOK* (Bulletin of PAPOK) but renamed *Techni kai Polit-ismos* (Art and Culture) later in the 1970s. A number of cultural societies collaborated with the body.[191] By contrast, RF insisted on the direction of the "autonomy" of cultural societies: while not rejecting their coordination per se, it decried the existence of a permanent body, which would regulate their activity. These differences with regard to the "progressive cultural move-ment" flared up dramatically in the late 1970s, during the second wave of emergence of such associations.

Apart from the societies that attracted young left-wingers of various directions, there were also those founded by a single youth organization. The KNE set up the DKN (Dimokratikes Kiniseis Neon, Democratic Youth Movements), as soon as it became legal. The DKN were to be found in the districts of Athens and Salonica, housed usually in a ground apartment of a block of flats. Inside, there was always a bookcase with the titles of *Synchroni Epochi* (Contemporary Era), the publishing house of the KKE. Turkish cof-fee was served to the people who gathered there. The DKN frequently held discussions about Marxist-Leninist ideology. They also produced announce-ments that posed certain demands, such as "democratization," "withdrawal from NATO," and "solidarity with the struggle of Cyprus for independence and sovereignty." Their activities appeared in *Odigitis* and *Rizospastis*.[192] Ini-tially, the DKN attracted unaffiliated young people, who were leaning to-ward KNE. Although there is no detailed information about the number of young people that were active in every DKN, accounts of local branches of RF state that in the lower-middle and working-class districts around Piraeus, the DKN flourished. To cite one example from the district of Kokkinia, these accounts claim that "soon after its inception, DKN reached a member-ship of 150 people."[193] In general, however, the more the 1970s advanced, the more DKN participants of the first wave joined the KNE. As no new cohorts came to replace them all branches of the DKN had ceased to func-tion by 1977–1978.

In the case of RF, the situation was more complex. Although the orga-nization espoused the creation of cultural societies, whose operation would not be directed by Parties and political youth groups, it did create some clubs itself, which were called the DIMOLEN (Dimokratiki Leschi Neola-ias, Democratic Youth Club). Such clubs were created in the districts around Piraeus, but, as the accounts of the local branches of RF state, they soon fell into disarray.[194] A DIMOLEN was also established in Exarchia, in the center of Athens, in 1976.[195] The status of these clubs was a contested issue at the First Panhellenic Conference of RF in 1976. Members of the left-wing "opposition" within RF supported the establishment of cultural societies, which would not be run by a particular youth organization, instead.[196] On the contrary, the recommendation of the central council claimed that it was legitimate for local RF branches to create a club themselves, if disagreements with other left-wing forces proved to be insurmountable. It was added that the long-term aim of the club would be to attract young people beyond RF members.[197]

The Youth of PASOK and the PPSP did not found their own cultural associations. AASPE, while not establishing its particular clubs, supported an organization that was founded by the EKKE in 1975 and was active in the domain of "culture": Laiki Allileggyi (Popular Solidarity). Even though the organization did not collaborate solely with people who were members of the EKKE, it followed closely the ideological line designated by the EKKE cadres. Its title was not chosen randomly: it was meant to conjure the memory of Ethniki Allileggyi (National Solidarity), a left-wing resistance organization founded on 28 May 1941. National Solidarity was preoccupied with welfare issues and, primarily, with the struggle against famine. It was one of the founding groups of the EAM. The activity of Laiki Allileggyi usually comprised concerts imbued with a didactic character, aiming mainly to promote the cause of striking workers or to be performed at gatherings in solidarity with Maoist militants who were facing trial in 1975–1976:[198] EKKE cadres and members had entered the American embassy in Athens on 21 April 1975, exactly eight years after the staging of the coup d'état, wishing to show that the United States was deeply involved in the establishment of the dictatorship. As a result, its leadership was subsequently prosecuted, but the Court of Appeals acquitted them in January 1976. The memory of the 1940s played a major role in the repertoire of the concerts organized by Laiki Allileggyi, since the preferred songs were left-wing partisan ones from this decade, alongside political songs of the 1970s and Greek folk music. Besides the concerts, Laiki Allileggyi held discussions at its headquarters in Athens, some of which concerned the youth and especially issues of sexuality.

While the Left had also created clubs and societies in previous decades as well, a novelty of the 1974–1977 period in Greece were the political youth festivals, organized by youth groups together with the Parties to which they were aligned. The festivals were the pedagogical tools through which left-wing Parties and youth organizations aimed at inculcating particular emotions in their members. They were based on a series of rituals, which embodied their cultural politics. The festival as such was a kind of gathering that actually had its roots in the French Revolution. It was a dominant feature of the cultural politics of the Social Democrats in Western Europe from late-nineteenth century and which Communist Parties and regimes embraced in the twentieth century as well.[199] Although the DNL had contemplated organizing such a festival in the 1960s, in the end these plans failed to materialize.[200] The first

Figure 2.2. From an event organized by Laiki Allileggyi in Athens on 8 October 1975 against the prosecution of the EKKE members. *Source:* Brochure of Laiki Allileggyi entitled "Na min perasei kai na syntrivei i ypouli katigoria tis ithikis aytourgias," 1975, p. 15.

left-wing youth festival in Greece, the Festival of KNE-Odigitis, took place in 1975. In 1977, RF followed with the Festival of Avgi-Thourios and the Youth of PASOK with "Giorti Neolaias" (celebration of youth), respectively. Left-wing youth groups were not the only ones who organized festivals: the Center-Right ONNED also began to host "Giortes Dimokratias" from 1978 onward. Still, there were political youth organizations, which neither approved of nor tried to organize youth festivals throughout the period from 1974 to 1981: the Maoist ones. The PMSP was loud in its condemnation of them: It argued that RF, the KNE, and the Youth of PASOK wasted too much energy in their preparation and, consequently, undervalued the rest of their political tasks, such as the day-to-day "struggle against high prices."[201] Since the festivals of Socialist and the Eurocommunist youth organizations appeared in the late 1970s, this section focuses on the Festival ofKNE-Odigitis; the others are approached in more detail in chapter 4.

The central activities of all political youth festivals in Greece took place in a district of Athens at the beginning of the academic year, either in September or early October. They were the culmination of a series of pre-festival events that were held throughout Greece, including lower-middle and working class districts of Athens and Salonica as well as smaller cities, such as Larissa. In the case of the KNE, its festivals were apparently highly successful in instilling the feeling of common belonging in its members, as evident in a number of interviews. G.K. and G.L., both male, mid-ranking KNE cadres in Athens and Salonica, respectively, in the mid–1970s and, most importantly, both supporters of political rivals of the KKE at the point of the interview, stressed the same point in their narratives: how the preparations and the very event of the festival strengthened bonds of solidarity among comrades of the KNE. The preparation was depicted to have required strenuous efforts and teamwork. G.K. narrates: "[I]n 1977, the festival of KNE took place in Peristeri. We constructed the festival site ourselves: it used to be a wasteland. We found dead horses while making the preparations. Every member was allocated a task. Some were supposed to welcome the visitors, others to clean the toilets. Everybody was doing something!" (G.K., A.M., Interview) Although G.K. is no longer a member of KKE, his activity in KNE during the 1970s features prominently in his carefully constructed sense of self. Subsequent frustration has not totally effaced the pride he had felt during that period about elements of the activity of the pro-USSR group. Once again, this is a case of what van Boeschoten describes as "parts of collective memory (that) remain unchanged."

Such ties were certainly affective, influenced by the emotions that the festival activities stirred, which *Odigitis* described as a "combination of *kefi* and revolutionary fervour."[202] In an emotionally charged text, this mixture appeared to stem from a variety of artistic genres that were presented at the festival of the KNE: "*Tryfera* [sweet] love songs," "protest songs" about Che (Guevara) by Maria Faradouri, but also songs describing imprisonment and torture of left-wingers, like "Kapnismeno Tsoukali."[203] Music was a context in which men and women, regardless of their political orientation, could express emotions, especially of grief and *kefi*, in modern Greece. The word *kefi* is typically translated into English as "joy." However, anthropologist Jane Cowan, who has studied *kefi* in the city of Sohos in northern Greece, argues that "more than just a label for a kind of high spirits, *kefi* has philosophical dimensions, particularly concerning the relation between self and collectivity."[204] While it "represents the natural predisposition of the [individual] heart," it is experienced more deeply within a group of people singing and dancing.[205] Its enactment, according to Cowan, is mainly associated with performances of masculinity in Sohos. Similarly, in his research on a rural community in the island of Lesvos, Evthymios Papataxiarchis has argued that the emotion of *kefi* is shared by heterosexual men who enjoyed an alcoholic drink, *raki*.[206] In the case of Sohos at least, women could also reach this emotional condition, but in contrast with men, not as a result of having consumed alcohol.[207] In the case of the KNE, *kefi*, even though it was equated with positive emotions, was connected with songs describing the "suffering" of the "Greek people" in general and the torture of left-wingers in particular. This "suffering," blended with the "correct guidance" of the KNE and KKE, would lead to the ultimate socialist transformation of Greece. In a sense, pouring tears over popular suffering mirrored the determination to struggle for the "joyful" future. Both male and female members of the group were licensed to perform in the same way, in order to reach this emotional condition, singing collectively and drinking wine.

Regarding the ritualistic performances during the festivals, the KNE wished to accentuate its self-representation as the continuity of the OKNE, EPON and DNL. *Odigitis* quoted a slogan of EPON, "Polemame kai tragoudame," namely "We fight and we sing," in 1975 to justify the very inception of the festivals; the newspaper argued that the Greek people always combined "struggle" with "singing."[208] The glorification of left-wing Resistance against the Tripartite Occupation was made palpable through stalls that were dedicated to the EAM and EPON. Perhaps their most striking feature was the exhibition of objects produced in the mountains by the partisans.[209] While venerating this past, the KNE also used the festivals, in order to present its analyses about the challenges of the present. Those were particularly outlined in the speeches of the general-secretaries of the KNE and the KKE marked the culmination and the closing of the festival. Numerous members and friends attended and listened, while waving red flags, raising their fists and chanting slogans of the group.[210]

Left-wing youth groups envisioned youth festivals as the consummate expression of the "progressive cultural movement" as a joint project, involving the organization and left-wing intellectuals and artists. In the KNE case, this was marked by a particular ritual, the publication of short, open letters by well-known intellectuals such as the composer Giannis Markopoulos and film director Theodoros Angelopoulos, addressing the members of the group.[211] These letters appeared in *Odigitis* both prior to and after the festival and they praised the effective organization of the event itself and the activity of the political group in general. In addition, the Festival of KNE-Odigitis showcased those artists that the pro-Soviet Communist youth group treated as the best examples of "progressive art." Famous intellectuals as well as less prominent artists, amateur and professional, partook in the festivals. Among the renowned singers and composers who participated in the first festivals of KNE-Odigitis, Giannis Markopoulos, Manos Loizos, Christos Leontis, Thanos Mikroutsikos, and Sotiria Bellou figured prominently. Those artists did not necessarily get along well with each other. Thanos Mikroutsikos defected from the EKKE to the KKE in the mid-to-late 1970s, where he would remain until 1984. His approach to "progressive" music was not identical to that of the KNE: he had been rather critical of some albums that appeared just after the collapse of the dictatorship and offered graspable political messages, such as "Ta tragoudia mas" by Loizos. Mikroutsikos argued that these were cases of *laikismos* (populism), which he defined as efforts to appease the "Greek people" by representing it in an idolized fashion. His approach was hardly compatible with the rigid definition of "culture" as conveying "progressive messages" that the KKE and the KNE were enamored of. Still, Mikroutsikos sided with the pro-USSR Party in an uneasy relationship. In the festivals that were organized by the KNE, many young musicians also appeared, such as Giorgos Dalaras, Vassilis Papakonstantinou, Charis Alexiou, and Ilias Andriopoulos.[212] Amateur bands, such as *Nikos Belogiannis*,[213] which comprised pupils and young workers playing *rebetiko* and partisan songs, performed onstage as well.

So far, I have described the consolidation of the influence of left-wing youth organizations in the first post-dictatorship years as well as to the main axes of their cultural politics. The following sections take a look both from above and from below: they probe the extent to which these policies really affected the leisure activities and sexual practices of young left-wingers in this period.

Notes

1. Alexis Heraclides, *Kypriako: Sygkrousi kai Epilysi* (Athens 2002), pp. 199–205.
2. Ibid., pp. 206–25.
3. About the development of various brands of nationalism in Cyprus, see Rebecca Bryant, *Imagining the Modern: The Cultures of Nationalism in Cyprus* (London, 2004); Peter Loizos, *Iron in the Soul: Displacement, Livelihood and Health in Cyprus* (New York, 2008).
4. Sotiris Rizas, *Enosi Dichotomisi Anexartisia: Oi Inomenes Politeies kai I Vretania stin anazitisi lysis gia to Kypriako, 1963–1967* (Athens, 2000), pp. 235–36.
5. Konstantinos Svolopoulos, *I elliniki exoteriki politiki, 1945–1981*, vol. 2 (Athens, 2001), p. 149.
6. Brendan O'Malley and Ian Craig, *The Cyprus Conspiracy: America, Espionage and the Turkish Invasion* (London, 1999), pp. 151–231.
7. Claude Nicolet, *United States Policy Towards Cyprus, 1954–1974: Removing the Greek-Turkish Bone of Contention* (Mannheim, 2001), pp. 414–51; Sotiris Rizas, *Oi Inomenes Politeies, I diktatoria ton syntagmatarchon kai to Kypriako zitima, 1967–1974* (Athens, 2002), pp. 175–240, 247–50.
8. Heraclides, *Kypriako*, pp. 314–15.
9. Voulgaris, *I Ellada tis Metapolitefsis*, p. 25.
10. Nikos Poulantzas, *La Crise des Dictatures: Portugal, Grèce, Espagne* (Paris, 1975).
11. Robert M. Fishman, "Rethinking State and Regime: Southern Europe's Transition to Democracy," *World Politics* 42, no. 3 (1990): pp. 426–34.
12. See Voulgaris, *I Ellada apo ti Metapolitefsi*, pp. 11–20.

13. Ibid., p. 36.
14. Close, *Greece since 1945*, p. 142.
15. Sotiropoulos, Nikolakopoulos, and Lyrintzis, "Eisagogi: I poiotita kai i leitourgia," pp. 19–42.
16. Close, *Greece since 1945*, p. 145.
17. Ibid., p. 142.
18. Voulgaris, *I Ellada tis Metapolitefsis*, p. 61.
19. Ibid., pp. 59–60.
20. Ibid., pp. 57–65.
21. Anti-American images circulated widely in left-wing publications in this period. They could be found in a broad range of newspapers and magazines, including *Thourios, Avgi, Rizospastis, Odigitis, Agonistis,* and *ANTI.* The one contained in this volume is just an example.
22. See the points of view of the cadre of KKE Grigoris Farakos as well as of the prominent left-winger Manolis Glezos in the article: "Aristera, Theseis kai antitheseis," *ANTI,* 21 September 1974, pp. 12–13, 15–16.
23. Voulgaris, *I Ellada tis Metapolitefsis*, pp. 28–31.
24. Ibid., pp. 37–42.
25. Ibid., pp. 45–46.
26. Ibid., pp. 44–45.
27. Sotiropoulos, Nikolakopoulos, and Lyrintzis, "Eisagogi: I poiotita kai i leitourgia," pp. 23–24.
28. Vassilis Karapostolis, *Katanalotiki Symperifora sti Neoelliniki Koinonia, 1960–1975* (Athens, 1983), p. 332.
29. Nikos Souliotis, "Dievrynsi tou koinou, ekleptynsi ton diakriseon: koinoniki kataskeyi tis zitisis stin athinaiki symvoliki oikonomia apo ta mesa tis dekaetias tou '70 os simera", in *Koinonikoi kai chorikoi metaschimatismoi stin Athina tou 21ou aiona,* ed. Dimitris Emmanouil et al., (Athens, 2009), pp. 279–320.
30. ASKI, Archive of Rigas Feraios, Central Council of RF, box 9, envelope 3 (1977–78), "Organotiki diarthrosi tou Riga Feraiou. Katagrafi ton organomenon dynameon," December 1978.
31. *Ylika tou A Metadichtatorikou Synedriou tis PPSP,* Athens 1977 p. 7.
32. Embassy of the German Democratic Republic in Athens, "Information über die griechischen Jugendorganisationen," 30 March 1979, DY 24, 22446, Bundesarchiv Berlin.
33. "Festival olis tis Neolaias," *Odigitis,* 11 September 1980, p. 11.
34. "Giorti Neolaias '77: Komma kai politistiko kinima," *Agonistis,* 18 February 1978, p. 3.
35. Kornetis, *Children of the Dictatorship*, p. 139.
36. "I PASP proti dynami sto exoteriko," *Agonistis,* 5 January 1979, p. 2.
37. Hadjiyanni in Charalambis, Maratou-Alipranti, and Hadjiyanni, *Recent Social Trends*, p. 60.
38. See Yfantopoulos, "I organotiki," pp. 94–99.
39. See "Theseis grafeiou OB Kokkinias," 1976 and "Theseis grafeiou OB Keratsiniou," 1976, both in the Personal Collection of Maria Repoussi.
40. Interview with S.K. in Kornetis, "Student Resistance," p. 363.

41. Rosenthal defines the "biographical turning points" as experiences that lead to a fundamentally different interpretation of the past, present, and future. See Gabriele Rosenthal, *Erlebte und erzählte Lebensgeschichte* (Frankfurt/M., 1995).

42. Horn, *The Spirit,* pp. 161–63.

43. Kornetis, *Children of the Dictatorship,* pp. 293–94.

44. See "Niki tis aristeras. Oi foititikes ekloges kai merika symperasmata," *Agonistis,* 26 December 1975. For the case of KNE, see "Prosklitirio enotitas kai koinis drasis," *Odigitis,* 3 February 1977. About RF, see "I enotita kai I politiki ton foititikon dynameon," *Thourios,* 3 February 1977, p. 7.

45. ASKI, Resolutions passed in the first Panhellenic conference of RF; Archive "Charilaos Florakis" of the KKE, Proto synedrio tis Kommounistikis Organosis Neolaias-KNE: Ylika kai ntokoumenta; "O imperialismos kai ta thymata tou," *Agonistis,* 12 May 1975.

46. See, for instance: "Panellinio Sosialistiko Kinima. Vasikes arches kai stochoi," *Agonistis,* 1–15 November 1974, pp. 2–4; "Programma ameson diekdikiseon tis KNE (schedio)," *Odigitis,* 23 October 1974, p. 9; "I simerini mas politiki kai I prooptiki tis," *Thourios,* 30 Januray 1975, p. 6.

47. See, for instance, the decision of the general assembly of the students of the School of Philosophy of the University of Athens on 15 December 1976 which, among others, stated that the assembly no longer recognized Nikolaos Karmiris as a member of academic staff and would not allow him to teach due to his activity under the dictatorial regime and "in general." See "I geniki syneleysi ton foititon tis Filosofikis," ASKI, Archive of Dimitris Fyssas, Box 6.

48. See, for example: "I Neolaia tou PASOK protopora stous agones tou Laou," *Agonistis,* 1–15 December 1975, p. 2.

49. "Prosklitirio enotitas kai koinis drasis," *Odigitis,* 3 February 1977, pp. 10–11.

50. Some quotes from *Rizospastis* on 24 October 1978, just after the municipal elections, are telling: It is maintained that "whoever voted for Theodorakis in the first round supported Beis in the second. It goes without saying." Theodorakis was the candidate of the KKE for the municipality of Athens, while Beis was supported by PASOK. The latter was finally elected, defeating Plytas, the candidate supported by New Democracy. See: cover page, *Rizospastis,* 24 October 1978.

51. See, for instance: Vicky Charisopoulou, *"Tis Metapolitefsis Chameni Genia"* (Athens, 2001).

52. While young Communists and Socialists were certainly interested in recruiting young workers, the age of the workers on strike and their relation to the Left requires further examination.

53. Christos Ioannou, *Misthoti Apascholisi kai syndikalismos stin Ellada* (Athens 1989), pp. 85–104.

54. Nikos Serdedakis, "I diadromi tou foititikou kinimatos sti metemfyliaki Ellada", in *I elliniki neolaia ston 20o aiona,* ed. Vangelis Karamanolakis, Evi Olympitou, and Ioanna Papathanasiou, pp. 160–82.

55. "Apofasi tou 1ou (9ou) Synderiou tou KKE Esoterikou," *KOMTHEPOL,* June–July 1976, pp. 6–7. It was the first Congress of KKE Es. since the split in 1968 and it would be the ninth Congress of KKE since its inception, had it remained unified; "I dimokratiki synergasia kai I enotita tis neolaias," *Thourios,* 15 January 1976, p. 3.

56. "O Charilaos Florakis milaei sto ANTI," *ANTI,* Dekemvris 1976, p. 54.

57. "Ntokoumenta ths B Panelladikis Syndiaskepsis ths EKON Rigas Feraios. Politiki Apofasi," *Agonas gia tin Kommounistiki Ananeosi,* May 1978, pp. 24–35.

58. The concept of "michanismoi entaxis," as introduced by Maounis, can be found in many articles written since the mid-1970s by young Eurocommunists leaning toward the "Opposition." One example, where the influence of Louis Althusser and Nikos Poulantzas is also manifest, is: "Paideia kai koinonikos choros," *Dimokratikos Agonas Londinou,* January–February 1976, p. 45–64.

59. Christos Lazos, "To neo prosopo tou dogmatismou," article written on 3 April 1978 and attached into *Thourios,* 6 April 1978.

60. *Mavri Vivlos,* Special edition of AASPE, 1977, p. 15, Personal Collection of Dimitris Aravantinos.

61. Voulgaris, *I Ellada tis Metapolitefsis,* p. 112.

62. Decision of the First Panhellenic Conference of RF, 1976, p. 4, Archives of Contemporary Social History (ASKI), Archive of the First Panhellenic Conference.

63. Voulgaris, *I Ellada tis Metapolitefsis,* pp. 93–94.

64. Pantazopoulos, "Gia to Lao," pp. 154–55.

65. Ibid.

66. Voulgaris, *I Ellada tis Metapolitefsis,* p. 69.

67. Neofasicst terrorist groups, such as Nea Taxis (New Order), also appeared. Their hallmark was cinema bombings.

68. Kassimeris, "Junta by Another Name?, pp. 745–62; Vangelis Kalotychos, "The Beekeeper, the Icon Painter, Family, and Friends: 'November 17' and the End of Greek History," in *Anti-Americanism,* ed. Andrew Ross and Kristin Ross (New York, 2004), pp. 179–94.

69. Robert Lumley, *States of Emergency: Cultures of Revolt in Italy from 1968 to 1978* (London, 1990), pp. 296–97.

70. George Kassimeris, *Europe's Last Terrorists: The Revolutionary Organization 17 November* (New York, 2001), pp. 70, 114. S. Pavlidis, "Atomiki tromokratia kai kratiki katastoli," *Agonas gia tin Kommounistiki Ananeosi* (February 1980): pp. 6–7.

71. See, for example, the series of seven articles appearing in *Odigitis* in November and December 1976, under the banner "I Sovietiki Neolaia simera."

72. "Sosialismos, Kapitalismos," *Odigitis,* 17 September 1976, p. 3.

73. "Ti simainei 'ston kathena analoga me tis anagkes tou,'" *Odigitis,* 16 April 1975, p. 9.

74. "Technes-Grammata-Zoi," *Odigitis,* 27 August 1975, p. 12.

75. "Sosialismos, Kapitalismos," *Odigitis,* 17 September 1976, p. 3.

76. "1917: 60 chronia sosialistikis oikodomisis," part 6, *Odigitis,* 10 June 1977, p. 15.

77. "Keimeno synomilias tou presveyti tis ESSD stin Ellada I.I. Unalchov me ton geniko grammatea tis KE tou KKE C. Floraki kai to melos tou Politikou Grafeiou tis KE tou KKE A. Ampatielo," in Afinian et al., *Oi scheseis,* pp. 260–61. The USSR supported financially other Communist Parties in Western Europe as well. According to Tony Judt, between 1971 and 1990, the Soviet Union provided the French Communist Party with 50 million dollars and the Italian Communist Party with 47 million dollars. See Judt, *Postwar,* p. 495.

78. According to Jenson, the shift of the French Communist Party toward Eurocommu-

nism marked some openness of the Party toward second-wave Feminism, but only in the period 1974–1978. For more, see Jenson, "The French Communist Party and Feminism," pp. 121–47.

79. "Plouralismos, Dimokratia kai Aytonomia ton Kommaton," *Thourios*, 15 January 1976, p. 8.

80. See, for example: "O imperialismos kai ta thymata tou," *Agonistis*, 12 May 1975.

81. The book appeared in English in 1973 and was translated into Greek in 1974. About the life of Andreas Papandreou, see Stan Draenos, *Andreas Papandreou: The Making of a Greek Democrat and Political Maverick* (New York, 2012).

82. "TO PASOK EINAI TO KINIMA TOU LAOU," *Agonistis*, 16 July 1975.

83. Ibid.

84. "Koini anakoinosi BAATH-PASOK," *Agonistis*, 12 May 1975; "Koino anakoino-then PASOK- BAATH Iraq," *Agonistis*, 25 December 1975.

85. "Vorras-Notos kai pagkosmia oikonomiki krisi," *Agonistis*, 30 July 1979; "OCHI stin EOK," *Agonistis*, 25 May 1979.

86. About this issue, see also: Nikiforos Nikiforos Diamantouros, *Politismikos dyismos kai politiki allagi stin Ellada tis metapolitefsis* (Athens, 2000), p. 67, 130.

87. ASKI, Archive of Dimitris Fyssas, box 12, "Fylladio tis DAP gia ta AEI," 1976.

88. ASKI, Archive of Dimitris Fyssas, box 12, DAP Mathimatikou, "Deltio," 3 May 1976.

89. Venetia Apostolidou, *Logotechnia kai Istoria sti Metapolemiki Aristera: I paremvasi tou Dimitri Hatzi, 1947–1981* (Athens, 2003), pp. 248–63.

90. According to data that the magazine published, its readership in the period from 1974 to 1976 was about 7,500 to 8,000 and in 1978 over 13,000; 67 percent of its circulation was in Athens and 17 percent in Salonica. The majority of its readers were young (under 25 years old) and well-educated. It appealed to all young left-wingers, but especially to those affiliated with or leaning toward KKE Es. See Ilias Karras, "To 'ANTI' kai oi anagnostes tou," *ANTI*, 3 June 1978, pp. 34–39.

91. Theodorakis composed this album, when he was transferred to Averoff prison in 1968.

92. Actually, it was not atypical for left-wing artists, who had lived in exile, to return to Southern European countries, after the collapse of the dictatorial regimes there. For instance, the Communist poet Rafael Alberti returned to Spain after the restoration of democracy there. See Santos Juliá, "History, Politics and Culture, 1975–1996," in *The Cambridge Companion to Modern Spanish Culture*, ed. David T. Gies (Cambridge, 1999), p. 112.

93. "50,000 atoma cheirokrotisan ti synaylia Theodoraki," *Kathimerini*, 14 August 1975.

94. See, for example, http://www.youtube.com/watch?v=5GOQKEKDnBU (last accessed on 25 September 2013).

95. See: http://www.youtube.com/watch?v=NLgerQJo7zM (last accessed on 20 March 2014). The song was from the album *Enas Omiros* (The Hostage, 1966). *Enas Omiros* was a theatre play, which was adapted from a longer one-act play entitled *An Giall* by the Irish author Brendan Behan. Theodorakis set into music poems included in the play, such as "On the Eighteenth Day of November" and "The Laughing Boy," which became a signature song-poem for the Greek Left.

96. For the entire Tragoudia tis Fotias movie, including this moment of the concert, see: https://www.youtube.com/watch?v=g8kiKAxBIF4 (last accessed on 12 February 2015).

97. "O Kilaidonis milaei gia ton Kilaidoni," *ANTI,* 1975, p. 39.

98. Eleftheria Rania Kosmidou, *European Civil War Films. Memory, Conflict and Nostalgia* (New York, 2013), pp. 133, 138, 143.

99. "Oi 15 emporikoteres tainies stin periochi Athinon-Peiraios-Perichoron," *Ta Theamata,* 10 December 1976, p. 53.

100. "Oi 15 emporikoteres tainies stin periochi Athinon-Peiraios-Perichoron," *Ta Theamata,* 21 December 1978, p. 76.

101. "Oi 15 emporikoteres tainies stin periochi Athinon-Peiraios-Perichoron, 1976–77," *Ta Theamata,* 5 December 1980.

102. For the conceptualizations of the "Greek nation" in the Conservative thought in Greece, see Despoina Papadimitriou, *Apo to lao ton nomimofronon sto ethnos ton ethnikofronon: I syntiritiki skepsi stin Ellada, 1922–1967* (Athens, 2006).

103. Lekkas, *To paichnidi me ton chrono,* p. 142.

104. See Antonis Liakos, "I Neoelliniki Istoriografia to teleytaio tetarto tou 20ou aiona," *Synchrona Themata* 76–77 (2001): pp. 72–91; Vangelis Karamanolakis, "Anamesa sto idiotiko kai to dimosio: to vioma tou Emfyliou," *Avgi,* 20 September 2009.

105. In fact, authors of the "Generation of the 1930s" had been increasingly preoccupied with Makrygiannis from the interwar period in their pursuit of "examples of genuine Greekness." See Mario Vitti, *I Genia tou Trianta* (Athens 2000), pp. 197–200.

106 In the case of the KKE and the KNE, relevant publications mentioned that the era "immediately after the liberation … [was marked by] the Civil War, the persecution, the imprisonment, the execution [followed and affected those who had established]… Free Greece." See "Enas parallilismos dyo vivlion," *Odigitis,* 25 February 1977, p. 18. Concerning the Youth of PASOK, an article in its newspaper praised EAM as the subject that helped "enhance the political conscience of the People," adding that the violent conflict in Greece that erupted "in 1946" was a chapter of a "national tragedy." In contrast with relevant texts in *Odigitis,* this article did not specify the term "national tragedy" and avoided any references to detention camps. See G. Sergopoulos, "Ta 33 chronia tou EAM," *Agonistis,* 1–15 November 1974, pp. 7–8.

107. Ioanna Papathanasiou, "Vioma, Istoria kai Politiki: I ypostasi tis prosopikis martyrias. Skepseis me aformi dyo vivlia tou Taki Bena," *Ta Istorika* 24–25 (1996): pp. 253–66.

108. For the case of the EKKE and the AASPE, see: ASKI, Archive of Dimitris Fyssas, box 10, "Ochi sto '1o synderio' tou 'K'KE Ex.," 1978, pp. 5–7. About the KKE(m-l) and the PPSP, see: "Festival: periigisi sto perivoli tou astorevizionismou," *Salpisma,* no. 7, autumn 1977, pp. 13–14.

109. In the case of the PCE, such an orientation should be associated with developments that had appeared already in the mid–1950s: at that point, the PCE endorsed the "National Reconciliation" doctrine and aimed to collaborate with forces that had initially supported the Francoist regime, but had subsequently distanced themselves from it, such as the Royalists. About the memory of the Spanish Civil War during

the *Transición,* see Paloma Aguilar, *Memory and Amnesia: The Role of the Spanish Civil War in the Transition to Democracy* (New York, 2002), pp. 237–50. Concerning the limited references to the Spanish Civil War in the years of the transition, see also: Helen Graham and Alejandro Quiroga, "After the Fear was Over? What Came after Dictatorships in Spain, Greece and Portugal," in *The Oxford Handbook of Postwar European History,* ed. Dan Stone (Oxford, 2012), pp. 502–25.

110. "Christos Maltezos: mia zoi dosmeni ston agona," *Odigitis,* 26 November 1976, p. 6.
111. Writing biographies and autobiographies is a staple of identity making in the Communist movement in general. See, for instance: Bernard Pudal and Claude Pennetier, *Autobiographies, Autocritiques, Aveux Dans Le Monde Communiste* (Paris, 2002).
112. "Tsaprazis Taxiarchis," *Odigitis,* 13 February 1976, p. 15.
113. Voglis, *Becoming a Subject,* p. 157.
114. John Saville, "Interviews in Labour History," *Oral History* 4 (1972): p. 95.
115. Jo Stanley, "Including the Feelings: Personal Political Testimony and Self-Disclosure," *Oral History* 24, no 1 (1996): p. 65.
116. Dido Sotiriou, "Oi 14 neolaioi prodromoi ths EPON," *Thourios,* 26 February 1976, p. 6.
117. ASKI, Archive of Dimitris Fyssas, box 10, "Ochi sto '10o synderio' tou 'K'KE Ex.," 1978, pp. 5–7; "Sto dromo tis EPON," *Salpisma,* 23 February 1977, p. 16.
118. The diverse left-wing organizations concurred during the period in question in labeling the dictatorial regime that had ruled Greece from 1967 to 1974 as a "fascist" one. Thus, struggles against it were part of an "antifascist" commemoration. A notable exception, as mentioned in chapter one, is Nikos Poulantzas, who did not describe the dictatorial regime that ruled Greece from 1967 to 1974 as a fascist one.
119. Kertzer, *Politics and Symbols,* p. 19.
120. "To Polytechneio Zei…," *Thourios,* 29 November 1974, p. 5. The issue whether citizens died, when the uprising was crushed, as well as the exact figure of the casualties, have prompted heated debates in post-authoritarian Greece, which continue in the 2010s. Historian Leonidas Kallivretakis presents a meticulous examination of those casualties as well as of their memory in: Leonidas Kallivretakis, "Polytechneio '73: To zitima ton thymaton: nekroi kai traymaties," in *Polytechneio '73: reportaz me tin istoria,* ed. Giorgos Gatos (Athens, 2004), pp. 38–55.
121. "Aristera, Theseis kai antitheseis," *ANTI,* 21 September 1974, p. 15.
122. "Serious fun" was introduced by historian Robert Edelman, who explored spectator sports in the USSR. It is my understanding that he has used the term in two ways: to demonstrate that the Soviet regime wished to imbue mass culture, including sport, with purpose, but also to argue that those sports actually let their spectators in the USSR have a kind of fun that "reminded them of their humanity, and reinforced a healthy and authentic utopianism that the rest of life often denied." Gorsuch borrowed the term, in order to show that the travel experience of Soviets in late Stalinism combined recreation with indoctrination. In terms of actual leisure experience, her use of the term is far less normative, in my view, than in the work of Edelman and is bereft of assumptions that such fun necessarily marked an "escape" from the rest of the lives of the people under study. Thus, the way I construe

the term rests upon her approach. See Robert Edelman, *Serious Fun: A History of Spectator Sport in the USSR* (Oxford 1993), pp. x, 250; Anne E. Gorsuch, *All This is Your World: Soviet Tourism at Home and Abroad after Stalin* (Oxford 2011), p. 47. Of course, there are marked differences between the contexts Gorsuch and Edelman and I are exploring, since my volume does not probe a Communist regime.

123. For instance: *Gia tin agonistiki taxiki patriotiki diapaidagogisi tis neolaias*, Athens 1977; "Apofasi tis Panelladikis Syskepsis tou RF," *Thourios*, 14 March 1975, pp. 8–9; *Ylika tou A Metadichtatorikou Synedriou tis PPSP*, Athens 1977 p. 88.

124. "Gyro ap' to tragoudi: poreia kai prooptikes," *Odigitis*, 4 June 1975, p. 7.

125. For example, see "30 chronia dogma Trouman, 30 chronia ethnikis ypoteleias," *Odigitis*, 11 March 1977, p. 19.

126. Thodoris Pagiavlas, "O imperialismos kai ta thymata tou," *Agonistis*, 12 May 1975.

127. "Gyro ap'to tragoudi: poreia kai prooptikes,"*Odigitis*, 4 June 1975, p. 7.

128. Mary Douglas, *Purity and Danger* (London, 1966).

129. Kornetis, *Children of the Dictatorship*, p. 141.

130. Both RF and KNE used the term alternately with "cultural imperialism" or the "culture of the imperialists."

131. "Amerikanikos Tropos Zois: to synchrono montelo," *Odigitis*, 22 July 1977, p. 10–11.

132. "Apofasi tis Panelladikis Syskepsis tou RF," *Thourios*, 14 March 1975, pp. 8–9; *Gia tin agonistiki taxiki patriotiki diapaidagogisi tis neolaias*, Athens 1977.

133. For the use of the term *ekpolitismos* by the EDA and the DNL, see Katsapis, *Ichoi kai apoichoi*, p. 285; Saint-Marten, *Lamprakides*, p. 95.

134. "Mia pseytiki kai xenoferti koultoura," *Mathitiki Genia*, 24 November 1975, p. 6.

135. Nikolakakis, "Tourismos kai elliniki koinonia," pp. 470–71.

136. "Narkotika: to 'taxidi' sto levko thanato," *Odigitis*, 22 April 1976.

137. *Mavri Vivlos*, Special edition of AASPE, 1977, pp. 14–15, Personal Collection of Dimitris Aravantinos.

138. See also a relevant critique in the high school pupil newspaper of PMSP: "Mathitiki Poreia kai porno," *Mathitika Neiata*, 4 May 1977. About the definition of the "American way of life" by N.EDA, see Katsapis, *Ichoi kai apoichoi*, pp. 284–85.

139. Ioanna Laliotou and Luisa Passerini, "Preface: An Experiment in Teaching and Learning," in *Across the Atlantic: Cultural Exchanges Between Europe and the United States*, ed. Luisa Passerini (Brussels, 2000), p. 14.

140. "Elefsina: pali oi Amerikanoi?" *Odigitis*, 11 June 1976, p. 7.

141. "Na sosoume ti neolaia ap' to 'leyko thanato': I elliniki nomothesia," *Odigitis*, 6 July 1977, p. 7.

142. "Plaka: I synoikia tis diafthoras," *Odigitis*, 30 July 1975, p. 5.

143. Ibid.

144. "I krisi tis astikis 'katanalotikis koinonias'," *Odigitis*, 28 May 1975, p. 13; "Kai 'evroporno'," *Odigitis*, 10 June 1977, p. 15.

145. "To 'evropaiko ideodes'," *Odigitis*, 1 July 1977, p. 17.

146. "I politiki mas gia tin entaxi stin EOK kai to politiko periechomeno tou 'Eyrokommounismou'," *Thourios*, 14 July 1977, pp. 4–5. For the stance of RF and KKE Es. toward the EEC, see also: S. Karpathiotis, "ELLADA-EOK," *KOMTHEPOL*, January–February 1977, pp. 19–29.

147. V.I. Lenin, "Ta kathikonta tis epanastatikis neolaias," reprinted by the local branches of KNE in Salonica in 1976. I have found this item in the personal collection of Nikos Samanidis; Konstantin Chernenko, "Merika zitimata tou Leninistikou styl douleias," *PES*, August 1976. The KNE also suggested Soviet textbooks translated into Greek, such as the following: *Marxistiki Ithiki* [Marxist morality], a publication of the Academy of Sciences of the USSR.

148. "Diakiryxi tou kentrikou symvouliou tis KNE," in *Gia tin agonistiki taxiki patriotiki diapaidagogisi tis neolaias* (Athens, 1977), pp. 10–11; the speech of Grigoris Farakos to the Central Council of KNE in 1977, in *Gia tin agonistiki taxiki patriotiki diapaidagogisi tis neolaias* (Athens, 1977). See, also: Grigoris Farakos, *I Neolaia kai to Ergatiko Kinima* (Athens, 1977). The latter was written in 1972, but circulated five years later.

149. "I omilia tou s. Dimitri Gondica sto 3o Festival," *Odigitis*, 22 September 1977, p. 11.

150. See, for example: "I KNE terastia diapaidagogitiki-agonistiki dynami tis neas genias," Speech of Charilaos Florakis in the First Congress of the KNE (Athens, 1976). I have found this item in the personal collection of Nikos Samanidis.

151. *Gia tin agonistiki taxiki patriotiki diapaidagogisi tis neolaias* (Athens, 1977).

152. Biopolitics is a concept that Michel Foucault employs in the *History of Sexuality* to depict how human life is subjected to mechanisms of power-knowledge. According to Foucault, a number of significant changes since the eighteenth century, such as the financial development, especially of the agricultural sector, rendered humans less vulnerable to diseases. The threat of death began to appear as more distant. As a consequence, a number of mechanisms have emerged, which regulate a broad range of issues that are connected with human life, defining "healthy" and "unhealthy" bodies and sexual patterns as well as (un)desirable demographic figures. Michel Foucault, *Istoria tis Sexoualikotitas*, vol. 1 (Athens, 1978), pp. 174–75.

153. Gayle S. Rubin, "Thinking Sex: Notes for a Radical Theory of the Politics of Sexuality," in *The Gay and Lesbian Studies Reader*, ed. Henry Abelove, Michéle Aina Barale, and David M. Halperin (New York, 1993), p. 13. The text was initially published in 1984.

154. "Periodika gia nees kopeles," *Odigitis*, 14 January 1977, p. 16.

155. "Proika: enas chreokopimenos thesmos," *Odigitis*, 13 August 1976, p. 16. About the classifications of sexual practices in the rhetoric of the KNE in general, see also: Papadogiannis, "Confronting 'imperialism' and 'loneliness'," pp. 229–30.

156. Vervenioti, "Left-Wing Women," p. 112.

157. "Ena methodeymeno provlima: Oi scheseis ton neon me to oikogeneiako tous perivallon," *Odigitis*, 1 April 1977, p. 7.

158. "Ideologiki Exormisi gia ton apoprosanatolismo tis neolaias," *Odigitis*, 15 April 1977, p. 13.

159. On the contrary, one could be either a cadre of RF or of KKE Es.

160. "O logos tou s. Char. Floraki sto Festival," *Odigitis*, 25 September 1975, p. 7.

161. Speech of Grigoris Farakos to the Central Council of KNE, in: *Gia tin agonistiki taxiki patriotiki diapaidagogisi tis neolaias* (Athens, 1977).

162. Lenin used this phrase in the Third All-Russian Congress of the KOMSOMOL. This was also the title of a series of articles in *Odigitis* about the Left and education.

See "Na mathainoume, na mathainoume kai pali na mathainoume," *Odigitis,* 27 May 1977; 3 June 1977; 10 June 1977; and 17 June 1977.

163. "O logos tou s. Char. Floraki sto Festival," *Odigitis,* 17 September 1976, pp. 14–15.

164. "I kopana, I tempelia kai i…theoria tous," *Mathitika Neiata,* 4 May 1977.

165. Felix Wemheuer, "Einleitung. Die vielen Gesichter des Maoismus und die Neue Linke nach 1968," in *Kulturrevolution als Vorbild? Maoismim im deutschsprachigen Raum,* ed. Sebastian Gehrig, Barbara Mittler, and Felix Wemheuer (Frankfurt/M. 2008), p. 11.

166. For more, see *Mavri Vivlos,* Special edition of AASPE, 1977, p. 9. Personal Collection of Dimitris Aravantinos.

167. "Gyro ap' to tragoudi: poreia kai prooptikes," *Odigitis,* 4 June 1975, p. 7.

168. "Na etoimasoume apo tora ti giorti tis 25 tou Marti," *Mathitiki Poreia,* 14 February 1976, pp. 8–9.

169. "To dimotiko tragoudi ekfrastis ton pothon kai ton agonon tou laou mas," *Agonistis,* 2 February 1978, pp. 11–12.

170. "Politistikes ekdiloseis," *Mathitika Neiata,* 23 September 1977.

171. After the Civil War, this hybrid genre emerged, combining aspects of *elafry* (light) song, which in the 1950s bore influences from cha cha, mambo, and rumba, and *rebetiko.* According to Dafni Tragaki, it was appreciated by well-off urbanites in lavish nightclubs. See Dafni Tragaki, *Rebetiko Worlds* (Newcastle, 2007), pp. 66–67.

172. "Gyro ap' to tragoudi: poreia kai prooptikes," *Odigitis,* 4 June 1975, pp. 8–9. For some more data about how Chiotis and other artists brought *rebetiko* songs closer to commercial mainstream, see Papanikolaou, *Singing Poets,* p. 67.

173. "Merikes skepseis gia to rebetiko kai tous rebetes," *Mathitiki Poreia,* 23 January 1975, p. 2; "Gnorimia me to rebetiko tragoudi," See also, *Agonistis,* 15 July 1975.

174. Tragaki, *Rebetiko,* pp. 109–23.

175. "Gyro apo ton thesmo tou 'Festival Ellhnikou Tragoudiou'," *Odigitis,* 2 October 1976, p. 13.

176. "Rebetissa ki antartissa," *Pantheon* 1975, pp. 110–12.

177. "Pablo Neruda," *Agonistis,* 15–30 September 1977, pp. 30–31.

178. Gavriilidis, *I atherapevti,* pp. 219–21.

179. "Differentialist racism" is a term employed by philosophers Étienne Balibar and Pierre-André Taguieff, used to describe a strand of racism, which is not premised on the purported biological superiority of a particular race, but on the assumption that the limits between different cultures are impenetrable and their traditions incompatible. See Étienne Balibar and Immanuel Wallerstein, *Race, Nation, Class: Ambiguous Identities* (London, 1991), especially pp. 20-21; Pierre-André Taguieff, "Les présuppositions définitionnelles d'un indéfinissable : le racisme", *Mots* 8 (1984): pp. 71–107.

180. About the former, see, for instance: "Ludwig van Beethoven," *Odigitis,* 15 April 1977, p. 12.

181. Such as "Jazz Club," owned by Giorgos Barakos in Plaka. Relevant data can be found in the magazine *Tzaz* (Jazz), which began to circulate in autumn 1977.

182. "Gia tin tzaz," *Odigitis,* 21 March 1978, p. 12.

183. Eric Hobsbawm, "Introduction: Inventing Traditions," in Hobsbawm and Ranger, *The Invention of Tradition* (Cambridge, 1992), p. 1.

184. For example, see "Technes-Grammata-Zoi," *Odigitis,* 8 October 1975, p. 12.

185. "Poious exypiretei o M. Theodorakis kai osoi ton akolouthoun … ," *Odigitis,* 8 October 1976, p. 5. For Theodorakis's statement, see "M. Theodorakis, Katigoro! … ," *Avgi,* 3 October 1976, p. 1.

186. "Prospatheia gia ti dimiourgia politistikis kinisis sta Petralona," *Avgi,* 9 September 1977, pp. 1, 8.

187. "2 chronia gonimis politistikis drastiriotitas," *Odigitis,* 21 May 1976, p. 12.

188. Anotati Scholi Oikonomikon kai Emporikon Epistimon, Athens School of Economics and Business.

189. Panteios School was a highest education institution, offering courses in political science and public administration. Since 1989 it has been renamed *Panteion University.*

190. "Oi politistikes drastiriotites ton scholon," *Dimokratikos Agonas,* 6 December 1976, p. 8.

191. Based on data found in the volumes of February and March 1977 of the magazine *Deltio pou ekdidetai apo tin Panellinia Politistiki Kinisi,* some of these associations were: Morfotiki Leschi Agion Anargiron (Educational Club in Agioi Anargyroi), Morfotikos Syllogos Neon Paralias Aspropyrgou (Youth Educational Association in Aspropirgos), Morfotikos kai Ekpolitistikos Syllogos Elefsinas (Educational and Cultural Society of Eleysina), Dimokratiki Protovoulia Kifissias (Democratic Initiative in Kifissia), Syllogos Neon Neas Filadelfeias (Youth Association in Nea Filadelfeia), Morfotikos Syllogos Gkyzi (Educational Association in Gyzi), Morfotikos Toustistikos Psychagogikos Syllogos Ilioupolis (Educational Tourist Recreational Association in Ilioupoli), Pneymatiki Estia Terpsitheas-Glyfadas (Intellectual Center in Terpsithea-Glyfada), Politistiko Kentro Peiraia (Cultural Center in Pireaus), Morfotiki Lecshi Neon Menidiou (Youth Educational Club in Menidi), and Ekpolitistikos Epimorfotikos Syllogos Korydallou (Cultural and Educational Association in Korydallos).

192. Based on data provided by *Rizospastis* and *Odigitis,* some of the DKN that appeared were active in the following districts in Athens: Nea Smyrni, Peristeri, Keratsini, Kolonos, Koukaki-Plaka, Kokkinia-Korydallos, Egaleo, Petroupoli, Pagkrati, Vyronas, Dafni-Neos Kosmos, Maroussi, Neo Iraklio, Petralona, Exarchia, Kallithea, Pireaus, Eleysina, Agia Varvara, Nea Ionia-Metamorfosi, Nea Liossia, Agioi Anargyroi, and Kamatero. It also appeared in districts in Salonica, such as Sykies. Their activities were advertised everyday on page 2 in *Rizospastis.*

193. "Theseis Grafeiou OB Kokkinias," 1976, Personal Collection of Maria Repoussi; "Theseis Grafeiou OB Keratsiniou," 1976, Personal Collection of Maria Repoussi.

194. Ibid.

195. It ceased to operate after some months and was refounded in 1977. See "I poreia tis OB Exarcheion apo ton Fevrouario tou 1977 os simera," official account of the local branch of RF in Exarchia about its activities. See ASKI, Archive of EKON Rigas Feraios, Sectors, 1975–79, box 6, envelope 12, report of the local branch in Exarchia Square.

196. "To neolaiistiko kinima sti synoikia kai o Rigas Feraios," Personal Collection of Maria Repoussi. The analysis was signed by the following members of RF: Aidonis Akis, Ginisakis Georgios, Daskalakis Spiros, Kalantzopoulos Georgios, Kalafaki Eleni, Karanasopoulos Fotis, Katsarelis Aris, Kontiza Katia, Maounis Antonis, Niaounakis Nikos, Panagiotou Panagiotis, Papaspyrou Spyros, Pachnis Vasilos, Tsirimonakis Mathios, Psarras Dimitris, and Psarianos Grigoris.

197. See the relevant volume of *Thourios* on 6 April 1978.

198. ASKI, Archive of Georgiou, box 1, envelope 4, brochure of *Laiki Allileggyi*; "Anakoinosi tis Epitropis Protovoulias gia ti Laiki Allileggyi," *Laikoi Agones*, 5 December 1975.

199. Mona Ozouf, *Festivals and the French Revolution* (London, 1988); Vernon Lidtke, *The Alternative Culture: Socialist Labor in Imperial Germany* (New York, 1985); Gundle, *Between Hollywood and Moscow.*

200. Saint-Marten, *Lamprakides,* pp. 96, 109. The group managed to organize the "Week of Greek Song" in Athens in August 1966, however.

201. "I neolaia olou tou kosmou agonizetai," *Mathitika Neiata,* 7 November 1977.

202. "Pantrema kefiou kai epanastatikis exarsis," *Odigitis,* 20 September 1977, p. 14.

203. Ibid.

204. Jane K. Cowan, *Dance and the Body Politic in Northern Greece* (Princeton, 1990), p. 107.

205. Ibid.

206. Evthymios Papataxiarchis, "O kosmos tou kafeneiou: Taytotites kai antallagi ston andriko symposiasmo," in *Taytotites kai Fylo sti Synchroni Ellada,* ed. Evthymios Papataxiarchis and Theodoros Paradelli, 3rd ed. (Athens, 2006), pp. 209–50.

207. Cowan, *Dance and the Body Politic,* pp. 204–5.

208. "Polemame kai tragoudame," *Odigitis,* 10 September 1975, p. 5.

209. "Pallaiki giorti kai syllalitirio oi ekdiloseis tou 3ou Festival stin Thessaloniki," *Odigitis,* 9 September 1977.

210. *10 chronia Festival KNE-Odigiti; 15 chronia KNE,* Personal Collection of Sifis Kotsantis.

211. See, for example: "Chairetizoun to Festival," *Odigitis,* 27 August 1976.

212. "Plousia symmetochi kallitechnon sto Festival tou 'Odigiti,'" *Odigitis,* 10 September 1975, p. 12; "Oi kallitechnes sto Festival ODIGITI," *Odigitis,* 17 September 1975, p. 18–19; *10 chronia Festival KNE-Odigiti,* pp. 10–15.

213. The band was named after Nikos Belogiannis, a prominent member of the KKE who fled Greece after the defeat of the Left in the Civil War in 1949. However, he returned in 1950, in order to help support the creation of local branches of the then illegal KKE. On 20 December 1950, he was arrested. He was put on trial and executed in March 1952. He kept a fresh red carnation everyday, which earned him the title "Man with the carnation." Pablo Picasso painted an image of his, which bore the same title.

Chapter 3

The Shadow of the Partisans

Perpetuating a trend of the early 1970s, the leisure activities of young Socialists and Communists in 1974–1977 largely revolved around a concern: to
distil a "progressive" message from the cultural products they chose. In the
aftermath of the dictatorship, left-wingers, including young ones, experienced an unprecedented freedom to openly express their views and cultural
preferences. They were particularly fascinated with films and songs, which
were linked with the activities of the left-wing partisans during the years of
the Tripartite Occupation (1941–1944). Young Socialists and Communists
were not only avid consumers, but also producers of such cultural products,
contributing significantly to the explosion of the memory of what they signified as anti-fascist struggle, an explosion that occurred in this period. This
process was not simply the outcome of a top-bottom imposition of left-wing
cultural politics, but also of grassroots endeavors of young left-wingers, especially in four domains, which, according to the publications of the Greek
Left in the 1970s and the oral testimonies I have collected, mattered most
in the leisure of "progressive" people: literature, theatre, music, and cinema.
In addition, during the first post-dictatorship years and similar to the 1960s,
young left-wingers linked leisure with sexuality. The pro-Soviet Communist
youth reproduced the most rigid taxonomies of sexual norms and the cultural products they were linked with. However, its members received such
guidelines selectively. In this sense, the left-wing youth witnessed complex
sexual transformations during those years: the comeback of a socially conservative language did not necessarily affect its practice.

A Youth Culture Enamored of Reading

Throughout the 1970s, reading and discussion was an essential prerequisite
of being a left-winger. In the mid–1970s, Socialists and Communists, in-
cluding young ones, dedicated many hours to painstaking readings of Lenin's
What Is to Be Done and *Imperialism* as well as *The Highest Stage of Capitalism*.
Of course, the Maoists were usually to be found with a pocket version of
Mao's *Little Red Book*. The pro-USSR Communists read the versions edited

by the KKE-controlled Synchroni Epochi (Contemporary Era), while members of RF opted for Themelio publications, which leaned toward the KKE Es. Young Communists were encouraged to read these works themselves and then held discussions to delve further into their significance, which was called "self-education."[1] Some of them, such as RF members in Paris, organized reading groups, in which Marx's *Das Kapital* was analyzed in depth.

In addition, the KKE published a journal dedicated solely to theory, *KOMEP* (*Kommounistiki Epitheorisi,* Communist Review), which KKE cadres but also members regarded as essential reading.[2] It was usually read in combination with *PES* (*Provlimata Eirinis kai Sosialismou,* Problems of Peace and Socialism), an international magazine that published articles written by pro-USSR Communists worldwide. Both magazines included plenty of articles by cadres of the Communist Party of Soviet Union as well as of pro-USSR Communist Parties worldwide, such as the Portuguese Communist Party (PCP, Partido Comunista Português).[3] Members and cadres of the KNE also devoured textbooks on Marxism-Leninism published in the USSR and translated into Greek, such as the one titled *What Is Communism?*, put out by the official Soviet Novosti publishing house, which appeared in Greece in 1975. Quite common was also the publication of interviews of high-ranking cadres of the Leninist Komsomol, the youth group of the Communist Party of the Soviet Union, in *Odigitis.*[4]

On the contrary, RF members were enamored of Antonio Gramsci, the structuralist Marxists Louis Althusser and Nikos Poulantzas, as well as other Western European Communist scholars who were critical of the Soviet model, such as the Italian Luciano Gruppi. They often quoted them as notable cases of a "nondogmatic" or "creative" understanding of Marxism-Leninism. The book *State, Power, Socialism,* authored by Nikos Poulantzas in 1978, was particularly influential among them. Poulantzas claimed that the state was not merely an apparatus in the hands of the bourgeois class, but a strategic battlefield for class conflict, "a specific material condensation of a given relationship of forces, which is itself a class relation."[5] He argued that a mixture of working-class struggle inside and outside state institutions was necessary, distinguishing, however, himself from Gruppi, whom he accused of neglecting the latter. In this vein, even representative democracy, according to Poulantzas, "however truncated by the dominant classes and by the materiality of the State, it still constitutes a mode whereby popular struggle and resistance are inscribed in that materiality."[6] RF members were also avid readers of Charles Bettelheim, who called into question the idea that the nationalization of the means of production was equivalent to "socialism" and the end of class exploitation, an approach that he called "economism." He argued that the Bolshevik Party legitimized technocratic elites and reproduced the same divisions of labor and social hierarchies as had capitalism.[7] The KKE Es. published a purely theoretical journal, *KOMTHEPOL* (*Kommounistiki Theoria kai Politiki*, Communist Theory and Politics). The latter served as a major interlocutor of the ideas of other Eurocommunist organizations, especially the PCI and PCE. It often included translated decisions and announcements as well as interviews with prominent cadres of these Parties.[8]

Young Maoists were also voracious readers, mainly of theoretical works of China's "Great Helmsman" as well as of publications of the Communist Party of China. The People's Republic of China had actually created a global network of distribution of theoretical and political publications. This network comprised the Foreign Language Press, founded in Peking in 1952, and the New China News Agency (Xinhua). According to Christos Mais, media studies specialist, the material circulated by this network featured prominently in the endeavors of Maoists worldwide, including Greece.[9] The Foreign Language Press published in Greek the "Quotations of Chairman Mao Zedong," also known as *The Little Red Book,* in 1969. This book shaped the credo of Greek Maoists in the first *Metapolitefsi* years as well. In addition, Maoists across the globe also seriously considered during the 1960s and the mid to late 1970s the *Peking Review,* a weekly English-language magazine first published in 1958. The *Peking Review* contained theoretical analyses, news concerning developments in China, as well as the official viewpoint of China on international affairs. EKKE and AASPE often translated extracts from the *Peking Review.*[10]

Young Socialists, on the contrary, enamored of dependency theories, read avidly texts particularly of Paul Sweezy. His work appeared in *Agonistis,* but also in another beloved outlet of Greek Socialists, the *Monthly Review.*[11] Alongside Leo Huberman, Sweezy was one of the two original editors of the journal, which was first published in New York City in 1949. From January 1975 to 1976, the *Monthly Review* also appeared in Greek under the name *Miniaia Epitheorisi,* edited by Aimilios Dimopoulos. The Greek version of the journal briefly ceased to circulate in 1976–1977, but it resumed in July 1977, edited both by Dimopoulos and Lefteris Rizas.[12]

Young left-wingers not only appreciated different texts, but also varied in the way in which they conceived of theoretical reflection. In the case of at least a number of RF members, especially the members of the peer groups that had been formed in the private high schools in the early 1970s, knowledge of currents of thought that extended beyond Marxism-Leninism, such as semiotics and psychoanalysis, was a source of prestige. In the interviews as well as in minutes of discussions of RF branches, these RF members appear to have attracted a high level of respect within their group due to the diverse range of their theoretical references. They styled themselves and were referred to by others as the "avant-garde" and those who had "studied or traveled a lot abroad" (T.S., Interview). It was mainly Paris that functioned as a symbol of high-caliber intellectual production among RF members. Indeed, the city was a place, where a spectacular variety of theories flourished in the 1970s.[13] Many Greek scholars, whose work seriously affected intellectual life in Greece during the 1970s, had studied in Paris and France in general in the 1960s and the 1970s. For instance, Aggelos Elefantis, one of the key contributors to the magazine *Politis* and highly influential figure among Eurocommunists and autonomous left-wingers, studied sociology and anthropology at the Sorbonne as well as history at the École Pratique des Hautes Études in the 1960s and early 1970s.

A grasp of complex theory and its display in RF publications was not universally welcomed in RF, however. In fact, it was challenged during the congresses of the group by the few RF members who did not come from the main urban centers and/or did not enjoy the same level of education. In 1978, a delegate from Larissa, a city in central Greece, to the First Congress of RF argued that articles in *Thourios* were not easily comprehensible for the nonstudent and the nonpoliticized youth: "there are so many complex analyses about Bergman there ... whom and how many do they interest?"[14]

Certainly in the KNE the same theoretical references could be a cause of embarrassment. Any aberration from the "classics" of Marxism-Leninism could earn them the appellation of a *koultouriaris,* which the pro-Soviet Communists construed as artsy-fartsy. T.M., a male, middle-class student, and member of KNE, recalls: "I was discouraged from turning to reading beyond Marxism-Leninism. I was depicted—in an informal way—among members of KNE as "bourgeois" and as similar to the members of Rigas (Feraios)" (T.M., N.R., Interview).[15]

Actually, the young pro-Soviet Communists demanded that Marxist-Leninist theory be transformed into easily graspable language for the lower-middle and working-class strata, a process that the KNE coined agitation. *Odigitis* also published a series of comics in 1975, titled "Familiarize yourselves with Marx," which explained extracts from texts by Marx in a simple way. This series were scorned by young Eurocommunists, who described them as nothing more than a Disney version of Marxian thought.[16] Moreover, it was often argued in *Odigitis* that young workers who had obtained a "basic knowledge" of these texts should be encouraged to become cadres, since the working-class youth was considered to be the category of the youth with the most revolutionary potential.[17]

Young left-wingers did not confine themselves to the reading of theoretical texts, but also expanded into literature. A Greek poet, beloved by the whole spectrum of the Left in the first post-dictatorship years, was Kostas

Varnalis. Varnalis (1884–1974) subscribed to Marxism in the interwar period and was a member of the EAM during the Occupation years in the early 1940s. He was awarded the Lenin Peace Prize in 1959. *Agonistis* called him "the poet of the people."[18] Extracts of his work were published in *Mathitiki Poreia,* the newspaper of high school pupils aligned or leaning toward RF.[19] The PPSP singled out especially his works during the period 1922–1926, such as "To Fos pou kaiei" (The Burning Light, 1922), in which, according to the young Maoists, he no longer solely recounted the suffering of the masses, but also demonstrated the revolutionary path. As they argued, he "gave a knife" to the people.[20] *Odigitis* also stressed 1922 as a turning point in his work, when, according to the newspaper, he ceased to idolize Ancient Greece and his literature became embedded in the ideology of the working class.[21]

Another Greek poet, Fotis Aggoules, was widely acclaimed by young Socialists and Communists. Aggoules (1911–1964) came from the lower social strata. He was aligned with the KKE; this cost him exile both by the British colonial authorities in Egypt, where Aggoules had joined the Greek Armed forces that had retreated there after the Occupation of the country in 1941, and by the Greek anti-communist governments in the aftermath of World War II. The Youth of PASOK venerated him, since it believed that both his work and his life vindicated the mixture of patriotism and internationalism that the group endorsed: "[H]e encouraged the people against the foreigners and their local lackeys," adding that "his experiences made him realize the vision of a "new motherland and a universal society."[22] Similarly, the KNE also lauded him for struggling against illiteracy, poverty, and the Tripartite Occupation of Greece.[23]

In addition, Giannis Ritsos was revered, especially among members of the KNE, who often invited him to the festivals of KNE-Odigitis.[24] The fact that the USSR granted him the Lenin Peace Prize in 1977 was met with enthusiasm in *Odigitis.*[25] The members of KNE and the cultural societies they controlled often organized "poetry nights," in which they read and discussed the work mainly of Ritsos and Varnalis. For example, the cultural committee founded by the administrative council of the student union of the School of Philosophy in Salonica held a tribute to Varnalis in 1976.[26] In its "self-education guides," the KNE also praised non-Greek militant poets and authors, especially Nazim Hikmet, Pablo Neruda, Vladimir Mayakovsky, and the French Communist Louis Aragon. The books that the KNE preferred were those that "clearly depicted class struggle," which, according to the organization, was best achieved through socialist realism. Although this current had been met with criticism from left-wing authors and reviewers in the 1950s and the 1960s, it continued to be viewed as the consummation of literature as well as a potent means of indoctrination by a segment of the left-wing youth in the *Metapolitefsi*.

In the case of the Greek authors, prose or poetry that referred to recent historical events represented a battlefield among young left-wingers. A notable example was *Katachtimeni chora* (Occupied Land) by Efi Panselinou.[27] The author dealt with the persecutions of left-wingers during the late 1940s as well as in the dictatorship years (from 1967 to 1974). The KNE lauded her book for displaying a "history marked by the indefatigable struggle of our people against imperialism."[28] By contrast, *Odigitis'* review of Dido Sotiriou's *Entoli,* which dealt with the first post–Civil War years, was much more ambivalent. Though the novel followed the trope of "anti-imperialist struggle," it was highly critical of the KKE leadership's stance in many circumstances, especially toward Nikos Ploumpidis (a cadre of the KKE who had been accused by the Party of being a British "agent" and a secret police spy). Unlike most of the leaders of the KKE, Ploumpidis remained in Greece after the end of the Civil War in 1949. He was arrested in 1952 and executed in 1954. KKE initially argued that his execution was fake. However, in 1958, following the process of de-Stalinization, Ploumpidis was rehabilitated. Still, his story caused embarrassment to KKE. *Odigitis* claimed that Sotiriou's book placed equal blame on "both perpetrators and victims."[29] By contrast, RF and the KKE Es. can be singled out in the mid–1970s for embracing literature, which approached the recent past from a self-critical perspective, especially the "literature of defeat," which arose in Greece during the 1960s. This concept encompasses left-wing authors, who expressed their anguish in the context of post–Civil War Greece as well as their doubts toward the Communist Party line. Authors who have been described as falling under this category include Manolis Anagnostakis, Titos Patrikios, Kostas Kouloufakos, Stratis Tsirkas, and Aris Alexandrou. Still, this label has sparked various controversies among left-wingers. Many of them did not accept that they are carriers of a "defeatist" spirit. Kouloufakos himself deemed the term "poetry of defeat" as "misleading," since he stressed that he "pinpointed weaknesses" of the Left, in order to help rectify them and not in order to breed pessimism.[30]

After the collapse of the dictatorship, RF and the KKE Es. endorsed those literary works as an opportunity for reflection on the mistakes of Communist politics. As a relevant article in *Mathitiki Poreia* stated: "They carry the emotion of frustration … which, however, does not eliminate the commitment to struggle … they are vehemently self-critical and critical … of "revolutionary" nomenclatures."[31] Interestingly, the article refrains from adopting the concept "generation of defeat." Similar to what Kouloufakos had maintained about ten years earlier, the article argued that those authors had not been rendered passive due to despair, but "continued to struggle." For RF members in the mid–1970s, those authors had been anti-heroes, albeit with a militant spirit. RF members showed great appreciation for the works of Stratis Tsirkas, especially his trilogy *Akyvernites Politeies* (Drifting Cities), published between 1960 and 1965, as well as *Chameni Anoixi* (Lost Spring), published in 1976. Similarly, young Eurocommunists were inspired by the often openly (self-)critical work of the poet and critic Manolis Anagnostakis, himself a member of the KKE Es. Without dismissing its activity completely, the poet was one of the few voices in the Greek Left in the 1970s who refrained from a glorification of the EPON, the left-wing partisan youth organization in the early 1940s. Having been himself an EPON member in the 1940s, it is telling that he claimed in *Thourios* that "we made many mistakes then, which we should examine in depth."[32]

Theatre: Performing Politics Onstage

Besides literature, theatre also featured prominently in the activities of the young Greek left-wingers throughout the 1970s. The intensifying radicalization of university students during the final years of the dictatorship had left its imprint on it. Numerous theatre performances functioned as a means of expressing dissent against the regime. An intimate link between politics and theatre emerged in full force during the initial years of the *Metapolitefsi*. Politicized troupes and their public were able to express their views freely, since they no longer faced censorship or jail due to their ideological orientation. As T.V., young man aligned with the PASOK in the mid–1970s, narrated: "Look. People were more joyful, more emancipated. During the dictatorship, you attended a theatre play (which criticized the regime), being apprehensive that someone could report you to the police" (T.V., Interview). In this vein, Socialist and Communist newspapers and magazines, which could now circulate freely, regularly published reviews of theatre plays as well as interviews with members of newly formed theatre companies. However, while theatre had largely served as a means of uniting pro-democracy voices in the early 1970s, it increasingly became a contested field among left-wing militants of differing orientation after 1974. In any case, the left-wing youth, similar to the preceding years, continued to play a major role in the politicization of theatre: they were involved in amateur theatre groups, which, according to Platon Mavromoustakos, an expert in theater studies, were flourishing during this period.[33] Some of those groups were the Theatre Section of the University of Athens, FOTHK (Foititikos Omilos Theatrou kai Kinimatografou, Student Club of Theatre and Cinema) in Salonica, as well as amateur troupes in particular university schools, such as at the Medical School of the University of Athens. In addition, young Socialists and Communists patronized the performances of professional theatre companies, such as the Eleythero Theatro (Free Theatre), Theatro Ereynas (Research Theatre), and Theatro Stoa (Arcade Theatre), which had been created during the dictatorship years by actors opposing the dictatorial regime and some of whose members were young left-wingers. The operation of those companies continued after the collapse of the dictatorial regime.[34]

This politicization of theatre in the aftermath of the dictatorship had two dimensions. The first was the collective reflection on the contemporary history of Greece through the lens of an anti-fascist, anti-imperialist discourse. Perpetuating a trend that had emerged in the early 1970s, various theatre performances referred, literally or allegorically, to "dependence" on "foreign" powers. They linked the rule of Otto,[35] the Bavarian monarch who sat on the throne of Greece from 1833 to 1862, with the Tripartite Occupation (1941–1944) and what they labeled as the control of the country by the "imperialist" United States since the late 1940s. Such a narrative was not manifest only in the work of amateur troupes formed by youngsters, but was also pervasive in the plays performed by professional theatre companies, featuring well-established authors. Testament to this tendency was "Our grand circus," a performance that caused the wrath of the dictators. It was written by Iakovos Kambanellis and first staged in spring 1973. Renowned actors, such as Jenny Karezi, as well as the musician Nikos Xylouris, participated. Kambanellis offered a historical sequence, which was deeply ingrained with a left-wing "patriotic" narrative. Gonda van Steen, an expert in Greek studies, notes: "[H]is focus is less on the yoke that outside enemies have imposed on Greece and more on internal repression. He highlights the various forms of submission and loss of dignity into which Greeks have pushed fellow-Greeks and also the conditions of foreign domination that obsequious Greeks have inflicted on their country."[36] Scenes referred to ancient Greece, the "Byzantine"[37] Empire as well as contemporary Greece, reproducing the doctrine of national continuity revolving around "grief and grievances." Moments of "sacrifice" were highlighted, such as the execution of Greek patriots by the Nazis. Still, its message was not pessimistic. The play actually hinted at a forthcoming uprising against the dictatorial regime. Indeed, according to Kornetis, it was particularly popular among radical university students; the play's slogans, especially "Psomi–Paideia–Eleftheria" (Bread–Education–Freedom) were employed by dissident students in the Polytechnic Uprising. As a result, the play's protagonists, including Jenny Karezi, were intimidated by the regime after the Polytechnic Uprising.[38] The "grand circus" made a triumphant comeback in the aftermath of the authoritarian regime. The performance now included a brief narration of the seven years of dictatorial rule, couched in sarcasm and in highly emotional terms.[39] It highlighted torture of dissidents and the student uprising in 1973, to the enthusiastic applause of the public, which included young Socialists and Communists. Policemen would no longer wait to question and imprison the protagonists.

Similarly, the work of Michail Hourmouzis (1804–1882) continued to attract the attention of left-wingers, including young ones. The Art Theatre[40] had performed a play of his in 1957, but it was amateur theatre companies, such as that of the private school Athens College,[41] that largely rediscovered him in the early 1970s. Hourmouzis was an ardent critic of the Bavarian officials who occupied high-ranking positions in the newly founded Greek state as well as of the Greeks that collaborated with them. The Free Theatre performed his *Tychodioktis* (Vagabond) in 1974–1975. The play, originally written in 1835, was meant to criticize the Greeks who filled the higher ranks of the administrative elites during Otto's rule. Hourmouzis's plays were not limited to left-leaning troupes; they were staged at the National Theatre[42] as well, which performed *Tychodioktis* in 1977.[43] Hourmouzis's work was not only increasingly performed but was also republished in the initial *Metapolitefsi* years. EKKE-leaning members founded the publishing house Na ypiretoume to lao (To Serve the People), which published *Tychodioktis* in 1979, edited by Giorgos Kotanidis.

In the first post-dictatorship years, new—and young—politicized theatre authors also made their debut. One of them was Mitsos Efthymiadis, born in Salonica in 1945, who authored, among others, the play *Oi Prostates* (The Protectors), performed by the Art Theatre in Athens in 1975. The play referred to the Greek War of Independence in 1821 and its aftermath, highlighting the ways in which Greece became dependent on—or, as he put it ironically, "protected" by—foreign powers. It particularly lambasted the role of the "bourgeois" class for having collaborated with the owners of landed property and compromising the "national" interest while exploiting the "people." A figure that represented the "bourgeois" class in the play is Poniropoulos, a merchant, whose surname alludes to a cunning person. The play was certainly meant to link the 1820s with the 1970s. In an explicit comment to *Panspoudastiki*, the KNE student newspaper, the director, Lazanis, said: "This is why I arranged that *Prostates* were performed onstage at the Art Theatre. Because I believe that the sellout that began after the 1821 Revolution has continued until today and has been a reality, unfortunately, for our country."[44] The Theatre Section of the University of Athens followed suit. In an interview published in *Avgi,* members of the Section claimed: "[W]e are guided by the progressive democratic student movement, which struggles for the democratization of the university and of Greece in general."[45] Its performances in the mid–1970s did not deviate from this spirit: For instance, in 1976 it staged Varnalis's allegorical play *Attalus III*. Attalus III was the last ruler of Pergamon, who in his will left his kingdom to the Roman Republic. Varnalis, who finished the play in 1968, wished to effectively link the "dependence" of the junta on "imperialists" through this act of Attalus III.

Young Socialists and Communists also engaged themselves as public— and, some of them, as actors, with the oeuvre of non-Greek playwrights. The Brechtian plays were certainly appreciated by young Greek left-wingers of all stripes in the mid–1970s. It was not atypical for left-wing-controlled high-school student unions to arrange that their members attend performances of his plays.[46] *Agonistis, Panspoudastiki,* and *Thourios* dedicated pages to analyses of the Brechtian theatre concepts, especially of the *Verfremdungseffekt*,[47] through which the playwright wanted to achieve the distantiation of the audience from what it regarded as familiar.[48] Similarly, amateur theatre groups, especially those established by young left-wingers, often performed Brechtian plays. For instance, the Theatre Section of the University of Athens presented *The Caucasian Chalk Circle* in Athens in May 1975.[49]

The politicization of theatre was not only limited to the ways in which the content of the plays was understood: its second dimension was the reflection on the relations among the members of the theatre companies. The initial *Metapolitefsi* period was full of challenges for troupes that experimented themselves with collective creation. According to the theatre expert Patrice Pavis, this term denotes "a production not created by a single person (playwright or director), but developed by an entire theatrical company. The text is often finalized after improvisation during the rehearsals, as each participant suggests changes."[50] This trend emerged after World War II and mainly in the 1960s and the 1970s and was connected with protest movements striving for direct democracy and self-management in this period. The Living Theatre in the United States, founded in 1947, as well as Théâtre du Soleil, established in France in 1964, are examples of companies that have followed this direction. Echoes of collective creation had also reached Greece by 1970, when the Free Theatre company was created, consisting of students from the National Theatre. Some of its members were Maoists. This company modeled itself on the Living Theatre and Théâtre du Soleil. A core component of its activity was, at least as stated in interviews given by the troupe to *Avgi* and *Agonistis*, the equality of its members, which was twofold: all the contributors were entitled to the same wage and they all decided on the text and the style of the performance without the guidance of a director.[51] Thus, in yet another manifestation of glocalization, this theatre group, which included advocates of China's "Great Helmsman", adopted this practice of collective creation that had appeared in the United States and France, when working on plays that it expected to stir reflection on the past and present of Greece.

The Free Theatre had been very active during the dictatorship. It staged John Gay's *Beggar's Opera* in 1970 and Petros Markaris's *The Story of Ali Redjo* in 1971 and 1972. In 1973, it presented *And You're Combing Your Hair*, a revue with political content, castigating the apathy of the lower-middle class in Greece at that point.[52] After the collapse of the dictatorship, they staged Hourmouzis's *Tychodioktis* (Vagabond) in 1974–1975 and *To Tram to Teleftaio* (The Last Tram) in 1976. The latter play featured characters from the magazine *Mikros Iros* (Young Hero), which had been published from 1953 to 1968. It contained fiction stories of young Greeks who had struggled against the Tripartite Occupation in the early 1940s. However, the activity of the Free Theatre became riddled with problems in the mid–to-late 1970s. According to an article in *Avgi*, a number of Free Theatre members declared that the company had deviated from its founding principles and they decided to withdraw.[53] Those members included D. Kamperidis, while others, such as K. Arzoglou, N. Lyras, A. Panagiotopoulou, I. Maltezou, and S. Fasoulis remained. Another member, Giorgos Kotanidis, had left already in 1975. As he narrates in his recently published autobiography, "what I realized during the performance (of *Tychodioktis*) in the winter is that … there was no real communication, as in the past."[54] He adds, however, that he was no longer interested in helping to rectify this issue: at that point, he was increasingly tied up in the activities of the Maoist EKKE, with which he had been affiliated since the dictatorship years. Indeed, he abstained from performances until 1978–1979. The remaining members of the Free Theatre renamed it Free Scene (*Eleytheri Skini*) in 1980.

In general, the operation of the Free Theatre propels ambiguities of Maoist activism into the limelight: while Greek Maoists in general were aligned with political organizations with rigid hierarchical structures, some of them played a major role in introducing collective theatre creation in Greece in the early-to-mid 1970s. In a sense, Greek Maoists both favored top-bottom decision making, similar to their West German counterparts, and—at least a few of them—facilitated manifestations of "participatory democracy," as Gerd-Rainer Horn argues that the Maoist and the Trotskyite "Far Left" did in working-class milieux in Southern Europe, such as in Italy, during the 1970s.[55] The case of the Free Theatre corroborates and complements his argument, demonstrating that Maoists helped spread anti-hierarchical attitudes not only in the factories in some Western European countries, as he argues, but also in the realm of theatre, at least in the case of Greece. To make the situation even more complicated, while the Maoist background of some actors had helped them shape such theatre initiatives, the priorities of Maoist militancy, especially in post-dictatorship Greece, was one of the parameters that led the Free Theatre into decline, at least as the trajectory of Giorgos Kotanidis demonstrates.

Nevertheless, the transition to democracy did not necessarily mark the demise of collective creation. Another company that experimented with such principles was the Popular Experimental Theatre, founded in 1975. It favored collective decisions on the interpretations of the plays as well as the styles of performance, without, however, precluding the existence of a person in charge of coordinating the stages of deliberation. The Popular Experimental Theatre staged various Brechtian works, such as *Mother Courage* in 1976 and *A Respectable Wedding* in 1976–1977. Collective creation was also considered by amateur university student troupes, in which Communist and Socialist students participated, such as the Theatre Section of the University of Athens. The latter tried to introduce a middle-ground approach between an all-powerful director and collective creation in the first *Metapolitefsi* years: the entire troupe elected a "directing team," comprising three to five members.[56]

One way or another, while it would be difficult to determine whether they functioned as the driving force or the stepping stone in the politicization of theatre, young Communists and Socialists were certainly an integral piece of the puzzle.

Conflating "Public" and "Private": Singing and Discussing

Music and song are central to social movements, according to sociologist Ron Eyerman and expert in theory of science Andrew Jamison, because songs may "embody in their lyrics and in the emotional force with which they were performed the values and virtues" of those movements.[57] The leisure pursuits of young left-wingers from 1974 to 1977 are certainly testament to this. Similar to the early 1970s, tavernas figured prominently in their daily schedule. During the final years of the dictatorship, left-leaning dissident students from different social backgrounds often met in such venues, which offered food and drink at low prices, to sing collectively. It was a practice that Kornetis beautifully describes as the "cathartic energy of the taverna ritual."[58] Tavernas, such as Doureios Ippos in Exarchia Square, Athens, as well as Domna in the Old Town, Suez in Analipsi, and Pagoulatos in Papafi (all three in Salonica), continued to be one of the favorite venues of young left-wingers after the collapse of the authoritarian regime.[59] Indeed, in almost every district of Athens and Salonica, there were tavernas frequented by young Socialists and Communists.

Meanwhile, discotheques continued to exist, attracting, however, numerous nonpoliticized people, who gathered there to listen mainly to soul music.[60] The Communist youth no longer frequented them. Regardless of their particular Party political affiliation, the tastes of those young people became growingly demarcated. This trend did not necessarily have to do with the imposition of official instructions. The members themselves experienced political commitment as incompatible with such forms of entertainment. Many narrators described the collapse of the dictatorship and the subsequent intense politicization as a "rupture." D.A., male, member of RF in the mid–1970s, and student, narrated: "I vividly remember that, as soon as the dictatorship collapsed and the fever of politicization increased, we stopped going to discotheques" (D.A., Interview). A.H., male, student, and cadre of KNE in the mid–1970s, described that during the mid–1970s he felt that time spent hanging out at discotheques was for people who "lacked an ideological background"; he also ceased patronizing them in 1975 (A.H., Interview). However, and in contrast with young Communists, members of the Youth of PASOK displayed a greater flexibility: young Socialists from different backgrounds narrated that they continued to patronize discotheques, even after the collapse of the dictatorship. One such case was I.A, female, pupil, and member of the Youth of PASOK in the mid–1970s (I.A., Interview). Similarly, T.V., young man affiliated with the PASOK in the same period, mentioned to me that: "Of course I frequented (discotheques). I liked it, when hanging around with a woman or with friends. Nowadays you go clubbing; back then, it was the dance floor" (T.V., Interview).

Meanwhile, while in the early 1970s it was common for left-leaning students affiliated to different left-wing groups to share the same table in a taverna. The relatively fluid condition of politicization in this period, however, was substituted by membership of a specific left-wing youth organization in the aftermath of the dictatorship. As a result, the "taverna ritual" was reshaped. It no longer functioned as a means of displaying opposition to the dictatorship, but of demarcating different left-wing youth identities. Eating and drinking at tavernas was indelibly linked with the activities of political youth groups. In this sense, left-wingers, both Communists and Socialists in this case, did not conceive of taverna-based activity as time apart; it was experienced as the continuity of the activities of their organization, of distributing flyers or of carrying on discussions held in the headquarters of their group. N.T., male, high-ranking cadre of RF in the mid to late 1970s, remembered that "it was very common, as soon as the duties in the headquarters ended, for us all to go to a nearby taverna" (N.T., Interview). Another interviewee with the same initials, male and member of AASPE in the mid–1970s, narrated that "before or after we did some work for the group, we would gather in the tavernas and discuss" (N.T., Interview).[61]

In the mid–1970s, young left-wingers would sit at the same table(s) with *epafes* (sympathizers) or members of the same political organization. *Epafes* were people leaning toward, but not aligned with, a particular group. However, communication between people sitting at different tables was not rare and the hoary old arguments about the transition to socialism and the avant-garde role of the Communist and Socialist groups no doubt echoed through the taverna. Young left-wingers monitored themselves, so as to re-produce accurately the writings of Marxism-Leninism and to disprove the arguments of their opponents. N.T., member of AASPE in the mid–1970s, narrated that "in the tavernas, you had to adopt a specific vocabulary" (N.T., Interview). B.L., female, student, and mid–ranking KNE cadre from 1977, was somewhat more nostalgic in her narration: "Our student life was very creative then, due to the intense politicization. I remember the debates in the tavernas. You had to be ready to respond: 'Lenin doesn't say what you claim!' You had to read and re-read the classic Marxist works: your whole life was a constant education. For me, the KNE was a school" (B.L., Interview).

The narrative by B.L. in general is a palimpsest of two levels: the first one appears to be a positive evaluation of her experiences as a cadre of KNE until the mid–1980s. In her narration, B.L. described the period extending from the mid–1970s until the mid–1980s as her best years in KNE, as also evident in this extract. However, there is also a level that revolves around 1989, the year when she left to join the splinter group NAR. The latter level accentu-ates a negative evaluation of her political experiences in KNE from the mid–1970s until the mid–1980s, which she names "excesses." Both levels coexist, without erasing each other.

The collective singing of "political song" was predominant in these gath-erings. *Rebetiko* songs, as in the preceding years, marked this affective invest-ment. However, partisan songs and Theodorakis's works were a much more important feature. After midnight and having consumed copious quantities of red wine, peer groups typically started singing. According to van Boe-schoten, the partisan songs of the 1940s had "expressed the growing expecta-tions of a peasants' movement."[62] In the last years of the authoritarian regime and, mainly, in the post-dictatorship period, however, they reappeared in an urban environment and were employed by the Left, including the Social-ist and Communist youth that was active in these settings, as a means to express its concerns. O.Y., male, student, RF member in the mid–1970s, and from the lower-middle and working-class Athenian district of Neos Kos-mos, narrated that: "We sang the EAM anthem, 'Apano sta psila vouna antartes Eponites.'[63] In doing so, we felt that we were partisans ourselves" (O.Y., Interview).

In addition, the songs of Stelios Kazantzidis were also part of the taverna left-wing repertoire. His songs had no direct political relevance, but their verses could be interpreted as expressing the "suffering" of the lower strata, as B.L., female, student, and KNE member from 1977, narrates: "Kazantzidis. We loved him. We would sing in the tavernas, 'Kato ap to poukamiso mou, i kardia mou svinei.'[64] He spoke about love, hardship at work. He was always grumbling in his songs, he was not a role-model, but we identified with him: we said that he expressed the disenchantment of people due to capitalism" (B.L., Interview).[65]

Kazantzidis was actually one of the favorite artists of many residents of the lower-middle and working-class areas in Athens and Salonica, regardless of age, gender, and ideological background.[66] However, it would be wrong to take for granted that their tastes were necessarily identical with those of young left-wingers. There were many artists, appreciated by the former, whom at least the left-wing youth organizations treated as examples of "rigged popular culture" or as "delinquent" individuals tarnishing the reputation of the "Greek people." An incident that occurred on an excursion, organized by RF, is telling. O.Y., male member of RF, university student, and activist in the district of Neos Kosmos, recalled that: "The RF branch in Neos Kosmos had organized an excursion to Xylokastro [a tourist resort near Corinth]. We attracted many young workers. During the trip, I chose the music we listened to and I preferred Theodorakis and partisan songs. The young workers sat at the rear of the bus; we were not a united group. At a point, they shouted, 'Stop this, let's listen to Michalopoulos!'[67] And they immediately turned on a transistor radio and started listening to him" (O.Y., Interview).

Although they would gather in peer groups of young men and women, young left-wingers would not articulate a political identity that would position "youth" as the social group that would bring the socialist transformation by itself. For young left-wingers, collective singing served as a means of identifying themselves with the "spirit of resistance" of the "Greek people" in general; this was viewed mainly through the lens of the continuity of the "anti-fascist, anti-imperialist struggle" since the 1930s, especially the activity of the Resistance fighters in the 1940s. Thus, they reproduced the story, which was predominant not only in the official language of the Socialist and Communist groups they belonged to, but was also very common in left-wing magazines, such as *ANTI* as well as in the works of unaffiliated left-wing intellectuals. Based on the perception that they belonged to a militant community that served "principles," they drew inspiration for their current and future protests, while experiencing a growing confidence in publicly expressing their ideological orientation. As A.A., female, KNE member in the mid–1970s, narrated: "[Y]ou listened to and sang songs that encouraged you to struggle" (A.A., G.K., Interview). G.K., male, mid-ranking cadre of KNE in the mid–1970s also recounted that "when singing partisan songs, you are responding to the cop, you are responding to everybody that might want to suppress your activity" (G.K., A.M., Interview). Similarly, S.M., male, university student and high-ranking cadre of the Youth of PASOK in the mid to late 1970s, claimed: "[W]e fervently wanted to sing partisan songs. We had developed the attitude to sing and discuss about the EAM. ... We had an issue in the Youth of PASOK and in PASOK during those years, to verify our left-wing identity" (S.M., Interview).

The "progressive" songs that all young Socialists and Communists liked were to a great extent identical. However, despite drawing on common reference points for all "progressive" people, this explosion of the memory of "anti-fascist, anti-imperialist struggle" that occurred after 1974 produced strong bonds among those who shared the same taverna table and belonged to or leaned toward the same organization. The way in which these songs were sometimes appropriated reproduced the divisions between the groups to which young left-wingers belonged. Members of RF would often yell "Long Live our Party, the KKE Es.," when singing "Bezentakos,"[68] while members of the KNE would say "Long live our Party, the KKE." The former would also ridicule the former king, by collectively singing "Na ton pame sti Vouli, na poulaei tin *Avgi*" (Let's send the king to the Parliament to sell *Avgi*), while the latter sang instead "Na ton pame sto Palati na poulaei *Rizospasti*" (Let's send him to the palace to sell *Rizospastis*)"; both were appropriations of the partisan version of the song "Yupi Ya Ya."[69] Besides that, the Maoists were exceptional in singing partisan songs of the Democratic Army of Greece, such as its anthem. They were clearly driven by their version of the memory of the 1940s, which glorified rather than silenced what they called the "second partisan uprising" in the late 1940s. In fact, the anthem of the Democratic Army also appeared in a compilation of partisan songs, entitled *Tragoudia tou Megalou Sikomou* (Songs of the Grand Uprising), which was produced by the Choir of the PPSP in 1977.

Young left-wingers sang collectively Greek political songs in boîtes as well. These were small, sometimes semi-underground venues, which first appeared in the Rive Gauche in Paris and emerged in Greece from 1962.[70] In Athens, boîtes hosted Neo Kyma (New Wave) artists, a trend in Greek music that included romantic songs written and sung by young musicians, like Dionysis Savvopoulos in his early years. After the collapse of the dictatorship, bands that sang left-wing partisan songs from the 1940s performed onstage there, accompanied by slides showing images of partisans. Thus, a space emanating from France became "localized"[71] and was resignified as the locus of "authentic" expression of a left-wing patriotic narrative, which attracted large masses of young Communists and Socialists. Partisan songs were on many radical students' lips already during the dictatorship years.[72] Still, they were sung with caution until its collapse. Panos Tzavelas, a legendary figure, who was himself a partisan in the 1940s and had been imprisoned from 1968 to 1971, mentioned in an interview he gave to *Agonistis,* that, as soon as he was released from prison, he tried to spread political songs and, sometimes, sang partisan ones.[73] After the collapse of the dictatorial regime, however, partisan music proliferated in boîtes, such as Limeri and Tabouri in Athens. Limeri was popular among RF members and Tzavelas appeared onstage there. In fact, an album of his, entitled "Tragoudia ap' to antartiko limeri tou," was released in 1975. As O.Y. remembers: "He would urge us to sing louder. 'Haven't you had enough lunch today?', he would shout" (O.Y., Interview). Young Communists would employ the clenched-fist salute while

Figure 3.1. Photo from the boîte Limeri, published in *ANTI* in 1975. Panos Tzavelas can be seen (with glasses and a clenched fist) singing alongside Manolis Glezos (second to his left), surrounded by young artists and listeners.

singing. Tabouri was patronized mostly by the young pro-USSR Communists and hosted a band, founded in the mid–1970s, which bore the same name. One more, less popular boîte was called Prasinos Ilios, conjuring the symbol of PASOK. Agrambeli was a similar venue in Salonica, which attracted young left-wingers of diverse persuasions.[74]

The emotion of living a "meaningful" life regulated the leisure activities of young left-wingers in a way that erased the division of the "public" and the "private." Many Communist and Socialist students, especially those who came from rural areas, rented an apartment together with friends of theirs, a trend that had started in the 1960s. There, they often gathered with their comrades. However, pupils and young workers were sometimes also part of such peer groups, as N.K. remembers about his apartment in Neos Kosmos. At friends' apartments, young left-wingers would "discuss, discuss a lot," as O.T., male, pupil, and mid–ranking cadre of KNE in Salonica in the mid–1970s, remembered (O.T., Interview). N.R., female, student, and member of the KNE in the mid–1970s and no longer member of KKE, narrated: "[W]e were rarely alone. We were almost always together with our comrades" (N.R., Interview). Hard-working young left-wingers would not party hard in their homes, though. Similar to their perception of the discotheques, French, Italian, and Greek pop music and parties seemed lacking passion, as narrators who were former members of RF and the KNE recounted, implying that they were too "light" to meet the challenges that they felt they were facing in these circumstances (N.T., Interview; A.H., Interview). Sixties rock music, like the Beatles and the Rolling Stones, was also waning in popularity: even in their homes, young left-wingers relied heavily on Greek "political song." Rock was not totally avoided, however: a particularity of the "home" as a space is the fact that some young left-wingers listened to rock music on their transistors when on their own. G.K., male, and mid–ranking KNE cadre in the same period, as well as D.K., male, and AASPE cadre in the mid–to-late 1970s, are such examples (A.A., G.K., Interview; D.K, Interview). The fact that G.K. is no longer a member of KKE may help him admit to activities that deviated from what was prescribed in the normative framework of his group.

Avid Cinephiles

Cinema certainly did not escape the attention of young left-wingers and their organizations. Similar to the early 1970s, watching movies at cinemas was one of the most important practices in the making of left-wing youth identities in the broad sense. However, the emergence of strong Socialist and

Communist youth groups in the aftermath of the dictatorship left its mark on this pursuit as well: their publications produced extensive texts that classified films. Movies were judged upon whether their content appeared to be coterminous with the political aims of the revelant groups. *Rizospastis, Odigitis, Avgi,* and *Thourios,* the newspapers of the KKE, KNE, KKE Es., and RF, respectively, all included a regular weekly column where films were reviewed. KNE members relied mostly on *Rizospastis* and RF members on *Avgi.* Dimitris Danikas, the film reviewer of *Rizospastis,* and Antonis Moschovakis, Michalis Dimopoulos, and Tellis Samantas, the film reviewers of *Avgi,* were the most influential among members of the KNE and RF, respectively. Tracking and shaping the affective investment of youth politicization in this period, reviews privileged films that approached the period extending from the 1930s to the 1970s from the perspective of the left-wing patriotic narrative. In this vein, Danikas maintained that the symbolism of *Kynigoi* was glaring: the encounter of the bourgeois hunters with the un-decomposed corpse of the dead 1940s partisan and their nightmares were a symbol of a potential popular uprising that could threaten the status quo.[75] Similarly, Moschovakis maintained that *Happy Day* was inspired by the condition in the detention camp of Makronisos, one of the several such camps that the Right, which had "ran amok," established in Greece during the Civil War of the late 1940s to crush "popular struggles for progress," adding that the torture carried out there precipitated that committed by the dictatorship.[76] *Agonistis,* the newspaper of the Youth of PASOK, concurred in praising the production and circulation of the Greek political cinema (NEK).[77] Nevertheless, there was no unanimity among young left-wingers with regard to what Greek progressive cinema consisted of: while also endorsing a message-centered approach to cinema that juxtaposed "progressive" with "reactionary culture," PPSP publications argued that some of the movies that were venerated by other left-wing organizations in Greece were actually "pseudo-progressive." They were particularly dubious about Angelopoulos's work. Referring to *Thiassos,* they described it as "disorienting," since it was "heavily loaded" with "neurotic conditions" and examples from ancient Greek tragedy that rendered its viewpoint "pessimistic."[78] The KNE had also expressed a somewhat cautious, though certainly less critical, view of that film, but greeted *Kynigoi* with enthusiasm.[79]

Greek movies, however, were not the only ones that were deemed to be "progressive." Perpetuating a trend that had first appeared in the last years of the dictatorship, films by Luchino Visconti, Pier Paolo Pasolini, Michelangelo Antonioni, Ingmar Bergman, Nagisa Oshima, Luis Buñuel, Sergei Eisenstein, and Andrzej Wajda were regularly shown and fascinated mainly young left-wingers in the mid–1970s.[80] The screened films were sometimes contemporary, but usually retrospectives containing films that dated back even to the early twentieth century. Some notable Western European movies, which were shown in Athens or Salonica during this period, were *Pierrot le Fou* (Pierrot the madman, 1965), *Alphaville* (1965), and *Les Carabiniers* (The Carabineers, 1963) by Jean-Luc Godard.[81]

There is no data concerning the exact number and the profile of people who attended such retrospectives. However, these screenings were usually advertised in left-wing newspapers and magazines with a youthful readership, such as *Odigitis, Thourios,* and *ANTI.* Young left-wingers displayed serious interest in movies from the "capitalist" world, which were endorsed, even by the KNE, on the condition that they revealed the "catastrophic" impact of capitalism on human relations. For instance, Charlie Chaplin appeared in *Odigitis* and in the Maoist *Mathitika Neiata* as representing the "Other America," which had not been brainwashed by capitalism. In articles about his work published just after his death in 1978, he was described as a "champion for peace," who was persecuted in the United States and had to migrate to Europe.[82] *Odigitis* also embraced the films directed by Alfred Hitchcock on the grounds that they did not breed passivity in the audience; rather, Hitchcock, according to *Odigitis,* "deconstructed the impression that in life everything functions well and he allowed his viewer to discover issues that s/he would have otherwise ignored."[83]

Furthermore, especially in the case of the KNE, Soviet movies were assigned a very important position, due to the representation of the USSR and Eastern European countries as the "embodiment of socialism." *Odigitis* represented Soviet socialist realist cinema as having reached the level of "perfection" in form and content, asserting that it "transmitted clear ideological messages" and "inspired spectators to become heroes!"[84] The fact that the KNE co-organized a tribute to Soviet cinema in 1976 is telling. However, as definitions of the "genuine socialist world" varied, so did the selection of the ideal national cinema for the purposes of facilitating the making of committed left-wingers, sometimes functioning as a Cold War battleground: glossing the USSR as a "social-imperialist" country, members of the Maoist PMSP and PPSP instead promoted the "Week of Albanian Cinema" that cinema Alkyonis organized in Athens in 1976.[85] Turning against *Avgi* and *Rizospastis,* whom they blamed for being "too critical" of the Albanian films that were screened, PPSP argued that they were a veritable expression of socialist realism: they bred "optimism" and demonstrated how the "Albanian people" resisted the blackmails of the clique of Khrushchev.[86] By contrast, the PPSP lambasted Soviet films of the post-1956 era as serving the interests of the "new bourgeois class" that it maintained that had won power in the USSR.[87] Still, Albanian and Chinese films did not play for Maoists in Greece such a preponderant role as for their counterparts in other European countries, such as in West Germany. The "Week of Albanian Cinema" was one of the very few instances that the Maoists in Greece promoted cultural patterns from Albania in cinema and in general. Moreover, Chinese ones were almost never mentioned in the publications or shown in the cultural activities even of those Maoist groups that continued to model themselves on the Communist Party of China throughout the 1970s, such as the EKKE and AASPE. In contrast with the Maoists in West Germany in the mid–1970s, who demonstrated an insatiable appetite for both Albanian and Chinese movies, China was virtually absent as a reference point in the domain of culture for their Greek counterparts.[88]

Young left-wingers rushed to watch the endorsed movies with unprecedented zeal, usually in groups of comrades. All the interviewees, regardless of class, gender, age, and rank, considered watching so-called "political" cinema as one of their favorite leisure activities. As was the case with "political song," watching and discussing "progressive" cinema allowed them to identify with the "anti-fascist, anti-imperialist struggle" of the Greek as well as of other "peoples." No matter their affiliation now and then, all narrators underlined that they regarded Angelopoulos and his *Trilogy of History* as a "landmark" of Greek cinema. O.Y., male, student, and member of RF in the mid–1970s, was crystal clear: "For me, *Thiassos* is the best movie I have ever seen!" (O.Y., Interview). Actually, even some young Maoists narrated in their oral testimonies that Angelopoulos's movies were meaningful to them. This was certainly the case for young people not aligned with, but leaning toward the PPSP and the AASPE. The official publications of those groups were not the only texts that defined their cinematic taste. A.D., female, student in the early-to-mid 1970s, and leaning toward PPSP, narrated that "concerning cinema, I was influenced more by my friends, who were affiliated with the KKE Es., rather than by PPSP members. I was fine with Angelopoulos" (A.D., Interview). Many Communist and Socialist students also attended the annual state-run film festival of Salonica, where NEK films usually made their debut. Likewise in the last years of the dictatorship, they gathered in the Upper Circle of the Society of Macedonian Studies to voice their opinions on the movies. In this sense, they were yet another example that attests to the argument put forth by Janet Staiger, an expert in film and television, that the "talk back at the screen" practice has outlived the silent films.[89] Left-wing students were also enamored of a number of cinemas, notably Aiantas in Salonica, and Studio and Alkyonis in Athens. However, similar to what was occurring in the tavernas from 1974 onward, young left-wingers who frequented both those cinemas and the Upper Circle of the Society of Macedonian Studies no longer mingled with other patrons that were aligned to different groups.

After the screening, the young left-wingers were once more involved in extensive discussions—and quarrels—about the "message" of the movie. T. R., male, university student, and cadre of the Youth of PASOK in the mid–1970s, narrated: "I remember, the first time that *Z* was screened, we stood for three hours outside the cinema after the end of the movie, discussing" (T.R., Interview). Similarly, O.Y., a male university student in the mid–1970s from the working- and lower-middle-class Athenian district of Neos Kosmos, member of RF in the mid–1970s and of B Panelladiki since 1978, recounted: "[We watched] cinema very often. Then, we discussed it in the tavernas, drinking red wine. I remember this situation with affection and nostalgia. I miss it: now we watch Makis Triantafyllopoulos,[90] and all those guys. We cannot reach the high level of that period" (O.Y., Interview). It is obvious that his narration is based on the distinction of "now," associated with what he perceived as the lack of active political engagement in the broader society in general in 2007, when I interviewed him, and "then." It is perhaps telling that O.Y. asked for our discussion to take place in the taverna Doureios Ippos in Exarchia, Athens, where he used to gather with his comrades and friends and talk about politics in the first post-dictatorship years. As in the 1970s, the interview was accompanied with drinking red wine.

However, discerning various layers of memory in the testimonies that I have elicited has brought to the fore a more complicated relationship to cinema. Many interviewees have joined other left-wing groups, such as the NAR, or no longer belong to the Left. These "biographical turning points" have allowed the accentuation of ambivalences, which they may have experienced already in the 1970s. The tropes of "instrumentalization of cinema by the Left" and the "overwhelming difficulty in understanding movies" that surface in many narrations are indicative: The "instrumentalization" trope appeared mostly in the testimonies of the better-educated narrators, male and female, who are no longer active in the Greek political scene or have joined the left-wing Party NAR. Those interviewees sounded a note of frustration, describing the political fever of their youth as having essentially led to a "superficial" understanding of cultural products. U.L., a male university student in the early and mid–1970s and high-ranking cadre of the KNE, at the point of the interview a member of the NAR, narrates: "Already in the 1970s you could witness many comrades dismissing movies or songs, which did not have a clear political message. They said that these were *koultouriarika*" (artsy-fartsy on this occasion, U.L., Interview).

On the other hand, some of those militants, mainly—but not only—those who did not make it to university and were young workers in the period under study, claimed that they tried hard, but largely failed to comprehend the meaning of the movies that the publications of their organization recommended. For instance, D.M., a male KNE member in the 1970s, who comes from the lower-middle and working-class district of Neos Kosmos, maintained: "I read what Danikas wrote in *Rizospastis*. We went to a movie, which Danikas claimed that is was of high artistic value. It showed some steppes: you didn't understand anything, unless you had read the ideological analysis. While my friends [from his district] laughed, I tried hard to be ready to analyze the movie, to distil the message. I got angry with them: I asked them to leave, [because] they could not understand socialist art!" [The narrator laughs here] (G.R., N.K., O.Y., D.M., Interview).

The element of laughter seems to be a key to understanding his narration: the difficulty of the narrator in the 1970s to capture the "meaning" of the movie had to be kept secret; he was a disciplined young Communist, who was expected to monitor himself by proving capable of understanding "socialist art" and of transmitting its meaning to non-Communists. However, he seemed to fail in both efforts, which made him angry. The fact that he no longer belongs to a Communist organization allows him to transform the embarrassment he experienced then into a somewhat ironic reflection, which is apparently established by his laughter.

While discerning "progressive" cinema, left-wing publications formulated its Other as well: the "American way of life," allegedly screened in pornography, horror movies—especially *Jaws,* which sold 326,996 tickets in 1975–1976 in Athens and Piraeus—martial arts films, and crime movies.[91] Did, however, young left-wingers actually refrain from watching those films, following the prescriptive publications of their organizations? Unfortunately, in general, there has been no research on the audience profile of such movies. Nevertheless, interviews seem to provide some evidence. In the case of porn movies, it is difficult to give a definite answer. Almost all the narrators claimed that they did not watch pornography in the mid–1970s. The settings of the interviews may have certainly imposed self-restrictions to the interviewees: when relatives or children were present it is possible that they would refrain from illuminating an activity, which is still considered in Greece to be incompatible with a "serious" masculinity. A different context, namely a discussion where only the male interviewer and a male narrator are present, could have brought a different outcome. However, the fact that many (male) narrators hold at present highly esteemed positions in the academia, the parliament, and the business world could once again make them unwilling to jeopardize their prestige through associating themselves with the watching of movies which are certainly not a signifier of high culture. The case is different for crime movies. As mentioned above, many young men watched such movies as teenagers in the late 1960s and the early 1970s.

Left-wing youth membership may have placed a premium on politically engaged films, but the response to crime movies varied. Many interviewees,
affiliated either to the KNE or RF in the mid–1970s, were scornful of them,
which they described as "trash" or "low-level." O.Y., male, member of RF
in the mid–1970s, remembered that "we sometimes watched such movies,
but we never took them seriously into account" (O.Y., Interview). Angelopoulos and James Bond were hardly natural bedfellows in the eyes of young
left-wingers, though not without exception. T.L., A.H., and H.Z., all male
and cadres of KNE in the mid–1970s, argued that they reserved a couple
of hours for themselves every day, during which they abstained from any
activity associated with their organization. This time arrangement did not
challenge the "discipline," as endorsed in the official texts, but, rather, supplemented and reinforced it. According to their narratives, it allowed them
to concentrate on their tasks for the rest of the day (T.L., Interview; H.Z.,
Interview). Working hard for the KNE required some time off.

Young Greek Socialists and Communists were not unanimous in seeking to distil "anti-fascist, anti-imperialist" messages from cinema movies at
that point, however. A number of young Eurocommunists were affected
by a heterodox approach, mainly voiced in the magazine *Synchronos Kinimatografos* and expressed by reviewers such as Christos Vakalopoulos[92] and
Thodoros Soumas, who were also affiliated with RF. Actually, the magazine
was appreciated both by supporters and by opponents of the central council
majority of RF, as evident in various oral testimonies (E.Q., B.Q., Interview;
N.T., Interview).[93] *Synchronos Kinimatografos* was the successor of the magazine *Ellinikos Kinimatografos* (Greek Cinema), which published five issues
prior to the establishment of the authoritarian regime in 1967. The former
first appeared in the early 1970s and continued to circulate after the collapse of the dictatorship. It contained detailed analyses of the work of several
Western European and Soviet film directors, such as Godard, Pasolini, and
Eisenstein.[94] In the mid–1970s, the magazine was modeled on the French
Cahiers du Cinema. At that point, notable contributors to the magazine,
such as Vakalopoulos, drawing on structuralist Marxism, construed cultural
products as neither inherently "progressive" nor "reactionary," but as "ambiguous," playing different roles in different contexts. Moreover, resonating
with the version of psychoanalysis endorsed by Jacques Lacan, they favored
a narration teeming with ruptures and moments of uncertainty. They argued that the prevailing tendency in the scenarios of NEK movies in the
mid–1970s was a "message-centered approach," classifying the film roles
in a Manichean fashion in the "heroes" of class struggle and their virulent
enemies. Vakalopoulos argued that: "Finding the 'message' has been connected in a one-dimensional way with the 'new,' 'progressive' and 'political'

cinema. The products of such cinema breed fanaticism. They resemble TV commercials."[95]

In lambasting such an approach, a number of *Synchronos Kinimatografos* contributors particularly dealt with the way in which Greek political cinema at that point narrated the Greek history since the 1930s. In this vein, *Kynigoi* received a lukewarm response in the magazine, precisely for the same reasons that Danikas appreciated it: for the contributors to *Synchronos Kinimatografos* it endorsed too linear a narrative which was similar to the "official Communist Party" line on memory.[96] By contrast, Vakalopoulos positively reviewed *Thiassos,* because, according to him, it "teemed with discontinuities."[97] While such critique of "message-centrism" appeared already in the mid–1970s, it became central to debates among left-wingers around "culture" especially from 1977, as is shown in the next chapter in detail.[98]

Young Left-Wingers on Vacation

Young Socialists and Communists, and especially the latter, largely dismissed leisure activities that were not conducive to the development of left-wing activity. They treated leisure as a key component of militancy. Still, there was an exception: their tourist patterns, which became only to an extent embedded in their ideology during the period in question.

In general, the increase in both the number of Greeks who went on holiday and of foreign tourists who visited Greece resulted in the spread of discussions about the ramifications of tourism for the Greek society. Already in the 1960s, as Nikolakakis has demonstrated, and throughout the 1970s, such debates ran across the political spectrum and involved a variety of social actors, such as the Church, political parties, and popular press.[99] On the one hand, tourism was represented as contributing to "modernization," especially in the sense of European convergence. Contact through tourism, it was argued, would allay the "low collective self-esteem" of Greeks in their encounters with other Europeans, by familiarizing the former with the latter. The popular center-left newspaper *Ta Nea* deemed this particularly important, due to the prospective entry of Greece into the European Economic Community in the early 1980s.[100] However, the link of tourism to "modernity" had negative connotations as well throughout the period from 1974 to 1981: tourist development was blamed for the emergence of youth venues, such as discotheques, where drugs were rumored to circulate. Plaka, whose discotheques continued to attract several tourists, was targeted throughout the period from 1974 to 1981 and was even described in Conservative and center-left newspapers as the "Greek Soho."[101] A third, widely held representation of tourism carried romantic connotations and linked it to notions of "freedom" and "discovery of the authentic Self" through a total disconnection from the "routines of the everyday life in the city." This link circulated in popular women's magazines, such as *Pantheon* and *Fantasio*. Vacations are a "psychological escape that makes you feel free," as an article in the latter asserted.[102] These magazines, often while referring to holidays, promoted a role model of a "liberated" femininity for young Greek women, who ideally would flirt and engage in premarital sexual relationships or reject male flirtation, without having to resort to the assistance of a male relative.[103] "Liberated" femininity, however, was usually associated by young male Greeks, who lived in tourist resorts, with foreign tourists, causing the emergence of *kamaki*.[104] According to anthropologist Sofka Zinovieff, the young male residents of the islands and the coastal areas in Greece, which attracted tourists, practiced *kamaki*.[105] In brief, it meant that a local young man would flirt with foreign female tourists, in order to attract them into ephemeral sexual relationships.[106] By "sexually conquering" women from Northern Europe or the United States, they envisaged that they took revenge for living in a poorer society. As Zinovieff notes, those men depicted such sexual acts in "violent metaphorical terms," such as "slaughtering."[107]

The representations of tourism as an "escape from routine" as well as the moral concern about its potential "corruptive" impact were issues raised by young Communists as well. Again, the KNE offered some of the most alarming images of this potential "corruption." It did not dismiss summer vacations, but, actually, aimed to reclaim them. A series of articles in *Odigitis* maintained that the "government," especially the EOT (Ellinikos Organismos Tourismou, Greek Tourist Organization),[108] and the "ruling class," deprived the youth of the "correct education and ideals."[109] Rather, they allegedly tried to spread the insidious "summer way of life," which the KNE portrayed as the "culmination" of the "American way of life." A major area of concern for KNE was, as already mentioned, the unstable sexual relationships. The group vehemently criticized the *kamaki* phenomenon: "[F]antasizing about the pretty English girl" results in the breaking of "decent" sexual norms, according to *Odigitis*.[110] The pro-Soviet young Communists actually reproduced an oft-repeated motif that was circulating at the time in diverse outlets in Greece, such as in *Ta Nea*: Summertime was an occasion to deviate from established sexual norms, a process that had started "elsewhere," in Northern Europe and the United States, and was conveyed to Greece by incoming "foreign" tourists.[111] While for popular women's magazines this was an opportunity, in *Odigitis* it was described as a "threat." In any case, and in a contradictory manner, pro-Soviet young Communists also accused the ruling class of "indifference" on the "right of the working class" to enjoy vacations, as it did not react to the fact that the "high cost of tourism" functioned as deterrent for them.[112] In order to counter these "detrimental" influences, the KNE itself set to organizing its own collective forms of tourism, meant to inculcate committed militants. The pro-Soviet organization hoped to offer low-cost vacations, aiming at providing young workers or students from the lower social strata with the opportunity of youth tourism.

One type of collective tourism was that of excursions to socialist European countries and, especially, the USSR. These excursions concerned university students in the last year of their studies. At least since the 1950s, university student associations had been arranging excursions abroad, mainly to Western Europe, for final-year students.[113] However, the major change in the environment of intensifying politicization was the destinations on offer, which, from 1974, lay primarily in Eastern Europe and the USSR. In 1975, a number of university faculty student associations, which included the Athens Law School and the Polytechnic in Athens, organized excursions to the Soviet Union. These holidays were promoted by the KNE and the PSK.[114] They attracted mainly, but not only, members and supporters of the group. They took place in the summer. Students were transported by airplanes belonging to the Soviet national carrier, Aeroflot, to Moscow and, then, traveled around the USSR by train or bus. The excursions also included meetings with the Greek political refugees, who had lived there since the end of the Civil War in 1949 and who were still banned from returning to Greece after 1974. After the defeat of the left-wing DSE (Dimokratikos Stratos Elladas, Democratic Army of Greece) in 1949, thousands of refugees fled mainly to Czechoslovakia, Yugoslavia, Poland, Hungary, Romania, East Germany, and the Soviet Union. They were initially stripped of Greek citizenship but the government of PASOK reversed this act in the 1980s and the political refugees were allowed to return to Greece, apart from those who, instead of "Greek," have coined themselves as "Macedonian." In 1975, *Odigitis* reported that the transportation and the accommodation of the Greek students were undertaken by Sputnik, the travel bureau of the Komsomol, the youth organization of the Communist Party of the Soviet Union. As a result, the cost was very low. Of course, these excursions were meant to acquire a didactic character. Long descriptions of them appeared in *Odigitis,* which are very interesting in the sense that they reproduced an image of the USSR as the locus of socialist perfection. The narration revolved around the concepts of "cleanliness" and "effective organization," which were argued to be "impressive" in all domains of social life. By contrast, it included scant references to the landscape or details of the cities and towns visited; it was more a prescriptive than a descriptive text, in the sense that it defined the form that socialism should, and would ultimately in the KKE's view, acquire in Greece.[115]

Actually, in 1977, the KKE was unique among left-wing organizations in establishing its own package tours agent, LEV Tours. Even though it did not address solely the youth, LEV Tours facilitated the forms of collective tourism organized by KNE, but the scope of its activities was not limited there. LEV Tours operated as an enterprise, which organized vacations abroad, often in the Eastern Bloc, but also in Greece. Its usual destinations, which appeared in its advertisements in *Odigitis*, were socialist European countries, such as Bulgaria and Czechoslovakia.[116]

It is difficult to assess the extent to which the participants in the excursions to Eastern Europe and the USSR were influenced by the representations of the Eastern Bloc that appeared in the publications of the pro-Soviet organizations. The collapse of the Soviet Communist system in 1989 has led to the proliferation of counter-narratives among participants about their experiences in the 1970s. A number of KNE cadres and members in the 1970s, who at the point of the interview belonged to other left-wing organizations, such as the NAR, bring the ambivalence, even the sense of disappointment they experienced during these tours, to the fore. U.L., male, high-ranking cadre, and university student in the early and mid–1970s, claimed that "I asked educated people about [Wim] Wenders in (East) Berlin and Moscow: they ignored him. Of Greek cinema, they only knew about a soft porn movie!" (U.L., Interview). Nevertheless, the collapse of the USSR and the proliferation of counter-narratives may, to an extent, obscure the significance of that country for the members of the KNE. The KNE promoted such excursions throughout the 1970s in a variety of university schools and often came into conflict with other young left-wingers, who were critical toward the Socialist bloc. In 1980, the final-year university students of the faculty of civil engineering at the Aristotle University of Salonica split over holiday preferences: one group organized an excursion to Thailand, while another, affiliated to the KNE, opted for Czechoslovakia (D.A., Interview).

Besides travel to the Soviet Union and Eastern European countries, collective tourism acquired another form: visits to resorts and sites close to Athens, which were organized in the summer by cultural societies in the working and lower-middle class areas and the university as well as by labor union youth committees and were promoted by Communist and Socialist youth groups.[117] The DNL had organized such excursions in the 1960s.[118] Nevertheless, they became much more common in the aftermath of the dictatorship. These trips did not attract only left-wing students, but also some nonaffiliated workers. The transportation was by bus and they usually lasted for one day. In general, all major left-wing youth groups aimed at bestowing an "educational" character to youth leisure. Therefore, they responded to the representations of holidays as an "escape from routine" and attempted not to totally challenge them, but mostly add the parameter of "culture." It is not by chance that the destination of many such excursions was the ancient theatre of Epidavros. The Cultural Group of Acharnon Street, controlled by the KNE, organized one trip there every year in the summer. The narration of a female member of the KNE, A.M., who was also very active in that society, is telling of the twofold character of these excursions: "We went to Epidavros every year, we watched a theatre play, then we enjoyed the sea and we returned home" (G.K., A.M., Interview).

Nevertheless, while not at all insignificant, collective tourism was apparently not the most popular form of holidays for young Communists and Socialists. By contrast, what most left-wing young people opted for were usually one or two weeks of vacation, organized by peer groups. It was a trend that began mostly since the early 1970s. The preference for such a type of holiday may be assumed by the fact that the majority of the articles in all left-wing youth newspapers referring to vacations offered advice for unofficially organized youth trips; a smaller number advertised or described collective forms of tourism. Youth peer groups most often comprised members of the same group or, at least, people within the range of the broader Socialist and Communist youth forces. These trips occurred at a point between late June, when university exams finished, and mid–August, when most young Communists and Socialist students returned to Athens and Salonica, in order to start preparing the youth festivals of their group. However, the opportunities for vacation varied, according to a number of parameters such as class. Many young workers, especially those who had not worked for the same employer for over a year, were not entitled to paid leave. They usually traveled to beaches in Attica in the evenings and returned the same night.[119] Moreover, many students, left-wing or not, from working-class families or rural areas, spent much, if not all of the summertime, with their family. Students from rural areas often helped their parents to cultivate their land (H.Z., Interview; D.P., Interview). Two other parameters were age and gender: women, especially high-school students as well as those who came from working-class districts or rural areas faced more restrictions from their families. B.L., who came from a working-class family in Piraeus, narrated that: "I had to wait until I was older, to get into university, in order to go on vacation with my peer group" (B.L., Interview). Finally, one's rank in a left-wing youth organization played an important role. In contrast with the ordinary members, the narrative of the then-cadres of both the KNE and RF differs significantly in stressing the lack of time for vacation in the period from 1974 to 1981: N.T., male, high-ranking RF cadre, claimed that he started going on summer vacation after 1980, when he toned down his active involvement with RF (N.T., Interview). The statements in these narratives are vindicated by the written sources, at least in the case of RF: documents of its central council reveal that cadres were allowed to abstain from their tasks for a limited number of days. A strict record of their presence at the summer activities of the group was kept.[120] This form of control certainly gave rise to complaints from young militants of all persuasions, even though it was also experienced as a necessary prerequisite of "struggle." "Shared possibilities," as defined by the Italian oral historian Alessandro Portelli, are obvious in the narrative of B.L. (B.L., Interview).[121] When I asked her whether she went on holidays, she replied: "Now you are asking about a traumatic experience. [She laughs]. We had to ask for permission. Even the employees in a multinational company would be entitled to more days off." However, she was steadfast to add that "There were these cons, but you experienced a group, which was ready to act throughout the year. We could organize protests even in the summer, like in 1978, when Law 815[122] was passed" (B.L., Interview).

Peer groups of young left-wingers traveled mostly to the Cyclades Islands in the summer. Folegandros, Schoinoussa, and Anafi, alongside Ios, Sifnos, and Santorini, were among the most popular for young left-wing tourists, as data from interviews show. In addition, *Odigitis* proposed travels to sites, which were the scenes of left-wing partisan activity in the 1940s. One such was the village of Panagia in Crete, where *Odigitis* claimed that the biggest battle in the island between the EAM and the German Occupation forces had taken place.[123] Nevertheless, young left-wingers did not apparently visit those locations frequently. T.L., male and high-ranking KNE cadre, narrated that "no, not at all, this was not an important criterion for us" (T.L., Interview). Due to his position, T.L. was expected to function as a role model and stick by the official language—which is what renders his statement most important.

All young left-wingers construed the excursions to the islands as pathways to unmediated contact with nature. Such naturalistic endeavors included free camping or even spending the night under the open skies in sleeping bags by the sea. Quite tellingly, T.V., young man affiliated with PASOK in the mid–1970s, narrated to me: "I have even slept in caves in Mykonos island!" (T.V., Interview). Concerning transportation, young Communists and Socialists opted for traveling on the deck of ships. In general, they preferred cheap options, regardless of their class origins. These elements perpetuated the anti-commercial travel culture, which had developed among a segment of left-leaning young dissidents from at least the early 1970s. However, this was not another aspect of a "progressive" identity that demarcated them from other youth cultures. Traveling to Greek islands and practicing (free) camping or renting very cheap rooms was a pattern, which extended to nonpoliticized peer groups as well. Again, the lack of relevant research leaves a significant lacuna, regarding a more concrete description of the tourist pursuits of non-left-wing young people. Nevertheless, advertisements for sleeping bags and tents as well as catalogues for camping sites were quite common in the 1970s in a broad range of magazines and newspapers: the center-left *Ta Nea,* the centrist *To Vima,* but also the entertainment and listings guide *Athinorama* are just some examples. These outlets described camping as a "very cheap," "adventurous," or "youthful," but refrained from any mention of the term "progressive" tourism.[124]

Vacations were actually such an exceptional case of leisure that young left-wingers construed them to an extent as time apart, as an "escape," where no rigid schedule of their activities applied. In a sense, this attitude was similar to the way nonpoliticized students described their holidays in a number of articles in *Thourios* and popular women's magazines. Still, three elements differentiated the travel experience of young Communists and Socialists: the collective memory of continuity of left-wing youth struggle from the 1930s to the 1970s accompanied them in their holiday resorts as well through collective singing; even by the beach, they opted for partisan or songs by Theodorakis. In the tavernas, again the discussion revolved around the issues of "democratization" and "anti-imperialist struggle," such as the Vietnam War or the Pinochet dictatorship in Chile. As B.L., who at the point of the interview was affiliated with the NAR, narrates with a hint of nostalgia, these holidays were characterized by "wonderful peer groups, wonderful discussions, [and] common interests" (B.L., Interview). In addition, young left-wingers remained keen on recruiting new members, even by the beach. K.K. and E.A., male and female respectively, both students in the early to mid–1970s and members of RF in the first post-dictatorship years, stressed that a recurring theme in their discussions, even during the holidays, was to "persuade people to join RF" (K.K., Interview; E.A., Interview). In a sense, vacations for young left-wingers were an in-between domain, neither solely characterized by individualistic indulgence nor structured only around collective pursuits. It was neither an escape nor a repetition of their everyday life.[125]

"Healthy" Sex, "Unhealthy" Sex

While left-wing organizations in Greece actively engaged themselves in the demarcation of a "progressive culture" in the aftermath of the dictatorship, they did not solely deal with leisure. Sexuality also featured prominently in their reflection, quite often in interconnection with leisure. Young Communists and Socialists envisaged the "progressive cultural movement," however they construed it, as a bulwark against the spread of sexual "immorality" through elements of the "American way of life," as previously mentioned.

The mid–1970s also witnessed the emergence of an alternative approach toward feminine sexuality, which began to influence a small segment of the Communist youth in this period and which certainly deviated from the "morality"/"corruption" model. This was second-wave feminism. In contrast with a number of left-wing women's organizations that were established in the aftermath of the dictatorship and focused on the position of women in production, a few socialist and radical Feminist groups appeared as well, which propelled the issue of feminine sexuality into the limelight.[126] Young women with university degrees, some of who had studied in Western Europe and came into contact with the Feminist ideas flourishing there, created these groups. The most prominent second-wave Feminist groups involving young Greek women in the mid–1970s were the Movement for the Liberation of Women, which rallied many radical left-wingers, especially Trotskyites; the Women's Committee of RF in Paris, which was founded in 1975;[127] and the Women's Committee of RF (in Athens), formed in 1977. Soon after its inception the Committee of RF in Paris ceased to be part of the apparatus of RF and became the Autonomous Women's Group. Its RF members, however, did not drop their youth organization affiliation. What these women developed was *dipli strateysi* (dual militancy). On the contrary, although operating autonomously, the Women's Committee in Athens remained attached to RF.

An important source of inspiration for these Committees and the Movement for the Liberation of Women was readings of the works of Juliet Mitchell and Sheila Rowbotham. The latter, in her book *Woman's Consciousness, Man's World*, combined a critique of the capitalist mode of production with the suggestion that women should explore their sexuality. Juliet Mitchell, in her book *Woman's Estate*, claimed that there are four pillars of female exploitation: production, reproduction, socialization of children, and sexuality. Unless all of them are radically changed, women's status will not improve. Mitchell and Rowbotham were, however, distanced from those advocates of feminism who attributed the exploitation of women solely to male repression.[128]

The main feature of all these groups was that they openly questioned the necessary link between feminine sexuality and motherhood.[129] As already shown, premarital sexual relationships were becoming increasingly common for women. However, unless women's sexuality was associated with motherhood, it continued to be a taboo topic in public discussions, including those involving left-wing youth organizations. The second-wave Feminist groups did not reject motherhood, but what they maintained was that women should decide whether and when coitus should lead to procreation. They stressed two issues in this period in Greece: the legalization of abortions and the popularization of the contraceptive pill. The Movement for the Liberation of Women published one of the first texts, in booklet form, on the means of contraception.[130] Moreover, leaflets published by the PCI and the UDI (Unione Donne Italiane)[131] regarding abortions and contraception were sent to members of the Women's Committee of RF by female comrades of theirs who studied in Italy from late 1976 or early 1977; some of them were translated into Greek and circulated in Athens (V.K., Interview). Actually, the contraceptive pill elicited differing reactions by second-wave Feminists across Western Europe. Feminists in West Germany, where the Pill had spread at a spectacular pace since the 1960s, detested its use as a means employed by men, in order to pressurize women to have sex with them.[132]

In practice, abortions in Greece took place quite often at that point, though in conditions that put women's health at risk, as the people who performed them were often not specialists. Since contraception was often not used, as it was considered to be incompatible with "natural" coitus, abortions functioned as a means of dealing with an undesirable pregnancy. Loizos and Papataxiarchis claim that during the late 1960s and the 1970s, when premarital sexual relationships became "increasingly possible for both men and women," Greece witnessed an "abortion syndrome," with about 150,000 abortions per annum being performed in the late 1960s and more than 300,000 in the 1970s.[133]

The influence of those second-wave Feminist groups was limited in the mid–1970s in Greece. Minutes of the RF central council indicate that male cadres of the group, especially Christos Lazos and the then-general-secretary, Manos Sotiriadis, were quite receptive to the agenda that Feminist Eurocommunists set.[134] However, the Feminist Eurocommunists were sometimes met with jeers at local branches. This complicated relationship will be analyzed in depth later in this book, as second-wave feminism really gained momentum and affected the official language of RF in the late 1970s.

Meanwhile, the official language of the KNE, PPSP, and AASPE relied to a lesser or greater extent on a normative model that counterposed the "corrupting American way of life" to the "morality inherent in Greek popular tradition"; by contrast, the publications of the Socialist and the Eurocommunist youth, apart from scant references to the "morally corrupting" porn movies, did not elaborate extensively on the desirable, "progressive" sexuality. Particularly the KNE assigned much importance to the "proper" moral behavior of its members, but the prescriptive level of its official language should not be equated with the description of the actual practices of its members. The period from 1974 to 1977 compared to the early 1970s, did not witness a conservative backlash in the sexual norms of young left-wingers, including the young pro-Soviet ones.

Premarital sexual instability was no terra incognita for the KNE, PPSP, and AASPE cadres in the mid–1970s, despite the dictates of the normative language of those groups. In fact, the activity of the left-wing groups in general, facilitated courtship among unmarried men and women. As O.T., male, pupil and mid–ranking KNE cadre until 1978, student and, subsequently, participant in Choros, narrates: "The KNE allowed male and female pupils to socialize and flirt. My colleagues who were members of the KNE used to gather at my home" (O.T., Interview). O.T. was at the time of the interview a member of the Coalition of the Left, Movements and Ecology, a constituent of the Coalition of the Radical Left (SYRIZA). During most of the interview he illustrated in a negative way his membership of the KNE as entailing strict discipline and the imposition of the moralistic norms that the official language of the group prescribed. However, he also elaborated on moments of informal interaction and courtship, of which he appeared nostalgic.[135]

Such flirting often developed into ephemeral sexual relationships. According to H.Z., male, university student aligned with the KNE in the mid–1970s, a comrade and friend of his used to boast to his friends about his sexual encounters with different women. As H.Z. narrates, he thought that his sexual life was so successful and intense that he likened his bed to Wembley Stadium (H.Z., Interview). According to the narrator, he was never reprimanded by the KNE about his attitude. The fact that the pro-Soviet Communist youth group tolerated unstable sexual relationships is also corroborated in open letters published in *Thourios* by KNE members who withdrew in the late 1970s, where it is mentioned that "very rarely" did they constitute a reason for expulsion or other forms of penalty in the group.[136]

The official regulations of sexuality, however, were certainly of some importance for KNE, AASPE, and PPSP members and cadres, who lambasted group sexual intercourse or parallel sexual relationships. There was no particular functionary in charge of supervising the sexual lives of the members: the latter themselves took the initiative and reported such incidents to the plenary meetings or to various cadres, such as the secretary of their branch or the secretary of the bureau of student/pupil/local branches. The narration of T.L., male, then-high-ranking cadre of the KNE, and at the point of the interview member of the NAR, is illuminating. Although all interviewees who are nowadays members of the NAR tended to stress that there were "excesses" in the way sexuality was approached in the official language of the KNE, T.L. remembered: "I asked for the expulsion of a member who had parallel sexual relationships with four female comrades. Comrades of the branch he belonged to kept complaining about his affairs to me. ... I accept that we all have passions, I do accept that, but this man could not act properly as a KNE member" (T.L., Interview).

The condemnation of group sex and parallel sexual relations was pervasive in the pro-Soviet Communist youth group: The interviews that I have conducted have revealed that even a member of KNE, who described himself in the late 1970s as being in a liminal condition between homosexuality and heterosexuality and, as such, deviating from the prescribed behavior patterns, did not hesitate to expel a female member involved in parallel sexual relationships.[137] When he narrated about his sexual life, he used the first person singular, whereas he often employed the first person plural to stress the "discipline" that existed in KNE and which he claimed that he liked very much. This case of "shared possibilities" provides another example that shows that the self-policing of sexuality in KNE had achieved a degree of consensus among its members. Maoist youth organizations developed a similar approach: cadres or members who cheated on their partners were asked to criticize themselves publicly (N.P., Interview; P.K., Interview).[138] By contrast, such practices did not appear either in RF or in the Youth of PASOK.

While their sexual relationships did not always lead to marriage, young pro-Soviet Communists and Maoists regarded it as an "essential" aspect of their lives, as prescribed in the official texts of the groups they were affiliated with. Available sources contain no data as regards the exact marital status of all members of left-wing youth groups. However, the assumptions that were voiced in several oral testimonies I have gathered provide some indication. In the case of young Eurocommunists, those who got married in the period from 1974 to 1981 refer to themselves as the "exception": N.E. employed this term to describe her marriage to another high-ranking cadre of RF in 1978 (N.E., Interview). At that point, the aforementioned peer groups of upper and upper-middle class pupils of private schools, most of whom subsequently became students in France and the United Kingdom and some of them cadres in RF, served as role models for many of their comrades. Those young Eurocommunist cadres had adopted behavior patterns, which they termed "emancipated" in the sense that they were not in accordance with established sexual norms: in this vein, they postponed or even rejected marriage, in order to distinguish themselves from what they labeled as their "bourgeois" families. Their influence among RF members is manifest in many interviews of former members of RF. One reason that arose in these testimonies was their positive representation of avant-garde intellectuals. T.S., male, student, and member of the group until 1978, said that "modern people, socially liberal, who had studied in the Leontios and other private schools, set the tone in RF" (T.S., Interview). Another category of role models within RF comprised those members or cadres who had been imprisoned by the dictatorship.[139] However, neither in their testimonies at the point of the interview nor in their self-presentation in RF publications in the 1970s did they link this suffering with restraint in sexual behavior, like the cadres of the KNE. On the contrary, their permissiveness set the tone in RF, mainly through discussions in peer groups comprising RF members. Ephemeral relationships soon ended up being regarded by members and opponents of the group as the typical standard of behavior of RF members regardless of class and rank. As N.T. narrated, "this was a core aspect of our *rigitiki*[140] identity, we took pride on it: we differed from the rest of the youth" (N.T., Interview). RF members who did not develop such a lifestyle felt that they were somewhat aberrant. O.Y., male, student, and member of RF until 1978, from the lower-middle and working-class district of Neos Kosmos in Athens, remembered: "[I]n RF there was permissiveness, sexual freedom. Changing partners was a common phenomenon. However, my experiences were quite different. I was involved in stable sexual relationships" (O.Y., Interview).

By contrast, marriage is regarded as a "normal outcome" of premarital sexual relationships in the narratives of those affiliated with the KNE, the Youth of PASOK, the AASPE and the PPSP. Some of them appear to have married as soon as they graduated from university. G.K., a male mid–ranking KNE cadre in Salonica, got married in the early 1980s to A.A., a female KNE cadre of working-class origins, soon after both graduated from university (A.A., G.K., Interview). In deciding on marriage, young left-wingers were not influenced solely by their political organization and activity, but also from other social actors, such as their families. The perception that marriage was the "respectful" pattern of sexual relationships was widely held in working-class and lower-middle class areas, let alone the rural ones, during the 1970s. In the case of the pro-USSR group, H.Z., male, coming from a working-class family, mid–ranking KNE cadre and student in the mid–1970s, and KKE cadre since the late 1970s, narrated that "my family had taught me to respect marriage. It is an issue of respect toward your partner" (H.Z., Interview). People aligned with or leaning toward the Youth of PASOK, who came from working- or lower-middle-class urban districts or from rural areas, also mentioned the importance that their families and relatives assigned to them getting married (D.P., Interview).[141] Parents—regardless of their political orientation—appear to have urged young left-wingers to get married, especially in cases of premarital pregnancy. In his testimony, D.K., a male and AASPE cadre in the mid–to-late 1970s, narrated: "[W]hen I was 20 years old, I established a relationship with a young woman; she had been active in the anti-dictatorship student movement; we were careless, she performed many abortions, the doctor reprimanded her. When I was 23 and she 23 and a half, we decided to have a child.... We got married due to the children; especially her father, a nice guy but conservative, would not accept our relationship otherwise" (D.K., Interview). Still, the marriage of young left-wingers sometimes helped weaken their ties with their parents. In stark contrast with what Hirschon describes in Kokkinia in the early 1970s, married couples did not necessarily live together with or very close to their parents. As B.L. narrates: "I got married young, in order to leave my house and live away from my parents" (B.L., Interview).

Nevertheless, the pro-Soviet Communist and the Maoist youth organizations also influenced their members' decision on getting married or not, albeit in a subtle way. While stating marriage as the optimum framework of sexual relationships, the KKE apparatus did not impose it. The members themselves employed it as a symbol that would signify strong bonds among male and female comrades, drawing upon descriptions of "love" that were found in various publications of their group: especially articles in *Odigitis, Rizospastis,* and *KOMEP* and translated relevant analyses of Soviet intellectuals, where a quote by Lenin, favoring "marriage of proletarians due to love" was often mentioned. A.A. and G.K. stressed in their interview that their marriage was an outcome of "love" that developed due to "strong bonds, common struggle, common interests," and was construed as yet another aspect of a "principled" life for them (A.A., G.K., Interview). The only form of intervention that occurred was in the form of discussion within peer groups of pro-USSR young Communists. U.L., male, aligned with KNE from the early 1970s, KKE cadre throughout from 1974 to 1981 and nowadays affiliated with NAR, was quite emotional during the interview about the issue and shed some tears, while narrating that: "This may sound dogmatic, but is based on sensitivity. I remember that we cared for each other, among comrades that we shared a common past since the dictatorship years. When somebody was involved in a long-lasting relationship, we would encourage him to get married, as a group of friends, not through the Party apparatus" (U.L., Interview).[142]

The affective investment of membership in KNE is evident once again: his critique against "dogmatic" modes of thought and practice may reflect to an extent ambiguities that he had experienced already in that period and which may have been underlined by his shift to the NAR in 1989. However, moments of militancy that stirred strong emotions to him during the 1970s continue to feature prominently in his narrative, constituting "parts of collective memory that remain unchanged." Moreover, both his narration and his reaction indicate that male members of the KNE experienced strong emotions due to their militancy and were licensed to do so. This is yet another example that calls into question the claim made by anthropologist

Catherine Lutz that emotion is assigned to femininity in the "West," which I view as somewhat essentializing.[143]

Similarly, the cadres of the PPSP and the AASPE, or the Parties that these groups were affiliated with, did not coerce their members to get married.[144] Resting upon a normative conceptualization of what "popular" was, members of these organizations joyfully did so, since they regarded marriage as a core component in their protracted effort to resemble an idealized, normative version of the "Greek people." "We tried to be serious, like the *laikoi* [people from the lower strata]," A.D., female, in the periphery of the PPSP in the mid–1970s, remembers (A.D., Interview). Similarly, D.K., male cadre of AASPE in the mid–to-late 1970s, narrated: "What occurred in the case of the AASPE was a mania, our effort to gain access to the lower social strata and to appear to be mature, that's why many of us got married ... It makes a difference to go to [the lower-middle and working-class district of] Egaleo and distribute our newspaper to the shops, as I did, carrying your babies with you, rather as a bachelor student" (D.K., Interview). Such perceptions are very similar to the attitude developed by Maoists in West Germany in the same period. Lambasting the open relationships and the promiscuity that advocates of the so-called "New Left" demonstrated, West German Maoists developed more restricted sexual norms and "sought their happiness in marriage."[145]

In the case of the KNE, another factor that may have rendered its members more prone to marriage was the issue of their relationships with elderly members of the KKE. There was a category of KKE members, whom many former pro-USSR Communists that I interviewed described as *geroi* (old men), namely elderly members of the Party who were not their parents, but who informally supervised their activities.[146] KNE members deeply respected these men—it was again a case of valorization of suffering. G.K., male mid–ranking KNE cadre in the mid–1970s, narrates: "This man was all day with me, from noon until night, for many years, I admired him; he was my God, because despite the tortures, he never repented. He was perfect. He would always advise me to marry Athina, because he thought we were both honest people" (G.K., A.M., Interview).

The gaze of the *geroi* was a factor that rarely, if ever, existed in the case of RF. On the contrary, many high-ranking cadres of KKE Es. were less patronizing in this respect. An indicative case was Kostas Filinis, who was a member of the political bureau of the central council of KKE Es. in charge of guiding the members of RF in the aftermath of the dictatorship. Filinis himself did not marry until he was in his sixties and, as N.E. narrates, "never intervened in our personal lives" (N.E., Interview).

What was the impact of the intensifying youth politicization in the mid–1970s on gender relations, though? Gender hierarchies, which had existed among young left-wingers in the last years of the dictatorship, continued throughout the mid–1970s. Masculinity was tested in the cut-and-thrust of public debate, aimed either at recruiting sympathizers or at ensuring the faith of the current members in the ideological line of their group. An excellent grasp of Marxism-Leninism, as advocated by each of the groups in question, was highly esteemed and was associated both by young male and female left-wingers with heterosexual male cadres, who possessed most of the higher-ranking positions in Communist and Socialist youth organizations at that point.[147] This trend was already present in the early 1970s. As a male young left-winger narrated to Kornetis: "To put it bluntly, in the post-'68 climate you could not date a woman if you hadn't read Althusser."[148] In the aftermath of the dictatorship, the theoretical inspirations may have varied, but this condition certainly perpetuated. Competence in debates in tavernas, amphitheatres, or in informal discussions, the *pigadakia,* not only helped determine which group many unaffiliated young left-wingers would join, but rendered these male cadres sexually attractive to female sympathizers and members. The male cadres were involved in unstable sexual relationships, which conferred prestige on them: O.M. and N.T., male university students in the mid–1970s and RF cadres, were both keen to mention the names of several male cadres of the group in their narrative, which they depicted as "very handsome" and very "successful with women." N.T. also prided himself on being O.M.'s "teacher" in the field of sexual relationships (N.T., Interview). By contrast, even the indication that a female member of a left-wing youth organization developed unstable relations could impair her progress upward to the higher ranks. R.L., one of the few female RF cadres in the 1970s, remembered that she assigned much weight to her attire throughout the period from 1974 to 1981, so that it would earn her the reputation of "seriousness" as opposed to the "frivolity" associated with an erotically charged appearance for women (R.L., Interview). In this vein, she tried to emulate the clothing style of her male comrades. This condition was not imposed by any set of guidelines. In the case of R.L., her attitude stemmed from her intention to resemble young male Eurocommunists, whom she regarded as more competent than women in politics. She narrates: "I remember that all female RF cadres during those years wanted to be like men, to be as tough, as competent, as effective speakers as men were. I wore blue jeans and never a mini-skirt or anything that would be too feminine, too sexually provocative" (R.L., Interview).[149] It is telling that N.T., male cadre and member of the central council of RF in the mid–1970s, recalls her as "a Communist, not a proper Feminist: she did not want to be singled out as a woman," implying that the aspect of comradeship was more important for her than gender (N.T., Interview).

In the case of the KNE, another element was assigned, especially—but not only—to heterosexual male cadres whose origins were in the working class: that of the "protector," especially of female members, in the event of violent confrontations.[150] N.K. recalls: "I had beaten up leftists[151] during a march; I was supposed to prove my working-class identity" (G.R., N.K., O.Y. and D.M., Interview). The association of working-class identity, as construed by KNE, with physical strength, was actually evident in the way that the publications of the organization presented the body of the worker: images of a muscular person, apparently a man, holding *Rizospastis* or *Odigitis,* are a notable example.[152] Nevertheless, the KNE expected its male members and cadres to behave as caring mates to their girlfriends, let alone their wives; discussion was supposed at least to serve as a core component of "love" and the "principled" life of the couple (A.A., G.K., Interview).

The enactment of the role of male "protectors" established hierarchies in relation to homosexual masculinity, lending support to the claim by sociologist R.W. Connell that the model of "hegemonic masculinity" is formulated in tandem with desirable or "emphasized femininities," but also as opposed to "subordinated masculinities."[153] H.Z., male, from a working-class family, mid–ranking KNE cadre and student in the mid–1970s, and high-ranking KKE cadre since the late 1970s, narrated: "When confronting RF members, we often said they were feminized men [*louloudes*]. We created stereotypes" (H.Z., Interview).[154] H.Z. probably mentioned this openly to me, because he is a close friend of my parents, a condition that vindicates the argument put forth by historian Valerie Yow, namely that historians should develop a "reflexive alert," taking seriously into consideration the ways they are influenced by the interviews and, in turn, how aspects of their identity affect the interviewees.[155]

In any case, the abovementioned confrontation was signified in a metaphorical sense as an act of sexual intercourse. The male opponents of the KNE were described as effeminate, namely "passive," an idea that reproduced the deeply entrenched belief in Greek society that signifies as "active" and "masculine" the person who "penetrates" in the act of coitus. This approach to subordinated masculinities should not, however, be linked only with the connotations of "working class" as a metaphor in the language of the KNE. It was also a staple of the representations of "manliness" that circulated in lower-middle and working-class districts of Athens and Salonica, in venues such as barber's shops and old-style cafés, and influenced members of KNE as well as other left-wing groups living there. O.Y., male, RF member until 1978, from the lower-middle and working-class Athenian district of Neos Kosmos, narrated: "[W]e gathered at a barber's shop, we discussed politics there with members of other groups, such as KNE and PASOK. The barber belonged to the KKE. Once, a member of RF asked him 'do you know that Giannis Ritsos is a fag?' The barber replied, 'I am afraid this is true.' ... To be honest," O.Y. now claims, "when I learnt that Ritsos was a homosexual, I was surprised in a negative way" (O.Y., Interview). Such representations, however, did not appear in the official texts of left-wing groups in the mid–1970s. During those years, homosexuality was almost never openly addressed by any Socialist or Communist youth organization in Greece, with the exception of a few articles in KNE publications, in which homosexuality was referred to solely as a theme of the "morally corruptive" pornography.[156] When "sexuality" was mentioned in left-wing publications during those years, it connoted heterosexual lifestyle norms, regarded implicitly as the sole "normal" ones.

In general, the sexual norms of the left-wing youth in the mid–1970s were not purely gender-specific. As already noted, heterosexual men, especially the cadres, had to conform to particular regulations (and prohibitions) in their sexual practice and expression. Nevertheless, heterosexual women and homosexuals suffered from substantially more limitations on their sexual life. What Rubin argues, that it is "essential to separate gender and sexuality analytically to reflect more accurately their separate social existence," is not really apt to illuminate the sexual norms and practices of the left-wing youth in Greece at that point. Both in their rhetoric and in their actual experience, sexuality and gender were entangled and mutually constitutive.[157]

Notes

1. "Odigos gia tin aytomorfosi," *Odigitis,* 24 October 1975, pp. 19–20; "Oi klasikoi tou Marxismou-Leninismou," *Thourios,* 14 March 1975, p. 23.
2. *KOMEP* first appeared in January 1921. It was published in the following periods: 1921–1925, 1929, 1931, 1932–1936, 1942–1947, 1974 until today.
3. For example, Alvaro Cunhal, "I anamorfotiki dynami tis kommounistikis ilikis," *KOMEP*, December 1974.
4. "1917: 60 years of socialist reconstruction," part 26, *Odigitis,* 27 October 1977, p. 18.
5. N. Poulantzas, *State, Power, Socialism,* Verso Classics edition (London, 2000), p. 73.
6. Ibid.
7. Charles Bettelheim, *Les luttes de classes en URSS—Première période, 1917–1923* (Paris, 1974). It was translated into Greek in 1975.
8. See, for instance: "Apofasi tou 14ou synedriou tou Italikou Kommounistikou Kommatos," *KOMTHEPOL,* June–July 1975, pp. 136–46; "Koini dilosi tou Italikou kai tou Ispanikou Kommounistikou Kommatos," *KOMTHEPOL,* August–September 1975, pp. 101–2.
9. Christos Mais, "The Marxist-Leninist Publishing Field During the 60s–70s in Greece" (MA diss., Leiden University, 2009), pp. 15–17.
10. See, for instance: Y. Wenyuan, "Gia tin koinoniki vasi tis antikommatikis klikas tou Lin Piao," *Laikoi Agones,* 4 July 1975, p. 3.

11. In the case of *Agonistis*, see, for instance: Paul Sweezy, "Chili: Ta dyo chronia tis kyvernisis laikis enotitas," *Agonistis*, 1–15 December 1974, p. 5.

12. For a brief account of the history of *Miniaia Epitheorisi*, see: Lefteris Rizas and Vangelis Chorafas, "1975: 30 chronia Miniaia Epitheorisi," *Miniaia Epitheorisi* 12, December 2005. The article is available online is the following link: http://www.monthly-review.gr/antilogos/greek/periodiko/arxeio/article_fullstory_html?obj_path=docrep/docs/arthra/MR12_30years/gr/html/index (last accessed: 13 November 2013).

13. To mention only some of them: semiotics (its prominent exponent, Roland Barthes, was elected in 1977 to the chair of Semiologie Litteraire at the Collège de France); psychoanalysis (Jacques Lacan gave public seminars to the Faculté de Droit from 1969 to 1980); and structualist Marxism (for example, the very influential in the intellectual debates in Greece, Nikos Poulantzas, taught at the radical University of Vincennes/Paris VIII and at the Ecole Pratique des Hautes Études).

14. ASKI, Archive of EKON Rigas Feraios, First Congress of RF, box 1. Speech of Kostas Kasidoulis, young worker, Larissa.

15. The same story of dismissal of such intellectual endeavors within KNE was repeated in an open letter of members of the organization who withdrew in 1978. See: "Idiaitera tis knitogenous Aristeras," *Agonas gia tin Kommounistiki Ananeosi*, May 1979, pp. 29–34.

16. See, for example, "Gnoriste ton Marx," *Odigitis*, 16 April 1975, p. 10. For the critique in Thourios, see: "O Marx sti Ntisneylant," *Thourios*, 14 August 1975.

17. "I ergatiki neolaia rachokokkalia tou neolaiistikou kinimatos," *Odigitis*, 25 February 1977, p. 14. I have found no such suggestions in RF publications. For the recruitment of young workers by RF, see, for instance, the article "Strofi stin ergazomeni neolaia," *Thourios*, 3 June 1976, pp. 4–5; ASKI, Archive of EKON Rigas Feraios, Central Council of RF, 1974–1975, box 9, envelope 1: Resolution concerning the orientation of the organization to the working-class youth.

18. "Efyge o Kostas Varnalis, o poiitis tou laou," *Agonistis*, 1–15 January 1975, p. 11.

19. "To ergo tou Varnali," *Mathitiki Poreia*, 23 January 1976, p. 9.

20. "Afieroma ston Kosta Varnali," *Spoudastikos Kosmos*, January 1975, pp. 24–25.

21. "Dyo chronia ap' to thanato tou K. Varnali," *Odigitis*, 17 December 1976, p. 13.

22. I. Georgakopoulos, "Fotis Aggoules. Enas laikos poiitis," *Agonistis*, 1–5 January 1976, p. 29.

23. "F. Aggoules: o poiitis tou agona," *Odigitis*, 25 June 1975, p. 12.

24. In the Third Festival of KNE-Odigitis, Giannis Ritsos presented a new poem that was dedicated to the pro-USSR youth organization and was titled "Ta paidia tis KNE" (it could be translated as "the members of the KNE"). See: *Odigitis*, 23 September 1977, p. 3.

25. See, for instance, the cover page of *Odigitis* on 13 May 1977, which stated: "Your honor is also our honor, poet."

26. See: Kostas Sarris, "Politistikes Drastiriotites ton foititon tis FLS kai IXGF, 1974–1999," in *Filosofiki Scholi Panepistimiou Thessalonikis. Ta prota 75 chronia* (Salonica, 2000), pp. 220–29. "Poetry nights" had been organized by left-wing students already in the 1960s and the early 1970s. See: Saint-Marten, *Lamprakides*, p. 100. In the aftermath of the dictatorship, such events were held by cultural societies,

in which not only pro-USSR young Communists, but also members of RF participated. See, for instance: "Politistiko Grafeio Polytechneiou: Mia ekdilosi gia ton Varnali," *Dimokratikos Agonas,* 8 February 1976, p. 2.

27. "Enas parallilismos dyo vivlion," *Odigitis,* 25 February 1977, p. 16.
28. "Odigos gia tin aytomorfosi," *Odigitis,* 24 October 1975, p. 19.
29. "Enas parallilismos dyo vivlion," *Odigitis,* 25 February 1977, p. 16.
30. Karali, *Mia imitelis,* p. 249.
31. "I poiitiki genia tis 'ittas,'" *Mathitiki Poreia,* 17 March 1976, p. 2
32. "Na stamatisei I mithologiki anaviosi katastaseon," *Thourios,* 3 February 1977, p. 14.
33. Platon Mavromoustakos, *To theatro stin Ellada 1940–2000: Mia episkopisi* (Athens, 2005), pp. 145–49.
34. Ibid., pp. 140–41; Series of articles entitled "Erevna: Me tis nees theatrikes omades," which appeared in *Avgi* on: 16 February 1975, 19 February 1975, 20 February 1975, 21 February 1975, 22 February 1975, 26 February 1975, 27 February 1975, 28 February 1975, always on page 2.
35. According the treaty of London (May 1832), Britain, Russia, France, and Bavaria placed Greece under the "guarantee" of the "Protecting" Powers (Britain, France, Russia); moreover, Greece would be governed by a Bavarian monarch. Since the prospective king, Otto, was underage, Greece was ruled from 1833 until 1835 by a regency council consisting of three Bavarians: von Armansperg, von Maurer, von Heideck. From 1835 to 1844, Otto ruled as an absolute monarch; from 1844 to 1862, he governed as a constitutional monarch. Following a coup in 1862, he fled to native Bavaria. The next monarch, George I, came from Denmark, terminating the period of Bavarian rule. For more, see: Clogg, *A Concise History,* pp. 46–55.
36. Gonda van Steen, "Joining our Grand Circus," *Journal of Modern Greek Studies* 25, no. 2 (2007): p. 315.
37. I put the term "Byzantine" in quotation marks, because this was not the term used by any social group in that Empire; its official name was the "Eastern Roman" Empire. The term "Byzantine" was actually invented after its collapse.
38. Kornetis, *Children of the Dictatorship,* pp. 187–88.
39. Part of this narration has been recorded and is accessible here: http://www.youtube.com/watch?v=XDR5sO6XJm0 (last access: 08 May 2013).
40. The Art Theatre had been established in 1942 and aimed at introducing contemporary foreign and Greek theatre trends to the public of Athens.
41. Mavromoustakos, *To theatro stin Ellada,* p. 142.
42. The National Theatre had been founded in 1930 by the Minister of Education, Georgios Papandreou and has been one of the most well-established theatre companies in Greece; it operated as a public entity from its inception until 1994, when it was transformed into a nonprofit organization.
43. See the online archive of the National Theatre and, especially, the following link: http://www.nt-archive.gr/playMaterial.aspx?playID=352 (last access: 8 August 2012).
44. "'Oi Prostates' tou M. Efthymiadi," *Panspoudastiki,* 28 November 1975, p. 10.
45. "'Anakrisi' tou P. Weiss kai nees prooptikes," *Avgi,* 30 May 1976, p. 10.
46. See, for example, the document of the agreement of the pupils of the Eighth Male High School of Salonica with the "Theatre of Salonica." The pupils, influenced by

the KNE, agreed to attend a performance of *Little Mahagonny*. I have found this document in the personal collection of Nikos Samanidis, high school pupil, affiliated with the pro-Soviet Communist youth organization in the mid–1970s.

47. The term has been translated in English as "alienation effect," "distancing effect," or "estrangement effect." To avoid confusion, I use the German original term, as employed by Brecht.

48. Nikos Lagadinos, "To Eleythero Theatro kai o Tychodioktis tou Mih. Hourmouzi," *Agonistis*, 1–15 January 1975; Roland Barthes, "Ta kathikonta tis brechtikis kritikis," *Thourios*, 3 April 1975, p. 11; "Ti einai apostasiopoiisi," *Panspoudastiki*, 11 January 1975, p. 2.

49. "To theatriko tmima tou Panepistimiou," *Odigitis*, 21 May, p. 12.

50. Patrice Pavis, *Dictionary of the Theatre: Terms, Concepts, and Analysis* (Toronto, 1998), pp. 62–63.

51. Nikos Lagadinos, "To Eleythero Theatro kai o Tychodioktis tou Mih. Hourmouzi," *Agonistis*, 1–15 January 1975; "Erevna: Me tis nees theatrikes omades," *Avgi*, 20 February 1975, p. 2.

52. Kornetis, *Children of the Dictatorship*, pp. 186–87; Mavromoustakos, *To theatro*, pp. 150–51.

53. "Vathia krisi sto 'Eleythero Theatro,'" *Avgi*, 23 January 1979.

54. Giorgos Kotanidis, *Oloi Mazi, Tora!* (Athens, 2011), p. 511.

55. Horn, *The Spirit*, p. 212.

56. "Theatriko Tmima Panepistimiou Athinas: I diadikasia anevasmatos ergon," *Thourios*, 3 June 1976, p. 14.

57. Ron Eyerman and Andrew Jamison, *Music and Social Movements: Mobilizing Traditions in the Twentieth Century* (Cambridge, 1998), p. 169.

58. Kornetis, "Student resistance," pp. 250–58.

59. For a list of tavernas in Salonica, which were patronized by left-wing students, see Aravantinos, "To Metapoliteytiko," p. 470.

60. "As milisoume gia ntiskotek," *Fantasio*, 8 July 1975, p. 78. The article mentions that there were eight discotheques in Plaka, such as "Karyatides," "Mekka," and "Apollon," as well as many more in the districts beyond the center of Athens.

61. The fact that they liked Kazantzidis's music also appears in written sources. See, for example: Ersi Hadjiargirou, "Me aformi to Polytechneio," *Agonas gia tin Kommounistiki Ananeosi*, November 1978, pp. 34–37. The extensive reflection by the participants in Choros, as shall be analyzed below, about their leisure activities in the mid–1970s provides many details about the "taverna ritual," which confirm data gathered in the interviews I have conducted.

62. Riki van Boeschoten, *From Armatolik to People's Rule: Investigation into the Collective Memory of Rural Greece, 1750–1949* (Amsterdam, 1991). Van Boeschoten mentions that different regions had different versions of the same partisan song.

63. "Apano sta psila vouna antartes Eponites" means: "partisan members of EPON struggling in the high mountains."

64. This phrase means: "Below my shirt, I am experiencing a heart attack."

65. Kazantzidis' songs were also very popular among Greek migrants in West Germany, regardless of their age and ideological orientation. See: Nikolaos Papadogiannis, "A (Trans)National Emotional Community? Greek Political Songs and the Politicisa-

tion of Greek migrants in West Germany in the 1960s and 1970s," *Contemporary European History* 23, no. 4 (2014): pp. 589–614.

66. In 1975 the album *Yparcho* (I Exist) was released. Stelios Kazantzidis sang all its songs and the album became immensely successful.

67. Panagiotis Michalopoulos sang some *rebetiko* songs, such as "Kapetanakis," which alluded to drug consumption.

68. The song is named after Michalis Bezentakos. The latter was a KKE cadre, who was charged with the murder of a policeman, but managed to escape from prison in 1932.

69. Its title does not have a particular meaning; it actually constitutes an expression of mockery. In post-1974 Greece, the partisan version has been sung by Panos Tzavelas and by Loukianos Kilaidonis.

70. Papanikolaou, "Schimatizontas ti neolaia."

71. Miller, "Consumption and Its Consequences," pp. 13–50.

72. Kornetis, *Children of the Dictatorship*, p. 200.

73. "To antartiko anikei s'olo to lao … ," *Agonistis*, October 1975.

74. The names of boîtes in Athens, where partisan songs were played, can be found in *Athinorama*. See, for example, "Boîtes," *Athinorama*, 28 October 1977, pp. 66–67.

75. Dimitris Danikas, "Stathmos ston elliniko kinimatografo oi 'Kynigoi,'" *Rizospastis*, 12 October 1977, p. 4.

76. Antonis Moschovakis, 'Happy Day, mia megali tainia', *Avgi*, 1 October 1976, p. 4.

77. Nikos Lagadinos, "O Neos Ellinikos Kinimatografos," *Agonistis*, 1–15 January, 1975.

78. "Syntomi anaskopisi tou ellinikou kinimatografou," *Salpisma*, issue 9, autumn 1977, p. 11.

79. "O Thiassos," *Odigitis*, 14 May 1975, p. 12; "Oi Kynigoi," *Odigitis*, 21 October 1977, p. 12. About left-wing cinema reviews during those years, you may also see: Papadogiannis, "Between Angelopoulos," p. 293.

80. For instance, see: "Mnimi Luchino Visconti," *ANTI*, p. 40. The article announces the screening of movies by Visconti in the framework of the "Visconti Week," organized by the Greek Film Archive Foundation and the Istituto Italiano di Cultura in Atene (The Italian Cultural Institute in Athens). See also the column "Eidiseis kai scholia" that appeared in every volume of the magazine *Synchronos Kinimatografos*. For similar retrospectives in Salonica, see the magazine *Kinimatografos*, published by an association named "Cinema Club of Salonica."

81. *Alphaville* and *Pierrot le Fou* were screened in the cinema Lila in Athens and were suggested in *Odigitis*. *Les Carabiniers* was screened by the Leschi (club) of the PSK, the pro-USSR Communist student group. Prior to their screening, a film reviewer, Vassilis Rafailidis, commented on it. See, for example: "Technes-Grammata-Zoi," *Odigitis*, 27 August 1975, p. 12.

82. "Tsarli Tsaplin," *Odigitis*, 5 January 1978, p. 13.

83. "Hitchcock choris telos," *Odigitis*, 16 May 1980, p. 18.

84. "Me aformi tin tainia tou V. Pudovkin 'I ptosi tis Agias Petroupolis,'" *Odigitis*, 2 October 1974, p. 2.

85. *Mathitika Neiata*, 18 May 1977, p. 7.

86. "I vdomada alvanikou kinimatografou," *Salpisma*, issue 7, spring 1977.

87. "'To Prim' I poso 'skouriase' t' atsali," *Salpisma*, 23 February 1977, p. 7, 12.

88. Andreas Kühn, *Stalins Enkel, Maos Söhne: Die Lebenswelt der K-Gruppen in der Bundesrepublik der 1970er Jahre (Frankfurt, 2005)*, p. 209.

89. Janet Staiger, "Writing the History of American Film Reception," in *Hollywood Spectatorship: Changing Perceptions of Cinema Audiences*, ed. Melvyn Stokes and Richard Maltby (London, 2001), pp. 19–32.

90. Journalist, renowned for sensational talk shows, where scandals are purportedly revealed.

91. "Oi 15 emporikoteres tainies…," *Ta Theamata*, 10 December 1976, p. 55.

92. For a comprehensive collection of Christos Vakalopoulos's articles, see: Kostas Livieratos, ed., *I oneiriki yfi tis pragmatikotitas* (Athens, 2005).

93. E.Q., male, was an opponent of the central council of RF, while N.T. a supporter.

94. See, for instance: "Afieroma ston Pier Paolo Pasolini," *Synchronos Kinimatografos*, November 1975–February 1976.

95. Christos Vakalopoulos, "To minima pou paei pantou," *Synchronos Kinimatografos*, September–November 1976, p. 16.

96. "O Synchronos Kinimatografos syzitaei gia to parelthon tou, tous *Kynigous*, ton Angelopoulo, nees peripeteies kai katastrofes," *Synchronos Kinimatografos* 17–18 (1978): p. 68.

97. Intervention of Christos Vakalopoulos in a discussion with Manolis Koukios, Maria Nikolopoulou, and Nikos Savvatis about Theodoros Angelopoulos, published in *Synchronos Kinimatografos*, January–May 1976 and republished in: Livieratos, *I oneiriki*, pp. 231–32.

98. About *Synchronos Kinimatografos*, see also: Papadogiannis, "Between Angelopoulos," p. 297.

99. Nikolakakis, "Tourismos kai elliniki koinonia," especially pp. 170–504.

100. N. Kampanis, "O tourismos mas therapeyei apo ta … complex," *Ta Nea*, 7 September 1976, p. 7.

101. "Technes-Grammata-Politismos," *Odigitis*, 10 September 1975, p. 12: see the statement of the singer Giorgos Dalaras. G. Douatzis, "Plaka: Na tin leme … Soho?," *Ta Nea*, 3 June 1980, p. 5. The conservative *Akropolis* decried the existence of many signposts in Plaka that were in English: "Eikona Sohou dinoun stin Plaka oi xenoglosses epigrafes," *Akropolis*, 11 July 1979.

102. "Kalokairi kai … antisylliptika," *Fantasio*, 8 July 1975, p. 18.

103. "Oraies oi diakopes, alla …," *Fantasio*, 1 July 1975, p. 14–15.

104. The literal meaning of the word in English is harpoon.

105. Sofka Zinovieff, "Hunters and Hunted: *Kamaki* and the Ambiguities of Sexual Predation in a Greek Town," in Loizos and Papataxiarchis, *Contested Identities*, pp. 203–20. Nikolakakis vindicates her argument, demonstrating that, already from the first post World War II decades, tourist resorts served for heterosexual men, both locals and visitors from other places in Greece, as loci of "sexual liberty," where they could make love with non-Greek tourists. See: Nikolakakis, "Tourismos kai elliniki koinonia," pp. 427–33, 435–38.

106. Nevertheless, Zinovieff also argues that the term has acquired a broader meaning in Greece and is equated with any kind of flirtation with Greek women, not necessarily in tourist areas, but in contexts, such as university parties as well, as shall be shown below in depth.

107. Zinovieff, "Hunters and Hunted," pp. 203–20.
108. *Ellinikos Organismos Tourismou,* namely Greek Tourist Organization. It is the state institution in charge of promoting tourism in Greece.
109. "Oi diakopes edo … ki ekei," *Odigitis,* 8 July 1977, pp. 10–11.
110. "Mia … yperochi aytapati apeleytherosis," *Odigitis,* 4 July 1980, pp. 6–7.
111. For instance: "Eisvoles gymniston sti Rodo," *Ta Nea,* 22 July 1977, p. 12.
112. "Oi diakopes edo … ki ekei," *Odigitis,* 1 July 1977.
113. For example, letter to K.A. from Cambridge (UK), 17 July 1973, personal collection of Giannis Papadogiannis. Papadogiannis was then a university student, studying Chemistry at the University of Salonica. The destination of the excursion he participated in as a final-year student was France, Italy, and the United Kingdom. In 1959 the Polytechnic School of Athens organized an excursion for its students to Egypt. Moreover, see "Kinisis Syllogon," Panspoudastiki, 2 December 1959, p. 4..
114. See, for example: "Ekdromi tis E Architektonon stin ESSD," *Panspoudastiki,* 11 May 1975, p. 8.
115. "Episkepsi sti S. Enosi," *Odigitis,* 21 May 1975, p. 16.
116. However, since relevant data is not accessible to historians, it is impossible from me to provide figures about the number of the members of the KNE who took part in these excursions.
117. For the case of RF in 1978, see "Oi Rigades organonoun ton eleythero chrono tous," *Avgi,* 28 July 1978.
118. Kornetis, "Student Resistance," p. 66.
119. "Synenteyxeis tou Thouriou me nees kai neous, se topous douleias, synoikies kai scholeia," *Thourios,* 25 June 1977, pp. 4–7; A. Angelopoulou, "Diakopes: ena zotiko provlima tis neolaias," *Pantheon,* 29 July–11 August 1975, pp. 56–57. The selection of the interviewees in both articles was not based on a particular methodology. Thus, what is narrated in the interviews quoted in *Pantheon* and *Thourios* does not necessarily reflect the travel cultures of students and workers in Greece during the 1970s. However, it yields valuable insights into differences among young people with regard to vacation opportunities and experience due to gender and social class.
120. Bureau of the Central Council of RF, "Kalokairines adeies stelechon." See: ASKI, Archive of EKON Rigas Feraios, central council of RF, box 12.
121. According to Portelli, "Oral history, then, offers a less a grid of standard experiences than a horizon of shared possibilities, real or imagined … each person entertains, in each moment, multiple possible destinies, perceives different possibilities, and makes different choices from others in the same situation." See: Alessandro Portelli, *The Battle of Valle Giulia: Oral History and the Art of Dialogue* (Madison, WI, 1997), p. 88.
122. A law bringing reforms in the structure of the universities as well as their examination system. The law was the target of massive protests at the end of the decade and is examined below in detail.
123. "Mikros Odigos," *Odigitis,* 9 July 1976, p. 14.
124. "Gia ena camping … demi saizon," *Ta Nea,* 7 June 1975, p. 17; C. Zografos, "Camping," *Athinorama,* 28 July–5 August 1978, p. 45.

125. Their holiday experience lends support to the argument put forward by historians Ellen Furlough and Shelley Baranowski that, rather than construing "vacation" and "tourism" as detached from everyday life, researchers should seek their interconnections. See: Shelley Baranowski and Ellen Furlough, introduction to *Being Elsewhere*, p. 19.

126. Women affiliated with or leaning toward left-wing parties created the KDG (Kinisi Dimokratikon Gynaikon, Movement of Democratic Women) in 1974. In 1976, two more women's groups were created: the OGE (Omospondia Gynaikon Elladas, Federation of Greek Women), affiliated to the Communist Party of Greece, and the EGE (Enosi Gynaikon Elladas, Union of Greek Women), affiliated to the Panhellenic Socialist Movement. For more details, see Margaret Poulos, *Arms and the Woman: Just Warriors and Greek Feminist Identity* (New York, 2007); Maria Repoussi, "To 'deytero fylo' stin Aristera. Ntokoumenta kai mnimes apo ti Feministiki paremvasi stin organosi tou Riga Feraiou, 1974–1978," *Elliniki Epitheorisi Politikis Epistimis* 8 (1996): pp. 121–53. For an in-depth analysis of the women's committees of RF throughout the period in question, see: For an in-depth analysis of the women's committees of RF throughout the period in question, see: Nikolaos Papadogiannis, "Red and Purple? Feminism and young Greek Eurocommunists in the 1970s," *European Review of History—Revue européenne d'histoire* 22, no. 1 (2015) : pp. 16–40.

127. The Committee was created following the relevant decision of the Central Council of the organization. This decision came after the establishment by the United Nations of the year 1975 as the International Women's Year. See: Repoussi, "To 'deytero fylo' stin Aristera," p. 128.

128. Sheila Rowbotham, *Woman's Consciousness: Man's World* (London, 1973); Juliet Mitchell, *Woman's Estate* (Harmondsworth, 1971).

129. For instance: Second text by Roxani Kaytantzoglou for discussion among the members of the Committee in Paris, p.1, Archive of Feminist Historians, Documents of the Women's Committee in Paris. Recommendation of the Women's Committee of RF to the Central Council of the organization, June 1977, pp. 13–16, Archive of Feminist Historians, Documents of the Women's Committee of RF, p. 6: "Gynaika, to miso tou ouranou," *Thourios*, 22 June 1978, p. 8.

130. In 1975, an article making an extensive reference to contraception was published in *Fantasio*. In this article, the contraceptive pill was portrayed as a very efficient and almost not at all dangerous method. See: "Kalokairi kai … antisylliptika," *Fantasio*, 8 July 1975, p. 18. For the booklet published by the Movement of the Liberation of Women, see Kinisi gia tin Apeleytherosi ton Gynaikon, *Antisylliptika mesa* (Athens, 1976). However, the autonomous Feminists, at least those that contributed to *Skoupa*, were very dismissive of *Fantasio*. They described it as a socially conservative magazine that actually upheld the institution of patriarchal family. See: Marilisa Mitsou-Pappa, "To ideologiko periechomeno tou 'gynaikeiou' typou: Mia proti proseggisi," *Skoupa*, January 1979, p. 70.

131. Left-wing women's organization, founded in the mid–1940s by members of the Communist and the Socialist Party. I have found in the collection of material used by members of the Women's Committee of RF two leaflets by the UDI: "Lo, la salute, la maternita, la sesualita, l'aborto' and 'Parliamo noi donne," written in March and May 1978, respectively.

132. Eva-Maria Silies, *Liebe, Lust und Last: Die Pille als weibliche Generationserfahrung in der Bundesrepublik 1960–1980* (Göttingen, 2010).
133. Loizos and Papataxiarchis, "Gender, Sexuality, and the Person in Greek Culture", p. 224; for the figure of abortions in Greece in the 1960s, see: V. Valaoras, A. Polychronopoulou, and D. Trichopoulos, "Abortion in Greece," in *Social Demography and Medical Responsibility: Proceedings of the Sixth Conference of the International Planned Parenthood Federation, Europe and Near East Region* (London, 1969), pp. 31–44. The figure for the 1970s is an estimate that appeared in the Feminist magazine *Dini*. See: Efi Avdela, Marina Papagiannaki, and Kostoula Sklaveniti, "Ektrosi 1976–1986. To chroniko mias diekdikisis," *Dini,* December 1986, pp. 8–28.
134. Recorded discussion between the Women's Committee of RF and the Central Council of the organization, June 1977, Archive of Feminist Historians, Documents of the Women´s Committee of RF.
135. Papadogiannis, "Confronting 'imperialism' and 'loneliness,'" p. 231.
136. "Politikes neolaies, apochoriseis," *Thourios,* 17 September 1981, p. 18.
137. He narrated that he was not attracted to women in that period, but he had not articulated a gay identity, either. As he mentioned, he was "searching."
138. N.P., female, and P.K., male, were both PPSP members in the late 1970s.
139. Several youngsters who were RF cadres in the post-authoritarian years had been tortured by the dictatorial regime. One occasion, when they narrated extensively their torture, was the trial of officers involved in the dictatorial regime. The trial took place in summer 1975. Such narratives may be found, for instance, in: Stavros Alatas, "Oi 6 'Rigades' pou vasanistikan stin ESA', *Avgi,* 10 August 1975, p. 5.
140. *Rigitiki* means that of RF.
141. Papadogiannis, "Confronting 'imperialism' and 'loneliness,'" p. 233.
142. Ibid., p. 234.
143. See Catherine Lutz, "Emotion, Thought, and Estrangement: Emotion as a Cultural Category," *Cultural Anthropology* 1, no. 3 (1986): pp. 287–89, 299–301. For works analyzing the relationship between masculinity and emotions in various "Western" contexts, see, for instance: Manuel Borutta and Nina Verheyen, eds., *Die Präsenz der Gefühle. Männlichkeit und Emotion in der Moderne* (Bielefeld, Ger., 2010); Evthymios Papataxiarchis, "O kosmos tou kafeneiou. Tavtotita kai antallagi ston andriko symposiasmo," in *Tavtotites kai Fylo sti Synchroni Ellada,* ed. Evthymios Papataxiarchis and Theodoros Paradellis (Athens, 1992), pp. 209–50.
144. It should be noted that none of the Greek left-wing organizations developed at that point a ritual similar to those of the "red" or "Communist" weddings, performed by the Italian Maoist organization UCI(m-l) (Union of Italian Communists [Marxist-Leninist]) in the early 1970s. In this ceremony, the officiant was a cadre of the group and the text of the rite of marriage linked family issues to the class struggle. See: Stefano Ferrante, *La Cina non era vicina* (Milan, 2008).
145. Kühn, *Stalins Enkel,* p. 83.
146. This was not a novel phenomenon. Elders had also constituted a mechanism of social control that existed in rural areas in Greece in the nineteenth and twentieth century, according to Gallant. See: Gallant, *Modern Greece,* p. 111.
147. For details about the representation of men and women in the Central Council of RF in the period 1974–1978, please see Nikolaos Papadogiannis, "The 'Women's

Question' and Young Greek Eurocommunists: Shifting Feminine Representations in 1974–78" (MA diss., Birkbeck, University of London, 2006). Moreover, throughout the period under study the most senior positions in all Communist and Socialist groups in question were occupied by men.

148. Kornetis, *Children of the Dictatorship*, p. 164.

149. Papadogiannis, "Confronting 'imperialism' and 'loneliness,'" p. 240.

150. In this context, masculinity appears to be inextricably linked with aggression. This representation is very similar to what Campbell describes in the case of *Sarakatsanoi* in the 1950s or to what Gallant argues in his research on knife fighting in nineteenth-century Greece. See: Thomas W. Gallant, "Honor, Masculinity, and Ritual Knife Fighting in Nineteenth-Century Greece," *The American Historical Review* 105, no. 2 (2000): pp. 359–82. However, whether this was the only version of masculinity in Greece until the second half of the twentieth century, as well as the similarities and differences in the making of masculinity in the rural and urban areas in Greece in the 1970s, certainly require further examination.

151. Presumably he means either Maoists or Trotskyites.

152. *Odigitis,* 11 September 1980, p. 13. This tendency apparently resonated with the male culture of pride that was pervasive among a segment of workers already in the 1960s, namely construction workers, who praised the robustness of the body. See: Dimitra Lambropoulou, *Oikodomoi. Oi anthropoi pou echtisan tin Athina: 1950-1967* (Athens, 2009), pp. 228–29.

153. Robert W. Connell and James W. Messerschmidt, "Hegemonic Masculinity: Rethinking the Concept," *Gender and Society* 19, no. 6 (2005): pp. 829–59.

154. Papadogiannis, "Confronting 'imperialism' and 'loneliness,'" p. 232.

155. Valerie Yow, "'Do I like them too much?' Effects of the Oral History Interview on the Interviewer and Vice-Versa," in *The Oral History Reader,* ed. Alistair Thomson and Rob Perks (New York, 2006), pp. 54–72.

156. "… Kai evroporno," *Odigitis,* 10 June 1977, p. 16.

157. Rubin, "Thinking Sex," p. 33; Kevin P. Murphy and Jennifer M. Spear, introduction to *Historicizing Gender and Sexuality,* ed. Kevin P. Murphy and Jennifer M. Spear (Oxford, 2011), pp. 1–11. However, Murphy and Spear argue that Rubin's call in "Thinking Sex" to avoid subsuming sexuality under the rubric of gender has triggered meticulous explorations of the potential interrelationship between the two fields.

Part III

The Late 1970s

Chapter 4

Breaches in the Wall

During the late 1970s, the cultural politics and the leisure pursuits of a segment of the Greek left-wing youth changed remarkably. No longer revolving around the effort to distil concrete "progressive" messages, young Eurocommunists and participants in a newly established loose network of autonomous left-wing groups construed art as a means of reflection on and even self-critique of their behavioral patterns. A statement published in *Thourios*—"it is essential to bear in mind that art should not be anticipated to produce volunteers to join the Red Army"—exemplified this trend.[1] They also approached "culture" as a testing ground for novel patterns of mass mobilization, which aimed at repositioning the individual militant toward collective action. In redefining their approach to culture, leisure, and politics, they were affected by a confluence of factors: a number of developments in the international Communist movement, especially the convergence of Eurocommunist Parties and the death of Mao Zedong; the comeback of rock music and the emergence of pubs and bars; and the debate among Greek left-wing intellectuals in the mid–to-late 1970s over the definition of "tradition."

Rock Versus Disco Fans

The musical landscape in Greece was shaken in the late 1970s by the growing—once again—popularity of rock music and the rapid spread of disco music. The success of the latter was associated to a great extent with the commercial success of the movie *Saturday Night Fever* (1977), starring John Travolta, which was accompanied by disco music played by the Bee Gees. The soundtrack of the movie was among the most popular non-Greek records for the year 1978, according to the magazine *Pop kai Rock*.[2] The movie itself sold 229,997 tickets in the first 392 days of its screening and was the third most commercially successful movie in Athens and Piraeus as of late December 1979.[3] In late 1970s Greece, the album *Bad Girls* by Donna Summer was also immensely popular, alongside the hits "I will survive" by Gloria Gaynor and "Rasputin" by Boney M.[4] Both disco and rock music were usually played in the discotheques, but not on the same day. Discotheques were a venue that had already existed since the late 1960s and early 1970s, especially in the center of Athens. Nevertheless, in the late 1970s, they spread to the districts and to smaller cities. For example in Volos, a city in central Greece, the number of discotheques rose from five in 1978 to ten in 1979; in Larissa, from five in 1978 to nine in 1979; and in Iraklio from nine in 1978 to eleven in 1979.[5] Indeed, some discotheques, at least in Larissa and Athens, organized dancing competitions, in which the winner was awarded the title of the "Greek Travolta."[6]

Meanwhile, rock music bounced back.[7] From 1977 to 1978, there was a proliferation of channels that enabled the contact between the Greek youth and rock music, such as the magazine *Pop kai Rock*. In the same period, television shows about rock music were also aired, such as "From the World of Pop" on YENED, which started in 1978 and was renamed to "Pop '80" in 1980.[8] YENED was one of the two TV channels in Greece in the 1970s, both of which were controlled by the state. Another relevant development was the emergence of numerous amateur and professional rock bands during the late 1970, especially in the districts of Athens and Salonica.[9] For example, the high-school pupil newspaper *Antiefimerida* in the Athens district of Zografou mentioned the Floating Feathers, The Sand, and Dalton as local amateur outfits.[10] This was not the first wave of amateur rock bands in Greece: they had also appeared in the early 1960s, due to the impact of the commercial success of the Beatles, but had faded by the mid–1970s.[11] Apart from the amateurs, many professional Greek rock bands also emerged. Some of them, Socrates Drank the Conium to name one, dated from the early 1970s. However, most of these bands, such as Spyridoula, Oriones, and Fatme were formed after 1976–1977. The annual poll by *Pop kai Rock* for the year 1979 indicated that Spyridoula was the most popular Greek band, followed by Socrates Drank the Conium.[12]

The musical tastes of young Greek rockers in the late 1970s were, however, mainly focused on non-Greek bands and particularly the major bands of the mid–1960s to early 1970s. In *Pop kai Rock*'s annual poll for the year 1978, its readers chose the Beatles, Jim Morrison, Deep Purple, and Janis Joplin, as their favorite non-Greek rock artists.[13] The Pink Floyd album *The Wall* was also very popular and it remained in the top position in the *Pop kai Rock* charts from at least June to November 1980.[14] Nevertheless, there were also fewer young rockers who were attracted to punk rock bands, such as the Stranglers. With a time lag, when compared to the United States, the United Kingdom, and Yugoslavia, where a punk scene emerged in the mid-to-late 1970s, punk music in Greece began to spread in 1979.[15] The popularity of punk rock would rise significantly beginning in the early 1980s, when the first Greek bands influenced to a lesser or greater extent by punk, like Trypes, came into existence.[16]

The rock music–following youth, or *rokades,* in Greece in the late 1970s, distinguished themselves clearly from the fans of disco music, or *kareklades.* According to information from articles, as well as from letters from rock and disco music fans published in *Pop kai Rock,* the former dismissed the latter as consumers of a music genre, which was simply a "product of multinational companies." They also lambasted the *kareklades* as people who displayed excessive concern for their outer appearance.[17] However, the issue whether there was a middle ground, namely a category of young people, who listened to both music genres, requires further examination.

In both cases, fans often claimed that their favorite music genre was conducive to "sexual emancipation." In a letter to *Pop kai Rock* replying to a disco music fan who favored Donna Summer as embodying sexual freedom, a rocker argued that "disco is irrelevant to sexual liberation. What kind of sexual liberation involves a chick, I apologize for my expression, who groans while singing, bring? My friend, I suggest that you listen to the Rolling Stones, listen to their 'Let's spend the night together', if you want to learn about sexual liberation."[18] Giannis Petridis, editor of *Pop kai Rock,* also maintained that there was a connection between rock music and permissiveness, extending to both heterosexual and homosexual tastes. The author cited numerous examples, such as those of Jim Morrison and Jimi Hendrix serving as sex symbols. "Morrison had a divine erotic sensitivity and his voice reached the limits of manic ecstatic yell"; Hendrix "demonstrated his sexuality through the performance, by playing as though he masturbated with the guitar, while enjoying this bizarre act."[19] Going to rock clubs and discotheques was yet another factor that accommodated courtship. As many letters show in a broad range of sources, including popular women's magazines and even pro-Soviet publications, female high-school pupils appeared willing to have the opportunity to dance and flirt in discotheques.[20] However, some parents were concerned about their children dancing in pairs, which they regarded as too sexually explicit, especially for female high-school pupils. This was a discourse reproduced by many newspapers as well, such as *Ta Nea,* where it was argued that "orgies" and the "rape" of young people, even female high school pupils, took place at such venues.[21] However, in contrast to the 1950s, the media no longer deemed it acceptable for fathers to resort to violence in order to "discipline" their daughters.

The relations of both amateur and professional Greek rock bands with the left-wing organizations were complicated. They were based on a form of mutual acceptance, especially in the case of RF and Choros, which will be examined later in detail in this and the following chapter, but not necessarily

identification. Rock bands and their following were a form of youth sociability, which did not gravitate around political affiliation. However, many Greek
rockers were not apathetic. Members of rock bands often made political references, either in their lyrics or in their interviews. Sometimes these were vague,
such as the concern for "peace" expressed by the members of Oriones in an
interview to *Pop kai Rock.* At times they were more explicit, such as when the
members of Spyridoula claimed that they opposed the practice of imprisonment.[22] Their complex relation to political youth organizations is manifest
in the interview given by the rock band 720 to *Thourios,* in which one of
its members argued that he would never appear at an event organized by
the Right, but he added that he had no particular preference for any certain
left-wing group.[23] As shall be shown, rock bands, mainly semi-professional or
professional ones, would appear frequently at the festivals and other cultural
events held by left-wing youth groups, even the KNE. The period from 1976
to 1980, when the Police performed on stage in Athens, saw no big concerts
by foreign and few by Greek rock bands.[24] Rock clubs were limited, too.
Thus, in this "comeback" to the rock music fever that Greece witnessed in the
late 1970s, the importance of events organized by left-wing groups was key to
the circulation of the music production of Greek rockers.

The re-emergence of rock music affected young left-wingers as well. Indeed, RF members were commonly patrons in a novel leisure space, the pubs
and bars, in which listening to rock music figured prominently. Such venues
started appearing from 1977 in Athens and Salonica. Domino and Lucky
Luke were among the first bars in Salonica, while Ippopotamos and Trip
opened in Athens. In contrast with the tavernas, bars did not serve red wine,
but concentrated on other alcoholic drinks, such as whiskey and cocktails.
They attracted mainly young people, some of whom were RF members and
Choros participants. As shown in the following sections, the pubs and bars
were fertile ground for the reflection of those left-wingers on how to recon-
figure politics.

Historicizing "Tradition"

The shifts of the late 1970s were not confined, however, to the leisure landscape in Greece: the mid to late 1970s witnessed an intellectual debate within
the Left, mainly in the magazines *ANTI* and *Politis,* where a number of historians and social anthropologists put forth a range of conceptualizations of
"tradition." *ANTI* published a number of articles in 1976 by intellectuals
from different ideological backgrounds. The author Dimitris Hatzis took the
initiative to host the debate in that magazine in March 1976. Kostis Moskov

defended the conventional position that Greek "national-popular culture" based on "Greek tradition" continued to form a crucial counterweight to the cultural production of the "global imperialist system" and the "dependent Greek bourgeois class."[25] Moskov was a sui generis intellectual, who employed a Braudelian approach to Greek history, which stressed a *longue durée* marked by the "resisting character" of the Greek nation. However, in stark contrast to the dominant views in the Left, he underlined the role of the Orthodox Church in the cultivation of this aspect.[26] Another approach was developed by Christos Giannaras: his anti-Enlightenment ideas were premised on the assumption that the "Greek tradition" was incompatible with any ideological current emanating from the "West," including Marxism.[27] On the contrary, a number of scholars, some of whom leaned toward the KKE Es., such as social anthropologist Alki Kyriakidou-Nestoros, historian Spyros Asdrachas, and literary theorist Alexis Politis, concurred in challenging the dominant conceptualization of "tradition" in left-wing patriotic discourse, namely as "immortal" and "inherently progressive." Instead, they defined it as a historically particular phenomenon, which would not outlive the social conditions that produced it. Kyriakidou-Nestoros associated "folk culture" with orally transmitted customs in rural areas and argued that "the folk culture no longer exists as a historical reality." She added that "the people who have moved from the rural areas to the urban centers have developed a way of life that comprises some remnants of traditional activities as well as appropriations of the lifestyle of the bourgeois class."[28] Politis maintained that "tradition" should not be approached in an essentialized fashion, as a set of patterns that remain unaltered. On the contrary, he argued that it was very important to explore the context which gave rise to them, maintaining that part of them emanated from and reproduced the cultural background of the feudal system. But he too concluded that by the 1970s "tradition," meaning cultural patterns that were orally transmitted from generation to generation, no longer existed.[29]

"Tradition" was an issue addressed in another left-wing magazine, *Politis.* The latter was first published in 1976. Many of its contributors, such as Michalis Papagiannakis and Aggelos Elefantis, had been educated in France. The magazine served as a forum, where currents of thought, such as psychoanalysis and structuralist Marxism, were presented. It is indicative that it published translated extracts and reviews of the works of Freud and Althusser as well as of Poulantzas and publicized the establishment of the Elliniki Etaireia Psychanalytikis Psychotherapeias (Hellenic Society of Psychoanalytic Psychotherapy) in 1977.[30] Its target group was narrower than that of *ANTI,* since *Politis* portrayed itself as a magazine connected with "Communist renewal." Concerning "tradition," the magazine hosted an article in 1980 by social anthropologist/folklorist Eleonora Skouteri, a student of Kyriakidou-Nestoros, under the notable title "I paradosi tis paradosis," which could be translated literally as "the tradition of tradition," but actually means "the transmission of tradition."[31] She repeated the argument that the analysis of "tradition" should consider the historical specificity of the context in which it emerged. One way or another, a growing number of left-wing actors called into question the "continuity of tradition" as the legitimizing factor of the cultural politics of the Left toward the end of the 1970s.

Iconoclastic Artists and Film Reviewers: Beyond the "Progressive Message"

Formulations of "tradition" were not, however, the only intellectual debate at that point that touched upon left-wing approaches to "culture." During those years, a growing number of left-wing artists and intellectuals reinvented their approach to politics and embraced a self-critical stance. I would like to label them as "iconoclastic" and "heterodox," since they challenged a perception that reigned supreme to a lesser or greater extent among left-wingers—including young ones—up to that point, namely that culture should revolve around "progressive" messages. Those artists and intellectuals neither desired nor managed to formulate a novel orthodoxy in terms of left-wing cultural politics, but certainly helped unleash protracted reflection on how the Left should construe "culture."

Indeed, it would be schematic to argue that all left-wing artists in the early and mid–1970s portrayed themselves as enlightened instructors, who would help forge committed militants. Savvopoulos did not subscribe to the normative conceptualization of "tradition," as endorsed by the Left.[32] In the late 1970s, he raised similar concerns in an interview he gave to *Thourios*. Savvopoulos argued for a more selective approach to "tradition." He proclaimed his work to be a creative "odyssey" through the production of hybrids, mixing Greek folk with rock music. Savvopoulos claimed that he did not attempt to recapture the past "as it was": he was not interested in "retro." He likened himself to Odysseus, claiming that he "returned to a port that was no longer the same." His iconoclasm extended to the ideological function of "culture." Savvopoulos opposed vehemently its definition as the source of "progressive messages."[33] He also took issue with the dominant form of left-wing politics in post-dictatorship Greece, which he mocked especially in his album *Rezerva* (1979). The album actually proved very popular: it topped the charts produced by *Pop kai Rock* for Greek albums in January and February 1980 and was the second most popular in March

1980. In the song "Politevtis" (Politician), he approached, in an ironic way, the appeal of the left-wing cadres, who were well-read and eloquent speakers, to young women. The lyrics went: "I will report you to the female student that has fallen in love with you. I will tell her that she is mistaken to be so enthusiastic about you! ... You take pride at speaking to the crowds: you speak to the people as though you were a rescuer." In another song, "Gia ta paidia pou 'nai sto Komma" (About the kids who belong to a Party) or "Lefke-galazie pontike mou" (My white-blue mouse), Savvopoulos urged the people who were aligned to a political organization to "escape the *kleisoura* [insularity] of the manifestos" and go to the "bar that stays open all night long." Savvopoulos was certainly ironic about organized left-wingers, but was not hostile to them. As is shown below in detail, he appeared at RF and Choros cultural events, such as the festival of *Avgi-Thourios* in 1980.

A similarly iconoclastic attitude is manifest and clearly expressed in the case of the magazine *Synchronos Kinimatografos* (Contemporary Cinema). In the mid–1970s, its main contributors, among them Christos Vakalopoulos, endorsed an approach toward films in particular and cultural products in general that was predicated on structuralist Marxism and mixed with influences from semiotics and psychoanalysis. However, the magazine soon developed a critical reflection on the employment of *any* theoretical framework, including this combination of semiotics, Marxism, and psychoanalysis. As Vakalopoulos replied to a reader's letter in 1979, the use of theory may function as a factor that obscures the film per se, treating it as simply a means to vindicate or refute a theoretical statement.[34] The contributors to the magazine went further to organize screenings and discussions of movies, which did not aim at "educating" militants, but, rather, at problematizing classifications of cinema movies even in genres and schools, such as "Nouvelle Vague" and "film noir." A notable case was the "Cinema Week" that *Synchronos Kinimatografos* held from 18 to 24 December 1978 at the Studio cinema. As Vakalopoulos put it in an interview, these discussions would serve as an "exit from the deeply entrenched idea that it is necessary to resort to a specific conceptual framework, in order to approach cinema."[35]

Still, the late 1970s witnessed the multiplication of voices, which opted for a less triumphalist understanding of "meanings" that could be distilled from cultural products. The poet Manolis Anagnostakis certainly featured prominently, discouraging left-wing cultural politics that were based on an "uncritical, mythologizing" memory of left-wing activity in modern Greek history.[36] Meanwhile, toward the end of the decade, Savvopoulos cooperated with Manolis Rasoulis and Nikos Xydakis in the composition of two albums, *Ekdikisi tis gyftias* (The Revenge of the Gypsies, 1978) and *Dithen* (Pretentious, 1979). They were an attempt to compose popular music, without the need to "purify" it or "elevate" it. Their songs referred to "love" and "loneliness" by using low-brow metaphors such as "the heart looks like a little broken piece of glass," as well as oriental sounds. In fact, their composers aimed to legitimize exactly those elements in popular music that Theodorakis wished to dispense with in his artistic-popular project. "Gypsy," which in Greek is used as a colloquial expression to signify low-quality taste, functioned as a means of subversion of the criteria of left-wing artists and their effort to produce art that followed the "ideal popular" model. In this case, the use of the term "Gypsy" apparently lacked any racist implications.

The account of the heterodox left-wing artists would be incomplete without a reference to Loukianos Kilaidonis. The shift in his work is indicative of the unfolding of youth politicization in the mid to late 1970s. In 1975 Kilaidonis had produced the album *Apla Mathimata Politikis Oikonomias* (Simple Lessons of Political Economy), which could hardly have been more overt in its intention to transmit "progressive messages" and encourage militancy. In his works in the late 1970s, however, he was no longer concerned about how to help workers spot the "opportunists" among them. The prevalent tone in his new work, delivered through a combination of humor and melancholy, expressed the doubt about the infallibility of any ideological doctrine. His 1978 album bore the title *Ftochos kai monos cowboy* (Poor lonely cowboy). In the verses of the song "Sti Vouliagmeni" (In Vouliagmeni), he was critical of what appeared to be the conformism of his friends. He employed the image of Lucky Luke to castigate in a pessimist fashion the fact that "all my friends have got married, they have become plump," while he still rides Dolly, Lucky Luke's horse, and whenever he feels sad, he "goes to the mountains." In the song "Ach, Rita!," included on his 1979 album *Psychraimia, Paidia* (Calm, Kids), he engaged in dialogue with feminism: he was ironic about Rita, whom he did not expect to "get married and become yet another housewife."

All the aforementioned iconoclastic artists had in common the fact that they did not offer an alternative model. They usually employed humor or melancholy to comment on lifestyle issues as well as left-wing politics, but without suggesting solutions to the concerns they raised. In stark contrast with France, where the New Philosophers such as Bernard Henri-Levy appeared in the late 1970s to target the Left and its hitherto dominance of the French intellectual circles, Savvopoulos, Kilaidonis, Rasoulis, Xydakis, and the reviewers of *Synchronos Kinimatografos* remained left-leaning or left-wing. Their relationship to a segment of the Left was reciprocal, as every side would draw on the approach developed by the other.

So far, a number of processes at work at the national and international level, which affected intellectual endeavors and the leisure landscape in Greece, have been outlined. The following sections examine their exact impact on different Communist and Socialist youth groups.

Young Eurocommunists in Front of the Mirror

It was the summer of 1977 when the KNE central council produced a very detailed set of guidelines regarding the desirable behavior patterns of its members. Both the then–young pro-USSR Communists and those who were aligned with other left-wing youth groups at that point often remember this text as the "Farakos Guidelines," after the KKE cadre who was in charge of the youth organization of the Party. This was a significant moment for the making of young left-wingers, but hardly in the direction that Grigoris Farakos might have anticipated or, at least, wanted. The sexual norms of KNE members, as shown above, conformed to the prescriptive texts only to an extent. However the "Farakos Guidelines," would prove, perhaps surprisingly, to be very influential among RF members: they served as a palpable expression of what they opposed in terms of behavioral patterns. Soon after, in the autumn of 1977, the young Eurocommunists became involved in the publication of a series of articles in which they openly confronted not only the guidelines, but also the cultural politics of the KNE in general. The elaboration of such guidelines by the KNE began in the mid–1970s, taking a detailed form in 1977; on the contrary, their critique by RF, Choros, the Youth of PASOK, and a segment of the Maoists unfolded throughout the late 1970s and was a key aspect in the forging of their identities.

The shift in RF was certainly facilitated by the wider historical juncture. At the international level, the bonds among Communist Parties, which were critical of the Soviet regime, especially due to the lack of pluralism and free and fair elections in the USSR, had already existed in the early-to-mid 1970s; common announcements of theirs had been published in KOMTHEPOL shortly after the collapse of the dictatorship in Greece in 1974.[37] However, in the late 1970s, these Parties crystallized their common ideological background. On 2–3 March 1977, Georges Marchais of the French Communist Party, Santiago Carillo of the Communist Party of Spain, and Enrico Berlinguer of the Italian Communist Party met in Madrid and signed a common declaration of their principles. They laid out the fundamental lines of their strand of communism, based on political pluralism and autonomy from the USSR. Gradually, drawing on Carillo's 1977 essay *Eurocommunism and the State,* they would demarcate the Socialist strategy they aimed at pursuing by calling themselves Eurocommunists. At the national level, the shaky electoral alliance between the KKE and KKE Es., the United Left, which had contested the 1974 elections, was dissolved. In the 1977 elections, the KKE fielded its own candidates, while the KKE Es. formed a coalition with smaller left-wing parties, which was called *Symmachia* (Alliance).[38] As the date of the election in November 1977 drew closer, the two Parties and their respective youth organizations flexed their muscles, emphasizing the different models of Socialist transition they opted for.

The deepening of the division between them extended to the domain of cultural politics. Responding to the KNE critique that its members were not disciplined enough to combat the "bourgeois" values of "individualism," RF cadres employed a language that was mindful of debates in the international Communist movement. Their articles began to develop the perception that a normative language that aimed at regulating the behavior patterns of the youth was yet another example of "Stalinism." Complying with the decision of the 20th Congress of the Communist Party of Soviet Union, the KKE had renounced Stalin. However, the KKE was often called "Stalinist" by its opponents, who wished to stress that it endorses an authoritarian model of administration. As the late 1970s progressed, it became increasingly common in RF publications to discuss how a "Eurocommunist" approach would differ in defining "culture." Whilst *Odigitis* maintained that it was necessary to "uproot the bars, the discotheques and the cafeterias, which [had] spread like mushrooms,"[39] the Greek Eurocommunists clearly opposed campaigns that favored restrictions and bans of particular leisure activities. On the contrary, a growing number of young Eurocommunists mounted a critique of the KNE, claiming that "genuine socialism" could not be established by "decrees."[40]

In this vein, perhaps for the first time in the history of Communist youth groups in Greece, the value of "tradition" as the cornerstone of their cultural politics was called into question. At this juncture, the "voice" of those young Eurocommunist cadres, who had been cautious toward a message-centered approach to cultural products from the mid–1970s, gained traction and, gradually, became the official line of the group. This development lends support to the argument by Long and Moore about sociality, namely that diverse forms of joint commitment should not be examined in isolation, but, rather, in interaction with emphasis on how they affect and potentially transform each other.[41] Such RF cadres set the tone of the cultural politics of the organization. Notable such cases were Christos Lazos and Christos Vakalopoulos. Both retained very close contacts with young Eurocommunists, who had studied abroad, such as Marisa Decastro and Kostas Livieratos. Lazos, a member of the majority in the central council, published a series of three articles under the rubric "The identity of the generation of '77." He attempted to define the behavior patterns of the youngsters in

Greece in 1977 and to explain what he viewed as the declining appeal of left-wing organizations among them. He argued the very term "American way of life" was incorrect: "[T]here is indeed the issue of American imperialist infiltration, which extends to the domain of culture; nevertheless, it is not detached from Greek popular culture; the dominant Greek culture combines both Greek and American elements … thus, it is not an 'American,' but a version of a Greek Way of Life."[42] He added in the same article that "the popular national tradition was never a unified whole, without imports from other cultures." Heterodox intellectuals certainly left their imprint on this reflection in *Thourios*. In fact, Lazos and Vakalopoulos interviewed Savvopoulos, the results of which were published in *Thourios*. The two young Eurocommunists concluded by arguing that Savvopoulos offered a novel and dynamic understanding of "tradition."[43] All relevant articles in *Thourios* since 1977 historicized the concept, similarly and in dialogue with the viewpoints of the intellectuals who had sought to explore the concrete context in which the "traditional" cultural products emerged. They perceived this act of contextualization as the counterweight to an "ahistorical," "museum" approach to "tradition" and "Greek history," allegedly endorsed by the KNE. Quite tellingly, they argued that the cultural patterns described by the "Farakos Guidelines" as "traditional," such as Greek folk dances, were not "innately progressive," but had been co-opted by the State and were "imposed" by the dictatorship from 1967 to 1974 on young people.[44]

But while they subverted the dichotomy "American way of life" as opposed to "Greek popular tradition," young Eurocommunists remained wedded throughout the late 1970s and early 1980s to an anti-American viewpoint with regard to the Greek economy and foreign relations, which revolved around the "popular struggle against imperialism." To an extent, their stance resembles that of the West German student protestors in 1968, who espoused political anti-Americanism, but were influenced by American cultural products.[45] The announcements of the central council, the decisions of the congresses and articles in *Thourios* reproduced without exception the argument that "American imperialists" supported "Turkish chauvinists" and put the sovereignty of Greece and Cyprus in danger, while U.S. companies exploited the natural resources of Greece. RF was adamant in condemning in 1980 the reentry of Greece into the military wing of NATO, from which it had withdrawn in 1974, after Turkey's invasion of Cyprus. "National independence" would continue to be a key demand in its language.[46]

Since RF no longer discerned a singular "Greek popular tradition," many articles in *Thourios* and *Mathitiki Poreia* in the late 1970s as well as early 1980s portrayed "people" as a diverse political and cultural category. As an announcement by the local branch of RF in the area of Ierotheos in Athens stated: "We know that the people are not a homogeneous whole, but comprise groups with different traditions, different tastes, and different preferences. Homogeneity, the claim that all should think and entertain themselves in the same way, is congenial to totalitarian regimes and, as such, is totally alien to our democratic and socialist ideals."[47]

The redefinition of the "people" as a heterogeneous category was predicated upon the theoretical influence of structuralist Marxism. Articles by both loyalists to the central council majority as well as of its opponents appropriated Althusser's writings on the "ideological state apparatuses." They argued that the French philosopher's theory pointed to the direction that cultural patterns, like all ideological products, were "ambiguous."[48] The opponents of the central council went further: drawing on the "integration mechanisms" approach, as had been formulated in the preceding years by Antonis Maounis, who was actually one of them, they claimed that the KNE aimed at rendering youngsters obedient to state institutions, which reproduced the dominant "bourgeois" values.[49] One way or another, the diffusion of mass consumption was not necessarily an anathema to young Eurocommunists. While it bred "depoliticization" and "individualism," it also challenged "conservative institutions," such as the "patriarchal family."[50] Similarly, formulations of tradition, according to young Eurocommunists, often served as an undesirable (for them) means of disciplining the youth. They strayed from a normative conceptualization of "tradition," which they lambasted as reproducing a model that positioned the Party as "rational" against Greek "youth" in need of "education" and "guidance." This, they asserted, was the spirit that had clearly animated the "Farakos Guidelines."[51] In discussing the desirable reconfiguration the RF, commentary acquired a self-critical flavor as well. Various RF members argued that the language employed in left-wing youth publications was alien both in style and content to youngsters who were not affiliated with a political group. Its normative tone was described as not allowing the youth to "express itself" about problems in interpersonal relations, such as "loneliness." Minutes from a discussion of members of RF in Salonica stated that: "Politics in the university have been deprived of a youthful aspect. Let's imagine how we think of the politicized student, as detached from the apolitical, let's think of the unlimited hours that the student assemblies last, let's think of the rejection of any pleasure in all this process. When speaking of culture, we do not mean just leisure, but the relations of the individual with the social background."[52]

Similarly, their version of the anti-fascist, anti-imperialist language also became more critical. Although Lazos, for instance, still regarded the militants of the OKNE, EPON, and DNL, as well as the activists of the Polytechnic Uprising in 1973 as role models in the struggle for "national independence," this did not fully apply to lifestyle issues. He argued that the "Resistance generation chose freely to subordinate its personal life to the historical mission of the antifascist struggle, which was correct at this historical juncture," adding that "the situation is very different nowadays, for the generation of '77."[53] By using the term "generation of '77," he aimed to define the Greek youth in general—employing a term, however, that was not utilized by any group of youngsters in Greece at that point to define itself.

Young Eurocommunists engaged themselves in such endeavors in order to tackle what they viewed as the crisis of the "youth movement," which they claimed started around 1977. To back their argument, they maintained that fewer students attended the general assemblies of their school and that the cultural societies in the urban districts had petered out.[54] This analysis, nevertheless, proved controversial and caused rancorous debates, especially between RF and the KNE. The latter group challenged the argument, mainly on the grounds that the number of young workers who were organized in the Left, especially the KNE and KKE, and who participated in protests, was rising significantly in the late 1970s.[55] In any case, RF claimed that deeply entrenched patterns in the practice of the Greek Left, including its cultural politics, were to blame for this purported decline, since, according to the young Eurocommunists, were growingly out of touch with what the youth desired or expected. In order to counter this trend, "dull" or "routine" politics had to be confronted, as was often stated in minutes of the RF central council from 1977: it was the so-called shift to "innovation" and "imagination," otherwise quoted as the "shift toward youth issues." Young Eurocommunists aimed at positioning the aspect of "organized struggle" in such a way, so that it did not "suppress" the "instincts" or "desires" of the youth.[56]

The refashioning of cultural politics that those aligned with RF endorsed tracked and shaped their shifting leisure activities. Their appreciation of rock music was certainly an integral piece of this puzzle. It functioned for them as a projection screen for their own ambivalence and doubts, stemming from the dominant social values and political practices in Greece in the 1970s as well as early 1980s. Opening a series of articles on rock music, *Mathitiki Poreia* stated: "[W]e invite those whose taste is not limited to the songs that just help them raise their fist, those who do not dismiss uncritically many cultural products as elements of the American Way of Life ... This is an open-ended dialogue."[57]

Numerous RF members enjoyed rock artists or bands of the mid– and late 1960s, which carried for them subversive connotations: they associated their work with the protest cultures of the Sixties, depicting it as the music of "Woodstock."[58] Nevertheless, in contrast with the Greek political song in the mid–1970s, they did not expect rock music to engender a particular "way of life." RF members did not resort to the lyrics of rock songs or to interviews of rock stars, in order to seek guidance and vindication of their political orientation. By contrast, the echoes of Jimi Hendrix and Jim Morrison were meant to open a debate about novel protest patterns, especially in relation to the realm of lifestyle practices. They were a point of departure rather than a means of promoting preconceived targets. Thus, the reflective consumption of rock music was first and foremost a way for young Eurocommunists to distance themselves from the taverna ritual. As E.Q., male, student in the early 1970s, high-ranking cadre of RF and prominent adherent of the "opposition" in the mid–1970s, claimed: "Rock does not shove in your face [the demand] 'come, friend, let's organize a revolution to overthrow the dictatorship' … Music became related with *diaskedasi* [entertainment] not just a means to express your opposition to the regime" (E.Q., B.Q., Interview).

Venues where young Eurocommunists listened to rock music were the pubs and bars. They did not gather there in order to consolidate their political affiliation or recruit new members, as happened in the tavernas. Personal accounts of RF members about their leisure pursuits, published in *Thourios* in 1978 and 1979, illustrate this, mentioning that "until 1977, we had been chasing new members; henceforth, our leisure is more relaxed."[59] What did young Eurocommunists do in the bars besides listening to rock music, then? K.M., male member of RF in the mid–1970s, explains that "in the pubs we would discuss cinema, not about the message, but about the form of the movies" (K.M., Interview). In a sense, pubs and bars were venues, where the self-representation of the young Eurocommunists as "avant-garde intellectuals," who could engage in complex theoretical discussions that extended beyond Marxism-Leninism, was vindicated. In *Thourios* RF members described this pub and bar environment as being "familiar" to them, due to this *koultouriariki,* namely high-caliber intellectual quality.[60] Nevertheless, the endorsement of bars by young Eurocommunists was not uniform. This divergence is evident in an event organized by RF in Terpsithea, a lower-middle and working-class district in Athens. The secretary of the organization argued in an article in *Avgi,* the newspaper of the KKE Es., that the youth should stay away from such venues.[61] It seems that members of the group, whose political activity lay in lower-middle and working-class districts where they lived and who had graduated from high school before the collapse of the dictatorship, were more cautious. On the contrary, going to bars, as well as forming rock bands, was much more common among RF members in the same areas who had started high-school after 1974. Still, besides the bars, many of the young Eurocommunists continued to gather in tavernas, such as around Exarchia Square in the center of Athens, which were close to a number of university schools and faculties (Law, Chemistry, Polytechnic, Athens School of Economics and Business) as well as their group headquarters. However, they would gradually refrain from singing partisan songs. Meanwhile, they visited boîtes less and less often. By the beginning of the 1980s, boîtes had declined in general.

RF members envisaged that construing "culture" as a means of reflection rather than of "instruction" would help them bridge the gap with peer groups of nonaffiliated young people, who appreciated rock music, but found the vocabulary and the activities of the organized youth unappealing. Such an approach permeated the cultural events that the young Eurocommunists organized in the late 1970s. Both articles in *Thourios* and interviews indicate that local RF branches held—or scheduled—many rock parties in their headquarters, such as in Salonica and in the district of Acharnes in Athens in 1978. A leaflet of the Democratic Union of the Higher Industrial School of Salonica argued that its members should "immediately take initiatives to organize parties within the premises of the university."[62] Participants were encouraged to dance in pairs and treat their body as a source of "pleasure" and not as something to "sacrifice" for the coming of the "future socialist society."[63] While dancing wildly, however, young people, politicized or not, were expected to start speaking in a "youthful" language, "free from taboos." The central council actively promoted such an approach: its announcements argued that "it is essential that we discuss with young people, when they entertain themselves, and then we must bring all the issues that have arisen in these discussions to the forefront of the activities of the group."[64]

A lone group of young Eurocommunists founded an amateur rock band in the working-class district of Kokkinia. Nevertheless, at events organized by RF, especially its festivals, it was mainly professional or semi-professional bands that performed. Actually, Greek rock bands participated in all festivals of Avgi-Thourios since 1977. At that year's event, the prominent Greek rock artists Pavlos Sidiropoulos and Vlasis Bonatsos appeared. The bands Apocalypsis, Pete and Royce, and Socrates Drank the Conium played onstage at the 1980 festival, while Iraklis kai I Lernaia Ydra participated in 1981. Professional Greek rock bands appeared onstage in RF's pre-festival activities such as the Vavoura Band in the Athens district of Holargos in 1980. The Eurocommunist youth group tried to subvert the taxonomy into "traditional" and "American," without inverting it. A broad range of music genres would be represented in the festivals of Avgi-Thourios: Hadjidakis' music in 1981; heterodox artists, such as Savvopoulos in 1980 and Kilaidonis both in 1980 and in 1981; *rebetiko* singers, such as Bagianteras and Pergialis in 1980 and Roukounas in 1981; and Greek folk singers, such as Domna Samiou in 1980. [65]

The Eurocommunist youth shift to rock music was not a Greek peculiarity: it also appeared in the case of Italian young Eurocommunists. In the mid–1970s, Italy witnessed a "sudden surge" in the popularity of rock and jazz festivals. *Re Nudo* (Nude King), an alternative magazine "heavily influenced by American hippie culture and its ideas of communal living, sexual liberation, drugs and mysticism,"[66] organized many of the festivals. *Re Nudo* became immensely popular in Italy in the mid–1970s: its claimed readership rose from about 50,000 to circa 100,000 from 1975 to 1978. The FGCI responded to the rock and jazz festivals held by this magazine by staging its own, such as in Pincio (1975) and in Ravenna (1976). The mottos of these events displayed the desire of the organizers to connect the reflection in rock music on interpersonal relations with the ideological discourse of the FGCI.[67]

In addition, in the late 1970s, the effort to channel youth tourism into forms that would combine this escape with "education" and "culture" was totally sidelined both in the publications and the activities of the young Eurocommunists. Rather, attempts were made to reconceptualize tourist "escape" in a radical way, as a means of helping to inject "imagination" into "dull" politics. As *Thourios* stated, "summer is a good opportunity … to change the routine way in which youth movements usually act." This was an open call to its readers to formulate new ideas on how left-wing political actors should function, which did not contain any concrete suggestions.[68] The shift was evident in the new form of the tourist supplement in *Thourios*. What stands out from the supplements from 1977 onward is its design. First of all, in contrast to the black-and-white format that was predominant in the left-wing youth press in the 1970s, they included more colorful images. Moreover, they included many pictures and comic strips, which were usually humorous or portrayed moments of relaxation: there was a clear rupture with the didactic language espoused by both the KNE and RF in the mid–1970s. Certainly, tourist guides were not a novelty introduced by the Eurocommunists, but had been published by various other Greek actors, such as the EOT, the Greek Tourist Organization. The EOT, however, catered to a broader range of tastes. For example, a pamphlet about Rhodes promoted images of luxury, stating that "of course, there is the casino at the Grand Hotel for all those who might like to try their luck at roulette, black jack and slot machines."[69] Nevertheless, the island of Aghistri near Athens was advertised from a different perspective: "All of this, along with the traditional simplicity of the people, makes for the magic which fills the Saronic Gulf with beauty."[70] On the contrary, the summer issue of *Thourios,* echoing romantic notions of the nineteenth century, promoted sites like Folegandros, Schoinousa, and Anafi, which were considered to be "remote" and, as such, "untainted by the tourist industry."[71]

The effort to distance themselves from a normative language was not manifest only in the Eurocommunist youth tourist supplements, but in its

Figure 4.1. Cover page of the tourist supplement, published by *Thourios* on 28 June 1979. It states: "Let's struggle with imagination. Let's change our lives. Let's change society." Used with permission from Dimitris Chatzisokratis.

publications in general. RF tried to reinvent itself as a group that tolerated a variety of lifestyles among its members and young people in general. Typical for these texts was the argument that "we are not going to pretend to be wise or provide you with guidelines about your leisure activities," as a leaflet written by the Democratic Union of the Higher Industrial School of Salonica stated.[72] Actually, in their articles, the young Eurocommunists opted for texts written in the first-person singular by members of the group or unaffiliated students, pupils, or young workers. This certainly stood in stark contrast to the first-person plural narrative ("we") or third-person singular that was hitherto predominant in the language of all left-wing groups. According to the Eurocommunist youth organization, the first-person-singular narrations were the "genuine expression of the youth, free from a normative language imposed by Parties and youth political groups." Young Eurocommunists frequently visited youth leisure venues, such as bars and discotheques, and gathered interviews from the patrons. They tried to refrain from commenting on them, in order not to be "judgmental": In one such article, called "Tonight we improvise through dancing," the authors stated: "[O]ur first stop is a very well-known discotheque in Plaka. The usual decoration, the very loud music, the colorful lights … We try to understand and not to judge."[73]

The conscious departure from a didactic language extended to the theatre and cinema reviews that appeared in *Thourios*. They particularly targeted the version of *Hamlet* that the Theatre Section of the University of Athens staged in 1978, which they said tried, following socialist realism, to classify the roles into those of "militant heroes" and "reactionary villains." They nicknamed the performance "Amletof," mocking its purportedly Soviet-inspired style.[74] As regards cinema, the reviews, especially by Thodoros Soumas, sought ambiguity instead of a "progressive message": they praised open-ended, nonlinear film narrative. The fundamentally different ways in which Andrzej Wajda's *Man of Marble* (1977) was reviewed in *Thourios* and in *Odigitis* are telling. The movie dealt with the effort of a female film director to find Stakhanovite workers. It shows that the Polish regime did not cultivate ideologically engaged subjects, but, rather, conformists or "marble men." Soumas appreciated its structure, depicting it as a "complex and refined narration."[75] *Odigitis* also offered a positive review of the movie, but on the grounds of its content: despite the critique that the movie mounted, it portrayed, according to the organ of the KNE, the ruling Polish United Workers' Party as capable of capturing the "weaknesses in the implementation of socialism" and of finding solutions.[76]

One more significant change in the publications of the Eurocommunist youth was the extensive use of humor, especially in the images that accompanied its publications. *Mafalda* by Quino was one of their choices and appeared in the leaflets of Democratic Union in the Higher Industrial School of Salonica.[77] They employed humor as another means of releasing what they viewed the "desires" of the youth and rendering politics "imaginative." In this vein, they aimed at shedding some serious dispute on dominant norms in Greek society in the domains of education, youth leisure, and sexuality. A leaflet put out in 1977 by DIMAK, the Eurocommunist pupil group, was decorated with an image of a "superhero" appearing vulnerable and exhausted. This was a reference to the hard work that the educational system required from pupils so that they could pass their final exams and be admitted to university.[78] Humoristic comic strips or slogans were published in various university student magazines (such as *Stasi* [Stop] at the School of Electrical Engineering in Athens or *Spoudi* [Study] at the School of Philosophy in Athens) to which RF members contributed. Through the use of humor, young Eurocommunists also voiced criticism of the behavior patterns prescribed in the official language of the KNE. For instance, the magazine of Democratic Struggle at the School of Fine Arts in Athens often made fun of the "Farakos Guidelines."[79] Apart from satirizing ideas and practices that they condemned, young Eurocommunists also employed a humorous lan-

Figure 4.2. Cartoon in *Thourios* commenting on the distinction between the "Greek traditional" and the "American way of life." The young person is thinking to himself: "I feel that the responsibility for the return to our popular tradition is a very heavy duty for me to bear," while listening to rock music. Source: "I elliniki neolaia anakalyptei xana tzaz kai rok," *Thourios,* 8 June 1978, pp. 6–7. Used with permission from Dimitris Chatzisokratis.

guage, in order to vindicate their politics. Quite often in the late 1970s they accompanied the program of forthcoming cultural events or festivals of *Avgi-Thourios* with funny images. Actually, a hint of self-satirizing was manifest in some of them. Rather than ridiculing their activities, however, RF members tried to promote them through a playful language.

Once again, inserting humorous images into left-wing youth publications was not confined to the Greek Eurocommunist youth during that period. In Italy the magazine of the Eurocommunist youth organization FGCI, *La città futura,* published supplements from 1978 onward, which contained solely comic strips (*fumetti*). These supplements, called *La città futura fumetto,* included comics that addressed political and ideological issues and were often accompanied with a humorous language. For instance, the supplement that appeared on 1 March 1978 was entitled "La rivoluzione: come, dove, quando" (The revolution: how, where, when). This publication mentioned: "When to start the revolution? The end of October is ideal, because peasants have finished with their work and are more available. Not beforehand, because there are still people returning from holidays." Next to this story, a funny image was inserted, which portrayed a figure that resembled Lenin looking for Trotsky, apparently in the summer, and being told that he is still on holidays by the sea.[80] Young Italian Eurocommunists were not, however, the first to use comic strips, in order to express their views on social and political issues. *Linus,* which had first appeared in April 1965, was a politicized comic magazine, partially influenced by the Californian counterculture of the 1960s. *La città futura* stated explicitly that they appreciated *Linus.* As in the case of rock festivals, Italian young Eurocommunists appropriated ideas and activities that were first introduced by alternative magazines and groups and became more experimental cultural producers and consumers. It is certainly not by chance that RF members followed a similar path in the same period. Given the close contact between the two groups, it would certainly not be groundless to argue that young Italian Eurocommunists functioned as role models for their Greek comrades, including the style of their publications.

The "shift" of RF "to the youth" also entailed more conventional activities as well, especially the campaign that RF ran from the late 1978 to late 1979. Young Eurocommunists treated youth as a particular category of citizens with specific rights. In this vein, RF put forth the *Katastatikos Chartis ton Koinonikon kai Dimokratikon Dikaiomaton tis Neolaias* (Constitutional Charter of Social and Democratic Rights of the Youth), which was divided into a number of chapters, entitled: "The Right to Education," "The Right to Work," "The Right to Free Time, Leisure and Culture," "The Right to a Humane Military Service," "The Rights of Young Women," and "The Right to Full Participation in Political Life From the Age of 18." The demands included devoting 15 percent of the annual budget to education; the abolition of entrance examinations to senior high school; full employment and that employees, regardless of age or gender, be paid the same wages for the same work; state support for cultural societies; the reduction of military service to eighteen months; and the legalization of abortions. Finally, it entailed the demand that the minimum voting age be reduced from twenty-one to eighteen years.[81] The latter point did not appear out of the blue in the late 1970s; all Communist and Socialist Parties and youth organizations, even some centrist forces, concurred in this demand and launched a number of relevant campaigns in the aftermath of the dictatorship. For example, RF alongside KNE, the Youth of PASOK, and the centrist youth group ESDIN (El-liniki Sosialistiki Dimokratiki Neolaia, Greek Socialist Democratic Youth) collected about 150,000 signatures, as Christos Lazos claims, in favor of changing the minimum voting age. However, the Center-Right government refused to amend the law.[82] RF organized open discussions in the universities and the districts to promote the charter. Still, these objectives of the organization failed to materialize in the late 1970s. As I will show in more detail, some of those demands were fulfilled only after PASOK won the elections in 1981.

Complex Encounters

Despite its purported openness, reaching out to the nonaffiliated youth proved a hard task for young Eurocommunists in practice. The "autonomous" cultural associations they had been endorsing already since the mid–1970s appeared for them to be a fertile ground for approaching them.[83] A serious issue that young Eurocommunists took up with most of the then-existing cultural societies in the university was the fact that the student administrative councils guided their activities. RF members claimed that this was a case of hierarchical, top-bottom relations, and argued that the decision-making of the student cultural societies should not depend upon any external institution, such as these councils, the PAPOK (the coordinating body of cultural associations that the KKE had helped establish) or any Party. The Eurocommunists elaborated on the line of "autonomy" and insisted on the formation of small, amateur cultural groups in the universities. Similar arguments about the "self-management [ayto-organosi] of youth leisure" appeared in the Decision of the Second Congress of RF held in 1980.[84] Nevertheless, apart from a limited number of cases, such as the FOTHK (Foititikos Omilos Theatrou kai Kinimatografou, Student Club of Theatre and Cinema) in Salonica, the influence of the Eurocommunists in the student cultural societies apparently remained minimal.

In the meantime, the cultural societies in the districts of Athens and Salonica had declined in popularity by 1977, with many of them shutting down and some continuing with a dwindling number of members. Young Eurocommunists tried to approach rock music fans in those areas. The central council encouraged RF members to reach out to young rockers and discuss lifestyle issues.[85] Again, however, the cultural politics of RF largely proved to be unsuccessful. The resolution of its first congress, held in 1978, named some cultural societies and magazines whose activities it approved, and where young Eurocommunists could be expected to be active: *Prospatheia* (Effort) of the male high school in the upper-middle class district of Filothei, *Ekkremes* (Pendulum) at the Moraitis private high school, *Roloi* (Clock) in Piraeus, *Politistiko Ergastiri* (Cultural Laboratory) in Nea Smyrni, and *Kathreftis* (Mirror) in the lower-middle class of Korydallos.[86] However, these were few and they would not significantly increase in number until the early 1980s.

This limited success may partly be attributed to the fact that the understanding of politics—and the concomitant openness to nonpoliticized young people—among young Eurocommunists did not shift as radically as the official sources suggested. S.L., male pupil, RF cadre in the working-class district of Kokkinia, and member of the central council majority, narrated that he found the members of local rock bands who had joined the Eurocommunist youth organization as not very keen to participate in discussions in the group headquarters. In his words, they were "*too* loosely politicized" (his emphasis. S.L., Interview), a condition which he then disliked while at the point of the interview he described them in an ambivalent manner as both "pivotal" and "lacking seriousness." A certain level of cautiousness toward young rock music fans was evident at the 1978 congress as well. A delegate named Thrassos maintained that: "Rock music is the American Way of Life. We will not become earring-wearing hippies. We are Greek Communists and not American intellectuals." He came from the lower-middle and working-class district of Kallithea. It seems, as in the case of pubs and bars, which some Eurocommunists from these areas continued to employ a normative language which was detested by the better-educated and upper-middle class students who influenced the official language of RF.[87]

However, the failure to communicate not only with most young rockers, but the diverse youngsters who were not aligned with a political group in general, can also be attributed to a factor inherent in the very effort to modify the ideological discourse of RF. In seeking complexity in cultural products in order to problematize the "progressive"/"reactionary" dichotomy as simplistic and therefore redundant, the young Eurocommunists ended up establishing different forms of classification. Actually, they sometimes became cautious, even dismissive, of settings, which they did not regard as conducive to a complex understanding of art. A telling case is that of open-air cinemas, which operated during the summer. At these venues, a broad range of films was screened. Interviewees O.Y. and N.T., male, students, RF member and cadre in the mid–1970s, respectively, narrated that the open-air cinemas provided them with the opportunity to watch many Greek political movies, which they had missed during the winter period (N.T., Interview; O.Y., Interview). Nevertheless, another young Eurocommunist, Vassilis Kapsambelis, argued in *Thourios* against open-air cinemas, maintaining that "whether it's a western or crime movie, porn or comedy, the audience watches everything while making jokes, smoking cigarettes and being indifferent. Open-air cinemas are the mass culture of the youth, like *Fantasio*."[88]

The other case was that of the discotheques. In all RF publications, only one source, namely the proceedings of the first RF congress, held in 1978, acknowledged that young Eurocommunists partook in club culture: Petros, a young worker and technical school student, mentioned that in the very little time he could dedicate to leisure, he visited a discotheque or a club.[89] However, the usual approach of the young Eurocommunists was substantially different. Members of RF took issue with the disco music that many discotheques played. Drawing on the debate between *rokades,* namely the rockers, and *kareklades,* the fans of disco music, the young Eurocommunists squarely aligned themselves with the former. Both the narration and the facial expressions of O.Y., male, student, and member of RF in the mid–1970s, or the interview as a deep exchange,[90] following the definition by Hilwig, are telling: "Disco? What are you talking about? This was a crime: this was profane!" (O.Y., Interview). While making this claim, he smiled, moderating the harshness that the terms he used carried. Still, he felt that he needed to conform to the "high intellectual standards" of his comrades, as he described them, which certainly excluded the enjoyment of disco music. Discotheques, even if they played rock, were still out of bounds. In an article published in *Thourios,* which professed "to understand," rather than to "judge" youth leisure activities, authors asserted that they felt much more comfortable in a bar than a discotheque, where people "did not develop any real communication, danced with each other, but without speaking, showing off their trendy clothes."[91] Discussion, whether as a means to analyze politics or even make fun or offer a complex analysis of a film, was an essential leisure pursuit of the young Eurocommunists. If dancing was not accompanied by a reflection on "sexual taboos," as apparently happened often in the discotheques, for young Eurocommunists it was no longer time apart but time wasted. While they aimed to dispense with a didactic language, when dealing with the leisure pursuits of youngsters that were not aligned to a political organization, young Eurocommunists continued in practice to be skeptical to a great extent toward the latter. Such lingering cautiousness seriously impeded their contact.

Turbulent Times: The Emergence of Choros

The efforts of the young Eurocommunists described earlier lay in reshaping the structure of a political youth organization, while sustaining an apparatus consisting of higher and lower ranks. In 1978, however, a very loosely organized network of groups and individuals emerged that criticized the organizational structure of left-wing youth groups, glossing them "hierarchical," or, most commonly, "bureaucratic."

In the late 1970s, left-wing organizations, while retaining their predominance in the universities and, at least as far as the KNE was concerned, some strength among young workers, were torn by a wave of splits and defections. The most serious split occurred in the case of RF, when, in the spring of 1978, the supporters of the "opposition" left the organization and created the EKON RF B Panelladiki. The latter acquired its title from its founding congress, which it named the B Panelladiki Syndiaskepsi (Second Panhellenic Conference), in order to demonstrate continuity with the first conference of the united RF held in 1976. In common with the central council majority, the members of the "opposition" demanded a "Communist renewal" through a distancing from the USSR, but they condemned the tactics of the "broadest possible anti-dictatorial unity" and "structural reforms." They accused the central council majority and, subsequently, RF, and especially the KKE Es., of adopting a *technocratic* line, which aimed at reforming state institutions; thus, it failed to confront the condition of *astikos eksynchronismos* (bourgeois modernization), which, as the internal opposition within RF had claimed in the preceding years, asserted that was predominant in Greece in this period. B Panelladiki argued that, ultimately, the reformed institutions would serve the capitalist system, having incorporated social groups that had been radicalized in the preceding years, such as the youth.[92] To the demand of the "gradual deepening of democracy" that would eventually lead to socialism, they counterposed a "revolutionary rupture" which would dispense with *entaxi* (incorporation) into the capitalist system.[93]

A notable event that precipitated the split was the occupation of the University of Patras in 1978. In January 1978, turmoil broke out in this institution, which initially took the form of class abstentions and extended in

March 1978 to the occupation of the university building in the city. The ma-jor demand of the protestors was framed as *metafora/katochirosi*: they claimed that students should not be required to pass all examinations every year in order to register for courses in the subsequent academic year. The Maoist or-ganizations AASPE and PPSP supported the occupation, as did the Demo-cratic Struggle, the RF-affiliated student group, which in that university was controlled by the "opposition."[94] They all argued that a stricter system of assessment and the resulting atmosphere of intense studying accommodated the "incorporation" of students.[95] The RF leadership condemned the deci-sion of the Democratic Struggle in Patras, however, arguing that only a tiny minority of students endorsed the occupation.[96]

The tensions increased in spring 1978. Those RF cadres and members who organized the Second Panhellenic Conference were automatically ex-pelled from the organization, because the majority of the central council did not recognize that conference as legitimate. The expelled young Euro-communists accused the KKE Es. and RF, which they termed "the KKE Es. Youth," of being bureaucratic institutions, similar to the KNE and KKE, since, despite their official language, they despised dissenting views. Con-cerning their number, estimates by the central council of RF indicate that the majority of the university students of the group, at least in Athens, joined B Panelladiki. Just after the parliamentary elections on 20 November 1977, there were about 700 university student RF members in Athens; only 230 remained after the split, with 250–300 estimated to have switched to the splinter group.[97]

What emerged out of this split was something novel in Greek experi-ence: a political youth group not affiliated with any Party. In fact, during the previous decades, left-wing youth groups without official links to any Party, such as Syndesmos Neon dia ton Pyrinikon Afoplismon Bertrand Russell, had appeared in Greece. Nevertheless, at least some of their members were aligned with a Party or its youth organization. By contrast, the members of B Panelladiki had no ties with any of the existing ones. Similarly, the few members of the KKE Es. who followed B Panelladiki—Vernardakis argues that they were about 300—refrained from creating a new Party.[98] Indeed, in what Vernardakis describes as the first period of B Panelladiki, namely from May 1978 until August 1979, its members tried to establish a new left-wing organization with Sosialistiki Poreia (Socialist Course) and the EDA (United Democratic Left).[99] However, these efforts did not prove fruitful. Meanwhile, from its inception, members of B Panelladiki debated the issue whether it should adopt a rigid organizational model based on democratic centralism, or a looser one, diffusing its activities across wider autonomous groups. A small section of the group, including Maounis, argued for the former, whereas a somewhat bigger contingent, including Kostas Livieratos and Giannis Gouzoulis, was in favor of the latter. The majority, however, which included Dimitris Psarras, advocated a middle ground. It was mainly during and after the 1979 occupations, which are analyzed below in detail, when in practice B Panelladiki became less visible as a distinct force; its members participated in common student groups, cultural societies and high-school pupil magazines alongside former members of other Socialist and Communist groups.

Internal strife spilled over into the Maoist organizations as well. This was not a Greek exception: since the death of Mao and the prevalence of Deng Xiaoping as well as the line that supported an opening to market-economy reforms in China, Maoists in Western Europe were at a loss how to approach the Party that until then served as their role model. In the case of West Germany, this shift was a reason of growing disenchantment among young Maoists; consequently, Maoist organizations gradually petered out.[100] In the case of Greece, the EKKE and its student group, the AASPE, experienced the most serious turbulences. The group accused both New Democracy and the KKE of being mouthpieces of the United States and the USSR, respectively. Drawing on the theory of the "three worlds," it portrayed China as leading the genuine "socialist" forces. However, the direction that China followed after Mao's death did not seem to confirm this line in the eyes of many of its members. The latter began to grumble that the Party had become a mouthpiece of China in a process they called *akolouthitismos.* However, their concerns fell on deaf ears, since their leadership continued to construe the Communist Party of China as its role model. As a result, numerous members withdrew from the EKKE and AASPE.[101]

The Youth of PASOK did not escape bitter infighting in the mid–to-late 1970s. Actually, the organization witnessed two massive expulsions of members in 1976 and in 1980. Members who had been expelled in 1980 or had since then disagreed with the leadership of the organization created in 1981 the *Kinisi gia tin stratigiki tou PASOK sto foititiko kinima* (Initiative for the strategy of the PASOK in the student movement), which was active only in the early 1980s. The Youth of PASOK reacted harshly toward them, naming them "vagabonds": since they no longer participated in PASOK, they were not entitled, according to the Youth of PASOK, to use its name.[102] The Kinisi rallied most of its members among students in Salonica, but, still, failed to gain momentum. In the university student elections that took place in Salonica in 1981, it harvested 2.9 percent of the vote, while in 1982 only 1.9 percent.[103]

In the case of the KNE, there was not such a serious split, but the organization did not escape resignations. No overarching reason can explain the defections from the pro-Soviet group. In the late 1970s, various members no longer attributed what they viewed as the failings of the group to particular cadres. Their critique became more penetrating and began to problematize the very ideological discourse of the group. The magazine *ANTI* is a valuable source for the understanding of the turmoil within the KNE, since it published many letters by young Communists who renounced it in this period. It appears that in 1979 many members in the Egaleo and Kallithea districts in Athens resigned.[104] A.M, male, high school pupil residing in Kallithea, was one of them. He argued that he had hitherto been a "zealot." However, in late 1978, when the police arrested a 17-year-old pupil, who was distributing KKE electoral material, he was disillusioned by the failure of the Party to actively seek his release. This stance triggered the anger of many pro-USSR Communists, who were in the same local branch as the pupil. A.M. narrates: "[F]or us, the Party seemed no longer reliable. It was not yet another insignificant shortcoming; it was not the mistake of a specific cadre. It was the Party itself that functioned in a problematic way" (A.M., Interview).

One of the apparently biggest splits in the KNE occurred in 1980, when about 400 members and cadres of the KNE and KKE signed a common declaration, the so-called "Text of the 400," explaining the reasons why they resigned from the organization.[105] The "400" were a rather heterogeneous group: some of them moved toward RF, while a segment ended their active involvement in politics. What is remarkable, not only in the "Text of the 400," but also in many letters to *ANTI* and in the testimonies that I have gathered, is the vocabulary employed to explain the disagreements with the KNE and KKE. The circulation of concepts such as "integration" into the capitalist system, "Puritanism," and "bureaucracy," which surfaced in the debates among left-wingers in the late 1970s, made some young pro-USSR Communists look afresh at their membership and attribute their particular negative experiences to the same issues.

From 1978 and 1979, many of those former members of RF, the KNE, the Youth of PASOK, AASPE, and PPSP, started forming Choros, a loose network of student groups and cultural associations. Still, young left-wingers who left or had been expelled from Socialist and Communist youth groups in the late 1970s and early 1980s did not necessarily participate in Choros: *Kinisi gia tin stratigiki tou PASOK sto foititiko kinima,* for instance, never joined the network. The student groups of Choros usually bore the title "autonomous" and were not aligned with any Party. Such a case was the AOFA (Aytonomi Omada Foititon ASOEE, Autonomous Groups of Students of the ASOEE), which also published its own newspaper, *Ta Nea*[106] (The News). B Panelladiki initially established its own student groups, called DA-APK (Dimokratikos Agonas-Anexartities Proodeytikes Kiniseis, Democratic

Struggle-Independent Progressive Movements). In general, the latter did not go on the electoral slate of DA-DE, the RF-leaning student group, although there were some certain exceptions.[107] However, DA-APK proved short-lived and, as is shown below in detail, B Panelladiki soon began to participate in the "autonomous" student groups alongside the rest of Choros.[108]

Choros also included some cultural societies in the universities from 1978, which were guided neither by the PAPOK nor by student administrative councils. The most notable one was the FOKTH (Foititikos Omilos Kinimatografou kai Theatrou, Student Club of Cinema and Theatre) in the Law School of Athens. The latter not only attracted participants in Choros, but also members of RF. Its activity extended to various arts. The FOKTH presented a number of plays, such as a selection of one-act plays by Karl Valentin in 1979.[109] According to a student magazine in the Law School, *Ioulos,* it also held a *rebetiko* concert as well as a concert of Joan Baez music in the same year.[110] As in the case of RF, B Panelladiki and Choros managed to establish only a limited number of student cultural societies in the universities. However, again like the Eurocommunist youth group, Choros proved more successful in accommodating the circulation of the work of rock bands, which appeared in the late 1970s, especially through the institution of the "weeks of student cultural work." This institution had arisen just after the collapse of the dictatorship, but the rivalries between Eurocommunists and pro-USSR Communists resulted in its termination in 1977. Following the joint efforts of Eurocommunist and autonomous students, it resumed in 1979, without the participation, however, of the student cultural societies which were controlled by the KNE. In 1979, a number of amateur bands, alongside one of the most popular—and politicized—professional Greek rock bands, Spyridoula, appeared.[111]

The participants in Choros described themselves as being bound together by the attitude of *amfisvitisi* (challenging). Its definition resonated with the concept of "mechanisms of integration" developed by supporters of the "left-wing opposition" in RF in the mid–1970s, which in turn derived from structuralist Marxist analyses on the ideological state apparatuses. Situationism, expressed in quotations from Guy Debord, also gained a degree of influence among Choros participants. Situationist ideas had been introduced in Greece by the anarchist magazine *Pezodromio* (Pavement) already in the early 1970s. Although the Situationists never commanded strong support among Greek youth, many interviewees, like O.T., male, pupil and cadre of KNE until 1977, and participant in Choros since 1978, remembered having read their work (O.T., Interview).[112]

The young autonomous left-wingers lambasted various avenues of what they construed as incorporation/integration into the capitalist system. They mainly targeted Law 815, introduced in August 1978, which brought changes to the structure of the university schools and to the system of student assessment. The "intensification of studies" also figured prominently in their rhetoric. Every faculty was divided into *tomeis* (sub-faculties), which would comprise at least five academic chairs. It also foresaw the limited participation of students in the decision-making of the faculties. As regards the examination system, the examination periods were reduced from three to two (with one additional for the final-year students). Finally, if students failed three or more examinations in the second period of every year, they had to repeat all the courses of that academic year. If they failed in two or more examinations twice, they would be expelled from the university.[113]

The enactment of Law 815 brought to the fore the two different strategies that were followed by left-wing youth groups. The KNE, RF, and the Youth of PASOK oriented the struggle toward postponing the immediate implementation of the law, with a view to achieving its abolition in the near future. Meanwhile, they both put forth alternative plans, such as the "Democratic Constitutional Charter" in the case of the KNE and KKE. These plans foresaw the abolition of academic chairs as well as the significant participation of students in the decision-making process of the faculties.[114] On the contrary, the AASPE and PPSP on the one hand and B Panelladiki and the autonomous student groups, on the other, were against the proposition of reforms. They supported the rallying of students around the demand for the immediate abolition of Law 815. In addition, they concentrated almost exclusively on the changes brought to the system of assessment. They argued that this would result in the easier incorporation of the students into the capitalist system. Studying would become more intense, as students would dedicate more time in order to prepare themselves for examinations; they would have little time or strength to reflect on the orientation and the flaws of the education system. Such purported disciplining sounded an unacceptable condition for militants enamored of challenging.

In challenging established left-wing politics, Choros participants did not call the role of the "working class" as the agent of social transformation into question; discussions about "integration" did not substitute, but actually complemented lengthy analyses of the "modes of production" and the condition of the workers in Greece, especially in *Agonas gia tin Kommounistiki Ananeosi*.[115] However, a small segment within Choros, which revolved around the radical left-wing group OPA (Organosi gia mia Proletariaki Aristera, Organization for a Proletarian Left) reconceptualized the term "working class" in age-specific terms. Its magazine, *Rixi*, provided extensive coverage of the squatters' movement in Switzerland, especially in Zurich and Amsterdam. It argued that the young people involved were the "social proletariat": they were unemployed and often excluded from educational institutions.[116] Their demands did not gravitate around "solidarity with the Third World" or the "making of the socialist state," but were connected with issues, such as leisure, family relations, police violence, and the operation of nuclear plants.[117]

The appearance of Choros marked the emergence of a new cleavage in the Greek political scene. Young autonomous left-wingers did not describe themselves as yet another "progressive" or "democratic" force. They did not pay even lip service to achieving unity with left-wing forces that they lambasted as "bureaucratic," which is especially manifest in the way in which they treated the EFEE, the National Student Union of Greece. Never had the very functioning of the student union been so loudly attacked by a left-wing group since the collapse of the dictatorship. Choros participants claimed that the body functioned as a "student parliament," serving the narrow interests of the Parties involved.[118] Similarly, Choros mounted a loud critique of particular left-wing organizations: the KNE epitomized everything they despised. The Eurocommunist youth organization and the Youth of PASOK also served as negative symbols. The KNE and the Socialist youth group responded in kind. The former was crystal clear in denouncing the participants in the network as "agents provocateurs" of the government. Publications of the pro-Soviet Communist youth referred to groups of "anarchoaristeristes" (anarcholeftists) or "anarchoautonomoi" (anarchoautonomous), which were inspired by magazines, such as *Rixi*, and which were approached by B Panelladiki, which, according to the KNE, had developed a similar ideological orientation.[119] The Youth of PASOK was rather skeptical toward B Panelladiki, too: young Socialists argued that dismantling the structures of the EFEE and "bowing to spontaneity" would bring confusion to "democratic" students and will strengthen their opponents.[120] This rift within the left-wing youth would appear in full force in late 1979, as will be discussed in detail.

Appreciating Perplexity in Memory and Culture

The autonomous left-wingers also criticized strongly behavioral patterns which they argued bred "conformity" with and "incorporation" into the capitalist system, but which the Left had been purportedly promoting. Based on *amfisvitisi,* participants in Choros extended their critique to the concept of "Greek popular tradition." In general, they argued that the Left treated this concept as a "fetish." A number of members of B Panelladiki, such as Diamantis Mpasantis, Kostas Livieratos, and Giannis Gouzoulis, published articles on this in *Agonas gia tin Kommounistiki Ananeosi.*[121] They maintained that "traditional" patterns developed in particular historical conditions and were inextricably linked with feudal and capitalist relations. Thus, they lambasted the approach of the KNE and KKE as "mere folklorism." Young autonomous left-wingers went further and decried any form of demarcation of a "progressive culture." Other publications of the B Panelladiki maintained that the construction of a "progressive culture" is an "idiotic pursuit."[122] These concerns were not expressed merely by the members of B Panelladiki, but were articulated by various publications of Choros in general. Those asserted that the pro-Soviet Communist Party and its youth group aimed at constructing "passive recipients of their messages," who relied on purported "experts" and suppressed their initiative. Regardless of the content of these "messages," this act facilitated apathy and "integration" into the system. A magazine published by Choros participants in Koukaki, Athens, likened the dominant cultural politics of the Left with the commercial TV shows, blaming them both for promoting monologue: "we are just recipients: of songs, show, stars, ideology."[123] Still, the autonomous young left-wingers did not put forward a clear alternative to those concepts. Choros' texts represented an incomplete, inconsistent collective self, or a "subject in motion," which was the outcome of the desire not to resemble the "parliamentary Left" on the one hand and an inability to articulate a different model on the other. The autonomous left-wingers usually articulated how they did *not* want to act. As Ersi Hadjiargirou argued in *Agonas gia tin Kommounistiki Ananeosi*: "We do not know how to run the cultural societies and whether they could be established again. We are searching for [the answer] through critique, self-critique and dialogue."[124]

Concomitantly, in comparison to the young Eurocommunists, B Panelladiki members developed a much more radical approach toward the culture of commemoration that had emerged in the initial post-dictatorship years. Most notably, they criticized the ritualization of the memory of the wartime Resistance in the early 1940s and of the Polytechnic Uprising (1973). They claimed that they were efforts to "subordinate" history to an eschatological meta-narrative that vindicated the guidelines of left-wing Parties, an act that reproduced "bureaucratic" relations. Writing in *Agonas gia tin Kommounistiki Ananeosi*, Gouzoulis argued that: "The Party must prove its capacity for struggle [and] its historical continuity. Thus, it resorts to the worst exploitation of the historical memory of the people ... It portrays history as existing outside real social conflicts, as a series of heroic acts and sacrifices ... It aims at the passive reception ... of the distorted version of history it offers."[125] A couple of B Panelladiki members, Kalas and Mastrantonis, went further to claim that such a commemoration had religious connotations: "It follows the same pattern as the representation of the Divine Drama; ascendance, fall, betrayal, comeback, victory, to mention the main points."[126] Voicing a vehement critique of this "instrumentalization" of time, as they labeled it, the members of B Panelladiki and the participants in Choros lacked a coherent collective memory that would give meaning to their activity.

Still, they were particularly fascinated with youth protest in Western Europe and the United States in the late 1960s, especially the "French May." Images and texts as well as accounts of "May 1968" spread through a variety of channels in Greece in the late 1970s. In 1978, grasping the opportunity afforded by the lapse of ten years since the youth revolts in Western Europe, the magazine *ANTI* published a number of articles about the aftermath of the "May" uprisings in France, as well as a number of leaflets distributed by the Movement 22 March[127] and the Trotskyites (JCR, *Jeunesse communiste révolutionnaire, Revolutionary Communist Youth*).[128] Most articles had in common the line of argument that, even though the uprisings did not topple the political status quo, they "shook established social and political norms." An additional source seems to have been the accounts of Greek students, who were in Paris in May 1968. One such narrative, by Michalis Papagiannakis, appeared in *Thourios,* the newspaper of RF, in 1978, as part of a retrospective of the 1968 rebellion in France. Throughout the Greek discussion of 1968 France was almost the exclusive center of attention. Representations of "1968" appeared in the publications of Choros as well. For the young autonomous left-wingers, they served as metaphors, apparently signifying the protest of the network against *ensomatosi* (integration). However, the participants in Choros did not portray "1968" as the substitute for the "partisan activity in the 1940s." Reflecting their disavowal of role models in general, the young autonomous left-wingers recalled 1968 in a fragmented fashion, through scattered images or slogans that appeared in their texts.[129] Those were not linked in an explicit way with the content of the text they supplemented. Sometimes, the very fact that these representations emanated from the youth revolts of 1968 in Western Europe was not even mentioned, as these images and slogans were employed without attribution. Such a use of symbols of 1968 is evident in the poster of the student group of B Panelladiki in 1979, which included the slogan "intensification, intensification, integration."[130]

Another similar case was the front page of the B Panelladiki founding charter, which featured the image of a young woman from the French May, without attribution and without any further reference to that particular youth revolt in the text itself.[131] In the publications of Choros, there are very few explicit references to or detailed analyses of the French May and its exact significance for the young autonomous left-wingers. While young autonomous left-wingers may have avoided attribution, judging that the origin of those symbols was well-known to the people they addressed, they never

Figure 4.3. Poster of the student group of B Panelladiki, 1979. *Source:* G. Floros, "Symperasmata apo tis foititikes ekloges," *Agonas gia tin Kommounistiki Ananeosi,* 6 May 1979, p. 7. Used with permission from Dimitris Psarras.

openly label their activity as the Greek equivalent to "1968."[132] In the meantime, while Choros participants eagerly appropriated images and slogans of
"1968," they largely failed or were indifferent to getting synchronized with
protest movements that had erupted in other European countries in the late
1970s. Rarely did their texts mention, for example, the "Movimento del
'77," which appeared in Italy in 1977, initiated by the extra-parliamentary
Left.[133] An exception seems to be the references to the squatters' movement
in Amsterdam and Zurich that appeared in *Rixi*, as mentioned above.

Another very important symbol for the members of B Panelladiki as
well as for the Choros participants in general emanated from the recent
Greek history: the Polytechnic Uprising in 1973. Its memory was not as
fragmented as that of "1968." Despite their differences with KNE, the Youth
of PASOK, and RF, the autonomous young left-wingers participated in the
annual march that took place on the anniversary of the Polytechnic Uprising on 17 November. In 1980 the march was marred by police violence. In
particular, the government decided that protestors would not be allowed to
pass in front of the U.S. embassy in Athens, a decision with which PASOK
and the KKE complied. Choros, alongside the Maoists, RF, and the KKE
Es., defied it. The police dispersed them and killed two protestors: the Cypriot student Iakovos Koumis and the young worker Stamatina Kanellopou-
lou.[134] Apart from their stance toward legal restrictions, there was another
telling difference in the way young autonomous left-wingers conceived of
the commemoration of the Polytechnic Uprising. For them, it was not another "moment" in a grand narrative that lauded the "militant character"
of the "Greek people" or the "effective organization of the struggle by the
Communist Party," but part of a memory that teemed with discontinuities and uncertainties. In this vein, they loudly criticized the slogan "EAM-
ELAS-Polytechneio" which left-wingers had used in the previous years. The
student rebellion against the dictatorship signified for them a "rupture" with
Party politics in the Left and their conciliatory stance. In a number of articles
Chrysanthos Lazaridis, member of B Panelladiki, stated that this uprising
was a cut-off point with what the author viewed as the rationale behind the
activity of the Left in post–Civil War Greece: the privileging of broader alliances that included some of the political expressions of the bourgeois class,
as well as the condemnation of every initiative that favored a direct confrontation with the regime.[135] However, the collapse of the authoritarian regime
had ushered in an era of Party politics with the protagonists of the Polytechnic Uprising joining the main political Parties of the Left and their youth
organization. This, as Lazaridis asserted, had tamed their confrontational
approach and led some of the militants to reinvent themselves as "bureau-
crats." As a result, according to another member of B Panelladiki, Giannis

Floros, the "parliamentary" Left held commemorations of the rebellion that failed to pose any threat to the status quo. To these "museum" events, as he called them, he counterposed the decision of Choros to defy the limitations imposed on the march of 17 November 1980.[136]

The adoption of an "emotionology" that aimed at eliminating "bureaucratic" aspects of politics that suppressed "spontaneity" and "initiative," extended to the leisure activities of the participants in Choros as well. In contrast with the KNE, even with RF, young autonomous left-wingers could hardly be described as pursuing particular cultural politics in the sense of the implementation of official decisions. The RF central council, which aimed at instilling "imagination" into politics, often published extensive texts clarifying to its members how to achieve this result. On the contrary, there were indeed relevant articles in Choros publications, which was nothing more than the expression of the personal viewpoint of the contributor. On no account were they relegated to the status of the official line, which had to be followed by all members.

In any case, rock music was one of the favorite cultural products of autonomous left-wingers.[137] According to a number of articles and interviews, they associated this music genre with youth protest movements that had emerged in the 1960s in the United States and in Western European countries.[138] As researchers of cultural appropriation would describe, drawing on the Birmingham School of Cultural Studies, Choros participants were active consumers that received rock music through a process of "bricolage": they "reaccented, rearticulated or trans-coded the material of mass culture to their own ends."[139] E.Q., male, high-ranking RF cadre until 1978, and member of B Panelladiki from 1978 to 1982, narrated that he listened to the "rock music of the Who, Jimi Hendrix and the Doors," which he called the "music of May '68." Of course, this connection could partially be attributed to the fact that the interview was conducted in 2008, the fortieth anniversary of the French May. It was a period that teemed with relevant discussions, which may have tempted the narrator to ground this aspect of his testimony on that event. Besides that, however, texts produced by Choros participants in the late 1970s also employed the link of late 1960s rock music with "Woodstock" and "1968"; nevertheless, they were rather evasive in analyzing the reasons why they established this link. While empathizing with the young rebels of the late 1960s in France or the United States through listening to rock music, participants in Choros, similar to RF members, did not signify this experience as helping transform them into dedicated militants of a "Greek May." Rock denoted norms that they opposed and not a particular framework that they endorsed. As argued in *Aythaireta,* the Athens area newspaper of B Panelladiki:

[T]hose forces that the crisis in the Left is unleashing ... need, besides their new political identity, a different form of leisure. It is this need that brings them close to rock music ... From the certainties of conformity to the contemplation of *rixi* [rupture]. From the demand for an alternative, democratic Law 815 to the occupations. ... That is how a homogeneous public is constructed. A public aware of the limits of music, which learns to entertain itself neither with the dance of the revolution nor with the dance of forgetting.[140]

In various Choros publications, the collective singing of partisan songs is described as epitomizing the period of the mid–1970s. This was an era of left-wing activity that, in their view, had failed to become really subversive and produced many "fake rebels" who had been co-opted and "cared about nothing else than their job." The shift of the youth to rock music, they argued, was one of the factors that marked it end and heralded the emergence of a "new anti-capitalist movement"—disregarding, however, the fact that several young rockers were not actively involved in politics.[141] Nevertheless, young autonomous left-wingers were ambivalent about the development of rock music from the 1970s, describing it as having been "co-opted" and "commercialized."[142] Consequently, some Choros participants shifted in 1980 to punk music, which, in a number of articles, they represented as an expression of a desirable "disharmony" against the "professionalization" of rock and its control by the cultural industry.[143] The young autonomous left-wingers seemed to appreciate what the punks in Greece and worldwide considered to be the core element of their subculture: provocation. The tiny subculture of Greek punk fans in the late 1970s wore safety pins and razor blades as jewelry and wore Mohawk haircuts, in a move familiar to their counterparts worldwide. Punk would actually reach its apogee in Greece somewhat later, in the first half of the 1980s. Many, but not all, young punks mingled with anarchist groups in squats that emerged since 1981 at the center of Athens and Salonica. Still, some of them adorned their clothes with the symbol of Swastika, not as a means of expressing their dedication to National Socialist ideals, but, once again, as an act of provocation.[144]

Besides rock, young autonomous left-wingers were also sympathetic toward the work of Savvopoulos, which they experienced as subversive due to its form and content. They described the fact the he mixed Greek folk with rock music as "original" and a "rejection" of the taxonomy of cultural products into "progressive" and "reactionary." Like RF, Choros prized the heterogeneity of tastes in its publications. This heterogeneity was no longer merely an issue of lifestyle practices, as in the early 1970s; being a "subject in motion" was embraced in Choros publications as a per se nonconformist stance.

As K.V. Dimitriou argued, "it is key to anybody who does not want to follow a conventional ideological approach to try and gather fragments and create a novel form of expression. The originality of the work of Savvopoulos and his contribution to art is the very fact that he has brought together cultural patterns that seemed to be incompatible … Greek folk song, rebetiko, pop and rock, to name some of them."[145] The young autonomous left-wingers usually preferred his album *Rezerva,* especially verses from the song "My white-blue mouse." An extract from *Aythaireta* gives a clear example: employing a phrase by Savvopoulos, it models the life-stories of Choros participants on the story described in the song, namely moving from "insularity of the manifestos" to the "bar that stays open overnight."[146] Again, as in the case of rock, Savvopoulos' music would not be praised for pointing toward a precisely defined alternative model. As *Rixi* stated, "Savvopoulos does not offer easy solutions to exhausted militants. He has rejected the "drugs that his friends are offering him," the "Party," and love as a solution to all problems. He does not let us rest! His songs are full of complex meanings."[147] And this was the reason why they were enamored of him: because his work carried a subversive quality that called into question, rather than constructed taxonomies.

The challenging of cultural taxonomies that had been set by the Left rendered them prone to problematizing the very concept of "heroes and martyrs," whose biographies had appeared en masse after 1974. Growingly skeptical of the role models of collective struggle—real or abstract figures that were active in Greece from the 1930s to the 1970s, especially during the wartime Resistance—Choros participants became fascinated by socially marginal groups or individuals, such as outcasts or bohemians. To be clear, rather than adopting their lifestyle, the young autonomous left-wingers resorted to them in order to portray themselves as "politically marginal." Choros participants experienced this status as both positive and negative. On the one hand, it signified their resistance to the "technocratic" and "bureaucratic" Left; on the other, it sparked an emotion of isolation and a concomitant melancholy, which runs through many of their texts from the late 1970s alongside the stories narrated nowadays by its former participants. The positive and the negative facet are both captured in the metaphors used by participants in Choros, in order to describe themselves as detached from Party politics, especially *exodos* (exit) and *syntrimmia* (ruins). Similarly, O.Y., male, member of B Panelladiki, remembers that "we were people beaten by the police, persecuted by the KNE … many had the psychology of the defeated" (O.Y., Interview). This emotion does not only appear in the oral testimonies of B Panelladiki members and other Choros participants. It was also reinforced through identification of anti-heroes in the cultural products that Choros participants appreciated. K.V. Dimitriou argued in *Agonas gia tin Kommou-*

nistiki Ananeosi that those young left-wingers, who refused to be uncritical followers of a particular Party, ended up feeling "isolated" and identifying themselves with "heretic" authors, such as Aris Alexandrou.[148] Young autonomous left-wingers were enamored with Alexandrou due to his life and his work. In the late 1940s and the 1950s, he was sent to detention centers for political prisoners, where, however, he encountered the hostility of his left-wing co-exiles.[149] Having been vehemently critical of the cultural policies of the Soviet Union in the late 1940s, he was punished with "isolation" by the other Communists who were imprisoned in Limnos, which meant that none of them were prepared to discuss with him.[150] Choros participants praised his uncompromising stance, even under those stern conditions of imprisonment, toward the Party apparatus.[151] The young autonomous left-wingers also appreciated his novel *To Kivotio* (The Mission Box), which was published in Greek in 1975 by Kedros. The book refers to the end of the Civil War in Greece. In contrast with the official line of the main left-wing organizations in Greece in the 1970s, Alexandrou does not approach this era from the perspective of the victimization of the left-wing partisans but from a rather self-critical standpoint. The novel describes the itinerary of a number of left-wing partisans who have been given the task by the Communist Party leadership to transport a box from one city to another. Those partisans are unaware of its content. In the end, their mission fails to materialize, as all of them die with the exception of the narrator. The latter opens the box, only to discover that it was empty. D. Mpasantis, a B Panelladiki member, in his review of *Kivotio,* lauded the author for illuminating a number of problematic aspects of Communist practice, which were not specific only to the Civil War years, but also applied to the post-dictatorship years: the bureaucratic structure and the discouragement of initiative.[152]

Another cultural pattern that facilitated the identification with the social fringe was a trend that appeared in Greek cinematic production in the late 1970s. Nikos Nikolaidis's *Ta Kourelia Tragoudane Akoma* (The Wrecked Are Still Singing, 1979) described the nostalgia of a group of middle-aged Greeks for their youth and the 1950s. Nikos Zervos's *Exoristos stin Kentriki Leoforo* (Exiled in the Central Avenue, 1979) portrayed a protagonist, metaphorically wandering in an avenue, struggling to find the ultimate truth in his profession, politics, and sexual emancipation, but always without success. These movies were not extremely popular, but, still, made an impact: *Ta Kourelia Tragoudane Akoma* sold 47,900 tickets in Athens, Piraeus, and their districts in the winter season 1979–1980, while *Exoristos stin Kentriki Leoforo* 16,010 in the same period and in the same areas.[153] They certainly did not address high politics and their tone was particularly pessimistic. Danikas, the film reviewer of *Rizospastis,* was very critical of both of them:

he lambasted the director of *Exoristos* for promoting the identification with drug consumption, pessimism, and individualism in the main part of the film.[154] By contrast, young autonomous left-wingers found those movies inspiring. Some of them narrated that they captured the emotions they felt at that point. I.A., a female university student in the late 1970s, member of the Youth of PASOK until 1980, and Choros participant subsequently, recounted that "we glorified the marginal: *Ta Kourelia* expresses this element. *Ta Kourelia* is the challenging (*amfisvitisi*) of everything, an emotion of decadence, a melancholy, which existed in our lives" (I.A., Interview).[155]

To an extent *rebetiko* music served as another means that helped Choros participants portray themselves as "politically marginal'" In a sense, their stance resembled the "mystique of marginality" approach of the Greek Left to *rebetiko* in the 1920s. As O.T., male, student and Choros participant from 1978, narrates: "[I]n 1978 we discovered some cassettes with old rebetiko songs, about cannabis dens. [For us they seemed to] combine the aspect of the social fringe with the challenging of Party politics, especially the style of the KNE and KKE. That's why we, the autonomous students, loved these songs" (O.T., Interview). This approach was the reason why Mikis Theodorakis, while praising *rebetiko* in *Techni kai Politismos*,[156] the magazine of the PAPOK, took it upon himself to lambast the autonomous left-wingers for "assigning" to it "a wrong meaning." The composer accused them of denoting this genre as the musical expression of the "free and militant citizen," whom they juxtaposed with the people, who were aligned with a Party.[157]

However, Choros participants did not listen solely to *rebetiko* songs with references to the "underworld," but, alike members of RF, the KNE and the Youth of PASOK, their preferences would extend to what they called "classic" or "old" *rebetiko* songs in general, meaning those that were produced in the interwar period. They would juxtapose this era with the postwar *rebetiko* production in Greece, namely the *arhontorebetiko* genre, which they also described as close to the commercial mainstream. The Communist and Socialist youth also appreciated dancing to "old" *rebetiko* in the late 1970s. This shift extended to groups of unaffiliated younger and older people as well. In addition to the type of tavernas, that had been the cornerstone of left-wing youth leisure since the early 1970s, the so-called *rebetadika* appeared from the early 1980s, with Douzeni and Taximi being two prominent cases in Athens. *Rebetadika* attracted young left-wingers of diverse persuasions, but their patrons were not necessarily active in politics. Meanwhile, resonating with the revived interest in the so-called "authentic" *rebetiko* that had appeared in Greece in the late 1960s, music bands playing *rebetiko* of the Interwar period, called *kompanies,* had begun to spread in Athens and Salonica from the mid–1970s onward. Later, they performed onstage in *rebetadika* as well. Opisthodromiki and Athinaiki Kompania were some notable bands.[158] *Rebetadika* were places where people could eat and drink, but also dance, mainly the *zeibekiko*. The latter was initially associated with heterosexual "manliness." Men danced the *zeibekiko* individually, improvising while following the rhythm of *rebetiko* songs. The dance denoted "authenticity," purportedly expressing the "profound" emotions of *dalgas* (grief) and *kefi*. For the young left-wingers in the late 1970s, however, *zeibekiko* was not necessarily connected with men. In many oral testimonies of young left-wingers of all persuasions, male and female, it was depicted as appropriate for the expression of the emotions of women as well. Tsitsanis himself appeared to approve of women dancing *zeibekiko* in the same period. In his album *12 nees laikes dimiourgies* (12 new popular creations), which was released in 1978, he included a song, in which he said that women could perform this dance even better than men.[159] Nevertheless, the transition was not necessarily as smooth as it was claimed. It is telling that hardly any female narrator remembered dancing *zeibekiko* in the 1970s. Some male narrators, members of left-wing youth groups in the 1970s, when describing actual women dancing to *rebetiko*, recalled another dance, namely the *tsifteteli*, an Ottoman dance performed solely by women, which became popular in Greece in the 1980s.

Young pro-Soviet Communists, Maoists, Eurocommunists, autonomous left-wingers, and Socialists, they all indulged in the improvisation of *zeibekiko*. However, they conceptualized the dance in diverse ways, in accordance with their political orientation. As far as Choros were concerned, *zeibekiko* was a leisure pursuit that was juxtaposed with the collective singing of partisan songs. O.Y., male, member of B Panelladiki in the late 1970s, narrated that: "we began to enjoy ourselves, *kefi* became predominant in our leisure: we visited rebetadika very often!" (O.Y., Interview). Again, *kefi* denoted for him spontaneity that was supposed to be the antidote to the discipline espoused by the KNE. One way or another, Choros participants appreciated those cultural products, which they felt that defied the cultural taxonomies that the Greek Left endorsed and, actually, undermined such classifications, an act they deemed congruous with challenging "bureaucratic" political organizations.

Notes

1. S.A., "Tainies Tromou: Oi pliveioi tou theamatos," *Thourios*, 3 July 1980, pp. 30–31.
2. The readers of *Pop kai Rock* voted it their fifth favorite album in October 1978 and their second favorite in November 1978. "Ta 10 prota stous xenous diskous," *Pop kai Rock,* November 1978, p. 96. It was voted the third most popular disco album for the year 1979, according to another poll held by the same magazine. "No. 1 ston xeno choro," *Pop kai Rock*, etisio teychos 1979, p. 16.

3. "Kinimatografiko Etos 1978–79," *Ta Theamata*, 31 December 1979.

4. "No. 1 ston xeno choro," *Pop kai Rock*, etisio teychos 1979, p. 16.

5. "Erevna DISCO," *Odigitis*, 10 August 1979, p. 14.

6. For the case of Larissa, the relevant announcement is reprinted (and vehemently criticized) in *Odigitis*. The advertised contest would take place on 6 January 1979 at the discotheque "Garden," beginning at 7 P.M. For more, see *Odigitis*, 5 January 1979.

7. Daloukas, *Elliniko Rok*, pp. 351–55.

8. Bozinis, *Rock pagkosmiotita*, p. 200.

9. Ibid., pp. 378–80.

10. "To Rock stou Zografou," *Antiefimerida*, 1979, pp. 4–5.

11. Bozinis, *Rock pagkosmiotita*, pp. 310–15, 378–80.

12. Special volume of *Pop kai Rock* for the year 1979, p. 22. Data based on a survey conducted by the magazine. The methodology used is not discussed, however. Thus, the issue whether the sample selected for this poll was representative is subject to discussion.

13. Annual volume of *Pop kai Rock* for the year 1978, p. 22.

14. In contrast with 1978, these charts were not based on the votes of the readers of the magazine, but on the sales of the albums. See "Xena albums" in the volumes of June, July, August, September, October, and November of the magazine *Pop kai Rock*.

15. About punk-rock in Yugoslavia, see Marko Zubak, "The Yugoslav Youth Press (1968-1980): Student Movements, Subcultures and Communist Alternative Media" (PhD thesis, Central European University, Budapest 2013), pp. 207–14. About punk in the UK, see Dick Hebdige, *Subculture: The Meaning of Style* (Abingdon, NY, 2007), pp. 62–70.

16. Bozinis, *Rock pagkosmiotita*, pp. 395–414.

17. See, for instance: Letter by Mariza Andrikopoulou, *Pop kai Rock*, July 1979, p. 12. "O Sokratis ipie to koneio alla oi 'Socrates' den to vazoun kato," *Pop kai Rock*, February 1980, p. 8.

18. "Grammata," *Pop kai Rock*, November 1979, p. 14.

19. Giannis Petridis, "I rock einai sex," *Pop kai Rock*, January 1980, pp. 6–10.

20. "Chryses vradies se rythmo disco," *Synchroni Gynaika*, November–December 1979, pp. 50–51. *Synchroni Gynaika* was the magazine of the women's organization affiliated with the KKE.

21. A. Skiadopoulou, "Ntiskotek," *Ta Nea*, 5 December 1978, p. 5

22. "Ellinika sygkrotimata," *Pop kai Rock*, February 1979, p. 73; "Spyridoula," *Pop kai Rock*, October 1980, p. 111.

23. "Apopseis gia ti rock," *Thourios*, 29 May 1980.

24. About the Greek rock bands, see Daloukas, *Elliniko Rok*, pp. 351–65.

25. Kostis Moskov, "Erevna: Laikos Politismos," *ANTI*, 6 March 1976, p. 42.

26. His views were adopted by a left-wing trend that appeared in the 1980s and was coined *neo-Orthodox*.

27. Christos Giannaras, "Erevna: Laikos Politismos," *ANTI*, 3 April 1976, pp. 36–37.

28. Alki Kyriakidou-Nestoros, "Erevna: Laikos Politismos," *ANTI*, 20 March 1976, pp. 44–45.

29. Alexis Politis, "Erevna: Laikos Politismos," *ANTI*, 17 April 1976, pp. 44–45.

30. See, for instance: "I psychanalysi einai anepithymiti stin Ellada," *Politis,* May 1978, p. 60.
31. Eleonora Skouteri, "I paradosi tis paradosis," *Politis,* March 1981, pp. 44–56.
32. "Mia syzitisi me to Dionysi Savvopoulo," *Agonistis,* 26 December 1975.
33. "Kato to retro, Zito I Odysseia," *Thourios,* 17 March 1977, p. 14–15.
34. Christos Vakalopoulos, "Theoritikos exoplismos kai kinimatografiki empeiria," *Synchronos Kinimatografos,* July–October 1979.
35. "Taxidi stis istories tou kinimatografou," *Agonas gia tin Kommounistiki Ananeosi,* February 1979, pp. 36–40.
36. "Na stamatisei I mythologiki anaviosi katastaseon," *Thourios,* 3 February 1977, p. 14. See also his ideas about a "nondogmatic" and pluralist approach to "culture," in a discussion among intellectuals affiliated with or leaning toward KKE Es., in: "Politistiki anaptyxi kai laiki protovoulia," *KOMTHEPOL,* November–December 1976, pp. 17–47.
37. See, for example: "Koini dilosi tou Italikou kai tou Ispanikou Kommounistikou Kommatos," *KOMTHEPOL,* August–September 1975, pp. 101–2.
38. The Alliance contained KKE Es., the Christian Socialist *Christianiki Dimokratia* (Christian Democracy), the post-dictatorship EDA, *Sosialistiki Poreia* (Socialist Course), which was formed by former members of PASOK that had been expelled, and *Sosialistiki Protovoulia* (Socialist Initiative).
39. "Nea Liossia: 25,000 neoi zitoun kalyteri psychagogia," *Odigitis,* 14 July 1978, p. 12.
40. V.K., "Kai pali gia ti laiki paradosi … kai ton 'amerikaniko tropo zois,'" *Thourios,* 8 September 1977, pp. 14–15.
41. Long and Moore, "Introduction: Sociality's New Directions," pp. 4, 7.
42. Christos Lazos, "I 'taytotita' tis genias tou '77," part 1, *Thourios,* 6 October 1977, pp. 10–11.
43. "Kato to retro, zito I Odysseia," *Thourios,* 17 March 1977, pp. 14–15.
44. Kostas Livieratos and Giannis Gouzoulis, "I KNE kai I symmorfosi tis neolaias. O kalos, o kakos kai o aschimos," *Thourios,* 22 September 1977, pp. 10–11; V.K., "Kai pali"; "I elliniki neolaia anakalyptei xana tzaz kai rok," *Thourios,* 8 June 1978, pp. 6–7; Lazos, "I 'taytotita,'" part 1, *Thourios,* 6 October 1977, pp. 10–11; part 2, 20 October 1977, p. 6; part 3, 3 November 1977, p. 13.
45. Mary Nolan, "Anti-Americanism and Americanization in Germany," *Politics and Society* 33, no.1 (2005): pp. 88–122.
46. ASKI, Archive of EKON Rigas Feraios, "Ntokoumenta, 1o synedrio ths EKON Rigas Feraios," 1978, pp. 8–9; RF publications were loudly critical of the reentry of Greece to the military wing of NATO in October 1980. See "To diko mas ochi," *Thourios,* 30 October 1980, p. 3; T. Chatzigeorgiou, "Skepseis meta apo tis kinitopoiiseis gia to NATO," *Thourios,* 13 November 1980, pp. 26–27.
47. "I elliniki neolaia," pp. 6–7.
48. Livieratos and Gouzoulis, "I KNE kai I symmorfosi tis neolaias," pp. 10–11; V.K., "Kai pali."
49. Livieratos and Gouzoulis, "I KNE kai I symmorfosi tis neolaias."
50. Ibid.

51. See, for instance, ASKI, Archive of EKON Rigas Feraios, "Ntokoumenta, 1o synedrio ths EKON Rigas Feraios," 1978.

52. ASKI, Archive of EKON Rigas Feraios, First Congress of RF, box 1: Speech of Lampsidis, "Culture and Student Life."

53. Lazos, "I 'taytotita,'" part 1, pp. 10–11.

54. See the common announcement, which was also signed by the DA (the student group leaning toward RF) published in *Avgi,* 13 February 1977.

55. The relevant archives are kept by the KKE today and no access to the researchers is allowed. Thus, it is not possible to shed light on the exact number of young workers who joined KNE in the late 1970s.

56. V.K., "Irthe I ora gia tin politistiki epitropi kathe scholis," *Thourios,* 10 January 1978, pp. 8–9; ASKI, Archive of EKON Rigas Feraios, 1978 Congress, box 11 (pre-Congress session of the Athenian local branches): Speech of Filis (high-school pupil).

57. "Anti-afieroma stous Beatles," *Mathitiki Poreia,* without date (most probably summer 1981), p. 16.

58. For instance, N.T., Interview. N.T., male, was a high-ranking cadre of RF from the early 1970s.

59. "Ascholeisai me tin politiki?," *Thourios,* 12 December 1979, p. 8.

60. "Apopse aytoschediazoume choreyontas," *Thourios,* 15 November 1979, pp. 10–11.

61. "Mastiga oi Amerikanoi gia tin Terpsithea," *Avgi,* 16 September 1978, p. 9.

62. ASKI, Archive of EKON Rigas Feraios, box 24, envelope 3, untitled leaflet of the Democratic Union of the Higher Industrial School of Salonica no 1.

63. The statement that the youth should not sacrifice its pleasure for the sake of future achievements was stated clearly in: Lazos, "I 'taytotita,'" part 1, pp. 10–11.

64. ASKI, Archive of EKON Rigas Feraios, "Programmatismos kalokairiou," 1978, central council of RF, box 9, envelope 3. About the approach of the young Eurocommunists toward rock music in general, see also: Nikolaos Papadogiannis, "Greek Communist Youth Identities and Rock Music in the Late 1970s," in *Between the Avant Garde and the Everyday: Subversive Politics in Europe from 1957 to the Present,* ed. Timothy Brown and Lorena Anton (New York, 2011), pp. 148–82.

65. "To Festival tis enotitas kai tis dimokratias," *Thourios,* 6 October 1977, pp. 8–9; *Thourios,* 17 September 1980, pp. 42–55; *Thourios,* 17 September 1981, pp. 6–14.

66. See Gundle, *Between Hollywood and Moscow,* p. 156.

67. Ibid. It would be worthwhile to examine whether other Eurocommunist youth organizations, such as in Spain and Finland, appropriated rock music in the late 1970s as a means of reconfiguring their ideological profile.

68. "Na agonistoume me fantasia kai tolmi: Na allaxoume ti zoi mas; Na allaxoume tin koinonia," *Thourios,* 28 June 1979, p. 3

69. "Greece Rhodes Kos," leaflet published by EOT, January 1979.

70. "Greek Saronic islands," leaflet published by EOT, May 1978.

71. "Erima nisakia," *Thourios,* 3 July 1980, pp. 5–6.

72. ASKI, Archive of EKON Rigas Feraios, box 24, envelope 3, untitled leaflet of the Democratic Union of the Higher Industrial School of Salonica no 2.

73. "Apopse aytoschediazoume choreyontas," *Thourios,* 15 November 1979, pp. 10–11.

74. "O 'Amletof' kai ta pontikia," *Thourios,* 8 June 1978, p. 4.

75. T. Soumas, "Anthropos apo marmaro," *Thourios*, 16 February 1979, p. 15.
76. Ibid. About the differing assessment of the movie by diverse Communist youth groups, see also: Papadogiannis, "Between Angelopoulos," p. 300. In fact, Poland triggered rancorous debates among Greek left-wingers in the late 1970s and early 1980s. The June 1976 protests that erupted there, the activity of the KOR (Komitet Obrony Robotników, Worker's Defence Committee) and, especially, the formation of the Solidarność (Solidarity) Trade Union in 1980 caused controversies among Greek left-wingers. The KKE and the KNE sided with the Polish government and welcomed the imposition of the martial law on 13 December 1981, as a means of eliminating "vagabonds" and the "extremist" voices within the Solidarity. See, for instance: "Metra Yperaspisis tou Sosialismou stin Polonia," *Rizospastis*, 15 December 1981, p. 1. However, other left-wingers, particularly those aligned with the KKE Es. and RF, were sympathetic toward the dissidents: Aggelos Elefantis, prominent intellectual and member of the KKE Es., authored an article in *Politis*, in which he hailed those developments as an opportunity of the working class to establish its own institutions free from state control. See Aggelos Elefantis, "Polonia: I koinonia ton politon enantion tou kratous Moloch," *Politis*, August–September 1980, pp. 26–30.
77. ASKI, Archive of EKON Rigas Feraios, box 24, envelope 3, untitled leaflet of the Democratic Union of the Higher Industrial School of Salonica no 2.
78. ASKI, Archive of Spyros Kakouriotis, envelope 1, leaflet published by the DIMAK titled: "Na peraso sto Lykeio," 1977.
79. An overview of relevant articles that appeared in those magazines can be found in: "Fantasia kai satira sta foititika entypa," *Avgi*, 4 March 1980.
80. "La rivoluzione: come, dove, quando," *La città futura fumetto*, 1 March 1978, p. 5.
81. "EKON Rigas Feraios, Ta dikaiomata tis neas genias," 1979; ASKI, Archive of EKON Rigas Feraios, "Voithitiko Keimeno gia tin analysi tou Katastatikou Charti," Central Council of RF, box 10, envelope 2 (the development of youth movements, 1979–80).
82. See Christos Lazos, "O 'R. Feraios' tha synechisei ton agona gia psifo ton neon sta 18," *Avgi*, 17 June 1977, p. 7.
83. See, for instance, V.K., "Irthe I ora," pp. 8–9.
84. ASKI, Archive of Rigas Feraios, "Ntokoumenta, 1o synedrio ths EKON Rigas Feraios," 1978, pp. 52–53; ASKI, Archive of Rigas Feraios, "N' allaxoume ti zoi mas. Eidiki apofasi tou 2ou Synedriou. EKON Rigas Feraios." Minutes from student assemblies of the Philosophy School of the Aristotle University of Salonica in the late 1970s, gathered by Kostas Sarris, capture the relevant debates between RF and KNE members. See Sarris, "Politistikes Drastiriotites," pp. 220–29.
85. ASKI, Archive of EKON Rigas Feraios, "Programmatismos kalokairiou," 1978.
86. ASKI, Archive of Rigas Feraios, "Ntokoumenta, 1o synedrio ths EKON Rigas Feraios," 1978, p. 54.
87. ASKI, Archive of Rigas Feraios, 1978 Congress, box 1 (pre-Congress session of the Athenian local branches), Speech of Thrassos, 1978.
88. V.K., "To kalokairino sinema kai i apousia tou film," *Thourios*, 25 June 1977, p. 22.
89. See ASKI, Archive of Rigas Feraios, 1978 Congress, box 1 (pre-Congress session of the Athenian local branches), Speech of Petros, Scholes OAED.

90. The term "deep exchange" was introduced by Alessandro Portelli, who wished to emphasize that, as the interview unfolds, there might be a role-reversal in the interviewing/interviewee relationship: the interviewee may feel that s/he has the authority to pose questions as well either to the interviewer or to other interviewees. Historian Stuart Hilwig appropriated the term, but used it to stress the nonverbal methods of communication during the interview. See Portelli, *The Battle of Valle Giulia*, pp. 72–78; Stuart Hilwig, "Are You Calling Me a Fascist? A Contribution to the Oral History of the Italian Student Rebellion in 1968," *Journal of Contemporary History* 36, no. 4 (2001): pp. 581–97.

91. "Apopse aytoschediazoume choreyontas," *Thourios*, 15 November 1979, pp. 10–11.

92. "Ntokoumenta ths B Panelladikis Syndiaskepsis ths EKON Rigas Feraios. Politiki Apofasi," *Agonas gia tin Kommounistiki Ananeosi*, May 1978, pp. 24–35.

93. Ibid.

94. The PASP also participated in the occupation in the beginning and took part in its coordinating committee.

95. T. Liontaris, "Panepistimio Patras. To chroniko tis katalipsis," *ANTI*, 25 March 1978, pp. 10–13. See also the newspaper *Katalipsi*, published by the protestors.

96. See, for instance, Kostas Karis, "Ena entatiko berdema," *Thourios*, 6 April 1978, p. 5.

97. ASKI, Archive of Rigas Feraios, Central Council of RF, box 10, envelope 2, "Organotiki Ekthesi."

98. Christoforos Vernardakis, *EKON RIGAS FERAIOS- B Panelladiki: mia istoriki proseggisi*, online article, which can be found in the following link: http://www.ver nardakis.gr/article.php?id=197 (last access: 27 September 2012).

99. This Party bore the same name with the umbrella group of the Left in the 1950s and 1960s, but did not constitute the same organization. The latter had dissolved after the establishment of the junta and most of its members had joined the Communist Party after 1974.

100. Wemheuer, "Einleitung," pp. 9–23.

101. "I prosfati diaspasi sto EKKE," *ANTI*, 4 January 1980, pp. 18–19; "Mia apantisi tou EKKE," *ANTI*, 18 January 1980, pp. 19–20.

102. ASKI, Archive of Fyssas, box 15, Announcement of the Youth of PASOK, 1981.

103. Aravantinos, "To Metapoliteytiko," p. 502, 524.

104. Some members who withdrew from the KNE announced their decision through letters published in *ANTI*. See, for example, "Dialogos," *ANTI*, 1 February 1980, p. 50.

105. "I politiki mas diafonia me to KKE," *ANTI*, 14 March 1980, pp. 20–26.

106. It should not be confused with the center-left newspaper that bore the same name.

107. For example, common lists appeared in the Schools of Architecture, Electrical Engineering, Mechanical Engineering, Physics, and Mathematics in the University of Athens. The issue whether these lists leaned toward DA-APK or DA-DE was contentious. See the exchange of views between Dimitris Papadimoulis, who was aligned to RF, and Kyra Adam, whose estimations favored DA-APK, in: "Flevaris '79, foititikes ekloges: mia apantisi kai mia antapantisi," *ANTI*, 17 March 1979, pp. 20–21.

108. Some of the participants in Choros did not participate in student elections. A case in point is the members of the radical left-wing group OPA (Organosi gia mia Proletariaki Aristera, Organization for a Proletarian Left).

109. Diamantis Mpasantis, "Merikes empeiries kai skepseis apo mia parastasi tou FOKTH Nomikis," *Agonas gia tin Kommounistiki Ananeosi,* May 1979, pp. 15–16.

110. "Politistiki Kinisi sti Nomiki," *Ioulos,* November 1978, pp. 19–22.

111. V.V., "D Evdomada Parousiasis Foititikis Politistikis Douleias," *Thourios,* 7 June 1979, p. 14. For the loud critique by the KNE, see "Mia apotychimeni prospatheia antiparathesis stin politistiki drastiriotita ton foititikon syllogon," *Odigitis,* 15 June 1979, p. 19.

112. Citations of articles that had been published in *Pezodromio* are also found in *Agonas gia tin Kommounistiki Ananeosi* throughout the late 1970s and early 1980s. The latter also contains references to the Greek translations of works of Situationists, such as: Guy Debord, *The Society of the Spectacle,* which had been translated into Greek in 1972. For such references, see, for instance: Diamantis Mpasantis, "O logos ton aligatoron," *Agonas gia tin Kommounistiki Ananeosi,* May 1980, p. 55.

113. "Schedion Nomou peri rythmiseos thematon aforonton eis tin organosin kai leitourgian ton Anotaton Ekpaideytikon Idrymaton," Athens 1978, Personal Collection of Maria Repoussi.

114. See the booklet published by KNE under the title: *Dekemvris '79: Agonistiki exarsi tou foititikou kinimatos* (Athens, 1980), pp. 9–10, 13.

115. For instance: M. Tsitsimelis, F. Pallas, "60 chronia agones … gia tous ergazomenous", *Agonas gia tin Kommounistiki Ananeosi,* November 1978, pp. 4–7.

116. OPA welcomed squats, which began in Greece since late 1981 and, thus, fall beyond the scope of this book.

117. "'Ta "frikia,'" *Rixi,* February 1980, pp. 38–41; "Zyrichi-Amsterdam, I exegersi tou 'koinonikou proletariou,'" *Rixi,* November 1980.

118. See, for example, the point of view expressed by a person who signed as Vassilis and claimed to be a member of B Panelladiki, in a recorded discussion about the occupations in 1979 that was published in *ANTI*: "Oria kai prooptikes enos kinimatos," *ANTI,* 18 January 1980, p. 25.

119. "Gia tis perithoriakes anarchoaristeristikes omades," *Odigitis,* 16 November 1979, p. 8.

120. ASKI, Archive of Dimitris Fyssas, box 15, Youth of PASOK, "Genikes theseis gia tis taseis tou reymatos amfisvitisis," 1979.

121. G. Gouzoulis, K. Livieratos, and S. Spanos, "Stasi," *Agonas gia tin Kommounistiki Ananeosi,* June–July 1978, pp. 47–55; Diamantis Mpasantis, "Merikes skepseis gia tin paradosi," *Agonas gia tin Kommounistiki Ananeosi,* October 1979, pp. 28–31; Mpasantis, "O logos," p. 55.

122. "Leschi Neon Kallitheas," *Ta Aythaireta ton synoikion ths EKON Rigas Feraios (B Panelladiki),* 1 May 1980.

123. Thodoris, "Politistikoi Syllogoi," *Exodos,* March 1980, pp. 10–12.

124. E. Hadjiargirou, "Me aformi to Polytechneio," *Agonas gia tin Kommounistiki Ananeosi,* November 1978, pp. 34–37.

125. G. Gouzoulis, "Enarxis ton Septemvrio …," *Agonas gia tin Kommounistiki Ananeosi,* September–October 1978, pp. 6–7.

126. G. Kalas and T. Mastrantonis, "Ta Festival ton politikon," *Agonas gia tin Kommounistiki Ananeosi,* October 1980, pp. 10–13.

127. It was a French anti-authoritarian student group, which was founded on 22 March 1968. It carried out the occupation of the administration building of the University of Nanterre in the spring of the same year. This event precipitated the uprising in May 1968.

128. Depsis, "I nostalgia tis exegersis,"*ANTI,* 20 May 1978, pp. 23–26; "Treis prokiryxeis tou Mai," *ANTI,* 20 May 1978, pp. 28–29; "O gallikos Mais kai oi Ellines tou Parisiou," *ANTI,* 20 May 1978, pp. 30–31.

129. Perhaps the only exception to this tendency is a chronicle of student protest in Italy in 1968, which was published in *Rixi.* See "O Italikos 'Mais' ton Foititon," *Rixi,* February 1980, pp. 88–103.

130. For a list of slogans that were written or chanted in Paris in May 1968, see Andrew Feenberg and Jim Freedman, *When Poetry Ruled the Streets: The French May Events of 1968* (Albany, NY, 2001).

131. *Enimerosi-Dialogos,* vol. 2, April 1978, cover page.

132. About the representations of "1968" in the publications of Choros, see also: Nikolaos Papadogiannis, "From Coherence to Fragments: '1968' and the Making of Youth Politicisation in Greece in the 1970s," *Historein, A Review of the Past and Other Stories* 9 (2009): pp. 76–92.

133. About the Movimento del '77, see Lumley, *States of Emergency,* pp. 295–312.

134. Some accounts of the events can be found in: Takis Benas, "Pos exelichtikan ta gegonota," *Avgi,* 19 November 1980. Takis Benas was a prominent left-winger, who had been active in EDA in the post–Civil War period. In the 1970s, he was a cadre of the KKE Es.

135. Chrysanthos Lazaridis, "Noemvris '78: Xechasmenes istories gia ena epikairo paramythi," *Agonas gia tin Kommounistiki Ananeosi,* November 1978, pp. 25–33.

136. Giannis Floros, "Polytechneio '80," *Agonas gia tin Kommounistiki Ananeosi,* November–December 1980, pp. 21–26.

137. It is indicative that *Agonas gia tin Kommounistiki Ananeosi* advertised record shops, where rock records were available, such as "Pop 11"; it also advertised books about rock music. See the advertisements on p. 2 in the volumes of May and July 1980.

138. This association was located both in written and in oral sources. For the former sources, see Mpasantis, "O logos," p. 55. See also the interview with E.Q. and B.Q., Athens, 29 October 2007.

139. Hugh Mackay, introduction to *Consumption and Everyday Life,* ed. Hugh Mackay (London, 1997), p. 6. Hebdige has also employed the term "bricolage" to show that youth subcultures in the United Kingdom, such as the punks, appropriated and resignified commodities, erasing or subverting their original meaning. See Dick Hebdige, *Subculture: The Meaning of Style* (Abingdon, NY, 2007), pp. 102–6.

140. "Thelete na me katapieite alla tha sas katso sto stomachi," *Ta Aythaireta ton synoikion tis EKON Rigas Feraios (B Panelladiki),* 1 May 1980.

141. "To xeperasma ths Metapolitefsis," *Rixi,* June 1980, p. 2.

142. "Elliniko rock: anaptyxi i adiexodo, prochorima i stasimotita," *Ta Aythaireta ton synoikion tis EKON Rigas Feraios (B Panelladiki),* 20 July 1980, pp. 6–7.

143. Ibid.

144. Bozinis, *Rock pagkosmiotita*, pp. 395–414.
145. K.V. Dimitriou, "O Savvopoulos kai to perithorio," *Agonas gia tin Kommounistiki Ananeosi*, May 1979, pp. 51–54.
146. "Thelete na me katapieite, alla tha sas katso sto stomachi," *Aythaireta ton synoikion tis EKON Rigas Feraios (B Panelladiki)*, 1 May 1980, pp. 6–7. High school pupil magazines related to a lesser or greater extent with Choros, like *Thranio*, published positive reviews of his work. For example, see M.L., "Ap' ti 'Rezerva' sto 'Fortigo'-15 chronia mousiki," *Thranio*, February 1980, pp. 9–10.
147. "D. Savvopoulos, Me tin ilikia tou kinimatos," *Rixi*, October 1979, pp. 83–95.
148. Dimitriou, "O Savvopoulos," pp. 51–54.
149. Alexandrou was briefly affiliated with the Communist Youth. Still, he was exiled for desertion from 1946 to 1951 and from 1953 to 1958.
150. Alexandra Ioannidou, "Political Aspects of Russian Literature Reception in Greece: Aris Alexandrou and Mitsos Alexandropoulos," *Slavica Gandensia* 32 (2005): pp. 89–104.
151. D. Mpasantis, "O Aris Alexandrou stin poreia tou kivotiou …," *Agonas gia tin Kommounistiki Ananeosi*, February 1979, pp. 33–36.
152. Ibid.
153. "Cheimerini periodos 1979–1980," *Ta Theamata*, 19 December 1980.
154. Dimitris Danikas, "Melodrama, alligoria, satira kai perithorio," *Rizospastis*, 11 December 1979, p. 4.
155. See also Papadogiannis, "Between Angelopoulos," p. 301.
156. PAPOK initially published the *Deltio*; it began to publish *Techni kai Politismos* in 1979.
157. "Mikis Theodorakis, 3 apantiseis gia tin entechni laiki mousiki," *Techni kai Politismos 4* (1979): p. 54.
158. See, for example: Angelos Sfakianakis, "Opisthodromiki Kompania," in *I Ellada sti dekaetia tou '80. Koinoniko, politiko kai politismiko lexiko*, ed. Vassilis Vamvakas and Panayis Panagiotopoulos (Athens, 2010), pp. 398–400.
159. "Modernes kai magkitisses," *12 nees laikes dhmiourgies*, CBS 1978.

Chapter 5

The "Moment" of the Occupations in 1979 and Its Echo

December 1979 witnessed an outbreak of student protest. Numerous university schools were occupied at the initiative of Choros participants and the Maoists. The initiators of those protests demanded the abolition of Law 815/1978, which, in their view, intensified studies and accommodated the integration of university students into the capitalist system. Self-management, humor/sarcasm, and a spirit of spontaneity were widespread in the occupied schools, reflecting the orientation of Choros. This was particularly manifest in the slogans written on the walls of those schools, such as: "Whoever has stolen a member of the KNE who belongs to me, please return him/her to me and keep the flowerpot. Thank you."[1] Such tendencies extended to the leisure activities that took place there: distilling a progressive message was no longer a concern for those young left-wingers. In brief, this moment of student protest was a multifaceted explosion of provocation. The occupations were a controversial event within the left-wing youth, however. The spontaneous activities in the schools occupied by Choros served for the KNE and the Youth of PASOK as a negative example of "disorientation." Still, the significant appeal of those protests, alongside developments in the international Communist movement, also functioned as a catalyst, stirring debates among the pro-Soviet Communists and the Maoists, especially about "youth" and "leisure." While they both continued to adhere to more or less normative conceptualizations of "leisure," they slowly began to demonstrate a degree of tolerance of lifestyle heterogeneity among their cadres and members.

The "Anti-Heroes" Take Action

Choros made its presence on the political landscape of the youth increasingly visible from September 1979, more than a year after Law 815 had been passed. In that month, the network, together with the PPSP and AASPE, organized the occupation of the academic chair of animal husbandry in the Faculty of Veterinary Medicine in Salonica as well as of the Faculty of Architecture in Athens. In the latter case, Professor Sinos, who was allegedly failing many students in examinations, was targeted. On 25 October, Choros held a demonstration, also attended by the Maoists, at which they voiced hostility against the EFEE. A clear expression of their views is manifest in the slogan "*Poulimeni* EFEE" (The EFEE is betraying the struggle!). Tension culminated in December 1979, a month marked by the wave of university occupations in Athens, Salonica, Patras, Ioannina, Xanthi, and Rethymno. At the beginning of the month, Choros and the Maoists geared their efforts toward supporting resolutions at the student assemblies calling for "immediate occupations." It was a battle closely fought against the PSK and PASP, which opposed this tactic as inopportune. On the contrary, RF took a middle-ground stance, supporting occupations, but only under the condition that the masses of students would participate in them. These they called *leitourgikes katalipseis* (functional occupations). The general assembly of students in the Faculty of Chemistry in Athens was the first to vote in favor—by a vast majority of 133 to 11—of occupying the faculty immediately for five days. The Polytechnic School of Xanthi and the Faculty of Geology in Athens followed suit on 4 and 7 December, respectively. On 8 December, after heated debates, the general assembly of students of the Faculty of Chemistry in Athens voted in favor of continuing the occupation for one more week. Soon, the Industrial School and the Faculties of Pharmacy, Forestry, Veterinary Medicine, and Surveying Engineering of the University of Athens decided to occupy their faculties "immediately." In closely contested assembly debates, Law as well as Physics students in Athens reached similar decisions, by 271 to 242 and 381 to 339 votes, respectively. The spread of occupations would paralyze the universities and force the PSK and PASP, which held the majority in the EFEE, to reconsider their stance: they eventually declared the occupation of all university schools in protest against Law 815 from 17 to 19 December.[2]

In the case of the assemblies, where Choros and the Maoists prevailed, "coordinating committees" were elected, in order to help organize the activities in the occupied buildings. These they juxtaposed with the "bureaucratic" administrative councils, since the student assemblies could recall their members at any point, while the councils were elected once annually. In addition, as the titles indicate, the members of the committees did not postulate themselves as a "guiding" body, but one that helped coordinate initiatives that the students themselves organized. This approach contrasted with that in the faculties that were controlled by forces loyal to the EFEE, such as the Higher Industrial School of Salonica, where the members of the administrative councils remained in charge. The latter members made their presence obvious by wearing armlets. One way or another, the critique against Law

815 was building up.[3] On 4 January 1980 the government was forced to render Law 815 inactive through an announcement made by prime minister Konstantinos Karamanlis.

The cultural side of the occupations was not at all negligible. In the occupied schools where they were in control, Choros participants were involved in a number of activities that aimed at challenging, in a provocative manner, what they viewed as "bureaucratic relations." In fact, the occupations witnessed an explosion of humorous, usually spontaneous, expression. Very often, the activists did not act in an organized manner. Rather they took the initiative to present their personal thoughts individually. The best example is the fact that many of them wrote their own slogans in the walls of the occupied schools. Student newspapers, such as *Ta Nea tis Katalipsis* (News of the Occupation), published by the students of the Law School of Athens, who were aligned with or leaning toward RF, alongside *Rixi* and *Thourios,* reveal many such slogans. These were either simply written on walls or on cartons, which also included photos. Some notable are the following (translated in English): "The members of the KNE beat people up, the rockets kill. Prevent the members of KNE from becoming rockets"; "You cops, we Apache"; "We are not Papua, we are not Zulu, we are the wild tribe of the Law School" (the latter was an appropriation of the song "Den eimaste Zoulou"[4] broadcast on the radio show "Edo Lilipoupoli"[5]); "We are red, not experts." As some of them make clear, the young autonomous left-wingers identified themselves with elements assigned to the representation of "primitiveness" (Zulu, Apache). The latter aspect was apparently the counterweight to the conformity that the behavioral patterns promoted both by the state and by some political youth groups, especially the KNE, purportedly cultivated.[6] In addition, in the Polytechnic School of Athens, the young autonomous left-wingers transformed a classroom into a labyrinth by using chairs, tables and stools and named it "the labyrinth of exams." Inside, a slogan stated: "Bread here, freedom at the exit, education-whatever," while a piece of stale bread hung from a chair. This was an inverted appropriation of the slogan that was chanted in the Polytechnic Uprising in 1973, namely "Bread-Education-Freedom."[7] In a humorous fashion, Choros participants made clear their disillusioned understanding that the militancy in the post-dictatorship period had not led to the realization of its basic aims. These slogans, however, triggered disagreements between Choros on the one hand and the Maoist groups on the other, which otherwise rallied against the EFEE. The PPSP and AASPE were put off by their provocative tone. Still, the members of the PASP and PSK were the most annoyed. They regarded such spontaneous expression and their tone as a direct challenge to the form of "organized" struggle that they espoused. As an announcement of the PSK in the Faculty of Chemistry on 7 December 1979 stated, its members denounced the writing of "provocative" slogans in the walls of the Faculty by "anarchists" and "marginal" elements.[8]

Humor and sarcasm extended to the rationale that lay behind the movies that the young autonomous left-wingers chose to screen. They actually reinvented the watching of so-called Greek "commercial" movies, such as *I kori mou i sosialistria* (My Socialist daughter, 1966), starring the famous actress Aliki Vougiouklaki, alongside propaganda movies that had been produced during the dictatorship, such as *Oi Gennaioi tou Vorra* (The heroes of the North, 1970). The former showed the daughter of an industrialist falling in love with a worker, who participates in strikes and demonstrations, whereas the latter referred to the occupation of areas of Northern Greece in the early 1940s by Bulgaria and the purported resistance of the local population. Choros participants screened them not to promote discussions of the "meaning" they conveyed but in order to satirize them.[9] This was clearly an act of "trashing," which film scholars define as demonstrating what the audience regards as the faults of the film.[10] The young autonomous left-wingers individually expressed themselves during the screenings of those movies, in order usually to comment in a provocative fashion on the tactics of the KNE. As N.T., male, AASPE member until 1979, and Choros participant subsequently (including during the period of the occupations), narrates: "[D] uring the occupations, there was fun, joking and chanting. It was not like in the previous years, [there was] no militaristic tone, [and] we never planned the slogans that we would chant" (N.T., Interview). The narration of N.T. was, however, more ambivalent toward Choros than it may appear in this extract. His narrative was actually shaped by two conflicting layers of memory: the first was the critique of the discipline demanded by the members of AASPE and the counterposition of his activity in Choros as a "liberating experience"; the second, however, is closely related with the fact that, at the time of the interview, he was a member of a left-wing Party, the Coalition of the Left, Movements and Ecology. Thus, during our discussion he often claimed that the participants in Choros tended to "exaggerate the negative elements in organized struggle."

Provocation was also meant to mark the other leisure activity that was a common feature of the occupations: rock parties.[11] Most notably, a group of autonomous students in the Law School of Athens held what they called a *kamaki party*, obviously employing the broader meaning of the term, namely flirting in general, as a way to subvert what they apparently viewed as conformity in the social interaction of male and female students. However, the way these parties were experienced was not unanimous for all participants in

Choros. This diversity may be linked to varying representations of "left-wing intellectuals" that circulated within the network. Some members of B Panelladiki were certainly not party animals. For instance, E.Q., who had been a high-ranking RF cadre, narrated that, although he liked the music, he actually forced himself to dance: "I hated it; it was as though I took medication" (E.Q., B.Q., Interview). Instead, he happily participated in discussions in bars about cinema movies, having delved into *Synchronos Kinimatografos*. For him, being a *koultouriaris* (on this occasion meaning to possess high-caliber intellectual quality) functioned as a crucial aspect of the way he viewed politicization. On the other hand, some of the young autonomous left-wingers, especially those who were not affiliated to B Panelladiki, regarded theoretical endeavors with suspicion. Such a stance marked a clear rupture with the prevalent attitude among young left-wingers since the early 1970s, which had been to educate themselves in theory and history. These young autonomous left-wingers were certainly not anti-intellectual, in the sense that they did not despise all scholarly analyses. However, as O.T., male and student in the late 1970s remembers: "[W]e prized action instead of reading. I regret that now, my knowledge in social theory is limited" (O.T., Interview). In this vein, another female student in the late 1970s, who was not affiliated to B Panelladiki but who participated in Choros, mentioned in her oral testimony that she danced to rock music in these parties as a way to criticize and subvert the valorization of the good grasp of theory in the Left: "I felt that it was enough with all these analyses, enough with the intellectuals, it was the revenge of simplicity" (I.A., Interview).

This multifaceted explosion of provocation soon came to an end, leaving, however, the network of the autonomous left-wingers more influential among youngsters than prior to its eruption: the influence of initiatives linked with Choros among students skyrocketed, as manifest in the results of the student elections of 1980, which are shown in table 2.2. The number of blank and invalid votes in these elections also increased from 1224 in 1978 to 2230 in 1980.[12] Some of them may have been cast by students who leaned towards those forces of Choros that detested student elections, although it is really difficult to determine the motivation of such voters, let alone whether they construed such an act as a political one. Besides that, the limits between the more organized forces, such as B Panelladiki, and unaffiliated students participating in Choros, were further blurred. As a result, an umbrella student group was founded in 1980, called Aristeres Syspeiroseis (Left Rallying), which attracted all autonomous left-wing students. Such a development, however, was not uncontested: various members of B Panelladiki, including Maounis and Psarras, argued that it should guard its distinct character. They accused other participants in Choros of acting in an excessively spontaneous way and of lacking interest in the elaboration of a concrete plan for the overthrow of capitalism.[13]

The year 1980 also signaled the diffusion of the activities of Choros, alongside the refraction of a language that was produced in the universities, into two more domains. The high schools witnessed a growing convergence of Eurocommunist and autonomous left-wing students, who rallied against what they called *aytarchiki ekpaideysi* (authoritarian education). The latter term conflated demands that had to do with pupil leisure and sexuality as well as their assessment at school from an anti-"integration" perspective; its exact content will be analyzed in chapter 6. More significantly, there was a remarkable shift in the organization structure for which these pupils opted. In the first post-dictatorship years, all major left-wing youth groups struggled for the establishment of *mathitikes koinotites* (pupil communities), namely councils elected by high-school pupils themselves. Communist and Socialist pupils were often at odds with the Ministry of Education and Religious Affairs about the rules that regulated the election and the responsibilities of these councils.[14] However, since the very late 1970s, Eurocommunist and autonomous left-wing pupils accused the KNE of having "bureaucratized" their operation. Similar to their counterparts in the university schools, young autonomous left-wingers, alongside young Eurocommunists, opted for the creation of cultural groups and pupil magazines that would be autonomous from these communities.[15] A number of such magazines spread in Athens and Salonica from 1979, mainly after the occupations, including: *Koukos* (Cuckoo) and *Antiefimerida* (Anti-newspaper) in the Athens district of Zografou, *Touvlo* (Brick), and *Thranio* (Bench). The contributors to some of them, such as *Antiefimerida,* also held rock parties and *rebetiko* nights. Once again, rock music appeared for them to carry anti-authoritarian connotations.[16] Many of these magazines were presented at the "festival of pupil magazines" that took place on 3 and 4 May 1980 in Athens.[17] Despite these stirrings, however, the high schools saw nothing close to the massive protests witnessed during the university occupations of 1979.

The end of the occupations also marked the spread of Choros activity to the districts, mainly of Athens. These were either centered on cultural societies or magazines. Participants in Choros created the Leschi (Club) of Kallithea in 1980, which functioned as a bar and concert venue featuring local amateur rock bands. They also established the Mousiko Kafetheatro (Music Café-Theatre) in Palaio Faliro and the Steki (Venue) in the working-class district of Neo Iraklio, which hosted similar activities. They participated in the cultural society ZEA in the lower-middle class area of Kypseli, which organized rock parties and published the magazine *TAM-TAM.* Similar cultural associations were founded in Nea Ionia, Korydallos, Egaleo, and Vyronas.[18]

All these societies were loose-knit groupings and collectivities.[19] Following the conceptualization of political scientist Dimitri Sotiropoulos, they were a case in-between formal and informal civil society. According to Sotiropoulos, the latter are "rather amorphous collective actors" that should be distinguished from the former, which comprises voluntary associations that are officially registered and whose operation is based on clearly defined structures.[20] The cultural associations of Choros were loosely knit, albeit not totally structureless. An administrative council existed in some of them. Nevertheless, this council was not stipulated to "guide," but merely to "coordinate" the diverse activities of the participants.[21] In any case, none of those associations followed the line set by a Party apparatus. They were the outcome of the experimentation of young left-wingers, who demanded personal autonomy without withdrawing from politicized collectivities. A.M., male, mid-ranking KNE cadre until 1979, and, subsequently, Choros participant, narrated the following about the Leschi (Club) in Kallithea: "In the Leschi, we had developed a feeling that we could do whatever we like, that there were no limits" (A.M., Interview). Once again, Choros activity seems to have valorized "spontaneity" as opposed to "conformity." The latter is evident in the target groups of these associations: categories of young people that existed in the 1970s in the districts of Athens and Salonica and for a variety of reasons were regarded as "subversive" by autonomous left-wingers. Those included youngsters involved in the so-called "pirate" radio stations, which were illegal and often shut down by the police. Such radio stations were usually local and played either rock or Greek popular music. One more group they addressed was the motorbike riders: young men, who saved their pocket money or wages to buy a scooter, dismissing the usually negative reactions of their parents. A third category was the young rockers. It goes without saying that the distinctions were not sharp and somebody could be, for instance, both a rocker and a motorbike rider. In the presentation of their cultural work, published either in *Aythaireta ton Synoikion* or in *Rixi,* a number of cultural associations leaning toward Choros regarded the fact that such young people were at odds with the police or their families as an indication of revolutionary potential.[22] The young autonomous left-wingers were usually more successful with the rockers. As in the case of the universities, Choros helped circulate the work of rock bands by staging rock concerts, such as in Palaio Faliro.

Apart from the cultural societies, which mainly organized leisure activities, the autonomous left-wingers also published magazines and newspapers in the districts: *Ta Aythaireta ton synoikion,* put out by members of B Panelladiki, featured prominently. There was also the local *Dialogos* (Dialogue) newspaper in Palaio Faliro, which its publishers claimed in *Rixi* that it had a readership of about 600 people.[23] Another example was *Exodos* (Exit) in Koukaki. These magazines brought into the fore environmental issues, especially toxic water basins in these areas. In general, and in contrast with the autonomous cultural societies, however, they dedicated very little or no space at all to leisure, with the exception of *Dialogos,* which reported on the concerts of rock bands in Palaio Faliro.[24] In any case, despite the spread of its activity beyond the university schools, the very network of Choros turned out to be short-lived and petered out in the early 1980s, with one of its core components, B Panelladiki, ceasing to exist in 1982.

A Dialectic of Rigor and Flexibility

While RF and Choros introduced various novelties in the leisure activities and the cultural politics of the Left, continuities and ruptures were neither identical nor did they occur at the same pace among young left-wingers of all persuasions. In fact, a number of key aspects of the ideological discourse of both the Youth of PASOK and the KNE on "culture" remained unchanged throughout the period from 1974 to 1981. Despite those signs of continuity, however, the cultural activities of both the KNE and the Youth of PASOK also witnessed vibrations toward the end of the decade, albeit not so strong, as in the case of RF. One way or another, the activity of Choros and, especially, the 1979 occupations featured prominently in the publications, particularly of the KNE, on "culture" in a contradictory manner: mainly as a negative role model, but also, implicitly, as one of the impulses for the reconsideration of shortcomings of its cultural politics.

Similar to the first post-dictatorship years, both the KNE and the Youth of PASOK combined cultural with political anti-Americanism in the late 1970s. They conditioned the "national independence" of Greece on the expulsion of the "imperialist" capital as well as the eviction of American military bases from the territory of Greece. In this vein, they vehemently opposed the reentry of Greece to the military wing of NATO in 1980.[25] Those forces were also stable in their opposition to Greece entering the European Economic Community. To struggle against what they viewed as political, financial, and cultural dependence of Greece, they arranged several events. PAMK (the high school pupil group aligned with PASOK) held an event in Piraeus in 1979, where its members decried "foreign" cultural patterns, defending what they coined as a "genuine Greek popular way of life."[26] Defining and promoting the genuine "progressive" culture of the Greek people continued to be major concerns both for the young Socialists and the pro-Soviet Communists, a stance which featured prominently in the songs they appreciated. A telling case was the work of Thomas Bakalakos, who composed the music and wrote the lyrics of the album *Oi prostates* (The Protectors, 1979). The songs of this album asserted that Greek farmers and workers were in a straitjacket, imposed by "foreign" protectors; to put an end to "exploitation," the "People" was called to rise up and "protect itself" from them. Bakalakos performed onstage in the cultural events organized by both the Youth of PASOK and the KNE during those years.[27] Likewise, cinema reviews that were published in the pro-Soviet Communist press bore a striking resemblance with those of the mid–1970s. A case in point is the film review of *O anthropos me to Garyfallo* (The Man with the Carnation, 1980), which narrated the biography of the prominent KKE cadre, Nikos Belogiannis, concentrating on his trial and execution in the post–Civil War era. The film sold 602,956 tickets in Athens, Piraeus, and their lower-middle and working-class districts from autumn 1980 to 1 February 1981, topping the box office films in those areas.[28] The KNE and the KKE venerated Belogiannis and evinced great interest in the way his biography was presented. Danikas found the movie quintessentially "progressive," arguing that it offered a positive role model of a militant with origins in the lower social strata, who was committed to the "anti-fascist, anti-imperialist" struggle.[29] *Odigitis* also praised the film for providing an "accurate" and "honest" account of post–Civil War Greece and shedding light onto the "heroic figure" of Belogiannis.[30]

In order to instill those "progressive" values, the KNE and KKE strove for the consolidating the network of cultural associations that they influenced. In contrast with the initiatives linked with RF and Choros, they continued to espouse a top-bottom structure. Thus, they intensified their efforts to strengthen the "progressive cultural movement" in cooperation with the PAPOK as well as with the municipal authorities that the KKE backed. KKE actually controlled the municipal authorities in many lower-middle and working-class areas in Athens and Salonica. In the mid– to late–1970s, Kaisariani and Peristeri were a few examples in Athens, alongside Ambelokipoi and Stavroupoli in Salonica. From 1979, the KNE and the PAPOK proved more successful than RF and Choros in running and, actually, reestablishing many of the cultural associations, whose operation had ceased in the period around 1977. The data from *Odigitis* and *Techni kai Politismos* indicate that the Athens districts had at least seven such cases of cultural societies: the Morfotiki Leschi Palaiou Falirou (Educational Club of Palaio Faliro), which had been founded in 1974, was reestablished in 1977 as the PSPF (Politistikos Syllogos Palaiou Falirou, Cultural Society of Palaio Faliro), and appears to have lasted until 1993, according to the minutes of its assemblies;[31] the cultural society of the lower-middle and working-class area of Haidari; the Pneymatiko Kentro Neon "Dimitris Glinos" (Cultural Society of the Youth "Dimitris Glinos") in the lower-middle and working-class area of Egaleo, founded in 1980; the Morfotikos Syllogos Gkyzi (Educational Society of Gkyzi); the society in Agia Varvara, a lower-middle and working-class district; the POA (Politistiki Omada Acharnon, Cultural Group of Acharnon), another lower-middle and working-class area in Athens, established in the late 1970s; and the Cine Club of Piraeus.[32] The common aspect of most of these associations was their clear organizational structure. All of them subscribed to the framework endorsed by the PAPOK, according to which the aim of art was to reproduce "anti-fascist" and "anti-imperialist" messages. With the exception of the POA, they were all administered by a council. The KNE was predominant in all of them, but RF members participated at least in the PSPF and the Cine Club of Piraeus. Those cultural associations demonstrated a remarkable activity: In 1981 the Cine Club organized numerous screenings of movies, such as *Thiassos,* in other lower-middle and working-class districts, like Kokkinia, Drapetsona, and Perama.[33] The Morfotikos Syllogos Gkyzi held the *Gkyziaka,* an annual local festival, where the work of amateur music bands and dance groups was presented. The *Gkyziaka* took place at least twice, in 1978 and 1979. A similar local festival, called the *Karaiskakeia,* was organized in 1980 by the society in Haidari under the auspices of the PAPOK. The PSPF held a summer festival in Batis, a seaside area of Palaio Faliro, called "Avgoustos '81" (August '81), which was supported by the KKE-backed municipal authorities of Palaio Faliro. In addition, on 9 and 10 August 1980, sixteen KKE/KNE-backed trade unions held the "Two Days of Workers' Cultural Production" in Salonica, which included special sections for the cultural work of young workers.[34]

Similarly, the cultural politics of the KNE proved quite successful in the university schools, where a lot of societies were administered by PSK-controlled student councils. These included, apart from the Theatre Section of the University of Athens, the cultural societies of the Polytechnic School, the School of Philosophy and of Medicine in Athens, the School of Philosophy in Salonica, as well as the Athens School of Economics and Business.[35] From 1980, associations leaning toward the KNE, supported by the central council of the EFEE as well as by the Theatre Section of the University of Athens, presented theatre plays, screened movies, and held concerts of *rebetiko,* rock, and political song in the *Irida* theatre in Athens.[36] Besides them, the PAPOK organized from 1978 an annual meeting of amateur theatre groups in Salonica, attracting both students and young workers. The meeting was held in close cooperation with local municipal authorities that were backed by the KKE, such as of Salonica and Stavroupoli.[37]

One more enduring component of the cultural politics of the KNE and the Youth of PASOK were youth festivals. The structure of the festivals of both organizations bore much in common: they were praised in open letters by left-wing or left-leaning artists as conducive to shaping determined militants, they showcased "progressive" as opposed to "reactionary" culture and they culminated with the speeches of the leaders of the youth groups as well as the Parties they were affiliated with. In fact, many "progressive" artists participated in both festivals, such as Christos Leontis, who appeared both in *Giorti Neolaias*, the Festival of the Youth of PASOK, and in the Festival of KNE-Odigitis in 1979, somehow reinforcing the feeling of common belonging among members and supporters of diverse left-wing youth groups, despite their often bitter debates.[38] However, infighting in the Youth of PASOK exacted a cost to the *Giorti Neolaias*: A number of young Socialists that lambasted the leadership organized their own festival in Salonica in 1980 and were subsequently expelled.[39] Nevertheless, such duality did not last long and from 1981 onward once again only one Festival of the Youth of PASOK took place every year.

A growing challenge for the cultural politics of the Youth of PASOK and the KNE was the comeback of rock music in Greece at the end of the 1970s. The Youth of PASOK responded more positively, despite its suspicion toward "foreign cultural products," and began to incorporate rock artists into the program of its festivals, such as in 1980, with the explicit aim to "present all music genres."[40] By contrast, the KNE and the KKE were more ambivalent. Similar to the preceding years, they approached several cultural and political developments, which they treated with skepticism or uncertainty, through the prism of drug consumption; the comeback of rock music was one of them. Their publications sounded a note of fear that some rock songs, such as "Cocaine" by Eric Clapton, were an open call to drug addiction.[41] They were also hostile toward bars and the open-air concerts of non-Greek rock bands, on the grounds that they encouraged drug circulation and the carrying out of violent acts.[42] In their stance on the open-air concerts, the KKE and KNE distinguished themselves from a role-model regime, that of the German Democratic Republic. In 1981, the East German band City appeared live in Greece. As it appears from correspondence, the East German regime asked the KNE to support the band, as a "commercial" success would contribute to "more independence" from West German music producers.[43] However, the KNE stuck to its position opposing all open-air concerts, even though it accepted that City's music was not "reactionary" and "contributed to the socialist cause" in the context of East Germany.[44]

Drugs served as a prism for the KNE to approach rock music in relation to the emerging network of Choros as well. In many articles as well as images in *Odigitis,* Choros participants, who were glossed as *anarchoautonomoi* (anarchoautonomous), were depicted as young, bourgeois-class, pot-bellied people. Resorting to Lenin's *"Left-Wing" Communism: An Infantile Disorder, Odigitis* glossed them as another case of *leftism*: one facet of their "spontaneous" reaction to the "anxieties" ultimately attributable to capitalism, was Choros' purported willingness to espouse violence.[45] The KNE maintained that such violence was incited by the consumption of drugs and alcohol, which it asserted were a staple of the rock parties that Choros organized at university schools amid or after the 1979 occupations.[46] The newspaper of the pro-Soviet Communist youth reported on the aftermath of such a party at the Department of Chemistry in Athens in February 1980: "Broken windows, office and laboratory doors, torn newspapers and posters, repulsive slogans against the EFEE and the KNE, bottles of wine and cognac, among others, demonstrated the vandalisms that had been committed. Venting here and now, by the protagonists of the lethal attack in the School of Physics and Mathematics."[47] The alleged "lethal attack" was a direct reference to the violent confrontations between members of the KNE and on the one hand and participants in Choros on the other in the occupied Department of Chemistry in Athens in 16 December 1979.[48] Male KNE cadres argued that the *anarchoautonomoi* were "drunk," had consumed "drugs," and were ready to attack; the cadres went further to argue that they had to "defend" themselves and "protect" the female members of the organization(T.L.,Interview). By contrast, Choros participants reversed the argument. They described the young pro-USSR Communists as prone to violence, since their group rendered them "disciplined" in such a fashion that they were expected to silence critique against them by any means. In this vein, young autonomous left-wingers claimed that a kind of "militaristic" masculinity had developed within the KNE. Indeed, in *Rixi* in 1980, male members and cadres of the latter group were depicted as marching like a Roman legion. The same trope appears in many interviews of then young autonomous left-wingers, both male and female.[49]

Rock music was not the only phenomenon that the KNE linked to drug consumption, though. In the late 1970s, disco music was designated as a "construct of the cultural industry" and as the "purest expression of the American Way of Life." The young pro-USSR Communists argued that *Saturday Night Fever* glorified the opportunities for upward social mobility of the individual within the capitalist system. It purportedly encouraged the youth to "abstain from struggle" and try to overcome its "serious problems" by forgetting them for some hours through disco dancing—an approach that the KNE termed *apochavnosi* (stupefaction) or *akindyni gia to systima ektonosi* (a vent that was harmless to the system). In the venues where disco

Figure 5.1. Representation of marching KNE members during the confrontation in the Department of Chemistry published in 1980 in the magazine *Rixi*. Source: "Katalipseis," *Rixi,* February 1980, p. 41.

music was played, according to the KNE, the youth were not only rendered impassive to the dictates of capitalism, but also got hooked on heroin, cocaine, cannabis, or LSD.[50]

Following the definitions offered by Passerini and Avdela, it can be argued that "youth" was a metaphor that captured not only the hopes, but also the anxieties of the KNE concerning the unfolding of "modernity" in Greece in the 1970s. These "anxieties," however, were transformed into "fear," to borrow the analysis of historian Joanna Bourke, through the construction of an "objective" threat. Bourke claims convincingly that "according to most commentators, the word 'fear' is used to refer to an immediate, objective threat, while 'anxiety' refers to an anticipated, subjective threat. Anxiety is described as a more generalized state, while fear is more specific and immediate. The 'danger-object' seems to be in front of us in fear states, while in anxiety states the individual is not consciously aware of what endangers him or her." She warns that historians should be, however, "extremely wary about imposing such distinctions on emotional states in the past," adding that what one group perceives as "fear" may be experienced as "anxiety" by another. What historians should examine, as she aptly remarks, are "social ... responses" by a particular group in a specific era, which establish the demarcation between those emotions. As she maintains: "[T]he only difference between a fear and an anxiety is the ability of individuals or groups to *believe* themselves capable of assessing risk or identifying a (supposed) enemy." Thus, transforming "anxiety" into "fear" is connected with "the ability to externalize threat, which provides a sense of personal invulnerability."[51] As members of the KNE in Nea Liosia stressed, "it is not enough to speak about a problem: you should clearly name who is to blame for it."[52] Thus, all the phenomena that were depicted as negative by the pro-USSR organization boiled down to one specific "perpetrator," the "imperialist centers" and their local collaborators in Greece, the "bourgeois class." In dealing with them, the normative language of the pro-USSR Communists in the late 1970s drew increasingly on a medical language. Articles consisting of interviews with psychologists frequently appeared in *Odigitis* claiming that capitalism caused "psychological problems," sometimes defined as "neuroses." KNE members and cadres were mainly inspired by Soviet sociologists and psychologists, such as Edward Rosenthal, and his work *Stochos: I fthora ton syneidiseon* (Target: The Corruption of Conscience), which was translated into Greek in 1979.[53] Extensive extracts of Rosenthal's works, specifically targeting the open-air concerts of the Rolling Stones and disco-dancing, appeared in *Odigitis, Rizospastis,* and *KOMEP.* Rosenthal employed a devolutionary narrative, claiming that such dancing, which he said was accompanied by drug consumption, demoted the youth to the status of its most "primitive" instincts, especially violence.[54] It was a viewpoint that vindicated the approach that the KNE endorsed in the mid–1970s as well, namely that "the instincts" or "spontaneity" had to be subsumed into "organized struggle." The latter was the only *diexodos* (outlet) in the *adiexodo* (impasse) that young people experienced due to capitalism.[55] In a sense, this argument was an inversion of that of some Choros participants, who had employed, mainly during the 1979 occupations, "primitiveness" as a positive symbol and counterweight to the "discipline" that the pro-USSR Communist youth group cultivated.

The concern for the spread of drugs was not confined to the KNE, but was voiced by several social and political actors, which imputed this development to various factors. Articles in the right-wing newspaper *Akropolis*, named the "weak" character of those affected as a main reason for this phenomenon.[56] However, the purported spread of drug consumption was usually blamed on factors specific to the social context. What the German historian Klaus Weinhauer has argued about West Germany in the period extending from the 1960s to the 1980s—namely that "debates about drugs figured prominently in a process of 'normative self-assurance' made to combat the erosion of social norms and values"—was also valid in the case of Greece in the late 1970s.[57] In this vein, the center-left newspaper *Ta Nea* blamed the alleged spread of the drug consumption on the "welfare" that bred "greediness" and "false needs" among the young people, who often failed to fulfill them and, consequently, fell prey to drugs.[58] Some of its articles asserted that discotheques and the non-Greek so-called *alitotouristes* (vagabond tourists) acquainted Greek youngsters with drugs.[59] Exarchia Square in the center of Athens, where the *anarchoautonomoi* gathered, was sometimes also described in these newspapers as a place where drug dealing flourished. For the KNE, the conditions in Exarchia gradually caused much more concern than Plaka had in the mid–1970s.[60] The so-called *alitotouristes* were usually young Europeans, male and female, who wandered around Greece in small groups, often by hitchhiking. They stayed in camping sites or even in parks in the urban centers and often practiced nudism. Influenced by countercultural trends, they opted for travel patterns alternative to commercial tourism. Greece was one of the beloved destinations for those "alternative" tourists, as Anja Bertsch describes them, during the 1970s and the 1980s.[61] However, they were not always greeted with enthusiasm in Greece. Local actors in the tourist resorts criticized them for not spending significant amounts of money and, consequently, not contributing to the development of their areas.[62] KNE publications blamed them for drug trafficking: "among those convicted of selling or using drugs, the majority was foreigners, especially *alitotouristes*."[63]

The scale of the actual drug consumption in Greece in the late 1970s is difficult to determine. *Odigitis* in 1977 reproduced data published by the police in Athens, Salonica, Corfu, and Patras about people trading or consuming drugs—neither KNE nor the police distinguished between "soft" and "hard."[64] The data are the following: 197 arrests in the year 1973 (29 aged 13–20, 79 aged 21–30, 89 older than 31); 255 in 1974 (31 aged 13–20, 108 aged 21–30, 116 older than 31); and 185 in 1975 (11 aged 13–20, 116 aged 21–30, 58 older than 31).[65] Such data, of course, do not cover many areas, such as various tourist resorts, and do not include people who may have consumed drugs, but were not arrested by the police. Thus, it is not possible to determine how widespread the use of drugs, as KNE defined it, was. *Ta Nea* published an article in 1979, claiming that, according to data offered by the police, about 10,000 people were on the verge of dying due to drug addiction in Greece.[66] However, the methodology that was followed to estimate this number was not referenced at all.

In any case, the KNE did not simply voice its biopolitical concerns in its publications. It participated in "committees against moral corruption" that appeared in many areas in Athens, such as in Nea Liosia, supported by municipal authorities, in order to struggle against what it labeled as the spread of drug abuse in Greece. These committees did not only address solely pro-Soviet Communists, but were open to broader social and political forces that shared a similar vantage point on drugs: for instance, the Orthodox Church was not necessarily precluded and, in the case of the Athenian district of Vyronas, local priests were invited to participate.[67] To achieve their goals, those initiatives also demanded the closure of bars and discotheques, where they argued that drugs circulated extensively.

Was this, however, a case of another moral panic, like that in the late 1950s, when rock 'n' roll reached Greece? Was the representation of the young rockers the functional equivalent of that of the "teddy boys" for the late 1970s in Greece? Toward the end of the decade, the KNE adopted a more complex approach toward rock music and did not view it solely as a "threat." In the meantime, young people who joined the group in the late 1970s, mentioned in their oral testimonies that they had been coming into contact with rock music through various channels: the rock music magazines, discotheques, and rock clubs, or through acquiring rock cassettes or sometimes records while still high school pupils.[68] In addition, the official language of the pro-Soviet Communist youth became to an extent more open to rock music. The viewpoint of prominent intellectuals and Communist functionaries certainly led in this direction. Mikis Theodorakis, whose work was highly esteemed by the pro-Soviet youth organization, openly argued in favor of the value of rock music. "Although I compose Greek music," Theodorakis claimed, "I like listening to rock music … the problem is with the one-sidedness."[69] The organ of the KNE also published in 1980 an interview with Alvaro Cunhal, the general-secretary of the pro-Soviet Portuguese Communist Party, who argued, when discussing about rock music that he was not a fan of rock music, but it was problematic to remain attached to "parochial tastes." He added that rock could render young people "enthusiastic" through its "beauty and rhythm," "alike other music genres," and that some rock music sub-genres were "perhaps mistakenly" associated with "drugs and violence."[70]

As a result, rock music, even though not described as part of the "Greek tradition," was not necessarily equated with the "American way of life," either, in the publications of the pro-Soviet youth group. The KNE employed the narrative of progressive co-optation of rock music, shared by young Eurocommunists and autonomous left-wingers as well: this theory claimed that, in the mid–1960s, a number of artists, such as John Lennon with the song "Working-Class Hero," had produced songs with "progressive" messages, castigating capitalism, racism, and imperialist wars, according to the organization.[71] However, the choices several prominent rock musicians had made since the early 1970s were lambasted in *Odigitis, Synchroni Gynaika* (the OGE[72] magazine, published by and addressed to women of all ages), and *KOMEP.* They were depicted as showing a dwindling interest in politics. They were also presented as having been co-opted by the cultural industry, which turned them into "idols," namely persons who catered solely for their individual interests and who indulged in "fake paradises" that they expected to experience through dug consumption. Still, *Odigitis* argued that there were exceptions to this alleged downfall of rock music. One notable instance was the work of Pink Floyd, including the album *The Wall.*[73] Their music and lyrics, according to the newspaper, castigated the "lack of communication" that the system causes, especially for young people.[74] Frank Zappa's *Sleep Dirt* (1980) was also appreciated in *Odigitis.*[75] From 1979, rock albums often appeared in its weekly music review column. They were also included in the newspaper's suggestions for Christmas gifts in the same year.[76] In 1980 *Odigitis* also published letters from members, who were fans of rock music and who underlined the "progressive aspects" of the work of post-punk and new wave artists of the late 1970s, especially the bands involved in "Rock against Racism" initiative, which had appeared in the United Kingdom in 1976.[77] However, even these pro-Soviet rock fans were rather selective in their appreciation of new wave. They argued that only a segment of new wave artists were "progressive," while others were apathetic or "nihilists," without clarifying which particular bands they portrayed as such.

In addition, rock and disco dancing were not rejected per se in the cultural politics of the KNE. On the condition that they did not take place in venues, where drug consumption occurred, they were increasingly proclaimed in the publications of the pro-USSR Communist youth organization as a "legitimate youthful" activity.[78] Indeed, from 1978 onward, KNE members in articles in *Odigitis, Techni kai Politismos,* and *Synchroni Gyn-aika* argued that singing partisan songs of the 1940s and the continuous reproduction of slogans that had to do with high politics were "stereotypical activities" and reproduced a *mouseiaki* (parochial) conceptualization of "tradition," which could not capture the "vitality" of young people. [79] These, in fact, were the very concepts used by RF and Choros as part of their critique of the cultural politics of KNE. This appropriation of terms by the KNE in the aftermath of the 1979 occupations may be construed as a case of *het-eroglossia,* to borrow a term introduced by philosopher and literary theorist Mikhail Bakhtin. As he argues: "Therefore his orientation toward the listener is an orientation toward a specific conceptual horizon, toward the specific world of the listener; it introduces totally new elements into his discourse; it is in this way that, after all, that various different points of view, conceptual horizons, systems for providing expressive accents, various social "languages" come to interact with each other."[80] In this vein, parties that also featured rock music soon began to take place in the cultural societies controlled by the KNE in the Athens districts, such as in Palaio Faliro and in Kolonos.[81]

Despite this cautious openness toward rock as well as disco dancing in the publications of the KNE, their reception by its members varied according to a number of parameters, such as geographical and social origin and gender. A.M., female member in the lower-middle class Athens district of Kolonos, narrated that after a pause of four years, she started dancing again. She cited numerous examples, such as her participation in a carnival party with rock and disco music in a discotheque in the center of Athens as well as in organizing a party, which included rock dancing, in the cultural club of which she was a member (G.K, A.M., Interview). Actually, for some categories of KNE members, namely the ordinary members of the group, especially female, dancing to disco or rock music in discotheques seems to have been quite common. As a variety of sources, including a letter to *Synchroni Gynaika* indicate, this practice was experienced in an ambivalent manner that included a degree of guilt, as a necessary "pleasure" after a week's hard work on the one hand, but as a "form of entertainment that stupefies" on the other.[82] Even if the aforementioned letter was forged by the editorial team, it is also obvious that it responded to the concerns of a segment of the young pro-USSR Communists. The case of S.T., female, university student and member of the KNE in the late 1970s, who was very active in the KNE-controlled cultural society in the middle-class suburb of Palaio Faliro, is also interesting. She narrated that, from the late 1970s a bar operated on the premises of the society, adding that "we often organized parties in the cultural society, at least once a month ... we mainly listened to rock music at them" (S.T., Interview).[83] On the contrary, G.K., male, mid-ranking cadre of the KNE, active in the lower-middle and working-class area of Kolonos, who was then partner and, at the point of the interview, husband of A.M., refrained from dancing in the late 1970s. His leisure activity revolved around tavernas (G.K., A.M., Interview).

The varying reception of rock music is illustrated in the debate concerning the "youth club" at the Festival of KNE-Odigitis in 1980. At the "youth club," visitors had the opportunity to dance to rock and jazz music in a place where "no drug circulation took place."[84] The club, however, was not met with unanimous approval. According to T.L., male and high-ranking cadre of KNE in that period, there was a level of tension over the issue among some KNE cadres who originated from the working class and whose activity lay in the districts of Athens, and some student cadres whose domain of activity was the universities (T.L., Interview).[85] The former constituted the most highly esteemed category in the value system of KNE and their practices had to be in accordance with the prescriptive texts published by the group; apparently, at least some of them had internalized such perceptions. These disagreements are captured in the testimony of T.L.: "It is somewhat schematic, but mainly working-class cadres said that it was us, the university students, who deviated from the party line by allowing such foreign dances at the festival. ... I responded that they should start dancing and stop being *skliroulides*" (T.L., Interview). The use of the word *skliroulides*, the diminutive form of *skliroi* (tough) is interesting. It seems to address in a critical to an extent way the self-representation of working-class male cadres as "protectors," eager to resort even to aggression to impose the party line. Simultaneously, it hints at the intimacy between the narrator and the young Communists he addressed. His critique was apparently not meant to sever their ties. In any case, at the 1981 festival, the "youth club" was much different and included solely *rebetiko* and Greek folk songs, which the leadership of the group wished to serve as the counterweight to rock music.[86] *Rebetiko* was also increasingly substituting partisan songs in the leisure pursuits of the KNE members toward the end of the decade. To an extent, the individual *zeibekiko* dance replaced collective singing for young pro-USSR Communists as well. But this had different implications in the case of the KNE than it did for the Eurocommunists and autonomous left-wingers. In the KNE the *zeibekiko* dance followed the singing of *rebetiko* verses, which expressed the suffering of the "Greek people" and encouraged "youth militancy." They did not construe the "profound" and "authentic" emotion of *kefi* as contradictory to "discipline," but as complementing and strengthening it: they sometimes danced *zeibekiko* and sang KKE slogans.[87] *Rebetiko* and rock music would not be regarded as mutually exclusive for long in the cultural politics of the KNE, however. Reports in *Odigitis* and

Rizospastis show that rock bands performed onstage in the festivals of KNE-Odigitis in the 1980s.[88]

Maoists (Re)Think Culture

A major development in left-wing politics in Greece in the late 1970s was the decline of the Maoist Parties and student organizations. Many ex-members of theirs had joined Choros by 1979. Maoist groups did not bounce back after the occupations of 1979. The EKKE and the AASPE were growingly abandoned in the early 1980s. Similarly, the KKE(m-l) and the PPSP suffered from internal splits and massive withdrawals, experiencing a serious crisis in the early 1980s. [89]

Shortly prior to demise, however, the Maoist Parties and youth organizations readdressed the ways in which they approached "culture." In the case of the PPSP and KKE(m-l), their cultural politics became more systematic. *Proletariaki Simaia,* the newspaper of the KKE(m-l), began publishing the column "Politistiki Zoi" (Cultural Life) on a regular basis, in response to "the demand of numerous of its readers."[90] Moreover, Istorikes Ekdoseis (Historical Publications), affiliated with the KKE(m-l), translated a growing number of theatre works. Among the books that were translated by it during this period were Dario Fo's *La giullarata.*[91] Such developments were also evident in the youth organization affiliated with the KKE(m-l): even though a choir of the PPSP existed in the mid–1970s, an all-encompassing cultural committee of the group was not founded prior to 1980. In 1978, the *Proodeytikos Kinimatografos* (Progressive Cinema) magazine also appeared. It was renamed *Proodeytikos Kinimatografos-Alloi Kairoi* (Progressive Cinema-Other Times) in the early 1980s. All members of its editorial board were affiliated with the KKE(m-l). The editorial board comprised Aris Maragkopoulos, Ada Klampatsea, and Nikos Vergitsis. All of them were around thirty years old in the late 1970s; Maragkopoulos, the eldest, had been born in 1948. Nevertheless, the magazine did not address solely the "youth." Most of the editors had studied abroad, either in Paris, such as Maragkopoulos and Vergitsis, or in Italy, like Klampatsea. The *Proodeytikos Kinimatografos* editors and contributors were partially iconoclastic: although they galvanized a heated debate, especially within KKE(m-l) and PPSP, around the topic of sexuality, as is shown in detail in the next chapter, they formulated yet another message-centered approach to the reception of cinema movies with the explicit aim to generate committed Communists.

At that point, young Maoists in Greece often exchanged views, especially on cinema, with their comrades in other Western European countries.

The magazine *Proodeytikos Kinimatografos* cooperated with the French *Feuille Foudre,* which had an explicit aim to accommodate a Maoist initiative in "culture." The latter was published by the *Group Foudre d' intervention culturelle* (Lightening Group for cultural intervention), which had been launched by the Maoist UCFml, namely the Union of Communists in France (Marxist-Leninist) in 1974, and in which a number of philosophers, like Bernard Sichère and Alain Badiou participated. In 1978 *Feuille Foudre* published a review by Aris Maragkopoulos, of Angelopoulos's film *Kynigoi.*[92] The common aim of *Proodeytikos Kinimatografos* and *Feuille Foudre* was to produce and promote a "militant" cinema that would not be linked with commercial networks and whose content would lambast "capitalism," "imperialism," and "revisionism." Such an effort had been made since the late 1960s by cinema collectives and magazines in France, whose work was predicated upon Maoist principles. "Militant" films were usually documentaries, often about the life of the workers. Groups involved in this project in France were, among others, Cinéthique and CRAC. "Militant" cinema provides an example of intercrossings, since it was a joint venture undertaken by actors across Western Europe. Authors, who contributed with articles to *Proodeytikos Kinimatografos,* were also involved in it: one of them, Dimitris Panagiotatos, alongside Denis Levy, were the film directors of the movie *L'Usine du Vampire* (The Factory of the Vampire), produced by CRAC in 1977. However, *Proodeytikos Kinimatografos* editors did not produce any such movie in Greece.

By contrast, "militant" movies were produced in Greece in the mid– to late–1970s by another segment of Maoists: a prominent example was Thodoros Maragos, a film director, leaning toward the EKKE, who was influenced by the transnational Maoist effort to produce a distinct cinema. Maragos was a member of the militant cinematic "Group of Six," which produced the realistic documentary *Agonas* in 1975. The documentary concentrated on strikes in the early *Metapolitefsi* years. However, the "Group of Six" was short-lived and its function ceased soon after the completion of *Agonas.* In the late 1970s and early 1980s, Maragos directed the films *Apo pou pane gia tin havouza* (Which is the way to the refuse dump, 1978); *Thanassi sfixe ki allo to zonari* (Thanassi, tie your belt more tightly, 1980), starring the renowned Greek comedian Thanassis Veggos; and *Mathe paidi mou grammata* (My kid, you should get educated, 1981). Maragos's movies were immensely popular: according to *Ta Theamata, Apo pou pane gia tin havouza* topped the list of box-office hits, selling 480,145 tickets in Athens and Piraeus in the winter season of 1978–1979, being the most popular Greek film for that period, while *Thanassi sfixe ki allo to zonari* sold 282,025 tickets in the same area in the winter season of 1979–1980.[93] His work was often praised in the publications of young Maoists affiliated with the EKKE, such as in the pupil magazine *O Agonas ton Mathiton* (High School Student Struggle).[94] However, *Proodeytikos Kinimatografos* was dubious about his work: although the magazine invited him to express his viewpoint on how he construed "militant cinema," it often voiced negative critiques of some of his movies. It reviewed *Apo pou pane gia tin havouza* as a sheerly "demagogic" one: it purportedly referred to some serious problems existing in Greek society, such as the distortion of the information presented on television, simply to stir up public opinion and without demonstrating clearly how capitalism causes all those issues. As such, it lacked, according to the magazine, "militant" credentials and was a "compromise with the dominant ideology."[95]

During the late 1970s, the KKE(m-l) and the PPSP perpetuated, to an extent, the viewpoint they had developed toward "culture" in the very first post-dictatorship years. Their relevant analyses continued to revolve around the promotion of "progressive culture" and the struggle against the "American way of life" or, put differently, "imperialism" in the domain of "culture." An article in the Maoist pupil newspaper *Mathitika Neiata* is telling: "Enemies of the tradition are the American sailors, who spoil our ports with their presence ... Clubs and disco are the enemies of our tradition."[96] They also accused the center-right government of shedding crocodile tears on Greek "tradition." In fact, the Ministry of Education and Religious Affairs designated the academic year 1978–1979 as the "year of Greek tradition." Directives to high school teachers, alongside articles in the government-controlled high-school pupil magazine *Eleftheri Genia* (Free Generation) urged pupils to collect old objects and stories about "traditional customs."[97] However, the Maoists dismissed these efforts, arguing that the government, which they accused of promoting "imported" leisure pursuits, was a foe of this "tradition."[98]

Still, while approaching "culture" from the same lens, the KKE(m-l) and the PPSP adopted a broader conceptualization of what a "progressive" artifact was: Similar to the KNE, they experienced an internal controversy about rock music. The participation of the PPSP in the student occupations in 1979 certainly functioned as a catalyst in those internal debates: PPSP cadres and members were confronted with the dilemma how to react to the rock parties that their allies, the autonomous young left-wingers, organized in the occupied university schools. The vibrations of those parties could be felt even in the pages of *Salpisma,* the magazine of the PPSP: while listening and dancing to rock music was sometimes detested per se, on other occasions it was stated that some 1960s rock music songs bore a "progressive" message, as manifest in Woodstock. Although articles in *Salpisma* concurred in arguing that rock music production was largely "commercialized" in the 1970s and lamented that "anti-fascist" The Clash were soon succeeded by the "superficially emotional" The Police, they were steadfast in finding positive, in their view, examples of rockers: they singled out Frank Zappa as a case of a 1970s "progressive" and "socially concerned" rock.[99] In practice, what had occurred in the KNE was also evident in the case of the PPSP: the music taste and the stance toward rock differed due to a variety of factors, such as social and geographical origin and age. Older cadres and members, especially those who came from rural areas, tended to be more cautious toward rock music. V.S., male, high-ranking cadre of the KKE(m-l) in the late 1970s, remembers divisions within the PPSP about rock music: "I think that we, the older ones, who were filling the leadership positions (of the KKE(m-l) and the PPSP), without wishing to impose our viewpoint, we felt that our approach differed from that of the younger cadres. However, there was no rancorous debate among us about that issue" (V.S., Interview). One way or another, in attempting to grapple with frustrating or at least perplexing for them developments in the Communist movement worldwide, Maoists in Greece increasingly dealt with "culture," sometimes ending up challenging basic tenets of the version of the Communist ideology they had endorsed in the preceding years.

Notes

1. "O OFI, oi skoupes kai o lavyrinthos," *Thourios*, 10 January 1980, p. 9.
2. Extensive analysis and accounts of the occupations can be found in *Rixi*, February 1980, pp. 4–103; *ANTI*, 18 January 1980, pp. 21–31; and *Thourios*, 10 January 1980, pp. 8–9.
3. The temporary academic staff in the Greek universities, called EDP (Eidiko Didaktiko Prosopiko, Special Teaching Staff), had gone on strike from February until May 1978 demanding that they become permanent. Many members of the EDP showed their solidarity toward the student occupations in 1979 by organizing *anti-mathimata*, namely "alternative classes," in the occupied schools. See Kostas Gavroglou, "Tomeis Edron: to adynato mias symviosis," *To Vima tis Kiriakis*, 30 March 1980. See also: Aravantinos, "To Metapoliteytiko," pp. 283–84, 287.
4. The title can be translated as "We are not Zulu."
5. "Edo Lilipoupoli" was the name of a show that was broadcast from 1976 to 1980 on the Third Program of the Greek Public Radio. These songs appeared in an album bearing the same name as the show in 1980.
6. "Oi Katalipseis," *Rixi*, February 1980, p. 17; "O OFI, oi skoupes kai o lavyrinthos," *Thourios*, 10 January 1980, p. 9.
7. "O OFI, oi skoupes kai o lavyrinthos," *Thourios*, 10 January 1980, p. 9. For both slogans that appear in this sentence I mention the translation of their original, Greek version, in English.
8. See the booklet published by KNE under the title: *Dekemvris '79: Agonistiki exarsi tou foititikou kinimatos* (Athens, 1980), p. 56.
9. Papadogiannis, "Between Angelopoulos," p. 301.

10. For an in-depth examination of this practice, see: Janet Staiger, "The Perversity of Spectators: Expanding the History of the Classical Hollywood Cinema," in *Moving Images, Culture and the Mind,* ed. Ib Bondebjerg (Luton, UK, 2000), pp. 19–30.

11. The fact that rock parties took place during the occupations is also recorded, for instance, in the following article: "Stigmiotypa apo tis Katalipseis: O OFI, oi skoupes kai o lavyrinthos," *Thourios,* 16 January 1980, p. 9.

12. Aravantinos, "To Metapoliteytiko," pp. 488, 500. The number of blank and invalid votes kept increasing in the elections of 1979 and 1980. See also: "Foititikes ekloges '79: Ti kainourio fernoun gia to foititiko kinima," *Thourios,* 16 February 1979, p. 12; "Apti tora I dynatotita gia mia nea poreia tou foititikou kinimatos," *Thourios,* 13 March 1980, p. 2.

13. A. Maounis, T. Platis, and D. Psarras, "Gia ton fetino Noemvri," *Agonas gia tin Kommounistiki Ananeosi,* November–December 1980, pp. 31–38.

14. See, for example, ASKI, Archive of Rigas Feraios, Central Council of RF, 1974–1979, box 5, envelope 4, resolution of the third regular session of the central council about high-school pupils, 1977, pp. 7–8.

15. For the case of RF, see, for example: ASKI, Archive of Michalis Sabatakakis, Box 5, envelope 7, report of the bureau of high-school pupils.

16. See, for instance, an interview of a pupil, who participated in Choros, in: "Syzitame gia ti zoi, to scholio, to mathitiko kinima," *Thourios,* 17 April 1980, pp. 4–5.

17. "Festival Mathitikon Efimeridon," *Thranio,* vol. 6, 1981.

18. "Geitonies," *Rixi,* March 1981, pp. 27–42.

19. See the discussion about the activity of Choros in the districts of Athens in the volume 6 of *Rixi,* published in March 1981.

20. As Sotiropoulos has asserted, the significance of the "informal civil society" in Greece is often neglected in scholarship, which privileges organized political actors. For more, see Dimitri A. Sotiropoulos, "Formal Weakness and Informal Strength: Civil Society in Contemporary Greece," discussion paper published in 2004 on the website of the Hellenic Observatory of the London School of Economics and Political Science, which can be found at the following address: http://eprints.lse.ac.uk/5683/ (last accessed: 2 October 2012).

21. See, for instance: "Lesches-Syllogoi," *Ta Aythaireta ton synoikion tis EKON Rigas Feraios (B Panelladiki),* 1 May 1980, p. 12.

22. See, for example, "Faliro," *Rixi,* March 1981, pp. 32–36.

23. Ibid.

24. See, for example, "I synaylia sto Mpati," *Dialogos,* September–October 1981, p. 15; see also the discussion about the activity of Choros in the districts of Athens in the volume 6 of *Rixi,* published in March 1981.

25. See, for example, "As mpoume apofasistika ston agona tis allagis," *Odigitis,* 18 September 1980, p. 4; "Empros gia ena gero kai maziko kinima tis Neas Genias," *Agonistis,* 21 September 1979, p. 8.

26. "Stathmos i ekdilosi tis PAMK Peiraia," *Agonistis,* 2 February 1979, p. 12.

27. "Laos PASOK stin exousia," *Agonistis,* 21 September 1979, p. 4; Program of the Festival of KNE-Odigitis, *Odigitis,* 13 September 1979, p. 13.

28. "Apo enarxeos tis heimerinis periodou mehri 1/2/1981," *Ta Theamata,* 20 February 1981, p. 8.

29. Dimitris Danikas, "Kritiki Kinimatografou," *Rizospastis,* 25 November 1980, p. 4.

30. "Technes … Grammata," *Odigitis,* 28 November 1980, p. 10.

31. Minutes of the assemblies of the PSPF, Personal Archive of Roura Sifnaiou.

32. See, for instance: "Provlimata kai prooptikes ton politistikon syllogon," *Odigitis,* 30 March 1979, pp. 16–17; "Politistikos Syllogos Palaiou Falirou," *Odigitis,* 23 January 1981, p. 12.

33. "Dyo antilipseis gia to politistiko," *Avgi,* 14 March 1980, p. 4.

34. "Ergatiko Politistiko Diimero sth Thessaloniki," *Odigitis,* 14 August 1980, p. 15.

35. About the School of Philosophy in Salonica, see Sarris, "Politistikes Drastiriotites," pp. 220–29.

36. "Ekdosi tis Panspoudastikis gia ton Politismo," 1980. Personal Collection of Aimilia Karali.

37. "I synantisi erasitechnikon thiason stin Thessaloniki," *Odigitis,* 29 May 1981, p. 14.

38. "O choros kai to programma tis Giortis," *Agonistis,* 7 September 1979, pp. 8–9; "Savvato 15.9," *Odigitis,* 7 September 1979, p. 13.

39. "1000 neoi estisan 'prasini politeia' sti N. Filadelfeia," *Ta Nea,* 3 September 1980, p. 13.

40. Cover page, *Ta Nea,* 15 September 1980.

41. Dimitris Panousakis, "Gia ton Amerikaniko Tropo Zois," *KOMEP* 1979, October 1979, pp. 44–54.

42. "Na sosoume ti neolaia ap' to 'leyko thanato,'" *Odigitis,* 27 May 1977, p. 11.

43. I would like to thank Prof. H. Fleischer and Dr. N. Bozinis for informing me about this correspondence and Dr. E. Rofouzou for providing me with the relevant material. For the correspondence from the East German side, see DY/30 Vorl. SED 34922, 17 March 1981, Stiftung Archiv der Parteien und Massenorganisationen der DDR im Bundesarchiv Berlin. See also: Papadogiannis, "Greek Communist Youth Identities and Rock Music," p. 89.

44. "Via kai Rok," *Odigitis,* 29 May 1981, p. 14.

45. "Lenin: 110 chronia. Syneidito kai aythormito," *Odigitis,* 18 April 1980, p. 8.

46. For instance: "Ektonosi 'edo kai tora,'" *Odigitis,* 22 February 1980, p. 8.

47. Ibid.

48. *Dekemvris '79: Agonistiki exarsi tou foititikou kinimatos* (Athens, 1980), p. 70.

49. I.A, Interview. I.A. is female, and she was a student from 1977 to 1981 from a lower-middle-class family, PASP member until early 1980 and subsequently Choros participant; "Katalipseis," *Rixi,* February 1980, p. 41.

50. See, for example: "Travolta I pos paraskevazetai ena indalma," *Odigitis,* 10 November 1978, p. 10.

51. Joanna Bourke, *Fear: A Cultural History* (London, 2006), pp. 189–92.

52. "Exormiseis sta 'stekia' kai ekdilosi gia ti diafthora," *Odigitis,* 29 August 1980, p. 6.

53. It was translated in Greek in 1979 by *Sychroni Epochi* editions.

54. A similar argument appeared in: Antonis Stemnis, "Gia tin anaptyxi tou politistikou kinimatos," *KOMEP,* October 1978, pp. 108–25. Stemnis described rock and disco dance as "dance until you drop under the effect of drugs."

55. Actually, *Odigitis* published a series of articles in 1980 titled "(A)diexodos sto adiexodo." See, for example: 1 February 1980, pp. 10–11; 15 February 1980, pp. 12–13.

56. "Narkotika: Ta pairnoun kai koritsia 13 chronon!," *Akropolis,* 16 December 1979, p. 7.
57. Klaus Weinhauer, "The End of Certainties: Drug Consumption and Youth Delinquency in West Germany of the 1960/70s," in Schildt and Siegfried, *Between Marx and Coca Cola,* p. 377.
58. "Voitheia! Soste mas apo ta narkotika," *Ta Nea,* 3 December 1979, p. 5.
59. Kostas Chardavellas, "Ntiskotek," *Ta Nea,* 4 December 1979, p. 4.
60. See the aforementioned series of articles titled "(A)diexodos sto adiexodo."
61. Anja Bertsch, "Alternative (in) Bewegung: Distinktion und transnationale Vergemeinschaftung im alternativen Tourismus," in *Das Alternative Milieu: Antibürgerlicher Lebensstil und linke Politik in der Bundesrepublik Deutschland und Europa 1968–1983,* ed. Sven Reichardt and Detlef Siegfried (Göttingen, 2010), pp. 116–17.
62. G. Garedaki, "Chania: oi alitotouristes," *Ta Nea,* 12 August 1980, p. 3.
63. "Na sosoume th neolaia apo to 'leyko thanato,'" *Odigitis,* 1 April 1977.
64. About the KNE, see, for instance: "'Malakes' theories me 'sklirous' stochous," *Odigitis,* 19 December 1980, pp. 14–15.
65. "Na profylaxoume ti neolaia ap' to 'leyko thanato,'" *Odigitis,* 1 April 1977, pp. 8–9.
66. M. Mathioudakis, "Se trochia thanatou," *Ta Nea,* 3 December 1979, p. 7.
67. "Na sosoume ti neolaia ap' ton 'leyko thanato,'" *Odigitis,* 27 May 1977, p. 9; "Exormiseis sta stekia kai ekdilosi gia ti diafthora," *Odigitis,* 29 August 1980, p. 9.
68. For example, B.L., Interview. B.L., female, was a university student and mid–ranking KNE cadre in the late 1970s.
69. "I Techni einai ena aitima opos to Psomi kai I Doulia," *Odigitis,* 30 March 1979, pp. 15, 18. See also: Papadogiannis, "Greek Communist Youth Identities and Rock Music," p. 87.
70. "Anoichti syzitisi me ton Alvaro Cunhal", *Odigitis,* 14 August 1980, p. 7.
71. D. Panousakis, "Gia ton Amerikaniko Tropo Zois," *KOMEP,* October 1979, pp. 44–54.
72. Omospondia Gynaikon Elladas, namely Federation of Women in Greece, aligned with KKE.
73. The album *The Wall* was very popular and it maintained the first position in the charts of *Pop kai Rock* from January until August 1980. The charts were based on the level of sales of the albums, as estimated by a team of *Pop kai Rock* in charge of statistics, in contrast with its annual polls, which were based on what the readers of the magazine voted.
74. "Diskoi," *Odigitis,* 18 January 1980, p. 12.
75. "Diskoi," *Odigitis,* 11 April 1980, p. 12.
76. In 1979, for example, two albums by The Police, namely "Outlandos d'Amour" and "Regatta de Blanc" alongside "The Fine Act of Surfacing" by the Boomtown Rats, were suggested. "Akoume mousiki?," *Odigitis,* 21 December 1979, p. 18.
77. "Disco, o antipodas tou Neou Kymatos," *Odigitis,* 24 August 1979, p. 13; "A New Wave machomenis mousikis," *Odigitis,* 11 April 1980, p. 9.
78. Papadogiannis, "Greek Communist Youth Identities and Rock Music," p. 88.
79. See "Ergazomeni neolaia, eleytheros chronos," *Odigitis,* 20 June 1980, p. 9.

80. Extract from Mikhail M. Bakhtin, *The Dialogic Imagination*, republished in *The Bakhtin Reader*, ed. Pam Morris (London, 1994), p. 76.
81. "B Panelladiki synantisi politistikon foreon," *Odigitis*, 11 May 1979, p. 17.
82. "Chryses vradies se rythmo disco," *Synchroni Gynaika*, November–December 1979, pp. 50–51.
83. An article in *Aythaireta* vindicates this claim. See "Synenteyxi me to periodiko 'Dialogos' tou P. Falirou," *Ta Aythaireta ton synoikion tis EKON Rigas Feraios (B Panelladiki)*, 20 July 1980, p. 11.
84. "Mia stasi sto 'steki' mas," *Odigitis*, 11 September 1980, p. 7.
85. It is notable that T.L. has been a member of the NAR (Neo Aristero Reyma, New Left Current) since 1989.
86. "Steki psychagogias, prospatheia pou petyche," *Odigitis*, 17 September 1981, pp. 18–19; Maria Damanaki, "Gia orismena simerina politistika fainomena," *KOMEP*, October 1980, pp. 70–78. See also: Papadogiannis, "Greek Communist Youth Identities and Rock Music," p. 89.
87. "Steki psychagogias, prospatheia pou petyche," *Odigitis*, 17 September 1981, pp. 18–19.
88. In the case of the Festival of KNE-Odigitis in 1988: A. Fraggos, "Rok-mplouz ap' tin Agglia," *Rizospastis*, 13 September 1988, p. 10; "'Aichmalotoi' tis rock," *Rizospastis*, 14 September 1988, p. 10. The rock bands that appeared onstage in this festival were TYA and the Mekons.
89. The en masse withdrawals from the AASPE were admitted in texts of its Central Council that were written at the end of the decade. Their exact number is not defined, but one of those texts mentions that a "significant minority" of "comrades," especially in Athens and Piraeus. See: ASKI, Archive of Fyssas, "Schedio Apologismou tis AASPE gia tin 8chroni drasi tis," pp. 1–4, 10–12.
90. "Politistiki Zoi. Gia tin kathierosi mias stilis," *Proletariaki Simaia*, 18 February 1978, p. 2.
91. It was translated into Greek by Mania Politou and published in Athens in 1981.
92. Aris Maragkopoulos, "Les choix d'angelopoulos: Les chasseurs," *Feuille Foudre*, spring/summer 1978, pp. 30–32.
93. "Cheimerini Periodos 1978–1979," *Ta Theamata*, 31 December 1979, p. 74; "Cheimerini periodos 1979–1980," *Ta Theamata*, 19 December 1980.
94. "Synenteyxi me ton T. Marago," *O Agonas ton Mathiton*, October 1977, pp. 12–13, 15.
95. Thodoros Maragos, "Gia ton agonistiko kinimatografo," *Proodeytikos Kinimatografos*, third term 1979, pp. 66–67; Ada Klampatsea, "Apo pou pane gia ti havouza," *Proodeytikos Kinimatografos*, first term 1979, pp. 80–86.
96. "I 'provoli' tis laikis mas paradosis," *Mathitika Neiata*, 2 February 1979, pp.4–5.
97. *Eleftheri Genia*, vol. 27, 1979. Relevant activities of high-school students were publicized in the booklet titled *Politistikes Drastiriotites*, published by the Ministry of Education and Religious Affairs in 1979.
98. "I 'provoli' tis laikis mas paradosis," *Mathitika Neiata*, 2 February 1979, pp. 4–5.
99. For instance: "Rock-1980?," *Salpisma*, November–December 1980, p. 31.

Chapter 6

Sex and the Left-Wing Youth Around 1980

An Era of Controversy

From 1978 onward, young Eurocommunists and Choros participants voiced critique of the dominant sexual norms in Greek society, which they asserted were also reinforced in the prescriptive texts of the Left, especially in the "Farakos Guidelines." Dispensing with such a normative language, they engaged in collective reflection on youth sexuality, containing open-ended questions and humorous narrations. Such developments gained momentum "around 1980," during and in the aftermath of the occupations, spreading also among a segment of the Maoists and young Socialists. Meanwhile, the Feminist and the homosexual liberation movements also challenged sexual norms, which they claimed that reproduced gender hierarchies in Greece in general and within the Greek Left in particular. Those movements were certainly not by-products of the occupations: not only had they predated them, but their demands largely failed to gain traction in the occupied schools. Feminists particularly intensified their activities in 1980, when they staged protests against the Family Law. The relationship between those movements and the heterosexual male members of the Greek Left was rather complex. Some of the latter, in lambasting "Puritan" norms and displaying sexual promiscuity, resorted to sexist stereotypes, expressed especially in spontaneous slogans or jokes. Nevertheless, at least a few young Eurocommunists tried to elaborate on a nonsexist model of masculinity, echoing mainly the demands of their female comrades who subscribed to second-wave feminism.

Overcoming Taxonomies

In describing sexuality in Europe, Herzog argues that the late 1970s heralded the "turn inward": diverse individuals "felt even more unmoored and disoriented about their bodies, desires, emotions, and relationships that before."[1] The situation appeared much more complex in Greece at that point, however. There were subjects, such as the Christian Orthodox groups, who sounded a note of anxiety for what they viewed as a disseminating "over-sexualization."[2] Meanwhile, what gained traction was a counter-argument, voiced by subjects such as journalists in women's magazines (as will be shown in this chapter) who represented sexuality as a source of pleasure that should not be constrained by "Puritan" sexual norms. One way or another, the popular press hosted numerous relevant surveys and extensive articles.[3]

Redefining sexuality and gender as well as repositioning leisure toward them certainly figured prominently in the rhetoric and practice of some Communist and Socialist groups in Greece at that point. In this vein, lambasting the "didactic" language of the "Farakos Guidelines," the publications of RF and Choros increasingly contained from 1978 onward an extensive reflection on sexual relationships: many of the first-person singular narratives of affiliated and nonaffiliated youngsters that appeared in Eurocommunist youth publications at that point referred to sexuality. These were usually published in the articles of Feminist Eurocommunists in *Thourios*, but were soon employed by male young Eurocommunists as well. Flirtation was a common topic; besides that and in stark contrast with the mid–1970s, descriptions of the human sexual organs, even of the very act of intercourse, appeared. Young women often narrated in detail their fears of sex. A person who signed as Elena, 18 years old and pupil, mentioned: "Thus, I decided to make love. The fact that I could hurt made me anxious. I was even more afraid of not being aware of how to react and of having to rely on Divine Providence, in order not to get pregnant. It was long before fear was transformed into pleasure, before I really started enjoying sex."[4] Young men often referred to their experiences in brothels. Somebody who signed as Panos, 24 years old, recounted: "[T]he first time I have ever made love was with a whore. I went to the brothel alongside a friend who had already been there, because I didn't know what to do there."[5] *Thourios* also contained the perspective of the sex labor. Maria, presented as a 26-year-old prostitute, displayed a degree of compassion: "I think that most men have their first sexual experience with us. We teach love to men. There are men who ask me to show them, because they know nothing. When they tell me so, I think, what the hell, I have ended up being a teacher of love. However, I feel sorry, because they are kids, 15–16 years old."[6] The persons who signed the articles were almost always heterosexual; homosexuality was regarded as legitimate in the Eurocommunist youth publications, but concerning a "minority." Such narrations usually revolved around the description of the "taboos" that were portrayed as "suppressing sexual desires." While the "New Left" in West Germany sought "anti-fascist bodies" in the late 1960s, those Greek left-wing actors embraced no grand narrative, none of the ideas introduced by Wilhelm

Reich or any language that would classify what forms of sexual intercourse would be the ideal ones.[7] In addition, in comparison to what happened in left-wing magazines elsewhere in Western Europe, such as the West German *Konkret,* sexually explicit photographs never accompanied relevant articles of Choros and RF.[8]

Self-reflection on sexuality also spread among pupils leaning toward or aligned with RF and Choros. The former had been publishing relevant articles in their magazine, *Mathitiki Poreia,* from 1977 onward. Gradually, and especially after 1979, when Choros participants gained momentum in high schools, Eurocommunist and autonomous left-wing pupils converged in their attacks on what they described as "authoritarian education" or "everyday fascism" in *Mathitiki Poreia,* in pupil magazines, and in the reports from Eurocommunist pupil cadres, containing the proposed policies of the group in the high schools. One such account, referring to the publication of pupil magazines states that: "anxiety, heavy work, sexuality, loneliness, leisure, are factors that have caused a growing challenging of everyday life ... in the pupil magazines that have appeared recently, humor and imagination are predominant ... pupils should opt for self-management and confront bureaucratic relations."[9] "Authoritarian education" contained the critique of a number of norms, which this segment of the left-wing youth claimed that jeopardized the personal autonomy of the pupils and ensured their "integration" into the capitalist system. Penalties, especially expulsions, and the assessment system, featured prominently in their critique. So did issues of gender and sexuality. Eurocommunist pupil publications demanded, without success, that sexual education be introduced into the curricula.[10] Eurocommunist pupils alongside the RF Women's Committee also strove for the abolition of gender-segregated schools. This was achieved in 1978 in a number of high schools and 1979 in almost all of them, following the issuing of the relevant regulation of the government. They also mounted a loud critique of female pupil uniform;[11] it was actually abolished after PASOK rose to power in 1981. Young Eurocommunists and autonomous left-wingers also extended their critique to what they viewed as "taboos" on pupil sexuality beyond the premises of high schools. Vacations were one of their favorite issues, since they were represented as an ideal locus for the development of sexual relationships: "sun, sea, happiness shake our bodies in the quest for pleasure."[12] In this vein, *Mathitiki Poreia* implied that pupils going on vacation without their parents enjoyed more freedom in their social interaction.[13]

In a sense, and with the active involvement of students or former students, pupils appropriated a conceptual framework that emerged in the domain of the universities and projected it onto their own interpersonal relations. For instance, in the case of B Panelladiki, Christoforos Vernardakis wrote articles in *Agonas gia tin Kommounistiki Ananeosi* about pupils, even when he was a student. On account of her studies in pedagogics, Marisa Decastro, Feminist Eurocommunist, was assigned by the central council tasks that were connected with the guiding of the Eurocommunist high-school pupils. In her capacity as a cadre, she promoted events, in which male and female pupils completed questionnaires about their sexual experiences and subsequently discussed them in public. She also introduced a column in *Mathitiki Poreia,* where lifestyle issues were discussed.[14]

In general, young Eurocommunists viewed sexuality as closely interwoven with their leisure pursuits. A male high school pupil claimed in *Mathitiki Poreia* that the songs "Let it be" (1969) and "Yesterday" (1965) by the Beatles accompanied the various stages of his experience of "falling in love."[15] Some RF members went further: by reflecting on rock music, they wished to simultaneously formulate a "revolutionary critique of interpersonal relations," dispelling sexual "taboos," without necessarily, however, putting forth

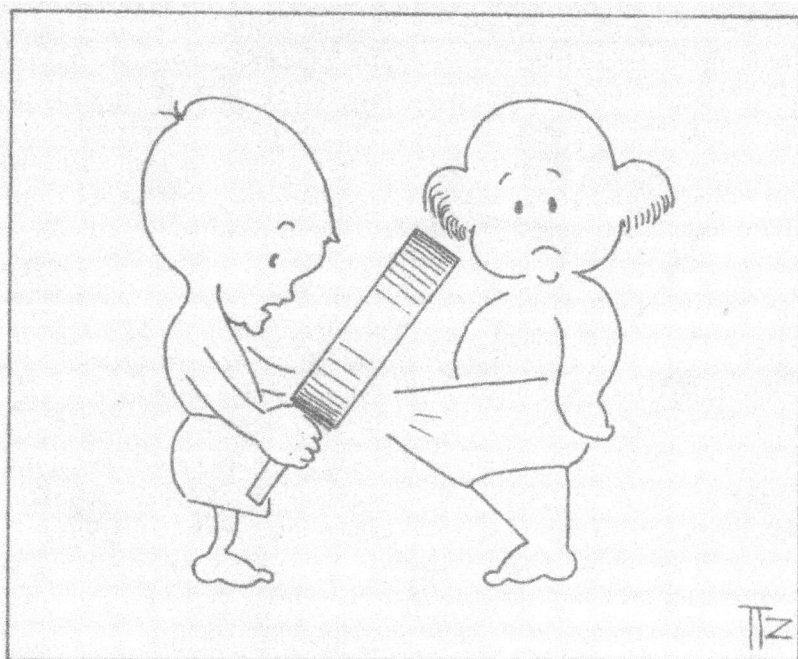

Figure 6.1. Comic publicizing an open discussion about sexuality organized by RF members in the Third Male Senior High School in Kokkinia in 1978. Source: "Ekdilosi gia ta afrodisia nosimata sto G lykeio Nikaias," *Thourios,* 6 April 1978, p. 11. Used with permission from Dimitris Chatzisokratis.

alternatives.[16] Once again, this music genre denoted for them a projection screen for their reflection and (self-) critique.

The prescriptive language of a segment of the Maoists vis-à-vis sexuality altered as well toward the end of the decade. During the mid–1970s the publications of the PPSP lambasted sexual patterns that deviated from stable, heterosexual relations leading to marriage and castigating the "revisionists" for making too much fuss for a "purported" liberation from a "petty-bourgeois" morality.[17] However, the relevant texts of the latter began to echo an embarrassment, mainly after the occupations in 1979. As in the mid–1970s, the discourse of the PPSP continued to be predicated on the dichotomy of "Greek popular" as opposed to "imported/foreign" cultural products. Nevertheless, quite interestingly and in contrast with the pro-Soviet Communists, they no longer connected "foreign" cultural products with biopolitical concerns. Those young Maoists increasingly feared that they were in the slippery slope, when trying to delineate "progressive" sexual patterns. A clear manifestation of this dubiousness is found in *Salpisma,* the magazine of the PPSP: in an article that appeared in 1981, the author made explicit his/her inability to suggest any sexual norms. S/he limited himself/herself to stating that neither the cohabitation of young people (and their apparently libertine spirit) nor the "couples of the beloved members of the KNE" are viable options, since they reproduce either a "liberal" or a "conservative" version of "bourgeois norms."[18] By contrast, the student and the pupil groups aligned with EKKE, AASPE, and AAMPE, perpetuated the discourse on sexuality that they had endorsed since the first post-dictatorship years. *O Agonas ton Mathiton,* the newspaper of AAMPE, published at that point an extensive text appeared idealizing marriage "due to love," which purportedly was predominant among working-class people, in contrast with the "bourgeois" sexual patterns, which demoted "love" merely to "sexual satisfaction."[19] The same organization actually organized a series of talks in order to "enlighten" its members in this direction.[20]

Young Socialists also rode on this wave of redefining left-wing politics in relation to sexuality. The apparatus of the Youth of PASOK had not guarded vigilantly the sexual activity of their members in the mid–1970s. What was new at the end of the decade was that young Socialists growingly articulated doubts about the dominant sexual norms in Greece in the publications of the group. A leaflet published by the Socialist student group in the Department of Mathematics of the University of Athens, labeled the approach that sexual relationships should necessarily be stable and leading to marriage as a "reactionary, bourgeois value," which had been incorporated into Marxism "like cancer."[21] This viewpoint was not peculiar to the Socialist students of Mathematics: it was also voiced in the festivals of the organization, where young Socialists questioned the norms that the Left had hitherto espoused, being particularly critical of the "Farakos Guidelines." In this vein, their festival in 1980 entailed a discussion entitled "Social issues of the youth: Is there also loneliness apart from imperialism?"[22] Similarly, in a series of articles published in *Avgi* about family relations in Greece, the representative of the Youth of PASOK, Giorgos Kanellopoulos, claimed that young people should not necessarily opt for marriage, mentioning long-term cohabitation of unmarried couples as an alternative. In stark contrast with the "Farakos Guidelines," stable relationships were not an objective for him.[23]

By contrast, the official language of the KNE remained largely unaffected from this critique of classifications of sexuality. In voicing its concern over drug consumption in the late 1970s, it reproduced taxonomies that juxtaposed stable, heterosexual relationships with the "unhealthy sexuality" of the allegedly drug-consuming "anarchists," whom it criticized for appreciating "group sex."[24] However, there was a modest change in the style of KNE publications. A new form of narrative, which may be called "patronizing autobiographies," began to appear in *Odigitis*. In contrast with the biographies of young "heroes and martyrs" of the OKNE and EPON, these had to do with contemporary, living persons. A number of young men and women employed first-person singular narratives as well as a number of terms, used by RF, Choros, and the Feminists, especially "taboos" and "loneliness." Nevertheless, it was made clear that sexual relations were understood within the framework of heterosexual relationships. Many young narrators appeared appalled at the "sex, drugs, and rock 'n' roll" lure that capitalism had created: for instance, a person who signed as "Dimitris (21 years old)" recounted: "I used to socialize with those people.... Offsprings of industrialists, tradesmen, whose parents are usually divorced; driven by anxiety and boredom, they seek happiness in parties, drugs, orgies and prostitution."[25] *Odigitis* also included testimonies from young people, whose vantage point differed from that of the KNE. For example, some narrators rejected marriage. However, the newspaper of the pro-Soviet Communist youth published their statements as examples of "morally corrupted" young people. In contrast with the Eurocommunist or autonomous left-wing youth publications, such testimonies were never meant to problematize the line of the organization.[26]

Did, however, young left-wingers change their actual sexual practices at that point? For many Choros participants, withdrawing from their former left-wing group had repercussions for their very sexual relationships as well. I.A. female, student from 1977 to 1981 from a lower-middle-class family, PASP member until early 1980 and subsequently Choros participant, as well as D.V., male, member of RF until 1978 and of B Panelladiki subsequently, concur in narrating that in the late 1970s they entered a period of what they coined "sexual experimentation" (I.A., Interview; D.V., Interview). This "experimentation," however, was not rigidly defined in the publications of Choros and was obviously self-regulated. Similar to the sphere of leisure, Choros did not aim at developing a coherent policy with regard to the sexual patterns of its members. Some narrators who were former autonomous left-wingers associated "experimentation" with overt parallel relationships, in the case of both men and women. I.A. remembers that "we had parallel sexual relationships and we did not hide this" (I.A., Interview). Still, several autobiographies, be they by young men or women, which appeared in the publications of RF and Choros or in oral testimonies that I have collected, did not indicate that they shifted from unstable heterosexual couples, which had been gaining ground from the early 1970s, to that of open parallel relationships.[27]

"Sexual experimentation" extended to another practice of young Euro-communists and autonomous left-wingers, that of nudism. As already shown, this phenomenon did not emerge at the end of the decade. The late 1970s, however, witnessed an expansion of that practice, especially among those high school and university students, who participated in Choros. The narration by O.Y., male, university student, from a working-class area of Athens, member of RF until 1978 and, subsequently, of B Panelladiki, is manifest: "In Fole-gandros we went to an isolated beach, we were all nude, boys and girls. We were all members of Panelladiki." The layers in his memory are interesting. Initially, he did not remember, when he started practicing nudism. However, as the interview progressed, this is what he narrated about the mid–1970s: "Now that we are discussing it, we never engaged in nudism then [as RF members in the mid–1970s]. The boys in the couples did not want to get undressed simultaneously in front of their girlfriends and the others. We did not discuss about this, but I knew it, it was implicit" (O.Y., Interview).[28]

Nudism was apparently also practiced by some high-school pupils of Choros from the end of the decade. In the narrative of some male high school pupils, who participated in Choros at that point, this practice and the re-emergence of rock music in Greece from 1977 were two sides of the same coin because both signified "emancipation" for them. Foreign young people, who hitchhiked around Greece and who practiced open camping, were no vagabond tourists for them; by contrast, they embodied this "lib-erating" combination of rock and nudism. For instance, as D.V., male and then-high-school pupil who participated in Choros, narrates: "They were foreign, young, 30–35 years old; they were not politicized, but they were alternative in their way of life. You saw youth, rock, nudism. It was a differ-ent atmosphere" (D.V., Interview). The meaning of "emancipation" for these young left-wingers, especially its complex relationship to "sexual freedom," requires a closer examination. The sexual norms of the nudists have actually been a contentious issue in diverse contexts across Europe, such as that of East Germany, where nudism flourished. Some of them organized parties, aiming at finding a partner and having sexual intercourse. Many East German nudists, however, had developed very strict norms and tried to totally distance nudism from sexual permissiveness.[29] In the case of Greece, high-school pupils who participated in Choros did not practice nudism in order to facilitate the direct attraction of a sexual partner. They construed nudism as a "direct relation to nature." Still, in a romantic fashion, "nature" denoted for them the "absence of taboos" that were portrayed as having been imposed by Christianity or "Stalinist" organizations onto sexuality: high-school and university students of RF and Choros, who practiced nudism, signified it as congenial to people who engaged in unstable sexual relationships and defied any regulation that sought to control their social interaction (I.A., Interview). This trope also appeared in the debate on nudism that arose in 1980, when the local branch of PASOK in Troizina, a tourist resort in the Peloponnese, allegedly demanded that the government ban nudism in the area. Its announcement employed a language premised on "Greek popular tradition," claiming that nudism was a "foreign" pattern that was conducive to "moral corruption."[30] A local Christian Orthodox initiative also issued a statement, in which it lambasted nudism and blamed it on "Western" influences that jeopardized "Greek Orthodox morality."[31] On the contrary, *ANTI* published the letters of left-wingers, who targeted both announcements and, especially, the one from the Socialists. A letter signed by someone who described himself as a "leftist in love," employed a similar language as I.A. in her testimony. The author claimed that "the Puritan forces," in which s/he included PASOK, the KNE, and KKE did not tolerate nudism as this was part of their effort to "restrict" youth sexuality by channeling it to one particular pattern, stable relationships that ultimately produced a marriage.[32]

The late 1970s and early 1980s were also marked by a wave of separations, and sometimes divorces, of couples of young Maoists. It was a period when a growing number of them got increasingly frustrated with their groups, which resulted in the demise of AASPE and the substantial decline of PPSP. "Membership of these organizations was the glue that held us together," according to D.K., male, member of AASPE and EKKE during the 1970s. "When this disappeared, many of us, who had got married young, divorced" (D.K., Interview). Subsequently, some of them got married again, while others opted for short-term relationships or cohabitation with a heterosexual partner.

One way or another, the publication of the "Farakos Guidelines" had a polarizing impact among young left-wingers, some of whom tried to question taxonomies of sexual practices that had been deeply entrenched in the

Greek Left by that point. Such reflection gained further momentum after the occupations of 1979. However, the aforementioned endeavors remain to be explored as to whether they dismantled gender hierarchies within the Left.

The Feminist Challenge

An important development in the late 1970s is the significant strengthening of diverse tendencies of the Feminist movement in Greece. In France, West Germany, and Italy, second-wave feminism gained momentum mainly after "1968" feeding off the language of "sexual emancipation" that was employed in these protests by male and female activists, but also responding to the reproduction of gender inequalities at the expense of women among these protestors, as historians Luisa Passerini and Gerd-Rainer Horn, historian and political scientist Bernhard Maleck, as well as political scientist and expert in women's studies Eva Maleck-Lewy have argued about the Italian, French, and West German cases.[33] By contrast, second-wave Feminist ideas spread in Greece later, shortly after the collapse of the dictatorship in 1974 and, mostly, toward the end of the decade and at the beginning of the 1980s.

In fact, a network of autonomous[34] second-wave Feminist groups, which, as already shown, first appeared in 1975–1976, flourished at the end of the decade. It comprised actors, such as the magazines *Sfigga* and *Skoupa*, Feminist university student groups, and the "Women's Publishing Group." According to the magazine *Sfigga*, such groups were: the Women's Group at the Law School in Athens, the Women's Group in Piraeus, the Women's Group at the Faculty of Medicine in Athens, the Women's Group in the Higher Industrial School in Piraeus, the Autonomous Group of Homosexual Women, and the *Vitamini Aygou gia Kanaria* (Egg Vitamin for Canaries).[35] Besides these, there were also autonomous women's groups in the Faculty of Biology, the Philosophy School, the ASOEE, and the School of Agriculture in Athens. Participants in the autonomous Feminist network were unaffiliated to any Party and, often, former RF or B Panelladiki members; a few of them, such as some contributors to the magazine *Skoupa*, had participated in the Women's Committee of RF in Paris and briefly in B Panelladiki. Nevertheless, Feminist RF members were also actively involved in the establishment of some autonomous Feminist student groups. The latter activists endorsed the autonomy of the decision-making of social movements from Party apparatuses, experiencing the condition of so-called *dipli strateysi* (double militancy). Still, a significant segment of second-wave Feminists were highly critical of all left-wing Parties and youth organizations, treating them, without exception, as "attached to the (patriarchal) status quo" and, thus, an impediment to the development of Feminist theory and activity. The contributors to *Skoupa,* for instance, were very skeptical toward Feminist Eurocommunists, disputing that their operation was genuinely "autonomous" from the Party or youth organization to which they were aligned.[36]

The activities of the autonomous women's liberation intensified in 1979–1980, with a series of protests against the Family Law, and with the establishment of the "Women's House" in 1980.[37] The Family Law foresaw that the husband is the "head" of the family and that the wife had to adopt his surname. The Constitution of 1975, however, saw that any legislation that reproduced gender inequalities had to be eliminated. The government assigned the task of locating and suggesting potential amendments to such laws to a committee headed by Professor A. Gazis. However, it proved reticent to implement the suggestions made by the Gazis Committee. Both autonomous Feminists and the women's organizations aligned to left-wing Parties reacted strongly. A coordinating committee was established, which included most autonomous Feminist groups as well as the KDG (Movement of Democratic Women), aligned with the KKE Es.; many relevant protests were organized, such as on 7 March and 6 October 1980.[38] It was not until PASOK came to power, however, that the Family Law was revised.

As in the mid–1970s, the autonomous Feminists demanded that women "control their body and sexuality" by determining when sexual intercourse leads to childbirth. In addition, the issue of rape and violence against women surfaced in their language.[39] Although they did not necessarily reject motherhood, many Feminists, including the Eurocommunist ones, recount that having children was not at all a priority for them during the 1970s.[40] The importance of second-wave feminism in Greece in the late 1970s extended beyond the members of autonomous women's groups, the readers of Feminist magazines and a segment of the Left. It also influenced institutions, such as popular women's magazines. The most notable example was *Pantheon*: particularly the articles authored by Aliki Xenou-Venardou promoted the legalization of abortion and spread of contraceptive means. The magazine also hosted an interview with Rowbotham.[41] In general, it had "absorbed a sprinkling of Feminist ideas," to appropriate a phrase used by cultural theorist Angela McRobbie, much earlier than the late 1980s or early 1990s, when such an influence appeared, according to McRobbie, on the pages of British women's and girls' magazines.[42] Still, *Pantheon* was not welcomed by the second-wave Feminists: for instance, *Skoupa* hosted an article, which asserted that, although *Pantheon* published a few articles on women from the perspective of the women's movement, its understanding of femininity was barely radical, as it revolved around motherhood and household activities.[43]

The emergence of the Feminist movement of the 1970s in Greece caused stirrings within the left-wing youth organizations as well. Choros and RF were to an extent sympathetic to the Feminists' cause. Young autonomous left-wingers invited second-wave Feminists to present their views during the student occupations. The *Avgi-Thourios* festival reserved space for the RF Women's Committee. In addition, the first congress of RF in 1978 passed a decision on the "women's issue," based on a draft written by the Women's Committee of the organization.[44] The impact of the second-wave feminism was not confined to the Eurocommunist youth. Some older (in age) female members of the KKE Es. also began to openly criticize what they described as "Puritan" morality of the Left. In 1980 *Avgi*, the newspaper of KKE Es., published a relevant discussion, where it was argued that the KKE in the period from 1949 to 1974 reproduced "bourgeois" values in the field of sexuality.[45]

The stance of the Spanish and the Italian Eurocommunist Parties and youth organizations featured prominently in the discussions within RF and the KKE Es. about gender relations.[46] In the case of the Italian Communist Party, both *Thourios* and *Avgi* frequently carried translated interviews with the senator Carla Ravaioli, member of the Party and prominent socialist Feminist; these were originally published in *l'Unità* or *Città Futura*, the newspapers of the Italian Communist Party and its youth organization, respectively. Similarly, in 1979 *Avgi* hosted an interview with Jose Maria Corpas, member of the executive committee of the central council of the UJCE (Unión de Juventudes Comunistas de España, Union of Communist Youth of Spain), the youth organization of the Communist Party of Spain. Corpas maintained that the fact that contraceptive pills had not become popular among women in Spain was a problem that had to be tackled.[47] More importantly, perhaps, Kostas Filinis, a high-ranking KKE Es. cadre, translated into Greek the resolution on the women's question of the 1978 PCE congress. The text proclaimed the PCE to be a "Feminist" Party and brought to the fore the demand that women should control their own body through the opportunity to resort to abortion or to the contraceptive pill.[48]

How did this encounter of second-wave feminism with communism affect the gender relations of RF members and Choros participants, though? Indeed, the narrative of some Eurocommunists seems to have been influenced by second-wave feminism. A number of personal narratives appeared, both in *Thourios* and *Mathitiki Poreia*, where male authors criticized (or purported to criticize) pornographic films as one of the foundations of an oppressive masculinity. Such statements are found not only in the newspapers of RF, however. Documents from discussions during the first and the second congress of the group (held in 1978 and 1980, respectively), indicate that at least some members, such as the high-school pupil who signed himself as Bloukos, approached pornography from a similar vantage point. He actually decried heterosexual male sexism, which he described as a form of disease that he labeled "masculinitis."[49] In a similar effort to reflect on gender hierarchies established through flirting, the cadre of RF, Tasos Ioannidis, argued in the Pre-Congress Athens Gathering of 1978 that the male young Eurocommunists should not call their female cadres "*sosialmanoulia*" or "*gkomenes*" (chicks).[50] Nevertheless, in contrast with a small segment of heterosexual men, who were affiliated with left-wing organizations in France and who established small groups, in which they gathered to challenge dominant norms of masculinity, young Eurocommunists did not go so far to establish similar structures.[51]

Such reflection on sexuality and gender in the Eurocommunist youth publications was not uniform, however. Issues, such as flirting and exposing the female body at the seaside in the summer stirred various reactions among RF members. A number of articles about summer vacations, published by Feminist RF members in 1979 and 1980, are indicative: "They flirt with me, they tease me. I just waaaaait! I am just the object of their male blindness."[52] By contrast, the contributions on the same issues by male members exhibit a significant ambivalence: the *kamaki*, in the narrower and broader sense, was depicted as both a "spontaneous" form of contact and as a process, which could result in practices that "insulted" women.[53] Other similar articles by Feminist Eurocommunists stressed in an ironic way the restrictions that many women, who felt their bodies did not correspond to the dominant criteria regulating female beauty, experienced when exposing their bodies on the beach. In an article in *Thourios,* a Feminist Eurocomunist appropriated the often repeated left-wing slogan, "the enemy is one, imperialism," which she transformed into "the enemy is one, the big arse."[54]

Nevertheless, in challenging what they termed "Puritanism," male RF members were not always receptive of concerns raised by Feminists. Due to the debate with the KNE on the "Farakos Guidelines," male RF members became more willing to satirize what they believed that were the sexual norms of the young pro-Soviet Communists, in a way, however, that did not necessarily avoid stereotypes and expressions that can be labeled sexist. Jokes that underlined the permissiveness of male young Eurocommunists, in contrast with the purported sexual conduct of their opponents, especially their female ones, circulated in peer groups of male young Eurocommunists.[55] Several heterosexual men, aligned with RF at the end of the 1970s, mentioned them happily in their oral testimonies. C.L., male, RF cadre and student in the early and mid–1970s, narrated: "[W]e in RF used to joke that former female members of the KNE and AASPE were the best chicks, the most promiscuous. When they leave their oppressive party apparatus, they become the craziest women" (C.L., Interview). In those jokes, young left-wing women were sometimes addressed as "chicks"—the very term that Ioannidis urged male RF members to avoid, when referring to their female comrades. This term carried specific connotations, singling out the sexual desirability of women at the expense of other aspects of theirs, such as their competency in politics. Neither the oral testimonies nor the Eurocommunist publications demonstrate any effort made at that point to resignify this term and attach to it a nonsexist meaning.

Such jokes and comments proliferated among Choros participants as well. A.M, male, member in KNE until 1978 and subsequently participant in Choros, described the KNE as a "monastery," where you could not "fuck any women" (A.M., Interview). Certainly, Choros was a fluid network, which makes it difficult to generalize on the attitudes of its participants. However, during a screening of the film *Oi Gennaioi tou Vorra,* when the character played by the actress Aimilia Ipsilanti, who was actually a cadre of the KKE in the late 1970s,[56] was raped by a Bulgarian soldier, some students linked to Choros shouted that it was "time for new rapes," a slogan directed not only against her, but KNE/KKE members in general.[57]

These jokes and slogans caused the wrath and the loud critique of autonomous Feminists.[58] In general, the persistence of stereotypes at the expense of women in the case of RF was also lambasted in first-person singular narratives that were written by female members of RF that subscribed to second-wave feminism. These can be found in a special women's column in *Thourios,* established in 1979.[59] The Feminist Eurocommunists demanded that unstable sexual relationships do not earn female RF members the representation of "political incompetence." They argued that, actually, young women in the group had to "masculinize" their outer appearance in order to become accepted by their male comrades as cadres.[60]

Remarkable vibrations occurred within the Maoists as well with regard to their stance to the Feminist movement. The reorientation of the Communist Party of China in the late 1970s fuelled doubts among Maoists in Greece not only about China as a role-model regime, but also about their conceptualizations of Marxism. This was a fertile ground, which in some cases accommodated intercrossings with other political movements, such as that of feminism. In this vein, actors linked mainly with the KKE(m-l) and PPSP began to voice a loud critique of the idealization of the "working mother," which had featured prominently not only in the discourse of KNE and KKE, but also of the Maoist groups. *Proodeytikos Kinimatografos* and a newly established in 1980 "women's group of PMSP" promoted Feminist perceptions of sexuality with vigor.[61] The text of the latter was actually published in

Salpisma, the newspaper of the PPSP.[62] Resonating with second-wave Feminist approaches, both that newspaper and the women's group argued that women's sexuality should not be subdued to motherhood and marriage. Certainly, this approach raised eyebrows, especially among high-ranking cadres of the KKE(m-l). One of them, V.S., narrated that, back in the 1970s, he viewed those initiatives with caution, since he believed that they could distract the attention of the Party and its youth group from the "class struggle," which lay at the core of "politics" (V.S., Interview).

The young Socialists did not express a particularly positive or negative assessment of second-wave feminism in their publications. However, according to S.M., male, university student and high-ranking cadre of the Youth of PASOK in the late 1970s, they disagreed on the formation of gender-specific groups; thus, they favored neither women's double militancy of second-wave Feminists nor the women's association aligned with PASOK, EGE (Enosi Gynaikon Elladas, Union of Greek Women) (S.M., Interview). Similarly, *Agonistis* was largely negligent toward second-wave Feminist publications or *Anoichto Parathyro,* the magazine of EGE.[63]

By contrast, the KNE was the most hostile left-wing organization toward second-wave Feminists. The pro-Soviet Communist youth group claimed that second-wave Feminists wished to substitute class with gender conflict. Concomitantly, it accused them of portraying men as being inherently in conflict with women, rendering the anti-capitalist struggle redundant or, at least, of secondary importance.[64] Articles in *Odigitis* lambasted the slogan "the personal is political," asserting that it was coterminous with what the Greek bourgeois class purportedly desired: to distract young people from the "organized anti-capitalist struggle" by channeling their "anxieties" into "individualistic" pursuits. However, the framework put forth by second-wave Feminists, Choros, and RF, influenced to an extent the language of the KNE. The issue of contraceptive pills and female uniforms, for example, began to be discussed in *Odigitis* and *Synchroni Gynaika.* The latter magazine expressed some cautious support to the Feminist call for the popularization of contraceptive pills, on the grounds that women should decide when to become pregnant. However, in stark contrast with second-wave Feminists, it stressed that its support for the use of contraceptive pills and the freedom of women to perform abortions was only conditional on the state actively promoting motherhood and taking steps to ensure that working mothers were financially supported. In part, *Synchroni Gynaika* was responding to letters sent to it from members and friends of the OGE, asking the magazine to delve into the issue.[65] Second-wave feminism had propelled the contraceptive pill into the limelight and the pro-USSR Communists found it hard to maintain the position that had been expressed in *Odigitis* in 1978, namely that issues of the uniform and the "blue pill" were of no real concern to working-class women.[66]

Homosexuality in the Limelight

The 1970s were an era during which important changes in the making of homosexual identities, at least gay ones, occurred in Greece. The ideal of forming couples gained ground among gays, amounting to a privatization of tenderness, as social anthropologist Kostas Yannakopoulos has labeled this process.[67] Moreover, distinct gay bars emerged in Athens in Salonica, like Banal. It is telling that in 1980 the homosexual magazine *Bananes* in Salonica published a list of bars, where gay cruising was common.[68] These bars, alongside gay sex shops in Athens, were the most important sites for the commercialization of the erotic expression of homosexuality, which developed in Greece from the mid–1970s.[69] Nevertheless, the homosexuals did not gain so much visibility in popular culture in Greece as had occurred in another Southern European postauthoritarian society at that point, namely Spain. Around the late 1970s and early 1980s, Spain, witnessed the emergence of a countercultural movement in Madrid, *La Movida Madrileña,* which was closely linked with gay and transvestite subcultures. The movement left its imprint on art. A main theme in *Movida*-influenced movies was the exploration of male homosexuality.[70] The work of the film director Pedro Almodóvar in that period is a case in point. Such a tendency, however, did not appear in the Greek cinema toward the end of the 1970s, which very rarely referred to homosexuals.[71]

In general, gays and lesbians continued to suffer throughout the 1970s from prejudices against them, which were deeply entrenched in Greece. Nevertheless, heteronormativity did not reign unchallenged: The gay and lesbian liberation movement took its first steps at that point. The AKOE (Apeleytherotiko Metopo Omofylofilon Elladas, the Front for the Liberation of Homosexuals in Greece), which mainly addressed male homosexuals, made its appearance in 1977. AKOE published the magazine *AMPHI.* The "Autonomous Group of Homosexual Women" was also founded in 1978 and was in charge of the magazine *Lavrys.* The lesbian liberation group was smaller than the gay one—in its first meeting only ten women participated, while its magazine was significantly more short-lived: While *AMPHI* circulated from 1978 to 1990, *Lavrys* was published only from 1982 until 1983.[72]

The initial committee for the establishment of the AKOE had appeared in autumn 1976 and the group came into existence shortly afterward. A main aspect of its activity was its vocal critique of a bill on the "protection from sexually transmitted diseases and the regulation of relevant issues" in 1977. AKOE maintained that the bill stigmatized homosexuality, foreseeing, among others, that males wandering in public spaces with the intention to sexually attract other males would be subject to imprisonment. The group collected signatures, including those of artists and scholars, as well as held events against the bill. One of the first of those gatherings, which they arranged together with transvestites, which were also targeted by the bill, took place at the theatre "Lusitania" in Athens on 25 April 1977.[73] Although in principle it did not exclude lesbians, the organization consisted mainly of male homosexuals. Their intellectual endeavors were connected to an extent with Foucault and his "History of Sexuality."[74] The AKOE set as a priority the introduction of the issue of homosexuality into the political agenda. "The emancipation of homosexual sexual desire" as well as the disconnection of "sexual intercourse from motherhood" were some of the topics that it brought into the fore and considered to be important political issues. In openly discussing about homosexuality, it approached the perspective of radical gay liberation groups in Western Europe, such as the FAHR (Front Homosexuel de l' action revolutionnaire, Homosexual Front of Revolutionary Action) in France. *AMPHI* often included interviews with or articles published by that organization.[75]

Although the magazine published photos of gay men kissing, it was quite cautious on reproducing the very idiom that many gays used, when flirting or having sex. On the contrary, the magazine of the AMOTH (Aytonomo Metopo Omofylofilon Thessalonikis, Autonomous Front of Homosexuals of Salonica), a much smaller homosexual liberation group, followed a different course: it enriched its articles with such phrases, such as *pidiomaste* or *pairnontai.*[76]

The AKOE represented itself as a "progressive" group. A segment of the left-wing youth actually welcomed their activity: RF and Choros were more open to AKOE. *Thourios, Agonas gia tin Kommounistiki Ananeosi,* and *Touvlo* published relevant articles or interviews with AKOE members. The homosexual liberation group also participated in the *Avgi-Thourios* festivals from 1979 onward, with the exception of 1980.[77] Still, a few Choros participants were biased against homosexuality: An autonomous left-wing pupil magazine, *Thranio,* published an article that labeled homosexuality "perversion," to receive vehement critique from another pupil magazine linked with Choros, *Touvlo.*[78]

A segment of the Maoists also treated the emergence of the gay liberation movement favorably. Upon the occasion of the release of the short film *Betty* (1979), which was directed by Dimitris Stavrakas and referred to the life of a homosexual transvestite called Betty, *Proodeytikos Kinimatografos* published

Figure 6.2. Image of two men kissing. Source: *AMPHI,* Summer–Autumn 1978, p. 73. Used with permission from Grigoris Vallianatos.

an extensive article aiming at dislodging stereotypes against homosexuality and tackling their vilification. The magazine argued against the perception that only those sexual relations that led to coitus are "normal"; it advocated the view that, unless sexual "pleasure" was the outcome of "exploitation,"

it was absolutely legitimate, no matter whether it stemmed from heterosexual or homosexual contacts. Moreover, it maintained that homosexuality was erroneously identified with prostitution and pedophilia.[79] Similar to
Thourios, Agonas gia tin Kommounistiki Ananeosi, and *Touvlo, Proodeytikos
Kinimatografos* sided with the gay liberation movement in Greece and published *AMPHI* advertisements in its pages.[80] Reconsidering issues of gender
and sexuality in general had, in fact, broader ramifications for the editors of
Proodeytikos Kinimatografos: the devaluation of the significance of the USSR
under Stalin as one of their role models. While the Soviet Union had initially displayed openness concerning sexuality issues, Stalin's regime from the
1930s onward changed stance: in venerating the "socialist family," it banned
abortions and persecuted homosexuals.[81] *Proodeytikos Kinimatografos* editors,
aware of this conservative turn, began, especially from 1980, to openly criticize Stalin's viewpoint and the Stalinist regime's conduct in the domain of
gender relations.[82]

Nevertheless, the ideas of *Proodeytikos Kinimatografos* on homosexuality
were certainly not met with unanimous acceptance by all young Maoists in
Greece in that period: A.M., male, coeditor of this magazine at that point,
remembers that working-class Maoists greeted them with jeers and found
their approach as totally unacceptable (A.M., Interview). In the publications
of the youth organizations of PPSP, however, neither was a reply issued nor
did a directly or indirectly homophobic article appear. Thus, Greek Maoists
differed to a lesser or greater extent from their comrades in West Germany
in this respect. Historian Andreas Kühn argues that the Maoists in West
Germany reinforced throughout the 1970s a "reactionary politicization" of
sexual and gender relations, allocating men the role of "breadwinners" and
women of "housekeepers." He adds that pejorative descriptions of homosexuals also appeared in the publications of West German Maoists during
that decade.[83] However, the interaction of *Proodeytikos Kinimatografos* with
the gay liberation movement was not the only exception to this tendency.
Already in the early 1970s, the "Far Left" organization VLR (Vive La Révo-
lution, Long Live the Revolution) in France, whose ideological background
was influenced by Maoism, but also by Situationism, came into contact with
the Feminist and the gay liberation movement. This was particularly evident in the twelfth issue of its magazine, *Tout!* (Everything!), published on
23 April 1971. According to historian Manus McGrogan, "the issue was a
multicoloured statement for gender and sexual freedom, from women's and
gay rights to transvestites and teenagers."[84] Nevertheless, combining all these
diverse influences proved an impossible task for the VLR and, actually, led to
its demise in the early 1970s.[85] In any case, a comparative and transfer history of Maoist approaches toward homosexuality across Western Europe in

the 1970s awaits to be authored and will hopefully illuminate the complexities of this relationship.

Still, despite the openness that some Maoists and Choros participants as well as the young Eurocommunists displayed toward homosexuals, the latter encountered well-entrenched prejudices against them, pervasive among numerous young left-wingers as well in Greece at that point. According to data contained in *AMPHI*, which, however, I was not able to corroborate, representatives of the EFEE, controlled by the pro-Soviet Communists and the Socialists at that point, once attempted to block their entrance to the commemoration site, arguing that "perverted" people could not be "progressive."[86] Moreover, similar to the mid–1970s, the publications of the KNE contained very few references to homosexuality. On rare occasions when they touched upon the issue, they deprived it of any positive connotations, linking it with prostitution, which they argued, flourished in the newly established pubs and bars.[87] Such a cautious, if not hostile attitude toward homosexuals has been evident in the publications of the KKE and KNE until today. In an article published in *Rizospastis* in 2009, it was argued that nobody (including the homosexuals) "should be executed for being different." Still, a number of homosexuals, according to the same article, pose demands, such as marriage between homosexuals, which are "utterly groundless."[88]

Notes

1. Herzog, *Sexuality in Europe*, p. 172.
2. See, for instance, the debate around nudism in Greece in the late 1970s that is analyzed later in this chapter.
3. In the case of the newspaper *Ta Nea*, see, for instance: Kostas Chardavellas, "Ellinida '80," *Ta Nea*, 21 August 1980, p. 5; "Oi Neoi tou '81," *Ta Nea*, 31 March 1981, p. 5.
4. "Kanontas erota proti fora: i stigmi tis myisis," *Thourios*, 9 July 1981, pp. 33–36.
5. Ibid.
6. "Kai oi pornes? Pos ekeines vlepoun ton protari?," *Thourios*, 9 July 1981, p. 36.
7. Pascal Eitler, "Die 'sexuelle Revolution'—Körperpolitik um 1968," in *1968: Ein Handbuch zur Kultur- und Mediengeschichte der Studentenbewegung*, ed. Martin Klimke and Joachim Scharloth (Stuttgart, 2007), pp. 235–46.
8. Ibid, pp. 237–39.
9. ASKI, Archive of EKON Rigas Feraios, Recommendation to the central council of RF by its high-school pupil committee, without date (probably 1980 or 1981).
10. For instance: ASKI, Archive of EKON Rigas Feraios, Box 25 (branch of Piraeus), folder 1, "Gia ta Dimokratika kai Koinonika Dikaiomata ton Mathiton," 15 January 1979.
11. "Mathitries: Na vgoume apo tin apomonosi," *Thourios*, 11 May 1978, p. 16.

12. Dafni, "Oneira kalokairinis nychtas," *Mathitiki Poreia*, 1980, without date (probably summer or autumn 1980), pp. 6–7.

13. I.V., "Cheri me cheri stin kathimerini mas zoi," *Mathitiki Poreia*, November 1980, p. 7.

14. "Mathitries: Na vgoume apo tin apomonosi," *Thourios* 11 May 1978, p. 16; see also the column "Cheri me cheri stin kathimerini mas zoi," which appeared in *Mathitiki Poreia* throughout the period 1977–81.

15. "Afieroma Beatles: ektos apo ton imperialismo yparchei kai i monaxia," *Mathitiki Poreia*, January–March 1981, pp. 8–9.

16. "Anti-afieroma stous Beatles," *Mathitiki Poreia*, without date (most probably summer 1981), p. 16.

17. See, for instance: *Ta Ylika tou A Metadichtatorikou Synedriou tis PPSP*, Athens, August 1977, pp. 88–89.

18. "'Prosopiki zoi': Adiexoda kai lyseis pou ta anaparagoun," *Salpisma*, January–February 1981, pp. 52–53.

19. "Oi scheseis anamesa sta dyo fyla," *O Agonas ton Mathiton*, December 1977, pp. 6–7.

20. See, for example: "Synechizetai me epitychia o kyklos dialexeon tis AAMPE," *Laikoi Agones*, 13 September 1979, p. 2.

21. ASKI, Archive of Fyssas, box 15, brochure published by PASP, Department of Mathematics, Aristotle University of Salonica, without date (possibly 1979).

22. "1000 neoi estisan 'prasini politeia' sti N. Filadelfeia," *Ta Nea*, 3 September 1980, p. 13.

23. He raised those concerns in his interview, extracts from which appeared in: "Theloun oloi, alla tolmoun merikoi," *Avgi*, 26 January 1981, p. 5.

24. "To prosopeio tou 'anarchismou,'" *Odigitis*, 10 February 1978, p. 11.

25. "Perithorio: (a)diexodos sto adiexodo," *Odigitis*, 1 February 1980, pp. 10–11.

26. See, for instance, "'Katafygio' I plevra tis koinonikis zois?," *Odigitis*, 8 August 1980, pp. 16–17; "Ta nea zeygaria simera," *Synchroni Gynaika*, January–February 1980, pp. 16–17. The latter was a recorded discussion with young couples. It is interesting, though, that the patronizing character of this recorded discussion was criticized in a letter to the magazine, which was published. The author of the letter claims that the testimonies seem to be "manipulated." See: M. Papadimitriou, "Apopseis gia ta 'Nea Zeygaria,'" *Synchroni Gynaika*, March–April 1980.

27. About RF, see, for example: "Kouventiazontas gia mas," *Thourios*, 29 May 1980, pp. 6–7; "Afieroma Beatles," pp. 8–9. About Choros, see, for instance: E.Q., B.Q., Interview.

28. The social background of the interviewee should be noted. Other RF members, such as those who had studied in private high schools, had been practicing nudism already in the early 1970s. However, nudism was a taboo even in the mid–1970s for the young people who lived in Neos Kosmos, the district where O.Y. came from and where he was active as a young Communist.

29. McLellan, *Love in the Time of Communism*, pp. 144–73.

30. Announcement of the local branch of PASOK in Troizina, reproduced in *ANTI*, 9 May 1980, p. 21.

31. Announcement of "Epitropi Agonos," a Christian Orthodox initiative that targeted nudism in Troizina, a tourist resort in Peloponnisos. The announcement was reproduced in *ANTI*, 9 May 1980, p. 21. Although I have not managed to find original copies of those two announcements, which were reproduced in *ANTI*, I did not trace any accusations that they were distorted, either.

32. Letter published on p. 60, *ANTI*, 6 June 1980.

33. Eva Maleck-Lewy and Bernhard Maleck, "The Women's Movement in East and West Germany," in Fink, Gassert, and Junker, *1968*, pp. 373–96; Horn, *The Spirit*, pp. 217-19. Similarly, Luisa Passerini stresses that student protests in Turin in the late 1960s bred sexual liberation for women, who often dispensed with monogamous relationships. However, this transitional period was marked by the absence of "love and respect" among women; the oral historian stresses the emotion of envy that many women felt for one another during the student movement. Luisa Passerini, *Autobiography of a Generation: Italy, 1968*, Hanover, NH, 1996, pp. 95–100.

34. This network should not be confused with Choros. "Autonomy" was a very popular concept in Greece in the late 1970s, employed by a broad range of actors.

35. See "Aytonomes gynaikeies omades," *Sfigga*, 1 July 1980, pp. 21–30; Intervention of Nassia Yakovaki at a gathering of the Women's Committee of RF titled: "I gynaikeia douleia mas sta panepistimia kai sto evrytero gynaikeio kinima," Personal Collection of Maria Repoussi.

36. "I parochimeni epikairotita tou ellinikou feminismou," *Skoupa*, December 1979, p. 98.

37. See: Vicky Kotsovelou and Maria Repoussi, "Feministika entypa, 1978–1985: mia proti proseggisi," *Diavazo*, 14 September 1988, p. 58; "Gia ti riziki anamorfosi tou Astikou Kodika," *Thourios*, 10 January 1980, pp. 4–5.

38. "Ena neo feministiko kinima gennietai," *Thourios*, 25 February 1981, pp. 9–13.

39. The Women's Group at the Law School in Athens held an open discussion on the issue of rapes on 8 October 1979.

40. Without necessarily rejecting motherhood, articles in *Skoupa* demanded that women themselves problematize their dominant representation as primarily mothers. See: "Mitrotita," *Skoupa*, January 1979, pp. 49–53.

41. See, for instance, Aliki Xenou-Venardou, "Antisyllipsi kai strouthokamilismos," *Pantheon*, 1980, 18-31 March 1980, pp. 32–33.

42. Angela McRobbie, *In the Culture Society: Art, Fashion and Popular Music* (London, 1999), p. 50.

43. "To ideologiko periechomeno tou 'gynaikeiou' typou. Mia proti proseggisi," *Skoupa*, January 1979, pp. 69, 72.

44. ASKI, Archive of Rigas Feraios, First Congress of RF, box 1, Resolution titled "Gia tin anaptyxi enos mazikou avtonomou kinimatos ton neon gynaikon. Gia tin kataktisi tis isotimias tis neas Gynaikas stin koinonia mas," June 1978, pp. 1–4.

45. "Astikes domes kai paranomia stirixan tin ithiki tis Aristeras," *Avgi*, 30 November 1980, p. 9.

46. I do not imply, however, that there were no gender exclusions in these organizations or that second-wave feminism was always met with enthusiasm. Gundle argues convincingly that the Italian Communist Party initially treated second-wave feminism as "heir to the youth movement and its errors" as well as an imported

phenomenon of American origin. See Gundle, *Between Hollywood and Moscow,* p. 150.

47. "I anergia odigei tous neous sti via," *Avgi,* 1 June 1980, p. 9.
48. The translated text was entitled *To KK Ispanias gia to Gynaikeio zitima.* It was published in Greek in 1980.
49. Speech by Bloukos, 1978, Archive of the First Congress of RF, 1978, box 1. See also Papadogiannis, "Confronting 'imperialism' and 'loneliness,'" pp. 240–41.
50. ASKI, Archive of EKON Rigas Feraios, Speech of Tassos Ioannidis, Pre-Congress Athens Gathering, 1978.
51. Alban Jacquemart, "Les hommes dans les mouvements féministes français" (PhD diss., École des Hautes Études en Sciences Sociales, Paris, 2011).
52. "Kamaki, peiragma, flert: sexismos I tropos epikoinonias?," *Thourios,* 9 April 1981, pp. 19–20. The article included two first-person singular narrations, one by a young woman and one by a young man.
53. Ibid.
54. "Sto plevro tis louomenis Ellinopoulas," *Thourios,* 3 July 1980, p. 27.
55. It is difficult to determine whether such jokes first appeared in the late 1970s. Nevertheless, since many of them refer to the "Farakos Guidelines," they apparently emerged or were resignified during the relevant debate.
56. Ipsilanti became a KKE MP in 1981.
57. Letter by an anonymous female student, *ANTI,* 18 January 1980, p. 54. In the article "Katalipseis" in *Rixi,* February 1980, p. 9, it is stated that, during the screening of the movie, some participants shouted *skistin,* which implies rape.
58. Leaflet titled *Gynaikes kai Politiki,* published by female students of RF in 1981.
59. "I kouventa mas," *Thourios,* 1 February 1979, p. 5.
60. E. Alitzoglou, A. Asser, M. Konstantelou, M. Decastro, and A. Trantzi, "Gia tin proothisi tis syneiditopoiisis ton gynaikon," *Thourios,* 22 June 1978, p. 6.
61. "Apo ta chronia ta palia ki ap' tin palia Diathiki oi Andres vrethikan psila ki emeis stin Apothiki," *Salpisma,* November–December 1980, pp. 28–30; "Amfisvitisi kai epoikodomima (me aformi tis katalipseis)," *Proodeytikos Kinimatografos,* first term 1980, pp. 17–23.
62. "Apo ta chronia ta palia,'" pp. 28–30.
63. EGE was led by Margaret Papandreou, the wife of the leader of PASOK. Some important documents outlining her activity in the women's movement are kept at Princeton Special Collections (Margaret Papandreou Collection).
64. The line of argument of the KNE and the KKE is epitomized in: Aleka Papariga, *Gia tin apeleytherosi tis Gynaikas,* Athens 1981. See also leaflets published by the PSK in the late 1970s, such as "Spoudastries, parte mazika meros ston agona" and "I Panspoudastiki S.K. kalei tis foititries." I have found these leaflets in the personal collection of Aimilia Karali.
65. "To antisylliptiko chapi," *Synchroni Gynaika,* May–June 1979, pp. 16–19. With regard to letters sent to Synchroni Gynaika, see: V. Papadiamanti, "Gia to chapi," *Synchroni Gynaika,* July–August 1979, p. 55.
66. "O Rigas Feraios kai i stratigiki tis antidrasis," *Odigitis,* 3 August 1978, p. 21.

67. Kostas Yannakopoulos, *Jeux du désir, jeux du pouvoir: corps, émotions et identité sexuelle des hommes au Pirée et à Athènes* (PhD thesis, Paris, Ecole des Hautes Etudes en Sciences Sociales, Paris, 1995).
68. *Bananes,* spring 1980.
69. Roxanne Kaftantzoglou and Kostas Yannakopoulos, "Forms of Erotic Expression," in Charalambis, Maratou-Alipranti, and Hadjiyanni, *Recent Social Trends,* pp. 532–35.
70. Peter W. Evans, "Culture and Cinema, 1975–1996," in *The Cambridge Companion to Modern Spanish Culture,* ed. David T. Gies (Cambridge, 1999), p. 275; Mark Allinson, "Star of Stage and Screen and Optimistic Punk," in *Constructing Identity in Contemporary Spain: Theoretical Debates and Cultural Practice,* ed. Jo Labanyi (Oxford, 2002), pp. 224, 229.
71. Nikolaos Tsiamis, "Eikones tis andrikis omofylofilias ston kinimatografo," (MA essay, Panteion University, Athens, 2007), pp. 66–68.
72. For the case of Lavrys, see: Venetia Kantsa, "I *Lavrys*: Mia Synoptiki Parousiasi enos Ellinikou Lesviakou Periodikou," *Dini* 8 (1995–96): pp. 73–95.
73. "I archi," *AMPHI,* spring 1978, pp. 4–5. However, the relationship between homosexuals who were transvestites and those who were not was not always smooth, as appears in an interview of Betty, whose life was the topic of a short film in 1979, in *AMPHI.* See: "Synenteyxi me tin Betty," *AMPHI,* spring 1980, pp. 60–61.
74. "I istoria tis sexoualikotitas tou Michel Foucault," *AMPHI,* Spring 1979, pp. 66–68.
75. "O Mais, I filosofia kai oi omofylofiloi. Synenteyxi me ton kathigiti Gilles Chatelet," *AMPHI,* Spring 1980, pp. 24–26.
76. Both mean "fuck." See: *Bananes,* spring 1980. However, the magazine was not always so articulate: sometimes it mentioned only the first letters of a provocative word, such as "g…" (*gamise,* fuck) or "ts…" (*tsimpouki,* blowjob).
77. "To ghetto den to thelisame emeis, mas to epivalane," *Thourios,* 18 October 1979, pp. 12–13; "Mia proti syzitisi me to AMPHI," *Agonas gia tin Kommounistiki Ananeosi,* November 1978, pp. 47–51; "Aytonoma Entypa," *Touvlo,* May 1981, pp. 19–21.
78. See "Omofylofilia: mia alli apopsi," *Thranio,* vol, 7, 1981, pp. 26–28; "Aytonoma Entypa," *Touvlo,* May 1981, pp. 19–21.
79. "Betty tou D. Stavraka," *Proodeytikos Kinimatografos,* third term 1979, pp. 38–40; "Skepseis gia to thema tis omofylofilias," Ibid., pp. 40–47.
80. *Proodeytikos Kinimatografos-Alloi Kairoi,* April 1981, p. 95.
81. About gender and sexuality in Stalin's Soviet Union, see, for example: Wendy Goldman, "Les femmes dans la société soviétique," in Bernard Pudal et al., eds, *Le Siècle des Communismes,* pp. 187–97.
82. "Gia tis sexoualikes scheseis, gia tin oikogeneia, gia ti gynaika," *Proodeytikos Kinimatografos-Alloi Kairoi,* April 1981, pp. 53–55.
83. Kühn, *Stalins Enkel,* pp. 82–87. Historian Aribert Reimann corroborates and complements the latter point, tracing a "stigmatization of homoerotic moments" already in the Kommune I in the late 1960s, a trend that continued among the advocates of Maoism in the 1970s. See: Aribert Reimann, "Zwischen Machismo und Coolness: Männlichkeit und Emotion in der westdeutschen 'Kulturrevolution' der 1960er- und 1970er- Jahre," in *Die Präsenz der Gefühle: Männlichkeit und Emotion in der Moderne,* ed. Manuel Borutta and Nina Verheyen (Bielefeld, Ger., 2010), pp. 242–43.

84. Manus McGrogan, "*Tout!* in context 1968-1973: French radical press at the cross-roads of far left, new movements and counterculture" (PhD diss., University of Portsmouth, 2010), p. 104.
85. Ibid., pp. 100–101.
86. "To Polytechneio kai i EFEE," *AMPHI,* March–May 1979, p. 6.
87. "Ta PUB sti Thessaloniki. Choros amfisvitisis I choros diavrosis," *Odigitis,* 8 June 1981, p. 12. A notable exception, however, is the very positive reference of Dimitris Danikas in Rizospastis to the short film about the life of the homosexual transvestite Betty. Danikas argued that it is a "bold film," delving into a phenomenon "repressed by the bourgeois ideology." See: Dimitris Danikas, "Rentzis-Mavrikos: Oi teleytaies kales stigmes tou Festival," *Rizospastis,* 10 October 1979, p. 4. Although Danikas's reviews were highly appreciated by the KNE members as well, his comments did not herald a reconfiguration of the stance of the pro-Soviet Communist youth toward homosexuality.
88. Review of *Milk* by Gus van Sant, *Rizospastis,* 15 January 2009, p. 30.

Conclusion

The 1970s and Their Aftermath

It was mid–September, 2011, when the events of the 37th Festival of KNE-Odigitis took place in Athens. Several of its core components seemed to be unaltered in comparison with the 1970s: the festival, aiming to promote and make clear the ideological orientation of the KNE and the KKE, culminated in the speeches of the general secretaries of those organizations. In addition, seeking to showcase cultural products that help foster militancy, namely ideological engagement and vigorous activity, it dedicated part of its musical program to those who "pursued class struggle without repenting." Some of the artists who appeared onstage were the same who had played a significant role in the festivals of the group in the first post-dictatorship years: Vassilis Papakonstantinou is certainly such a case. However, younger artists also featured prominently, such as the rock band Jethro Talibans. In contrast to the late 1970s, rock music is no longer a cause of controversy among KNE cadres and members.[1] The politicized youth festivals are perhaps one important parameter in the cultural politics of the Greek Left that was set in the first post-dictatorship years and still exists. Still, they are just one piece of a complex puzzle: that of the politicization of leisure and sexuality in Greece in the 1970s.

Throughout its existence, the Greek Left has approached "culture" in a bisemic way, equating it simultaneously with the arts and with behavior patterns. The analysis of its cultural politics presupposes an understanding of this term which considers both levels. Raymond Williams's approach is very illuminating in this sense, since he links "culture" with lived experience; moreover, his work raises the question of the relationship between a "whole way of life" and forms of signification, such as films, songs, and theatre. The 1960s posed new challenges to the Left in Greece, especially in relation to its cultural and youth politics. Greece witnessed growing urbanization and the spread of mass consumer trends among all social strata from the 1960s. Into this environment, rock music and Hollywood movies also arrived and contributed to the formation of youth identities circulating in newly established commercial youth venues. Young left-wingers in the 1960s rejected such venues as elements of an American way of life that promoted individualization and "sexual corruption," defined as sexual relationships deviating from the pattern of the stable heterosexual couple. On the contrary, the Left claimed to represent the "genuine expression of the Greek nation." It promoted or constructed cultural products, especially songs, which reproduced the purported "militant spirit" of the Greek "national popular tradition" in their verses.

The establishment of the dictatorship in 1967 resulted in the banning of all political parties. Youth politicization ceased for a while, only to bounce back in the early 1970s, mainly among university students. The majority of left-wing students were unaffiliated in this period and no Party apparatus regulated their leisure activities. Their lifestyle was indelibly linked with a number of practices, which included listening to *entehno laiko* and *rebetiko* songs, watching Greek political cinema (NEK) coupled with Italian neorealism and French Nouvelle Vague, and avidly reading Marxist-Leninist texts. Their contact with rock music also became more frequent, linked with the spread of representations of "Woodstock" and the "French May" in Greece. Far from being culturally Americanized, young left-wingers in the early 1970s privileged a narrative based on "Greek tradition" on the one hand and experimented with hybrid cultural products, such as the music by Dionysis Savvopoulos, on the other. As a result, Papanikolaou describes the Greek left-wing youth in the early 1970s as a "subject in motion," namely lacking a stable point of reference. Nevertheless, left-leaning dissident students in the last years of the dictatorship seem to have oscillated between being "in motion" and seeking stable foundations by reconceptualizing contemporary Greek history. In the meantime, the social interaction of young men and women at university, courtship at parties and images of "sexual liberation" that were linked with the "Global Sixties" reinforced a trend that had emerged in the 1960s: the reshaping of the dominant conjugal model in Greek society. Although most young people did not flatly reject marriage, flirting and premarital sexual relationships became more and more legitimate, both for heterosexual women and men.

The restoration of democracy tracked and helped shape the cultural politics of the Communist and Socialist youth groups as well as the actual leisure activities and sexual patterns of their members. In the period extending from 1974 to 1981, the cultural activities of the left-wing youth proliferated, spreading particularly in the universities, but, also, leaving their imprint on the lower-middle and working-class districts of Athens and Salonica. One way or another, young Socialists and Communists drew on conflicting left-wing understandings of "culture" that dated back to the Sixties and the authoritarian period, which they further shaped, introducing or endorsing novel representations of body and gender as well as new types of settings in which their leisure activities took place. In terms of the leisure and sexuality of the left-wing youth, 1974 was a semi-rupture: the mid–to-late 1970s witnessed neither a continuation nor a substantial reconfiguration in comparison to the preceding decades, but an in-between condition.

Developments in left-wing youth cultural politics were certainly related to the new political condition that dawned in Greece in 1974. Left-wing youth organizations became massive once again after the fall of the authoritarian regime. The collapse of the dictatorship also signaled the decline of anti-communism as the official ideology as well as the legalization of Communist organizations, which had been banned since 1947. No longer wishing to enforce ideological conformity on all Greek institutions, the post-dictatorial state resembled a condition which the political scientist Giannis Voulgaris depicts as a "duality of power." The Center-Right New Democracy formed the government throughout the period from 1974 to 1981. At the same time, the Left prevailed in intellectual circles and student unions. Young Socialists and Communists played a pivotal role in the production, circulation and consumption of cultural patterns, which they signified as "progressive."

During the first post-dictatorship years, namely from 1974 to approximately 1977, the leisure activities of the young left-wingers were subordinated to the reproduction of overt political messages. Their leisure pursuits were a case of "serious fun," combining recreation with indoctrination. All Socialist and Communist organizations in this period undertook the effort to define the genres that comprised "progressive culture." In doing so, they largely reproduced the conceptualizations of the "American way of life" and the invention of "Greek popular tradition" put forth by the Greek Left in the preceding decades. Similarly, they continued to endorse an "ideal popular" model, as defined by Panagiotopoulos, lauding a desirable representation of the "Greek people" and its purported cultural expression, which did not necessarily represent the actual taste of the lower and middle social strata in Greece at that point. To help promote "progressive culture," all left-wing youth groups, in close collaboration with a "parent culture," the Parties they were affiliated with, tried to establish what they coined as a "progressive cultural movement," which resulted in the formation of numerous cultural associations in the universities and in various districts of Athens and Salonica. Similar institutions had existed in the 1960s as well, but these had ceased to operate after the establishment of the dictatorship. However, in marked contrast with the pre-dictatorship years, left-wingers, including young ones, faced remarkably fewer limitations on their activities. In this vein, the cultural politics of Socialist and Communist youth groups reinforced a major novelty of the political condition of the *Metapolitefsi*: An integral piece of the delegitimization of anti-communism in post-dictatorship Greece was the explosion of memory of "anti-fascist struggle," a main pillar of which were anti-fascist commemorative events praising left-wing Resistance against the Tripartite Occupation of Greece in 1941–1944 and the Polytechnic Uprising in 1973. Young Communists and Socialists featured prominently in the organization of such events, which included live performaces of Greek political music, such as partisan songs of the early 1940s. Another new aspect in left-wing youth cultural politics in the mid–1970s was the organization of youth festivals for the first time in the history of the Greek Left. The same years saw the emergence not only of new structures, but also of new understandings of the "progressive cultural movement." As early as the mid–1970s, RF offered approaches that diverged from those of the KNE and the Maoists on how such associations should function. RF maintained that decision-making should not be regulated by any external structures, including those of political Parties, which was called the principle of "autonomy."

The effort to distill "progressive" messages through "culture" was not imposed on young left-wingers in a top-bottom fashion; it also tracked the endeavors of those militants in the final years of the dictatorship. Young Socialists and Communists regarded these activities as markers of a "progressive" identity, which they connected with activism aimed at the "national liberation" of Greece, especially from U.S. influence, as well as the "socialist transformation" of the country, however they construed this. These pursuits entailed in particular the collective singing of Theodorakis's and left-wing partisan songs of the 1940s in tavernas as well as watching Italian neorealist, French Nouvelle Vague, Soviet socialist realist, and Greek political films. To an extent, their taste was glocal: performances of Greek "progressive culture" also occurred in a space that had been imported from France in the 1960s—the *boîtes*.

Certainly, the left-wing politicization of leisure in the mid–1970s influenced broad masses of the Greek youth. Many young Greeks, who had not necessarily been affiliated with or leaning toward a Socialist or Communist organization in the early 1970s, embraced the cultural activities that left-wing groups labeled as "progressive." The popularity of Greek, Italian, and French pop music, which had reached its apogee in the early 1970s, dropped sharply in the aftermath of the dictatorship. Nevertheless, youth leisure activities did not become uniform in this period: discotheques remained a popular attraction for numerous young Greek people. What actually occurred was the growing demarcation of the tastes of young Greek Communists and Socialists from that of diverse young Greeks who were not aligned with a political group. Young left-wingers dismissed cultural products that they did not regard as "progressive" and tended to avoid socializing with those young people that they deemed "apathetic." However, there were exceptions: some leisure activities, especially the travel culture that young Socialists and Communists shared, were only partly related to political activity, and resembled the tourist activities of young people who were not members of a political organization.

In defining "culture," the Left linked leisure with sexuality, since it portrayed the former as conducive to desirable and undesirable sexual patterns. Although the sexual patterns of the young left-wingers were not a mere derivative of their leisure pursuits, the latter played an important role in shaping the former. The strengthening of left-wing youth organizations produced mixed results with regard to the sexual norms of their members, which could be described neither as a wave of sexual liberation nor as a surge of social conservatism. Some left-wing youth groups, especially the KNE, but also the Maoist ones, published numerous texts in the initial post-dictatorship period, in which they praised stable heterosexual relationships, leading to marriage, which they embedded with emotionally laden terms as the appropriate expression of "love." Therefore, they resorted to a normative discourse that the Greek Left had employed at least since the late 1950s. However, the members of those groups often negotiated this framework in practice and it was not uncommon for them to develop unstable sexual relationships without being reprimanded by the higher ranks of the organizations they were affiliated with. By contrast, the Youth of PASOK and RF developed a significantly less patronizing attitude toward the sexual practices of their members.

From 1977, although the influence of Communist and Socialist youth groups did not dissipate, the cultural politics of some left-wing youth groups and the leisure pursuits of their members entered a period of reconfiguration, which can be attributed to a confluence of a number of factors: developments in the international Communist movement as well as a shifting leisure landscape and intellectual debates over "tradition" in Greece. Eurocommunist Parties of diverse countries established closer contacts in the mid– to late–1970s; the common background of those organizations was that they mounted a loud critique of the USSR, while seeking a "democratic path" to socialism. Greek Eurocommunists sought an active role in this process and sought to radically redefine Communist politics. RF members proved to be trendsetters for a segment of the Greek Left, developing, among others, novel cultural politics, at least in theory. Such endeavors were undertaken particularly by peer groups of young Eurocommunists, especially those who had come in contact with structuralist Marxism, semiotics, and psychoanalysis. Their approach, already evident in the mid–1970s, clearly became the official line in RF toward the end of the decade. Young Eurocommunists developed synergies with iconoclastic intellectuals, who did not wish to serve as instructors of norms and values and who explicitly challenged "tradition" as the pinnacle of left-wing identity. Cultural patterns that emerged or reappeared in Greece during the late 1970s, such as pubs and bars, also facilitated reflection on protest patterns. A catalyst for the emergence of left-wing cultural politics that did not aim to reproduce "progressive" messages was the reaction of the Eurocommunist youth to the publication of detailed guidelines for the comportment of young people by the KNE and the KKE in 1977. Based on a conceptual background that stressed ambiguity, RF members were no longer interested in spotting "progressive" and "reactionary" cultural products. No longer fascinated with "serious fun," they opted for leisure pursuits in-between time apart and time dedicated to ideological engagement. Their shifting approach to culture and leisure was a testing ground for the mass mobilization patterns they embraced during mid– to late–1970s, especially the relationship between collective action and the individual militant. At the end of this decade, this segment of the left-wing youth stood "in front of the mirror" and sought ways, though often unsuccessfully, to cater to diverse youth lifestyles rather than urging its members to conform to a particular "progressive" model. This process cannot be described as a "retreat into the private," but a reconfiguration of politics and the relationship of the individual with the collective. Such experimentations were not specific to Greece: they were manifest among young Eurocommunists in other European countries as well, such as in Italy, with whom their Greek comrades were in close contact. RF members partook in a Eurocommunist youth moment that has been largely unexplored in historiography.

From 1978, youth politics became very turbulent, which again was linked with developments at the international level: the disillusionment with post-Mao China that led to the decline of Maoist groups in Greece. Coupled with a big split in RF, this resulted in the gradual emergence of a network of autonomous left-wing groups and magazines, which mainly attracted university students. Although left-wing or left-leaning youth organizations in Greece that were not officially linked with a particular Party had appeared in the preceding decades, it was for the first time in the history of the Greek Left that a left-wing youth group was established without any of its members having any kind of association with a political Party. This network did not portray itself as a subject that intended to mobilize solely the youth, however, and its participants refrained from questioning the role of the "working class" as the agent of social transformation. However, its appeal beyond students was limited throughout its existence. In general, this subject, self-defined as Choros, was a rather loose one: it lacked an apparatus that would produce an official line. As a result, its publications were rather heterogeneous. Still, all of them were predicated to a greater or lesser extent on two concepts, *amfisvitisi* (challenging) and *aytonomia* (autonomy): the challenging of normative models that aimed at controlling sexual relationships as well as of hierarchical Party structures, including those of the Left. In this vein, Choros did not produce a coherent cultural policy, which would regulate the leisure activities of its participants. It was self-consciously a "subject in motion," which did not seek stable foundations in a clearly articulated narrative. Rather, Choros voiced a loud critique against the intervention of left-wing Parties, especially of the KKE, which attempted to shape the lifestyle of the youth. Concomitantly, the cultural tastes of the young autonomous left-wingers were diverse. They combined American, Western European, as well as Greek cultural influences. One way or another, they were marked by humor—even sarcasm on some occasions—but also a deeply entrenched melancholy, an emotion of being trapped in an impasse, which justifies the fact that Choros participants were fascinated by the social fringe. The leisure activities of young autonomous left-wingers were particularly manifest in the university occupations in 1979, which were organized by Choros and the Maoists. In brief, both targeted Law 815, introduced in August 1978. Young Maoists and autonomous left-wingers maintained that it promoted the intensification of studies and facilitated the integration of students into the capitalist system. They demanded its immediate abolition and organized university occupations in December 1979 in protest against it. In fact, the occupations witnessed an explosion of humorous expression. Screening and watching movies in order to make fun of the protagonists and the movie plot rather than capture a "progressive" meaning, was a key feature of the leisure of Choros participants in the occupied schools. One way or another, the young autonomous left-wingers, similar to the young Eurocommunists, sought ways to associate the individual with the collective in a more flexible manner and deemed leisure to be fertile ground for such experimentation. By the early 1980s, the Maoist youth groups had been decimated. Meanwhile, the cultural politics of the flourishing Youth of PASOK as well as of the KNE pendulated between rigor and flexibility. Those groups continued to classify cultural products as "progressive" and "reactionary," but they began to integrate into their cultural events products that they had hitherto despised, especially rock music. The KNE was influenced by the increasing tolerance toward rock music exhibited by its role-model regimes as well as by pro-Soviet Communist politicians across Europe. This vacillation of the young pro-Soviet Communists was also linked with the complex impact of the occupations of 1979 on the pro-Soviet youth. Leisure activities in the occupied schools functioned as a negative example, but also as an impetus for self-critique of the cultural politics which the KNE had hitherto pursued.

In general, the tendency of young left-wingers to dismiss the leisure pursuits of unaffiliated young people, which was particularly evident in the mid–

1970s, was partially reversed toward the end of the decade. Members of left-wing youth groups made the effort, not always successfully, to mingle especially with unaffiliated young rockers, a youth culture that had made a comeback in Greece since 1977. A proportion of these young rockers evinced an interest in politics, albeit not necessarily in joining a left-wing youth organization. The potential interaction of the left-wingers with other categories of unaffiliated young people, such as football fans—the "youth of the football pitches"[2] as they were labeled in a somewhat schematic and judgmental manner by the KNE—is also an important topic awaiting historiographical exploration. In general, the very heterogeneity of the subjects of the left-wing youth, the diverse ways in which they approached the unaffiliated youngsters, as well as the varying ways in which the latter approached politics in general and the Left in particular, demonstrate that it is rather problematic to employ a schematic, binary taxonomy that juxtaposes "politicized" with "apathetic" youngsters, when referring to Greece in the period in question. Rather, to describe the relationship between youth and politics, it makes more sense to construe it as a continuum bounded by committed members of organized groups and apathetic youngsters at each end and containing several in-between conditions.

In any case, in the late 1970s, the effort of a segment of the left-wing youth to develop a non-normative conceptualization of "culture" was not confined to leisure pursuits. Greece witnessed no "turn inward" in discussions around sexuality at that point, similar to what Herzog describes that occurred elsewhere in Europe at the end of that decade: a segment of the left-wing youth in Greece, especially young Eurocommunists, autonomous left-wingers, Socialists, and some Maoists, voiced loud critiques of the sexual norms that the Greek Left had hitherto endorsed, which they named "conservative" and constraining. Ephemeral relationships between young unmarried left-wingers were no longer an oddity from at least the early 1970s. However, with the exception of the concerns that had been raised in the mid-1970s by small Feminist groups that rallied radical left-wing women, it was only in the late 1970s and, especially, around 1980, that official texts of left-wing organizations hosted contributions that openly put into question the concept of stable relationships leading to marriage. Singing and dancing to rock music served for them as an avenue to reflect on sexual "emancipation." However, they did not develop a concrete definition of what they regarded as desirable sexual patterns. In the same period, second-wave feminism and the homosexual liberation movement gained momentum in Greece, also influencing some young Eurocommunists, Maoists, and autonomous left-wingers. The advocates of those movements challenged motherhood as the necessary outcome of feminine sexuality. Those processes of challenging gen-

284 | Militant Around the Clock?

der and sexual norms were not necessarily in harmony with each other, however. Moments of friction were evident especially among some young male heterosexual left-wingers: they wavered between the use of sexist jokes to display promiscuity and the endeavors to use communications patterns that would not reproduce gender hierarchies. Such friction is yet another testament to the fact that the transition to democracy did not necessarily help "democratize" all dimensions of sexual and gender relations.

One way or another, the various approaches of the left-wing youth to leisure and sexuality demonstrated the hopes they derived from the political potential of the youth. However, this was certainly not an era during which "youth" was unequivocally represented as a positive force for change. A novelty in comparison with the 1960s was that, as the decade progressed, Socialist and Communist youngsters increasingly diversified with regard to their understanding of "youth": several of them became loudly critical of the idea that "youth" should be, apart from a source of hope, a cause of moral concern. Concomitantly, they detested the meddling of "parent cultures" that aimed to regulate the comportment of youngsters. Still, immensely popular youth organizations, such as the KNE, found it legitimate to act alongside the Parties they were affiliated with against phenomena they depicted as challenging what they viewed as the desirable behavior for Greek youth

Metapolitefsi after 1981

The late 1970s certainly signaled a rupture in some dimensions of the *Metapolitefsi* in Greece. Some of the Choros participants even argued in 1980 that the transformation of the ideological landscape in Greece was such that the "crisis" or even the "overcoming" of the *Metapolitefsi* had occurred.[3] Research should not uncritically embrace this statement, however. In particular the first half of the 1980s witnessed a dialectic of continuities and ruptures with regard to left-wing youth militancy, leisure, and sexuality—and their interdependencies. Some aspects of the *Metapolitefsi,* as they had crystallized in the mid–and late 1970s, perpetuated in the following decade. Left-wing parties dominated collective action in the 1980s; student unions were no exception, as is shown in table 7.1 below. In addition, all Socialist and Communist youth groups continued to hold festivals and evince serious interest in their cultural politics, an attitude they have been displaying until today.

Still, the early 1980s were not devoid of novelties in politics, leisure, sexuality, and gender relations: Greece became an official a member of the European Economic Community in 1981. PASOK won the elections in the same year, terminating a long period of right-wing or centrist governments. It implemented many demands set by the left-wing youth as well as the Feminist groups, a process which could be labeled as institutionalization.[4] Academic chairs were abolished with the introduction of Law 1268/1982. The Socialist government also liberalized family relations through the revision of the Family Law in 1983. As part of its revision, the obligation of the bride's family to provide a dowry was formally abolished.[5] According to Panagiotopoulos and Vamvakas, the 1980s witnessed the "democratization" of the state apparatus, as the examples above also illustrate, as well as its "expansion."[6] New state institutions were established, such as the General Secretariat for Youth, which was founded in 1982 and was in charge of devising the government policies with regard to youth. In addition, while in the period from 1974 to 1981 local cultural societies were neither created nor subsidized by the state, the Socialist government established many state-funded cultural centers across Greece, both in rural and in urban centers. These *politistika kentra* (cultural centers) held concerts, film screenings, exhibitions, and seminars, and organized excursions.[7]

Nevertheless, it would be inaccurate to describe the 1980s merely as a decade of institutionalization. New protest movements arose, such as that of the *enstoloi polites*, namely of young people doing their military service. The latter aimed at improving the experience of conscripts in the army, dispensing, especially, with the harassment of the soldiers by officers. While being a novelty of the 1980s, this protest culture echoed endeavors of the late 1970s autonomous student movement: According to Panayis Panagiotopoulos, Pavlos Pantazis, Nikos Rotzokos, and Giorgos Agelopoulos, some male participants in the 1979 occupations, who did their military service in the early 1980s, were among its protagonists.[8] What also arose around 1981 was the growing influence of anarchist groups among young Greeks. A number of squats, introduced by anarchists, appeared mainly in Exarchia Square in Athens. The Socialist government proved extremely hostile to them, launching a crackdown, named "Operation Virtue," in 1985. The early-to-mid 1980s also witnessed the emergence of a novel radical left-wing subject among university students: ASF-S (Aristeres Syspeiroseis Foititon-Spoudaston, Left Convergence of University and Higher Technical School Students). ASF-S should not be confused with the autonomous student groups linked with Choros: it mainly comprised students that were affiliated with a particular Party, most often the Trotskyite OSE (Organosi Sosialistiki Epanastasi, Organization Socialist Revolution) or the Maoist A/synecheia. ASF-S stopped functioning as a united group in 1987. In addition, anti-nuclear protests also proliferated in Greece in the 1980s, linked with the escalation of Cold War hostilities in the late 1970s. Ronald Reagan, who assumed the presidency of the United States in 1981, decided to deploy MGM-31 Pershing as well as cruise missiles in Western Europe, primarily in West Germany, as a response to the Soviet RSD-10 Pioneer ballistic missiles, stationed in Eastern Europe and the USSR.[9] The intensification of the arms race between the Cold War blocs caused a wave of anti-nuclear protest worldwide from the late 1970s onward and, especially, in the early-to-mid 1980s.[10] Such activities were widespread in Western European countries. For instance, in West Germany, according to historian Lawrence Wittner, about 300,000 people demonstrated in Bonn against the deployment of Pershing and cruise missiles. The Greens, who had campaigned for unilateral rejection of the deployment of the abovementioned missiles in West German territory, received 5.6 percent of the vote in the federal election of 1983 and entered the Bundestag (federal parliament) for the first time. In Greece, the anti-nuclear protest attracted strong support as well. Three were the main groups, which organized relevant protests: first of all, the EEDYE (Elliniki Epitropi gia ti Diethni Yfesi kai Eirini, Greek Committee for International Détente and Peace), which had been formed in 1955 and was linked with the pro-Soviet Communist Party of Greece; moreover, AKE (Adesmeyti Kinisi Eirinis, Non-Aligned Peace Movement), which was dominated by the KKE Es., emerged in 1981; finally, KEADEA (Kinisi gia tin Eirini, ta Anthropina Dikaiomata kai tin Ethniki Anexartisia, Movement for Peace, Human Rights and National Independence) was also established in 1981 by members of PASOK. Meanwhile, cultural transfers between Greek and Turkish left-wingers existed throughout the 1980s. The face-to-face interaction among Turkish political refugees and Greek Socialists and Communists intensified particularly after the coup d'état that was staged in Turkey in September 1980. Such contact included concerts, where the music of Mikis Theodorakis featured prominently.[11]

The 1980s signaled remarkable changes in the making of consumers in Greece as well. The rural areas witnessed significant financial development, due to the advent of tourism; the hefty EEC subsidies to the agricultural sector as a result of the Common Agricultural Policy (CAP); and to the return of many emigrants to their natal villages, who brought with them their capital.[12] Poor girls from the villages no longer rushed to the urban centers to become domestic servants; they were substituted in this work by Filipino female immigrants.[13] Consequently, the leisure pursuits of young people in the urban and rural areas tended to converge. This trend began with the diffusion of discotheques in smaller cities of the Greek periphery in the late 1970s and continued with the spread of cafeterias, even in the villages, in the 1980s, as a number of social anthropologists describe.[14]

However, the most significant shifts in politics and consumption occurred after 1985. The late 1980s were challenging for left-wing organizations.

Most of the KNE members broke away to form the NAR in 1989. Nevertheless, the KKE and KNE outlived the collapse of communism in Eastern Europe and continue to exist. RF and KKE Es. also experienced splits in the late 1980s. In 1987, the majority of their members decided to drop the word "Communist" from the organization's title. The biggest contingent of the KKE Es. reinvented itself as the EAR (Elliniki Aristera, Greek Left), while its youth organization, which attracted many former members of RF, was called RAN (Rizospastiki Aristeri Neolaia, Radical Left Youth). However, not everybody welcomed this decision: the minority in KKE Es. split and created KKE Es.- A.A. (KKE Es. Ananeotiki Aristera, KKE Es. Left Renewal), whose youth group retained the name EKON RF. Communist university student groups were also affected by those transformations: After the split in the KNE in 1989, PSK also ceased to exist. Its members founded, along with students aligned with or leaning toward EAR, the AEPS (Aristera Enotika Psifodeltia, Left Unity Lists), which ran in the student elections of 1989 and, subsequently, the PKS (Proodeytikes Kiniseis Synergasias, Progressive Allied Movements), which participated in the elections of 1990. Meanwhile, together with students affiliated with or leaning toward KKE Es.-A.A., NAR students formed the AAEPS (Aristera Antisynainetika Enotika Psifodeltia, Left Anti-Compromise Unity Lists). The drop in the electoral strength of the KNE students in 1990 is notable. Concerning Socialist groups, the PASP suffered from an abrupt decline in its influence in the mid–to-late 1980s as well. However, it has managed to remain one of the strongest student groups in Greece until the early 2010s.

Table 7.1. Results of university student elections, 1982–1990

	1982	1983	1984	1985	1986	1987	1988	1989	1990
DAP-NDFK	13.1	18.1	23	26.9	28.9	31.4	34.1	40	45.7
PASP	27.1	24.5	25.8	26.9	20.4	18.3	14.6	15.3	19.2
PSK	31.6	30.4	29.1	27.2	29.1	30.4	31		
DA-DE	14.3	14.7	12.4	12.1	10.1	8	2.2		
ASF-S	11.2	4.4	3.8	3.4	3.5				
AEPS								30.3	
PKS									12.4
AAEPS									12.2
Turnout	53,025	57,845	73,372	86,651	87,186	80,258	68,246	66,626	54,614

Note: Percentage of votes received by each of the student groups mentioned and voter turnout in the student elections in the period 1982–90. The table refers to the percentage of votes harvested by the most popular student groups only, which is the reason why percentages do not add up to 100 percent. Table prepared by the author based on data from Aravantinos, "To Metapoliteytiko", pp. 496–535.

The mid–1980s actually witnessed a broader restructuring of the political landscape in Greece. Communists no longer situated themselves in ideological proximity with the governing party, PASOK. They claimed that the latter had failed to effect socialist transformation in Greece. The most remarkable cut-off point was perhaps the municipal elections in 1986, when the KKE for the first time since 1974 refused to support Socialist candidates in the second round, asking for its supporters to abstain. As a result, New Democracy won the three biggest municipalities, namely Athens, Salonica, and Piraeus. In the same period, the Center-Right student organization increased in strength significantly and has actually dominated university student elections since 1987, as shown in table 7.1. In addressing the youth, the Center-Right did not neglect cultural politics: the youth group of New Democracy, ONNED, continued to actively engage itself in the organization of its festival, "Giorti Dimokratias," throughout the 1980s. In stark contrast to relevant left-wing events, however, the Center-Right youth allowed companies to advertise themselves within the festival premises and hosted Greek popular music artists, such as Antypas, whom the Left scorned as "commercialized."[15]

In addition, consumer traits in Greece altered remarkably in the mid–1980s. The era of frugality was over. A growing segment of low- and middle-class people in Greece, regardless of age, actively tried to become familiar with lavishness.[16] Showing off through wearing of expensive clothes became much more common, even for supporters of PASOK. From that period onward, many Socialists would not feel guilty in frequenting venues whose names aimed at manifesting wealth, such as the nightclubs named "Privilege." A number of magazines, which appeared in the late 1980s, like *Click*, promoted such a lifestyle. According to historian Panayiotis Zestanakis, such outlets were very popular especially among men. These magazines circulated representations of masculinity that valorized bachelorhood as well as a luxurious lifestyle and lambasted the subject-position of the male provider; they were also ardently supportive of the use of cosmetics by men.[17]

Due to these sweeping changes, some scholars have defined the mid–to-late 1980s as the point in which post or late modernity appeared in full force in Greece, even though relevant research has not been extensive. Sociologist Nicolas Sevastakis relates the dawning era of postmodernity in Greece with the overcoming of the *Metapolitefsi*. He views the latter as an era marked by a "liberating explosion," during which the defeated in the Civil War could express their views freely. This period was marked by collective action and protest as well as by the proliferation of collective memory from the perspective of the Left. By contrast, from the mid–1980s onward, according to Sevastakis, political radicalism subsided. The major political forces approached citizens as "individuals." The coming of postmodernity, in his view, although linked with developments at a global level, manifests a peculiarity in Greece: the ridicule of left-wing militancy, especially in magazines, such as *Click,* which played an important role in this transition.[18] The political scientist Giannis Voulgaris has observed a similar transition from "Greece of the Metapolitefsi," a period which lasted from 1974 to 1989, to "globalized Greece," from 1989 onward. From 1974 until at least the mid–1980s, according to Voulgaris, a "left-democratic" discourse was prevalent in Greek society; its key elements were the claim to represent "genuine patriotism," the veneration of the "collective" and the dismissal of entrepreneurship. However, this discourse subsided toward the late 1980s and gave place to growing individualism.[19] The latter, according to Voulgaris, coexists with the pervasive influence of national and religious stereotypes, which is not an occasion of duality, but an aspect of a late/post-modern era, which has dawned in Greece as well.[20]

Theoretical endeavors of Greek scholars about the emergence of late/post-modernity reflect broader scholarly debates in the "West" about the temporal limits of "modernity." An issue that has triggered rancorous debate among the latter is whether a clear-cut rupture with "modernity" and the emergence of a postmodern era can be discerned. A second issue, which has also been controversial among them, is whether such a rupture can be associated with changes in systems of economic production and the rise of post-Fordist[21] models. Fredric Jameson, a literary critic and political theorist, construes postmodernity as a distinct era. He describes postmodernism as the "cultural logic of late capitalism." The latter has appeared since the 1960s and is marked by the hitherto unparalleled global character of the activities of multinational corporations. Jameson argues that "the older master-narratives of legitimation no longer function in the service of scientific research—nor, by implication, anywhere else."[22] Postmodernism, by contrast, is characterized by pastiche: a "play of random stylistic allusion" which does not reflect an "external" reality.[23] On the contrary, sociologist Anthony Giddens claims that modernity has not come to an end, but, rather, reached a second phase, which he labels "high" or "late" modernity. He has discerned reflexivity as a crucial element of modernity, claiming that "most aspects of social activity, and material relations with nature" are subject to "chronic revision in the light of new information or knowledge." In the context of late modernity, the latter "task has to be accomplished amid a puzzling diversity of options and possibilities," under conditions of "uncertainty and multiple choice."[24]

Several academics tend to construe the coming of post/late modernity in Greece, often using those two terms interchangeably, as an indication of the ebb tide of mass mobilization. By contrast, scholars dealing with other European countries do not share, at least totally, this assumption. Cultural critic Jo Labanyi argues that, in the case of Spain, "the postmodernist sense of living after the 'end of history' was expressed in the *desencanto* (disenchantment) years from 1979 to the PSOE's (Spanish Socialist Workers' Party) election victory in 1982 by the *pasotismo* (dropping out) that succeeded the immediate post-1975 political and sexual euphoria."[25] However, she also argues that "a number of writers," such as Eduardo Mendoza, "have used the pastiche of mass cultural forms" to construe historical events from a politicized perspective.[26] Academics dealing with Northern Europe have gone even further, linking in various ways the dawning of a post or a late modern era not with the demise, but with the very activity of radical subjects. Siegfried reiterates the argument that the coming of a "postindustrial" or "reflexive" modernity in Northwestern Europe is related to the "alternative" milieux that emerged around the 1970s and which put into question the very foundations of "modernity."[27] In light of such approaches, it may be more fruitful to see whether a late or post modern condition in Greece was not necessarily incompatible with collective action. The late 1970s in that country witnessed serious subversions of social conventions and political norms, which were not pursued by "alternative" milieux, but by a broad range of subjects involved in left-wing youth politics. Those groups did not reject metanarratives per se, but, rather, seem to have developed protest patterns akin to a "puzzling diversity of options." This subversion acquired three forms: transgression of bipolar models classifying cultural products; formulation of anti-fascist narratives, which were replete with doubt and self-criticism; and rearticulation of the relationship between collective action and the individual, especially through the inception of less centralized political structures. Indeterminacy and hybridity were key aspects manifest in the political activities, in the domains of leisure and sexuality notwithstanding, of a broad range of the Greek left-wing youth, especially among the Eurocommunists and the autonomous young left-wingers. In this sense, they could be depicted as spearheading a late modern project, albeit perhaps not the one that eventually became hegemonic in Greece.

Did, however, the activity of those left-wingers also lead to the particular late modern condition, which was predicated on "individualization" and became prevalent in Greece toward the end of the 1980s, despite their intentions? Unlike what historian Niall Ferguson has suggested about the 1970s as an era in global history that paved the way for crises that occurred in the subsequent decades, the endeavors of the Choros participants and the young Eurocommunists was not at the root of the crisis of the *Metapolitefsi*.[28] The unfolding of post or late modernity in Greece did not occur in a teleological manner, but was replete with contingency. For instance, some of the Choros participants in the late 1970s were active in magazines, like *Scholiastis,* in the 1980s. The latter was a left-wing magazine, open to protest movements that were active in Greece at that point and not linked with any political Party. Articles about sexuality and leisure featured prominently in it and were a core component of the effort undertaken by the magazine to explore novel forms of relating the individual to collective action. However, such an attempt cannot be viewed as merely a precursor to magazines, such as *Click,* as Michalis Bartsidis aptly remarks.[29] *Scholiastis* treated with derision luxurious lifestyles and political apathy, which were celebrated by those outlets, which tracked and shaped post or late modernity, as established in Greece.

Moreover, a closer exploration of cultural events, which were introduced by the left-wing youth in the mid–1970s and which continue to exist, such as the youth festivals, may be conducive to a more nuanced understanding of the relationship between lavish lifestyles and radical politics. The spread of the former in the late 1980s in Greece is usually correlated with the decline of the latter, especially due to the vitriolic critique of radical politics that magazines like *Click* voiced, according to Sevastakis.[30] However, it is questionable whether those phenomena are mutually exclusive. The recent participation of the hip hop music bands Goin' Through and NEVMA in the Festival of KNE-Odigitis in 2012 has stirred relevant debates: In an article published in *Avgi,* at present the official newspaper of the Coalition of the Radical Left, the author chastised the invitation of those bands to the festival, since the members of Goin' Through were described as "often showing off ... furs, necklaces."[31] The bands issued a rebuttal, in which they claimed that their work encompasses socio-political reflection.[32] Implicitly, both sides sought to disassociate left-wing militancy from luxury, linking themselves with the former. What remains to be examined, however, is the actual practice of the fans of those hip hop bands, especially whether they regard wearing poshy clothes as incompatible with being radical and whether they practice both, without experiencing this as a contradiction. Whatever the case, the further examination of the resilience and the elasticity of left-wing youth festivals in Greece since the mid–1970s may yield valuable insights into both the influence and the orientation of the Greek Left since 1974.

In any case, the relationship between left-wing youth politics, leisure, and sexuality during the 1970s, but also in their aftermath, has been complex and multifaceted. One of the possible ways to make it tangible is to follow the orientation change in the work of Loukianos Kilaidonis, which tracked, but also contributed to, the shaping of this relationship. After the collapse of the dictatorship, he acted as an artist, who was confident that his work could instill "progressive" messages and help pave the way for socialism. However, his confidence had evaporated by 1978, when he reinvented himself as a "poor lonely cowboy." At least for a segment of the left-wing youth, the late 1970s were an era of reflection and self-critique; it was the time for the anti-heroes. In the early 1980s, he organized an open party at the EOT beach club in Vouliagmeni in collaboration with the local sailing club. The scale of the event was massive: it is estimated that around 50,000 to 80,000 people participated. This was no repetition of the huge concerts in the sport stadiums in the mid–1970s, in which Mikis Theodorakis had been the protagonist: songs were not meant to galvanize resistance and protest, but, rather, address individuals and make them have fun.[33] Nevertheless, left-wing youth cultures followed multiple trajectories: numerous other young left-wingers, such as the KNE supporters, sought in the meantime their ideal partisans, in order to combat the insidious effects of *Emmanuelle* and other "imperialist inventions." Kilaidonis's music has featured prominently in diverse left-wing understandings of "culture." While mobilizing their members and supporters against the "crisis of capitalism" in 2013, the KNE also resorted to his didactic album *Apla Mathimata Politikis Oikonomias* (Simple lessons in political economy, 1975).[34]

One way or another, the examination of conceptualizations of "culture" proves to be key to a comprehensive and nuanced understanding left-wing militancy, including that of the youth in Greece since 1974. The Greek Left has assigned much weight to "culture" as a means of triggering collective action: It is not by chance that the eruption of protests, in which the Left has figured prominently, such as the mobilization of pupils in the early and late 1990s and the demonstrations against the bailout agreements since 2010 has usually been accompanied by events, such as concerts. Scholars who analyze the long-term impact of left-wing youth militancy of the 1960s–70s in Greece and who consider its relationship with protest movements elsewhere in Europe will certainly continue to address the relationship between left-wing politics and culture. Similarly, an in-depth analysis of the politicization of sexuality and leisure in other post-authoritarian Southern European societies during the 1970s, namely Portugal and Spain, ideally in comparison with Greece, will help develop a more profound understanding of the transitions from dictatorship to democracy in those countries.[35]

Notes

1. http://jethro-talibans.blogspot.gr/ (last accessed on 11 August 2012).
2. "I Neolaia, to Kinima Neolaias kai I Kommounistiki Neolaia Elladas (KNE)," *KOMEP*, 1976, p. 14.
3. "To xeperasma tis Metapolitefsis," *Rixi*, June 1980, p. 2.

4. The term is not used in either a positive or a negative way in this book.
5. Dimitra Samiou, *Gynaika, Fylo kai Politiki (18os–20os aionas): Istoriografikes proseg-giseis: mia eisagogi* (Mytilini, 2006), p. 67.
6. Vassilis Vamvakas and Panayis Panagiotopoulos, introduction to *I Ellada sti dekaetia tou '80*, ed. Vassilis Vamvakas and Panayis Panagiotopoulos (Athens, 2010), p. XLIV.
7. Evangelos Lagos, "Politistika Kentra," in Vamvakas and Panagiotopoulos, *I Ellada sti dekaetia tou '80*, pp. 477–78.
8. Giorgos Agelopoulos and Nikos Rotzokos, "To kinima gia to strato ti dekaetia tou '80: politikes, ideologikes kai organotikes diastaseis," in Karamanolakis, Olympitou, and Papathanasiou, *I elliniki neolaia ston 20o aiona*, pp. 345–68; Pavlos Pantazis and Panayis Panagiotopoulos, "Neolaia kai stratiotiki thiteia 1980–1987: Ypokei-menikotita kai ekdimokratismos ton thesmon stin koinonia tis epithymias," in ibid., pp. 369–75.
9. See, for instance: Raymond L. Garthoff, "The Failure of the Détente of the 1970s," in *The Cold War: The Essential Readings*, ed. Klaus Larres and Ann Lane (Oxford, 2001), pp. 159–80.
10. Lawrence S. Wittner, *Toward Nuclear Abolition: A History of the World Nuclear Dis-armament Movement, 1971 to the Present* (Stanford, 2003). Philipp Gassert, Martin Klimke, and Wilfried Mausbach have also recently launched a relevant research proj-ect, entitled "The Nuclear Crisis: Cold War Cultures and the Politics of Peace and Security, 1975–1990." For more details, see http://www.nuclearcrisis.org/ (retrieved on 31 August 2012).
11. See, for instance: Leonidas Karakatsanis, *Turkish-Greek Relations. Rapprochement, civil society and the politics of friendship* (Abingdon 2014).
12. Gallant, *Modern Greece*, p. 216.
13. For the case of Greek female domestic servants, see Pothiti Hantzaroula, "I kataskeyi tis ypotagis: Oikiakes ypiretries stin Ellada, 1920–1945," (PhD diss., European University Institute, Florence, 2001).
14. Epitropoulos and Roudometof, "Youth Culture," pp. 119–44; Jane K. Cowan, "Going out for Coffee? Contesting the Grounds of Gendered Pleasures in Everyday Sociability," in Loizos and Papataxiarchis, *Contested Identities*, pp. 180–202; Christina Vlachoutsikou, "I katanalosi: metafora gia to monterno kai rogmi sti gynaikeia afaneia," *Synchrona Themata* 66, no. 1–3 (1998): pp. 87–103.
15. Nikolaos Papadogiannis, "Festival Neolaias," in Vamvakas and Panagiotopoulos, *I Ellada sti dekaetia tou '80*, p. 629.
16. Souliotis, "Dievrynsi tou koinou," pp. 299–300. Souliotis aptly remarks, however, that the lifestyle of the middle and the working class did not become identical with that of the upper class. For instance, customer service in upper-class leisure venues was much more personalized in comparison to those catering for low- and middle-class customers.
17. See Panagiotis Zestanakis, "Ekdoches tou andrismou sta ellinika lifestyle entypa tis dekaetias tou '80: Playboy, Status, Klik (1985–1990)," (MA diss., University of Crete, Rethymno 2008).
18. Nicolas Sevastakis, *Koinotopi Chora: Opseis tou Dimosiou Chorou kai Antinomies Ax-ion sti simerini Ellada*, Athens 2004.

19. Voulgaris, *I Ellada apo ti Metapolitefsi*, pp. 330–43. Giorgos Diakoumakos has reached similar conclusions in his PhD thesis. According to him, teenagers of the late 1980s are associated with the development of a "mainstream" youth culture, which has become hegemonic in Greece. This youth culture is based on individualism and conformism, namely the support for the dominant political forces. This endorsement is not an active one, though, since it does not entail mass mobilization with the aim to help realize the targets of those political forces. See Giorgos Diakoumakos, "Politistikes praktikes kai politikes antilipseis: Oi kentrikes ellinikes (politikes) ypokoultoures," (PhD diss., University of Athens, 2010), pp. 192–99.

20. Voulgaris, *I Ellada apo ti Metapolitefsi*, p. 343.

21. For the concept of the post-Fordist society, see Ash Amin, ed., *Post-Fordism: A Reader* (Oxford, 1994).

22. Foreword by Fredric Jameson in Jean-François Lyotard, *The Postmodern Condition: A Report on Knowledge* (Manchester, 1984), p. xii.

23. Fredric Jameson, *Postmodernism, or, the Cultural Logic of Late Capitalism* (Durham, NC, 1991), p. 18.

24. Anthony Giddens, *Modernity and Self-Identity: Self and Society in the Late Modern Age* (Cambridge, 1991), pp. 10–34, 70–108.

25. Jo Labanyi, Helen Graham, and Antonio Sanchez, "Conclusion: Modernity and Cultural Pluralism," in *Spanish Cultural Studies: An Introduction: The Struggle for Modernity*, ed. Helen Graham and Jo Labanyi (Oxford, 1995), p. 396.

26. Jo Labanyi, "Narrative Culture, 1975–1996," in Gies, *The Cambridge Companion*, p. 153.

27. Detlef Siegfried, "Das gute Leben im falschen. Dänemark-Wahrnehmungen im westdeutschen Alternativmilieu," in Reichardt and Siegfried, *Das Alternative Milieu*, p. 89.

28. Ferguson argues that phenomena of the 1980s, 1990s, and 2000s, such as the collapse of the Soviet Union and the spread of Islamic terrorism, should be imputed to developments that had appeared already in the 1970s. Thus, he labels the latter as a "'seedbed' of future crises," without necessarily construing "crises" in a negative way. See Niall Ferguson, "Introduction: Crisis, What Crisis? The 1970s and the Shock of the Global," in *The Shock of the Global: The 1970s in Perspective*, ed. Niall Ferguson et al., (Cambridge, MA, 2010), p. 20.

29. Michalis Bartsidis, "Scholiastis," in Vamvakas and Panagiotopoulos, *I Ellada sti dekaetia tou '80*, pp. 573–74.

30. Sevastakis, *Koinotopi Chora*, p. 60.

31. http://www.avgi.gr/ArticleActionshow.action?articleID=710636 (last accessed on 2 February 2013).

32. http://www.rizospastis.gr/wwwengine/story.do?id=7007150 (last accessed on 2 February 2013).

33. Olympia Konstantopoulou, "Party sti Vouliagmeni," in Vamvakas and Panagiotopoulos, *I Ellada sti dekaetia tou '80*, pp. 443–45.

34. That was part of the event "Tholoi kairoi, prosexe ergati ..." [Dire times, worker beware ...], which took place on 20 January 2013 in Athens. For more details, see http://www.902.gr/eidisi/neolaiapaideia/7057/epitropi-festival-kne-politistiki-paremvasi-me-epikentro-tin#/0 (last accessed: 8 February 2013).

35. For instance, historian Pamela Radcliff has argued about Spain that a social history of this transition, which would delve into the "juncture between economic development, political reform and social transformation … still remains largely unwritten." See Pamela Radcliff, "Associations and the Social Origins of the Transition during the Late Franco Regime," in Spain Transformed. The Late Franco Dictatorship, 1959-75, ed. Nigel Townson, Houndmills, 2010, p. 158. This is true of Portugal, too. I believe that a cultural and social history of the links between left-wing politics, leisure, and sexuality will be a core component of such an approach.

Bibliography

Primary Sources

Archives and Collections

Archive of Avgi, Athens

Archive "Charilaos Florakis" of the KKE, Athens

Archive of the KKE(m-l), Salonica

ASKI (Archeia Synchronis Koinonikis Istorias, Archives of Contemporary Social History), Athens:
    Archive of EKON Rigas Feraios
    Archive of Sabatakakis
    Archive of Brillakis
    Archive of Kakouriotis
    Archive of Fyssas
    Archive of Georgiou
    Resolutions passed in the first Panhellenic conference of RF
    "Ntokoumenta, 1o synedrio ths EKON Rigas Feraios" (Documents, 1st Congress of
        EKON Rigas Feraios)
    Resolutions passed in the second congress of RF

Bundesarchiv Berlin:
    DY/30 Vorl. SED 34922, 17 March 1981, Stiftung Archiv der Parteien und
        Massenorganisationen der DDR

Delphys Archive, Athens

Archive of EMIAN (Etaireia Meletis tis Istorias tis Aristeris Neolaias, Society for the
Examination of the History of the Left-Wing Youth), Athens:
    Archive of Chatzopoulos

ESYE Archive, Athens

Fondation Hellénique Archive, Paris:
    Posters of the Greek students residing at the Fondation Hellenique in the early 1970s

Istituto Gramsci Toscano:
    La città futura, 1977–1979

Princeton Special Collections, Princeton:
    Margaret Papandreou Collection

Personal Collections:
    of Areti Anastasiadou and Giorgos Karoubis
    of Dimitris Aravantinos

of Dimitris Dimitriadis and Niki Simou
of Aimilia Karali
of Giannis Kallipolitis
of Sifis Kotsantis
of Kostas Livieratos
of Aris Maragkopoulos
of Giannis Papadogiannis
of Maria Repoussi
of Nikos Samanidis
of Donald Sassoon
of Roura Sifnaiou

Periodicals

Agonas gia tin Kommounistiki Ananeosi
Agonas ton Mathiton
Agonistis
Akropolis
AMPHI
ANTI
Antiefimerida
Athinorama
Avgi
Bananes
Deltio tis KDG
Deltio tis PAPOK
Dialogos
Diavazo
Dimokratikos Agonas
Eleftheri Genia
Exodos
Fantasio
Gia tin Apeleytherosi ton Gynaikon
Gnomi
Gryllos
I Katalipsi
Ioulos
Kathreftis
KOMEP
KOMTHEPOL
Laikoi Agones
Manina
Mathitiki Genia
Mathitika Neiata
Mathitiki Poreia

Odigitis
Panspoudastiki (pre-dictatorship)
Panspoudastiki (post-dictatorship)
Panspoudastiki Vretanias
Pantheon
PES
Politis
Pop kai Rock
Pezodromio
Proletariaki Simaia
Rixi
Rizospastis
Salpisma
Sfigga
Skoupa
Spoudi
Synchroni Gynaika
Synchronos Kinimatografos
Ta Aythaireta ton synoikion tis EKON Rigas Feraios (B Panelladiki)
Ta Nea
Ta Theamata
To Vima
Techni kai Politismos
Thourios
Thranio
Touvlo
Vradyni

Published Sources

Aleka Papariga. *Gia tin apeleytherosi ton gynaikon* [For the Emancipation of Women]. Athens, 1981.
EKON Rigas Feraios. *Ta dikaiomata tis neas genias* [EKON Rigas Feraios. The rights of the youth]. Athens, 1979.
Gia tin agonistiki taxiki patriotiki diapaidagogisi tis neolaias [About the militant class patriot education of the youth]. Athens, 1977.
Dekemvris '79: Agonistiki exarsi tou foititikou kinimatos [December '79: Militant eruption of the student movement]. Athens, 1980.
To KK Ispanias gia to Gynaikeio zitima [The Communist Party of Spain about the women's issue]. Athens, 1979.

Interviews by the Author

B.N-C., Athens, 8 April 2009

T.L., Athens, 8 April 2008
H.Z., Salonica, 18 August 2008
I.A, Athens, 27 April 2008
O.T., Salonica, 15 May 2008
E.Q. and B.Q., Athens, 29 October 2007
U.L., Athens, 3 December 2007
R.L. Athens, 31 May 2006
N.E., Athens, 20 July 2006
B.L., Athens, 5 December 2007
T.D., Athens, 22 November 2007
O.M., Athens, 17 July 2006
N.T., Athens, 1 June 2006
N.K., Athens, 7 December 2007
A.H., Athens, 3 April 2008
A.A. and G.K., Salonica, 10 April 2008
L.L., Athens, 14 April 2009
D.V., Athens, 19 August 2008
L.C., Salonica, 28 December 2007
D.M., Athens, 13 September 2006
B.N., Athens, 4 April 2008
L.M., Athens, 17 May 2008
S.L., Athens, 13 April 2008
T.M. and N.R, Athens, 3 December 2007
A.S., Salonica, 15 December 2008
G.K. and A.M., Athens, 20 March 2008
D.A. Salonica, 12 May 2008
O.Y., Athens, 13 November 2007
N.R. and M.S., Salonica, 15 September 2009
G.R., N.K., O.Y. and D.M., Athens, 3 December 2007
D.P., Salonica, 15 September 2009
S.T., Athens, 12 July 2008
A.S., O.P., H.U. and S.T., Athens, 12 July 2008
K.K. Athens, 11 December 2008
E.A., Athens, 10 December 2009
V.K. Athens, 18 July 2006
A.P., Athens, 2 June 2006
T.S., Athens, 30 March 2008
A.T., Athens, 31 March 2008
K.M., Salonica, 9 January 2008
A.M., Athens, 22 May 2008
T.I., Athens, 13 December 2008
D.D. and N.S., Salonica, 3 September 2008
K. F., Athens, 4 May 2008
L. K., Athens, 6 April 2008
S. S., Athens, 3 May 2008
V.S., Salonica, 4 January 2012

S.M., interview via telephone, 11 October 2011
P.K., interview via telephone, 13 October 2011
N.P., interview via telephone, 12 October 2011
G.K., interview via telephone, 12 October 2011
A.M., interview via telephone, 10 October 2011
A.D., Salonica, 17 September 2011
T.R., Salonica, 17 September 2011
T.V., Athens, 7 September 2011
D.K., Athens, 8 September 2011

Secondary Sources

Abu-Lughod, Lila. *Veiled Sentiments: Honor and Poetry in a Bedouin Society.* Berkeley, CA, 1986.
Afinian, Basil G., Vassilis Kontis, Konstantinos Papoulidis, Nina D. Smirnova, and Natalia Tomilina, eds. *Oi scheseis KK kai KK Sovietikis Enosis sto diastima 1953–1977* [The relations between the KKE and the Communist Party of the Soviet Union 1953–1977]. Salonica, 1999.
Agelopoulos, Giorgos, and Nikos Rotzokos. "To kinima gia to strato ti dekaetia tou '80: politikes, ideologikes kai organotikes diastaseis" [The movement in the armed forces in the 1980s: Political, ideological, and organizational dimensions]. In Karamanolakis, Olympitou, Papathanasiou, *I elliniki neolaia* [Greek youth], pp. 345–68.
Aguilar, Paloma. *Memory and Amnesia: The Role of the Spanish Civil War in the Transition to Democracy.* New York, 2002.
Alarcon, Norma. "The Theoretical Subjects of *This Bridge Called My Back* and *Anglo-American Feminism.*" In *The Second Wave: A Reader in Feminist Theory*, ed. Linda J. Nicholson, pp. 288–99. New York, 1997.
Alivizatos, Nikos. *Oi Politikoi Thesmoi se Krisi, 1922–1974: Opseis tis ellinikis empeirias* [The political institutions in crisis, 1922–1974: Facets of the Greek experience]. 3rd ed. Athens, 1995.
Amin, Ash, ed. *Post-Fordism: A Reader.* Oxford, 1994.
Anderson, Benedict. *Imagined Communities: Reflections on the Origin and Spread of Nationalism.* London, 1991.
Andritsos, Giorgos. *I Katochi kai I Antistasi ston Elliniko Kinimatografo, 1945–1966* [Occupation and resistance in Greek cinema 1945–1966]. Athens, 2004.
Apostolidou, Venetia. *Logotechnia kai Istoria sti Metapolemiki Aristera: I paremvasi tou Dimitri Hatzi, 1947–1981* [Literature and history in postwar Left: The intervention of Dimitris Hatzis, 1947–1981]. Athens, 2003.
Aravantinos, Dimitris. "To Metapoliteytiko foititiko kai syndikalistiko kinima" [The student and trade union movement of the Metapolitefsi]. In *75 chronia: To panepistimio tis Thessalonikis stin avgi tou neou aiona* [75 years: The University of Salonica at the dawn of the new century], ed. Ioannis K. Hassiotis and Dimitris Aravantinos, pp. 465–560. Salonica, 2002

Asimakoulas, Dimitris. "Translating 'Self' and 'Others': Waves of Protest Under the Greek Junta." *The Sixties* 2, no. 1 (2009): pp. 25–47.

Athanasatou, Gianna. "Ellinikos Kinimatografos (1950–1967): Laiki Mnimi kai Ideologia" [Greek cinema (1950–1967): Popular memory and ideology]. PhD diss., University of Athens, 1998.

Avdela, Efi. "'Corrupting and Uncontrollable Activities': Moral Panic about Youth in Post-Civil-War Greece." *Journal of Contemporary History*, vol. 43, no. 1 (2008): pp. 25–44.

———. *Dia Logous timis: Via, Synaisthimata kai Axies sti metemfyliaki Ellada* [For reasons of honor: Violence, emotions, and values in post–Civil War Greece]. Athens, 2002.

———. *"Neoi en kindyno"': Epitirisi, anamorfosi kai dikaiosyni anilikon meta ton polemo* ["Youth in danger": Discipline, rehabilitation, and youth justice after the war]. Athens, 2013.

Avdela, Efi, and Angelika Psarra, eds. *Siopires Istories: Gynaikes kai Fylo stin istoriki afigisi* [Silent histories: Women and gender in historical narration]. Athens, 1997.

Bakhtin, Mikhail M. *The Dialogic Imagination*, republished in *The Bakhtin Reader*, ed. Pam Morris, pp. 74–80. London, 1994.

Balibar, Étienne, and Immanuel Wallerstein. *Race, Nation, Class: Ambiguous Identities*. London, 1991.

Baranowski, Shelley, and Ellen Furlough, eds. *Being Elsewhere: Tourism, Consumer Culture, and Identity in Modern Europe and North America*. Ann Arbor, MI, 2004.

Berghahn, Volker R. *The Americanization of West German Industry, 1945–1973*. Leamington Spa, UK, 1986.

Bermeo, Nancy. "Classification and Consolidation: Some Lessons from the Greek Dictatorship," *Political Science Quarterly* 110, no. 3 (1995): pp. 435–52.

Bertsch, Anja. "Alternative (in) Bewegung: Distinktion und transnationale Vergemeinschaftung im alternativen Tourismus." In *Das Alternative Milieu. Antibürgerlicher Lebensstil und linke Politik in der Bundesrepublik Deutschland und Europa 1968–1983*, ed. Sven Reichardt and Detlef Siegfried, pp. 115–130. Göttingen, Ger., 2010.

Bettelheim, Charles. *Les luttes de classes en URSS—Première période, 1917–1923*. Paris, 1974.

Bistis, Nikos. *Prochorontas kai Anatheorontas* [Moving and revising]. Athens, 2010.

Borsay, Peter. *A History of Leisure*. Houndmills, UK, 2006.

Bourke, Joanna. *Fear: A Cultural History.* London, 2006.

———. "Fear and Anxiety: Writing about Emotion in Modern History." *History Workshop Journal* 55 (2003): pp. 111–33.

Bozinis, Nikos. *Rock pagkosmiotita kai elliniki topikotita: I koinoniki istoria tou rock stis chores katagogis tou kai stin Ellada* [Rock globality and Greek locality: The social history of rock in its countries of origin and in Greece]. Athens, 2007.

Bracke, Maud Anne. "One-dimensional Conflict? Recent Scholarship on 1968 and the Limitations of the Generation Concept," *Journal of Contemporary History* 47, no. 3 (2012): pp. 638–46.

Brake, Mike. *The Sociology of Youth Culture and Youth Subcultures: Sex and Drugs and Rock 'n' Roll?* London, 1985.

Bren, Paulina. "Looking West: Popular Culture and the Generation Gap in Communist Czechoslovakia, 1969–1989." In *Across the Atlantic: Cultural Exchanges Between Europe and the United States,* ed. Luisa Passerini, pp. 295–322. Brussels, 2000.

Brubaker, Rogers, and Frederick Cooper. "Beyond 'Identity.'" *Theory and Society* 29 (2000): pp. 1–47.

Bryant, Rebecca. *Imagining the Modern: The Cultures of Nationalism in Cyprus.* London, 2004.

Campbell, John K. *Honour, Family and Patronage: A Study of Institutions and Moral Values in a Greek Mountain Community.* Oxford, 1964.

———. "Traditional Values and Continuities in Greek Society." In *Greece in the 1980s,* ed. Richard Clogg, pp. 184–207, London, 1983.

Capuzzo, Paolo. "Youth Cultures and Consumption in Contemporary Europe." *Contemporary European History* 10 (2001): pp. 155–70.

Caute, David. *The Dancer Defects: The Struggle for Cultural Supremacy during the Cold War.* Oxford, 2003.

———. *The Year of the Barricades.* New York, 1988.

Charalambis, Dimitris, Laura Maratou-Alipranti, and Andromachi Hadjiyanni, eds. *Recent Social Trends in Greece 1960–2000.* Quebec, 2004.

Charisopoulou, Vicky. *"Tis Metapolitefsis Chameni Genia"* [The Lost Generation of the *Metapolitefsi*]. Athens, 2001.

Chatzisokratis, Dimitris. "I syntonistiki epitropi" [The co-ordinating committee]. In *Polytecnheio '73: Reportaz me tin istoria* [Polytechnic '73: Report with history], ed. Giorgos Gatos, pp. 214–19. Athens, 2003, 1st ed. 1983.

Clarke, John, Stuart Hall, Tony Jefferson, and Brian Roberts. "Subcultures, Cultures and Class." In *Resistance Through Rituals: Youth Subcultures in Post-War Britain,* ed. Stuart Hall and Tony Jefferson, pp. 3–59. London, 2006.

Clogg, Richard. *A Concise History of Greece.* Cambridge, 1992.

———. *Parties and Elections in Greece: The Search for Legitimacy.* London, 1987.

Close, David H. *Greece since 1945: Politics, Economy and Society.* London, 2002.

Cohen, Stanley. *Folk Devils and Moral Panics: The Creation of Mods and Rockers.* Oxford, 1987.

Connell, Robert W. (Raewyn), and James W. Messerschmidt. "Hegemonic Masculinity: Rethinking the Concept." *Gender and Society* 19, no. 6 (2005): pp. 829–59.

Cosma, Yvonne. "Eikones gia to fylo mesa apo ton elliniko kinimatografo stin dekaetia tou '60: fylo kai sexoualikotita sto eidos tis aisthimatikis komenti (1959–1967)" [Gender images through the Greek cinema in the 1960s: Gender and sexuality in the genre of sentimental comedies]. PhD diss., University of Athens, 2007.

Courtois, Stephane, Nicolas Werth, Jean-Louis Panné, Andrzej Paczkowski, Karel Bartošek, and Jean-Louis Margolin. *Le Livre noir du communisme: Crimes, terreur, repression.* Paris, 1997.

Cowan, Jane K. *Dance and the Body Politic in Northern Greece.* Princeton, 1990.

———. "Going out for Coffee? Contesting the Grounds of Gendered Pleasures in Everyday Sociability." In Loizos and Papataxiarchis, *Contested Identities,* pp. 180–202.

Dafermos, Olympios. *Foitites kai Diktatoria: To antidiktatoriko foititiko kinima 1972–1973* [Students and the Dictatorship: The antidictatorship student movement, 1972–1973]. Athens, 1999.

Daloukas, Manolis. *Elliniko Rok: Istoria tis neanikis koultouras apo ti genia tou Chaous mehri to thanato tou Pavlou Sidiropoulou, 1945–1990* [Greek rock: History of the youth culture from the Chaos generation until the death of Pavlos Sidiropoulos, 1945–1990]. Athens, 2006.

Davis, Belinda. "Reconsidering Habermas, Gender and the Public Sphere: The Case of Wilhelmine Germany." In *Society, Culture, and the State in Germany, 1870–1930*, ed. Geoff Eley. Ann Arbor, MI, 1996.

———. "Violence and Memory of the Nazi Past in 1960s–70s West German Protest." In *Coping with the Nazi Past: West German Debates on Nazism and Generational Conflict, 1955–1975*, ed. Philipp Gassert and Alan E. Steinweis, pp. 210–37. Oxford, 2006.

de Grazia, Victoria. *Irresistible Empire: America's Advance through 20th-Century Europe*, Cambridge, MA, 2005.

Delveroudi, Lisianna. "Kinimata Neolaias kai kinimatografos stin Ellada tis dekaetias tou 1960" [Youth movements and cinema in Greece during the 1960s]. In Karamano-lakis, Olympitou, and Papathanasiou, *I elliniki neolaia* [Greek youth], pp. 309–17.

Demertzis, Nikos, and Yiannis Stavrakakis. "I erevna gia ti neolaia- synoptiki anadromi" [The research on youth- brief review]. In *Neolaia, o astathmitos paragontas* [Youth, an unpredictable factor], ed. Nikos Demertzis, Yiannis Stavrakakis, Bettina Davou, Antonis Armenakis, Nikolas Christakis, Nikos Georgarakis, and Nikos Boubaris, pp. 15–29. Athens, 2008.

Demetriou, Demetrakis Z. "Connell's Concept of Hegemonic Masculinity: A Critique." *Theory and Society* 30, no. 3 (2001): pp. 337–61.

Diamantouros, Nikiforos. *Politismikos dyismos kai politiki allagi stin Ellada tis metapolitef-sis* [Cultural duality and political change in post-dictatorship Greece]. Athens, 2000.

Dimitriou, Panos. *I diaspasi tou KKE* [The split of the KKE], vol. 1–2. Athens, 1978.

Douglas, Mary. *Purity and Danger.* London, 1966.

Draenos, Stan, *Andreas Papandreou: The Making of a Greek Democrat and Political Maverick.* New York, 2012.

Dumazedier, Joffre. "Leisure." In *International Encyclopedia of the Social Sciences*, ed. David L. Sills, vol. 9. New York, 1979, p. 251.

Durrer, Lorenz. "Born to be Wild: Rockmusik und Protestkultur in der 1960er Jahren." In *1968: Ein Handbuch zur Kultur- und Mediengeschichte der Studentenbewegung*, ed. Martin Klimke and Joachim Scharloth, pp. 161–74. Stuttgart, 2007.

Edelman, Robert. *Serious Fun: A History of Spectator Sport in the USSR.* Oxford, 1993.

Edkins, Jenny. *Poststructuralism and International Relations. Bringing the Political Back In.* London, 1999.

Eitler, Pascal. "Die 'sexuelle Revolution'—Körperpolitik um 1968." In *1968: Ein Handbuch zur Kultur- und Mediengeschichte der Studentenbewegung*, ed. Martin Klimke and Joachim Scharloth, pp. 235–46. Stuttgart, 2007.

Eley, Geoff. *Forging Democracy: The history of the Left in Europe, 1850–2000.* Oxford, 2002.

Eley, Geoff, and Keith Nield. *The Future of Class in History: What's Left of the Social?* Ann Arbor MI, 2007.

Epitropoulos, Mike-Frank G., and Victor Roudometof. "Youth Culture and Lifestyle in Modern Greece." In *American Culture in Europe: Interdisciplinary Perspectives*, ed.

Mike-Frank G. Epitropoulos and Victor Roudometof, pp. 119–44. Westport, CT, 1998.

Eyerman, Ron, and Andrew Jamison. *Music and Social Movements: Mobilizing Traditions in the Twentieth Century.* Cambridge, 1998.

Faulenbach, Bernd. "Die Siebzigerjahre—ein sozialdemokratisches Jahrzehnt?" *Archiv für Sozialgeschichte* 44 (2004): pp. 1–37.

Feenberg, Andrew, and Jim Freedman. *When Poetry Ruled the Streets: The French May Events of 1968.* Albany, NY, 2001.

Ferguson, Niall, S. Charles Maier, Erez Manela, and J. Daniel Sargent, eds. *The Shock of the Global: The 1970s in Perspective.* Cambridge, MA, 2010.

Ferrante, Stefano. *La Cina non era vicina.* Milan, 2008.

Fink, Caroline, Philipp Gassert, and Detlef Junker, eds. *1968: The World Transformed.* Washington, DC, 1998.

Fishman, Robert M. "Rethinking State and Regime: Southern Europe's Transition to Democracy." *World Politics* 42, no. 3 (1990): pp. 426–34.

Foucault, Michel. *Istoria tis Sexoualikotitas* [History of sexuality]. Vol. 1. Athens, 1978.

Fowler, David. *The First Teenagers: The Lifestyle of Young Wage-Earners in Interwar Britain.* London, 1995.

Fraser, Ronald, Daniel Bertaux, Bret Eynon, Ronald Grele, Béatrix le Wita, Danièle Linhart, Luisa Passerini, Jochen Staadt, and Annemarie Troeger. *1968: A Student Generation in Revolt.* London, 1988.

Friedl, Ernestine. *Vassilika: A Village in Modern Greece.* New York, 1962.

———. *Women and Men: An Anthropologist's View.* New York, 1975.

Furlough, Ellen. "Making Mass Vacations: Tourism and Consumer Culture in France, 1930s to 1970s." *Comparative Studies in Society and History* 40, no. 2 (1998): pp. 247–86.

Gallant, Thomas W. "Honor, Masculinity, and Ritual Knife Fighting in Nineteenth-Century Greece," *The American Historical Review* 105, no. 2 (2000), pp. 359–82.

———. *Modern Greece.* London, 2001.

Gann, Lewis H., and Peter Duignan. *The Rebirth of the West: The Americanization of the Democratic World, 1945–1958.* Cambridge, MA, 1992.

Garthoff, Raymond L. "The Failure of the Détente of the 1970s." In *The Cold War: The Essential Readings,* ed. Klaus Larres and Ann Lane, pp. 159–80. Oxford, 2001.

Gasparinatos, Konstantinos, Ioannis Ioannidis, and Konstantinos Tsakiris. *I katastasi tou systimatos dianomis stin Ellada* [The condition of film circulation in Greece]. Athens, 2000.

Gavriilidis, Akis. *I atherapeyti nekrofilia tou rizospastikou patriotismou* [The unremedied necrophilia of radical patriotism]. Athens, 2006.

Gay, Peter. *The Bourgeois Experience. Vol. 1: Education of the Senses.* Oxford, 1984.

Geertz, Clifford. *The Interpretation of Cultures: Selected Essays.* New York, 1973.

Giddens, Anthony. *Modernity and Self-Identity: Self and Society in the Late Modern Age.* Cambridge, 1991.

Gies, David T., ed. *The Cambridge Companion to Modern Spanish Culture.* Cambridge, 1999.

Gilcher-Holtey, Ingrid. *Die 68er Bewegung: Deutschland-Westeuropa-USA.* Munich, 2001.

———. "May 1968 in France: The Rise and Fall of a New Social Movement." In Fink, Gassert, and Junker, *1968: The World Transformed*, pp. 253–76.

Gkefou-Madianou, Dimitra. "Ennoiologiseis tou Eaytou kai toy 'Allou': Zitimata taytotitas sti synchroni anthropologiki theoria" [Defining the Self and the 'Other': Identity issues in contemporary anthropological theory]. In *Eaytos kai "Allos": Ennoiologiseis, Taytotites kai Praktiki stin Ellada kai tin Kypro* [Self and "Other": Definitions, identities and practice in Greece and Cyprus], ed. Dimitra Gkefou-Madianou, pp. 15–110. Athens, 2003.

Gómez Gutiérrez, Juan José. "The Influence of Socialist Realism in Italy during the Immediate Postwar Period." In *Transnational Moments of Change: Europe 1945, 1968, 1989*, ed. Gerd-Rainer Horn and Padraic Kenney, pp. 65–77. Oxford, 2004.

Gorsuch, Anne E. *All This is Your World: Soviet Tourism at Home and Abroad after Stalin.* Oxford, 2011.

Gouard, David. "La 'Banlieue Rouge' face au renouvellement des générations Une sociologie politique des cites Maurice Thorez et Youri Gagarine à Ivry-sur-Seine." PhD diss., University of Montpellier 1, 2011.

Graham, Helen, and Alejandro Quiroga. "After the Fear was Over? What Came after Dictatorships in Spain, Greece and Portugal." In *The Oxford Handbook of Postwar European History*, ed. Dan Stone, pp. 502–25. Oxford, 2012.

Graham, Helen, and Jo Labanyi, eds., *Spanish Cultural Studies: An Introduction: The Struggle for Modernity.* Oxford, 1995.

Gundle, Stephen. *Between Hollywood and Moscow: The Italian Communists and the Challenge of Mass Culture, 1943–1991.* Durham, NC, 2000.

Gunther, Scott E. *The Elastic Closet: A History of Homosexuality in France, 1942–present.* London, 2009.

Hadjikyriacou, Achilleas. *Masculinity and Gender in Greek Cinema: 1949-1967.* New York, 2014.

Hall, Stuart. "Introduction: Who Needs Identity?" In *Questions of Cultural Identity*, ed. Stuart Hall and Paul du Gay, pp. 1–17. London, 1996.

———. "The Meaning of New Times." In *New Times: The Changing Face of Politics in the 1990s*, ed. Stuart Hall and Martin Jacques, pp. 116–34. London, 1989.

Hantzaroula, Pothiti. "I kataskeyi tis ypotagis: Oikiakes ypiretries stin Ellada, 1920–1945" [The construction of submission: The domestic servants in Greece, 1920–1945]. PhD diss., European University Institute, Florence, 2001.

Hatcher, Evelyn Payne. *Art as Culture: An Introduction to the Anthropology of Art.* Westport, CT, 1999.

Hebdige, Dick. *Subculture: The Meaning of Style.* Abingdon, NY, 2007, first published in 1979.

Heilbronner, Oded. "From a Culture *for* Youth to a Culture *of* Youth: Recent Trends in the Historiography of Western Youth Cultures." *Contemporary European History* 17, no.4 (2008): pp. 575–91.

Hellbeck, Jochen. "Working, Struggling, Becoming: Stalin-era autobiographical texts." *Russian Review* 60, no. 3 (2001): pp. 340–59.

Hellman, Stephen. *Italian Communism in Transition: The Rise and Fall of the Historic Compromise in Turin, 1975–1980.* Oxford, 1988.

Heraclides, Alexis. *Kypriako: Sygkrousi kai Epilysi* [The Cyprus question: Conflict and resolution]. Athens, 2002.

Herzfeld, Michael. "Semantic Slippage and Moral Fall: The Rhetoric of Chastity in Rural Greek Society." *Journal of Modern Greek Studies* 1, no. 1 (1983): pp. 161–72.

Herzog, Dagmar. "Between Coitus and Commodification: Young West German Women and the Impact of the Pill." In Schildt and Siegfried, *Between Marx and Coca Cola*, pp. 261–86.

———. *Sexuality in Europe: A Twentieth-Century History.* Cambridge, 2011.

Hess, Franklin. "Singular Visions, Multiple Futures: Culture, Politics, and American Mass Media in Modern Greece." PhD diss., University of Iowa, 1999.

Hilwig, Stuart. "Are You Calling Me a Fascist? A Contribution to the Oral History of the Italian Student Rebellion in 1968." *Journal of Contemporary History* 36, no. 4 (October 2001): pp. 581–97.

Hirschon, Renée. *Heirs of the Greek Catastrophe: The Social Life of Asia Minor Refugees in Piraeus.* New York, 1998.

Hobsbawm, Eric, and Terence Ranger, eds. *The Invention of Tradition.* Cambridge, 1992.

Horn, Gerd-Rainer. *The Spirit of '68: Rebellion in Western Europe and North America, 1956–1976.* Oxford, 2007.

Houlbrook, Matt. *Queer London: Perils and Pleasures in the Sexual Metropolis, 1918–1957.* Chicago, 2005.

Hunt, Lynn. "Introduction: History, Culture, and Text." In *The New Cultural History*, ed. Lynn Hunt, pp. 1–22. Berkeley, CA, 1989.

Iatrides, John O. *Greece in the 1940s: A Nation in Crisis.* Hannover, NH, 1981.

Ilardi, Massimo, and Aris Accornero. *Il Partito Comunista Italiano, Struttura e storia del' organizzazione 1921/1979.* Milan, 1982.

Ioannidou, Alexandra. "Political Aspects of Russian Literature Reception in Greece: Aris Alexandrou and Mitsos Alexandropoulos." *Slavica Gandensia* 32 (2005): pp. 89–104.

Ioannou, Christos. *Misthoti Apascholisi kai syndikalismos stin Ellada* [Paid employment and trade unions in Greece]. Athens, 1989.

Jacquemart, Alban. "Les hommes dans les mouvements féministes français". PhD diss., École des Hautes Études en Sciences Sociales, Paris, 2011.

Jameson, Fredric. *Postmodernism, or, the Cultural Logic of Late Capitalism.* Durham, NC, 1991.

Jarausch, Konrad. *After Hitler: Recivilizing Germans, 1945–1995.* Oxford, 2008.

Jarausch, Konrad, and Hannes Siegrist, eds. *Amerikanisierung und Sowjetisierung in Deutschland 1945–1970.* Frankfurt, 1997.

Jenson, Jane. "The French Communist Party and Feminism." *Socialist Register* 17 (1980): pp. 121–47.

Jobs, Richard I. *Riding the New Wave: Youth and the Rejuvenation of France after the Second World War.* Stanford, CA, 2007.

Johnson, Alan. "'Beyond the Smallness of Self': Oral History and British Trotskyism." *Oral History*, 24, no. 1 (1996): pp. 39–48.

Jørgensen, Thomas E. *Transformations and Crises: The Left and the Nation in Denmark and Sweden 1956–1980.* New York, 2008.

Judt, Tony. *Postwar: A History of Europe since 1945.* London, 2007.

Kallivretakis, Leonidas F. "Provlimata istorikopoiisis tou Rock fainomenou: Empeiries kai stochasmoi" [Problems of historicizing the Rock phenomenon: Experiences and thoughts]. *Ta Istorika* 20 (1994): pp. 157–74.

Kalotychos, Vangelis. "The Beekeeper, the Icon Painter, Family, and Friends: 'November 17' and the End of Greek History." In *Anti-Americanism,* ed. Andrew Ross and Kristin Ross, pp. 179–94. New York, 2004.

Kalyvas, Stathis N. "Emfylios Polemos (1943–1949): To telos ton mython kai I strofi pros to maziko epipedo" [Civil War (1943–1949): The end of the myths and the shift to the masses]. *Epistimi kai Koinonia* (2003): pp. 37–70.

Karakatsanis, Leonidas. *Turkish-Greek Relations. Rapprochement, civil society and the politics of friendship.* Abingdon, 2014.

Kantsa, Venetia. "I *Lavrys*: Mia Synoptiki Parousiasi enos Ellinikou Lesviakou Periodikou," [Lavrys: a brief presentation of a Greek lesbian magazine], *Dini* 8 (1995–96): pp. 73–95.

Karali, Aimilia. *Mia imitelis Anoixi … : ideologia, politiki kai logotechnia sto periodiko Epitheorisi Technis* [An unfinished Spring: … ideology, politics and literature in the magazine Epitheorisi Technis]. Athens, 2005.

Karamanolakis, Vangelis. "Anamesa sto idiotiko kai to dimosio: to vioma tou Emfyliou" [Between the private and the public: the experience of the Civil War]. *Avgi*, 20 September 2009.

Karamanolakis, Vangelis, Evi Olympitou, and Ioanna Papathanasiou, eds. *I elliniki neolaia ston 20o aiona: Politikes diadromes, koinonikes praktikes kai politistikes ekfraseis* [Greek youth in the twentieth century: Political pathways, social practices, cultural expressions]. Athens, 2010.

Karapostolis, Vassilis. *Katanalotiki Symperifora sti Neoelliniki Koinonia, 1960–1975* [Consumer behavior in modern Greek society, 1960–1975]. Athens, 1983.

Kassimeris, George. *Europe's Last Terrorists: The Revolutionary Organization 17 November.* New York, 2001.

———. "Junta by Another Name? The 1974 *Metapolitefsi* and the Greek Extra-parliamentary Left." *Journal of Contemporary History* 40, no. 4 (2005): pp. 745–62.

Katsapis, Kostas. *Ichoi kai apoichoi: Koinoniki istoria tou rock 'n' roll phenomenou stin Ellada, 1956–1967* [Sounds and overtones: Social history of the rock 'n' roll phenomenon in Greece, 1956-1967]. Athens, 2007.

———. *To "provlima neolaia". Monternoi Neoi, paradosi kai amfisvitisi sti Metapolemiki Ellada, 1964-1974* ["Youth as a problem." Modern youngsters, tradition and challenging in postwar Greece]. Athens, 2013.

Kazakos, Panos. *Anamesa se Kratos kai Agora: Oikonomia kai oikonomiki politiki sti metapolemiki Ellada, 1944–2000* [Between the state and the market: Finance and financial policies in post–World War II Greece, 1944–2000]. Athens, 2001.

Kelperis, Christos, Aliki Mouriki, Yiannis Myrizakis, Thodoros Paradellis, Olympia Gardiki, and Afroditi Teperoglou. "Neoi: Diathesi Chronou, Diaprosopikes Scheseis" [Youth: Time economy, interpersonal relations]. *Epitheorisi Koinonikon Erevnon* 57 (1985): pp. 83–144.

Kertzer, David I. *Politics and Symbols: The Italian Communist Party and the Fall of Communism.* New Haven, CT, 1996.

Kitromilidis, Paschalis M. *Neoellinikos Diafotismos* [Modern Greek Enlightenment]. Athens, 1996.

Klimke, Martin. *The Other Alliance: Student Protest in West Germany and the United States in the Global Sixties*. Princeton, NJ, 2011.

Koenen, Gerd. *Das rote Jahrzenht: Unsere kleine deutsche Kulturrevolution 1967–1977*. Frankfurt, 2002.

Kokkali, Angeliki. "Ellinikos Kinimatografos kai Antidiktatoriko Foititiko Kinima" [Greek cinema and the antidictatorial student movement]. *Epitheorisi Koinonikon Erevnon* 92–93 (1997): pp. 127–50.

Koliopoulos, John, and Thanos Veremis. *Greece: The Modern Sequel: From 1831 to the Present*. London, 2002.

Komninou, Maria. *Apo tin Agora sto Theama: Meleti gia ti sygkrotisi tis dimosias sfairas kai tou kinimatografou sti Synchroni Ellada, 1950–2000* [From the Forum to the Spectacle: Research on the construction of public sphere in contemporary Greece, 1950–2000]. Athens, 2001.

Konstantopoulou. Olympia. "Party sti Vouliagmeni" [Party in Vouliagmeni]. In Vamvakas and Panagiotopoulos, *I Ellada sti dekaetia tou '80* [Greece in the 1980s], pp. 443–45.

Kornetis, Kostis. *Children of the Dictatorship. Student Resistance, Cultural Politics, and the "long 1960s" in Greece*. New York, 2013.

———"Student Resistance to the Greek Military Dictatorship: Subjectivity, Memory, and Cultural Politics, 1967–1974." PhD diss., European University Institute, Florence, 2006.

Kosmidou, Eleftheria Rania. *European Civil War Films. Memory, Conflict and Nostalgia*. New York, 2013.

Kotanidis, Giorgos. *Oloi Mazi, Tora!* [All together, now!]. Athens, 2011.

Kriegel, Annie. *Eurocommunism: A New Kind of Communism?* Stanford, CA, 1978.

Kroes, Rob. "American Mass Culture and European Youth Culture." In Schildt and Siegfried, *Between Marx and Coca-Cola*, pp. 82–105.

Kühn, Andreas. *Stalins Enkel, Maos Söhne: Die Lebenswelt der K-Gruppen in der Bundesrepublik der 70er Jahre*. Frankfurt, 2005.

Labanyi, Jo, ed. *Constructing Identity in Contemporary Spain: Theoretical Debates and Cultural Practice*. Oxford, 2002.

Lagos, Evangelos. "Politistika Kentra" [Cultural Centers]. In Vamvakas and Panagiotopoulos, *I Ellada sti dekaetia tou '80* [Greece in the 1980s], pp. 477–78.

Lambropoulou, Dimitra. *Oikodomoi. Oi anthropoi pou echtisan tin Athina: 1950-1967* [Construction Workers. The People Who Built Athens: 1950-1967]. Athens, 2009.

Lawrence, Jon. "Political History." In *Writing History: Theory and Practice*, ed. S. Berger, H. Feldner, and K. Passmore, pp. 183–202. London, 2003.

Leggewie, Claus. "A Laboratory of Postindustrial Society: Reassessing the 1960s in Germany." In Fink, Gassert, and Junker, *1968: The World Transformed*, pp. 277–94.

Lekkas, Pantelis. "O ypertaxikos charaktiras tou ethnikistikou logou" [The supra-class character of the nationalist discourse]. *Mnimon* 16 (1994): pp. 95–106.

———. *To paichnidi me ton chrono: Ethnikismos kai neoterikotita* [The game with time: Nationalism and modernity]. Athens, 2001.

Leventakos, Diamantis. *Opseis tou Neou Ellinikou* Kinimatografou [Facets of the New Greek Cinema]. Athens, 2002.

Liakos, Antonis. "I Neoelliniki Istoriografia to teleytaio tetarto tou 20ou aiona" [The modern Greek historiography in the last quarter of the twentieth century]. *Synchrona Themata* 76–77 (January–July 2001): pp. 72–91.

Lidtke, Vernon. *The Alternative Culture: Socialist Labor in Imperial Germany.* New York, 1985.

Livieratos, Kostas, ed. *I oneiriki yfi tis pragmatikotitas* [The dream side of reality]. Athens, 2005.

Loizos, Peter. *Iron in the Soul: Displacement, Livelihood and Health in Cyprus.* New York, 2008.

Loizos, Peter, and Evthymios Papataxiarchis, eds. *Contested Identities: Gender and Kinship in Modern Greece.* Princeton, NJ, 1991.

———. "Gender, Sexuality, and the Person in Greek Culture." In Loizos and Papataxiarchis, *Contested Identities*, pp. 221–34.

Long, Nicholas J., and Henrietta L. Moore. *Sociality: New Directions.* New York, 2012.

Lumley, Robert. *States of Emergency: Cultures of Revolt in Italy from 1968 to 1978.* London, 1990.

Lutz, Catherine. "Emotion, Thought, and Estrangement: Emotion as a Cultural Category." *Cultural Anthropology* 1 no. 3 (August 1986): pp. 287–309.

———. *Unnatural Emotions: Everyday Sentiments on a Micronesian Atoll and Their Challenge to Western Theory.* Chicago, 1988.

Lyotard, Jean-François. *The Postmodern Condition: A Report on Knowledge.* Manchester, 1984.

Lyrintzis, Christos, Ilias Nikolakopoulos, and Dimitris Sotiropoulos. "Eisagogi: I poiotita kai I leitourgia tis Tritis Ellinikis Dimokratias" [Introduction: The quality and the functioning of the Third Hellenic Republic]. In *Koinonia kai Politiki: Opseis tis G Ellinikis Dimokratias, 1974–1994* [Society and politics: Facets of the Third Hellenic Republic, 1974–1994], ed. Christos Lyrintzis, Ilias Nikolakopoulos, and Dimitris Sotiropoulos, pp. 19–42. Athens, 1996.

Maase, Kaspar. *BRAVO Amerika. Erkundungen zur Jugendkultur der Bundesrepublik in den fünfzigen Jahren.* Hamburg, 1992.

———. "Establishing Cultural Democracy: Youth, 'Americanization' and the Irresistible Rise of Popular Culture." In *The Miracle Years: A Cultural History of West Germany, 1949–68,* ed. Hanna Schissler, pp. 428–50. Princeton, NJ, 2001.

Mackay, Hugh, ed. *Consumption and Everyday Life.* Milton Keynes, UK, 1997.

Mackridge, Peter. "Eisagogi, Neoteri Epochi" [Introduction, modern times]. In *Istoria tis Ellinikis Glossas* [History of the Greek language], ed. Michalis Z. Kopidakis, pp. 234–43. Athens, 1999.

———. *Language and National Identity in Greece, 1766–1976.* Oxford, 2009.

Mais, Christos. "The Marxist-Leninist Publishing Field During the 60s–70s in Greece." MA diss., Leiden University, 2009.

Maleck-Lewy, Eva, and Bernhard Maleck. "The Women's Movement in East and West Germany." In Fink, Gassert, and Junker, *1968: The World Transformed,* pp. 373–96.

Maloutas, Thomas. "Koinonikos diachorismos stin Athina" [Social distinction in Athens]. In *Koinoniki Domi kai poleodomiki organosi stin Athina* [Social structure and town planning in Athens], ed. Thomas Maloutas and Dimitris Oikonomou, pp. 67–140. Athens, 1992.

Mannheim, Karl. *Essays on the Sociology of Knowledge.* New York, 1952.

Maragkopoulos, Aris. "Paidia tou Marx kai tis Coca-Cola" [Children of Marx and Coca Cola]. *O Politis* 99 (April 2002): pp. 21–24.

Marantzidis, Nikos. *Dimokratikos Stratos Elladas, 1946–1949.* Athens, 2010.

Marwick, Arthur. *The Sixties: Cultural Revolution in Britain, France, Italy, and the United States, c.1958–c.1974.* Oxford, 1998.

Mavromoustakos, Platon. *Schediasmata Anagnosis* [Sketches of reading]. Athens, 2006.

———. *To theatro stin Ellada 1940–2000: Mia episkopisi* [Theatre in Greece 1940–2000: A concise presentation]. Athens, 2005.

Mazower, Mark, ed. *After the War Was Over: Reconstructing the Family, Nation, and State in Greece, 1943–1960.* Princeton, NJ, 2000.

———. "Changing Trends in the Historiography of Postwar Europe, East and West." *International Labor and Working-Class History* 58 (2000): pp. 275–82.

———. *Inside Hitler's Greece: The Experience of Occupation, 1941–1944.* New Haven, CT, 1993.

McGrogan, Manus. "*Tout!* in Context 1968–1973: French Radical Press at the Crossroads of Far Left, New Movements and Counterculture." PhD diss., University of Portsmouth, 2010.

McLellan, Josie. *Love in the Time of Communism: Intimacy and Sexuality in the GDR.* Cambridge, 2011.

McRobbie, Angela. *In the Culture Society: Art, Fashion and Popular Music.* London, 1999.

Mergel, Thomas. "Überlegungen zu einer Kulturgeschichte der Politik", *Geschichte und Gesellschaft* 28 (2002): pp. 574–606.

Miller, Daniel. "Consumption and Its Consequences." In *Consumption and Everyday Life,* ed. Hugh Mackay, pp. 13–50. London, 1997.

Mitchell, Juliet. *Woman's Estate.* Harmondsworth, 1971.

Mitrofanis, Giorgos. "Politikoi kratoumenoi: Metemfyliako kratos, diktatoria" [Political prisoners: Post–Civil War state, dictatorship]. In *Istoria tou Neou Ellinismou, 1770–2000* [History of modern Hellenism, 1770–2000], vol. 9, ed. Vassilis Panagiotopoulos, p. 131. Athens, 2003.

Mouzelis, Nicos. *Modern Greece: Facets of Underdevelopment.* London, 1978.

Murphy, Kevin P., and Jennifer M. Spear, eds. *Historicizing Gender and Sexuality.* Oxford 2011.

Nairn, Tom. *Faces of Nationalism: Janus Revisited.* London, 1997.

Nicolet, Claude. *United States Policy Towards Cyprus, 1954–1974: Removing the Greek-Turkish Bone of Contention.* Mannheim 2001.

Nikolakakis, Michalis. "Tourismos kai elliniki koinonia tin periodo 1945–1974" [Tourism and the Greek Society during the period 1945-1974], PhD diss., University of Crete, 2013.

Nikolakopoulos, Ilias. *I kachektiki dimokratia: kommata kai ekloges, 1946–67* [The weak democracy: Parties and elections, 1946–67]. Athens, 2001.

Nolan, Mary. "Anti-Americanism and Americanization in Germany." *Politics and Society* 33, no. 1 (March 2005): pp. 88–122.

———. *Visions of Modernity: American Business and the Modernisation of Germany.* Oxford, 1994.

O'Malley, Brendan, and Ian Craig. *The Cyprus Conspiracy: America, Espionage and the Turkish Invasion.* London, 1999.

Ozouf, Mona. *Festivals and the French Revolution.* London, 1988.

Panagiotopoulos, Panayis. "Oi egkleistoi kommounistes kai to rebetiko tragoudi: mia askisi eleytherias" [The imprisoned communists and the rebetiko: an exercise of freedom]. In *Rebetes kai rebetiko tragoudi* [*Rebetiko* musicians and songs], ed. Nikos Kotaridis, pp. 259–301. Athens, 2007.

Panourgia, Neni. *Dangerous Citizens: The Greek Left and the Terror of the State.* New York, 2009.

Pantazis, Pavlos, and Panayis Panagiotopoulos. "Neolaia kai stratiotiki thiteia 1980–1987: Ypokeimenikotita kai ekdimokratismos ton thesmon stin koinonia tis epithymias" [Youth and military service 1980–1987: Subjectivity and the democratization of the institutions in the welfare society]. In Karamanolakis, Olympitou, and Papathanasiou, *I elliniki neolaia* [Greek youth], pp. 369–75.

Pantazopoulos, Andreas. *"Gia to Lao kai to Ethnos": I stigmi Andrea Papandreou, 1965–1989* [For the people and the nation: The moment of Andreas Papandreou, 1965–1989]. Athens, 2001.

Papadimitriou, Despoina. *Apo ton lao ton nomimofronon sto ethnos ton ethnikofronon: I syntiritiki skepsi stin Ellada 1922–1967* [From the people of the *nomimofrones* to the nation of the *ethnikofrones*: The Conservative thought in Greece 1922–1967]. Athens, 2006.

Papadimitriou, Lydia. *The Greek Film Musical: A Critical and Cultural History.* Jefferson, NC, 2006.

Papadogiannis, Nikolaos, "A (Trans)National Emotional Community? Greek Political Songs and the Politicisation of Greek migrants in West Germany in the 1960s and 1970s." *Contemporary European History* 23, no. 4 (2014): pp. 589–614.

———"Between Angelopoulos and *The Battleship Potemkin*: Cinema and the Making of Young Communists in Greece in the Initial Post-Dictatorship Period (1974–1981)." *European History Quarterly* 42, no. 2 (2012): pp. 286–308.

———. "Communist Youth Identities and Rock Music in Greece in the late 1970s." In *Between the Avant Garde and the Everyday: Subversive Politics in Europe from 1957 to the Present*, ed. Timothy Brown and Lorena Anton, pp. 77–91. New York, 2011.

———. "Confronting 'Imperialism' and 'Loneliness': Sexual and Gender Relations Among Young Communists in Greece, 1974–1981." *Journal of Modern Greek Studies* 29, no. 2 (2011): pp. 219–50.

———. "Festival Neolaias" [Youth Festivals]. In Vamvakas and Panagiotopoulos, *I Ellada sti dekaetia tou '80* [Greece in the 1980s], pp. 626–29.

———. "From Coherence to Fragments: '1968' and the Making of Youth Politicisation in Greece in the 1970s." *Historein, A Review of the Past and Other Stories* 9 (2009): pp. 76–92.

———. "Red and Purple? Feminism and young Greek Eurocommunists in the 1970s." *European Review of History—Revue européenne d'histoire* 22, no.1 (2015): pp. 16–40.

————. "The 'Women's Question' and Young Greek Eurocommunists: Shifting Feminine Representations in 1974–78." MA diss., Birkbeck, University of London, 2006.

Papanikolaou, Dimitris. "Schimatizontas ti neolaia: O Theodorakis, o Savvopoulos kai 'tou '60 oi ekdromeis" [Shaping the youth: Theodorakis, Savvopoulos and the 'travelers of the 1960s], unpublished article.

————. *Singing Poets: Popular Music and Literature in France and Greece.* Oxford, 2007.

Papataxiarchis, Evthymios. "O kosmos tou kafeneiou: Tavtotita kai antallagi ston andriko symposiasmo" [The world of the old-style *cafés*: Identity and exchange in the gatherings of men]. In *Tavtotites kai Fylo sti Synchroni Ellada* [Identity and gender in contemporary Greece], ed. Evthymios Papataxiarchis and Theodoros Paradellis, pp. 209–50. Athens, 1992.

Papathanasiou, Ioanna. "Vioma, Istoria kai Politiki: I ypostasi tis prosopikis martyrias: Skepseis me aformi dyo vivlia tou Taki Bena" [Experience, history and politics: The personal testimony: Reflections based on two books published by Takis Benas]. *Ta Istorika* 24–25 (1996): pp. 253–66.

Papathanasiou, Ioanna, Polina Iordanidou, Anta Kapola, Tasos Sakellaropoulos, and Angeliki Christodoulou. *I Neolaia Lambraki ti dekaetia tou '60: Archeiakes tekmirioseis kai avtoviografikes katatheseis* [The Lambrakis Youth in the 1960s: Archival material and autobiographical testimonies]. Athens, 2008.

Paradeisi, Maria. "I chrisi tou parelthontos ston politico logo: ta gegonota tis dekaetias tou 1940 ston politico logo ton kommaton tou Kentrou (1950–1964)" [The use of the past in political discourse: the events of the 1940s in the discourse of the Center parties (1950–1964)]. In *Mnimes kai Lithi tou ellinikou Emfyliou* [Memories and oblivion of the Greek Civil War], ed. Riki van Boeschoten, Tasoula Vervenioti, Eytychia Voutyra, Vassilis Dalkavoukis, Konstantina Mpada, pp. 271–92. Athens, 2008.

————. "I politiki os simptoma stis komodies tou ellinikou theatrou kai kinimatografou" [Politics as a symptom in the comedies in Greek theatre and cinema]. *To Vima ton Koinonikon Epistimon* 5, no. 17 (1995): pp. 163–74.

Passerini, Luisa, ed. *Across the Atlantic: Cultural Exchanges Between Europe and the United States.* Brussels, 2000.

————. *Autobiography of a Generation: Italy, 1968.* Hanover, NH, 1996.

————. *Fascism in Popular Memory: The Cultural Experience of the Turin Working Class.* Cambridge, 1986.

————. "Youth as a Metaphor for Social Change: Fascist Italy and America in the 1950s." In *A History of Young People in the West,* vol. 2, ed. Giovanni Levi and Jean-Claude Schmitt, pp. 281–340. Cambridge, MA, 1997.

Paulus, Julia, Eva-Maria Silies, and Kerstin Wolff, eds. *Zeitgeschichte als Geschlechtergeschichte. Neue Perspektiven auf die Bundesrepublik.* Frankfurt, 2012.

Pavis, Patrice. *Dictionary of the Theatre: Terms, Concepts, and Analysis.* Toronto, 1998.

Pavone, Claudio. "The General Problem of the Continuity of the State and the Legacy of Fascism." In *After the War: Violence, Justice, Continuity and Renewal in Italian Society,* ed. Jonathan Dunnage, pp. 5–21. Hull, 1999.

Pechlivanos, Miltos. *Apo ti Leschi stis Akyvernites Politeies: I stixi tis anagnosis* [From Leschi to Akyvernites Politeies: The punctuation of reading]. Athens, 2008.

Pells, Richard. "Double Crossings: The Reciprocal Relationship between American and European Culture in the Twentieth Century." In *Americanization and Anti-Americanism: The German Encounter with American Culture after 1945*, ed. Alexander Stephan, pp. 189–201. New York, 2005.

Peristiany, John G., ed. *Honour and Shame: The Values of Mediterranean Society.* London, 1965.

Perks, Robert, and Alistair Thomson, eds. *The Oral History Reader.* London, 2006.

Piccone Stella, Simonetta. "'Rebels Without a Cause': Male Youth in Italy around 1960." *History Workshop Journal* 38, no. 1 (1994): pp. 157–78.

Poiger, Uta. *Jazz, Rock, and Rebels: Cold War and American Culture in a Divided Germany.* Berkeley, CA, 2000.

Portelli, Alessandro. *The Battle of Valle Giulia: Oral History and the Art of Dialogue.* Madison, WI, 1997.

———. "The Massacre of Fosse Ardeatine: History, Myth, Ritual and Symbol." In *Contested Pasts*, ed. Katharine Hodgkin and Susannah Radstone, pp. 29–41. London, 2003.

Poulantzas, Nikos. *Fasismos kai Dimokratia* [Fascism and Dictatorship]. Athens, 1975.

———. *La Crise des Dictatures: Portugal, Grèce, Espagne* [The crisis of the dictatorships: Portugal, Greece, Spain]. Paris, 1975.

———. *State, Power, Socialism.* Verso Classics edition. London, 2000.

Poulos, Margaret. *Arms and the Woman: Just Warriors and Greek Feminist Identity.* New York, 2007.

Pudal, Bernard, Michel Dreyfus, Bruno Groppo, S. Claudio Ingerflom, Roland Lew, Claude Pennetier, and Serge Wolikow. Introduction to *Le Siècle des Communismes*, ed. Bernard Pudal, Michel Dreyfus, Bruno Groppo, Claudio S. Ingerflom, Roland Lew, Claude Pennetier, and Serge Wolikow, pp. 9–19. Paris, 2000.

Pudal, Bernard, and Claude Pennetier. *Autobiographies, Autocritiques, Aveux Dans Le Monde Communiste.* Paris, 2002.

Radway, Janice A. *Reading the Romance: Women, Patriarchy and Popular Literature.* London, 1987.

Radcliff, Pamela. "Associations and the Social Origins of the Transition during the Late Franco Regime." In *Spain Transformed. The Late Franco Dictatorship, 1959-75*, ed. Nigel Townson. Houndmills, Basingstoke and New York, 2010, pp. 140–62.

Raftopoulos, Dimitris. *Anatheorisi Technis: I Epitheorisi Technis kai oi anthropoi tis* [Revising art: *Epitheorisi Technis* and its people]. Athens, 2006.

Reimann, Aribert. "Zwischen Machismo und Coolness: Männlichkeit und Emotion in der westdeutschen 'Kulturrevolution' der 1960er- und 1970er- Jahre." In *Die Präsenz der Gefühle: Männlichkeit und Emotion in der Moderne*, ed. Manuel Borutta and Nina Verheyen, pp. 229–52. Bielefeld, Ger., 2010.

Reddy, M. William. *The Navigation of Feeling: A Framework for the History of Emotions.* Cambridge, 2001.

Repoussi, Maria. "To 'deytero fylo' stin Aristera: Ntokoumenta kai mnimes apo ti Feministiki paremvasi stin organosi tou Riga Feraiou, 1974–1978" [The "second sex" in the Left: Documents and memories of the Feminist activity in Rigas Feraios, 1974–1978]. *Elliniki Epitheorisi Politikis Epistimis* 8 (1996): pp. 121–53.

Righart, Hans. "Moderate Versions of the 'Global Sixties': A Comparison of Great Britain and the Netherlands." *Journal of Area Studies* 13 (1998): pp. 82–96.

Rizas, Sotiris. *Enosi Dichotomisi Anexartisia: Oi Inomenes Politeies kai I Vretania stin ana-zitisi lysis gia to Kypriako, 1963–1967* [Union Partition Independence: The United States and Britain seeking a solution for the Cyprus Question, 1963–1967]. Athens, 2000.

———. *Oi Inomenes Politeies, I diktatoria ton syntagmatarchon kai to Kypriako zitima, 1967–1974* [The United States, the dictatorship of the colonels, and the Cyprus Question]. Athens, 2002.

Robertson, Roland. "Glocalization: Time-Space and Homogeneity-Heterogeneity." In *Global Modernities,* ed. Mike Featherstone, Scott Lash, and Roland Robertson, pp. 25–44. London, 1995.

Rojek, Chris, ed. *Leisure for Leisure: Critical Essays.* New York, 1989.

Rosenthal, Gabriele. *Erlebte und erzählte Lebensgeschichte.* Frankfurt, 1995.

Ross, Kristin. *May '68 and its Afterlives.* London, 2002.

Rowbotham, Sheila. *Woman's Consciousness: Man's World.* London, 1973.

Rubin, Gayle S. "Thinking Sex: Notes for a Radical Theory of the Politics of Sexuality." In *The Gay and Lesbian Studies Reader,* ed. Henry Abelove, Michéle Aina Barale, and David M. Halperin, pp. 3–44. New York, 1993.

Saint-Marten, Katerina. *Lamprakides: Istoria mias genias* [Lamprakides: The history of a generation]. Athens, 1983.

Samiou, Dimitra. *Gynaika, Fylo kai Politiki (18os–20os aionas): Istoriografikes proseggiseis: mia eisagogi* [Women, gender, and politics (18th–20th century): Historiographical and political bibliographical approaches: An introduction]. Mytilini, 2006.

Samuel, Raphael. "The Lost World of British Communism." *New Left Review* I, no. 154 (1985): pp. 3–53.

Sarris, Kostas. "Politistikes Drastiriotites ton foititon tis FLS kai IXGF, 1974–1999" [Cultural activities of the students of the School of Philosophy and of the Institutes of Foreign Languages, 1974–1999]. In *Filosofiki Scholi Panepistimiou Thessalonikis: Ta prota 75 chronia* [School of Philosophy at the University of Salonica: The first 75 years], pp. 220–29. Salonica, 2000.

Sassoon, Donald. *One Hundred Years of Socialism: The West European Left in the Twentieth Century.* London, 1997.

Saville, John. "Interviews in Labour History." *Oral History* 1, no. 4 (1972): pp. 93–106.

Schildt, Axel, and Detlef Siegfried. *Between Marx and Coca-Cola: Youth Cultures in Changing European Societies, 1960–1980.* New York, 2007.

———. "Introduction: Youth, Consumption, and Politics in the Age of Radical Change." In Schildt and Siegfried, *Between Marx and Coca-Cola,* pp. 1–35.

Schmidlechner, Karin M. "Austrian Youth in the 1950s." In *Power and the People: A Social History of Central European Politics, 1945–56,* ed. Eleonore Breuning, Jill Lewis, and Gareth Pritchard, pp. 182–99. Manchester, 2005.

Serdedakis, Nikos. "'I diadromi tou foititikou kinimatos sti metemfyliaki Ellada" [The trajectory of the student movement in post-Civil War in Greece].' In *I elliniki neolaia* [Greek Youth], ed. Vangelis Karamanolakis, Evi Olympitou, and Ioanna Papathana-siou, pp. 160–82.

Sevastakis, Nicolas. *Koinotopi Chora: Opseis tou Dimosiou Chorou kai Antinomies Axion sti simerini Ellada* [Trivial country: Aspects of the public space and value ambiguities in contemporary Greece]. Athens, 2004.

Sfakianakis, Angelos. "Opisthodromiki Kompania." In Vassilis Vamvakas and Panayis Panagiotopoulos, eds., *I Ellada sti dekaetia tou '80* [Greece in the 1980s], pp. 398–400.

Silies, Eva-Maria. *Liebe, Lust und Last: Die Pille als weibliche Generationserfahrung in der Bundesrepublik 1960–1980*. Göttingen, 2010.

Sirinelli, Jean-François. "La France des *sixties* revisitée." *Vingtième Siècle: Revue d'histoire* 69 (2004): pp. 111–24.

Souliotis, Nicos. "Dievrynsi tou koinou, ekleptynsi ton diakriseon: koinoniki kataskeyi tis zitisis stin athinaiki symvoliki oikonomia apo ta mesa tis dekaetias tou '70 os simera" [Expansion of the public, refinement of distinction: The social construction of demand from the mid-1970s until today]. In *Koinonikoi kai chorikoi metaschimatismoi stin Athina tou 21ou aiona* [Social and geographical transformations in Athens of the twenty-first century], ed. Dimitris Emmanouil, Ersi Zakopoulou, Thomas Maloutas, Roxani Kaytantzoglou, and Andromachi Hadjiyanni, pp. 279–320. Athens, 2009.

Spiegel, M. Gabrielle, ed. *Practicing History: New Directions in Historical Writing After the Linguistic Turn*. New York, 2005.

Stacey, Jackie. *Star Gazing: Hollywood Cinema and Female Spectatorship*. London, 1994.

Staiger, Janet. "The Perversity of Spectators: Expanding the History of the Classical Hollywood Cinema." In *Moving Images, Culture and the Mind*, ed. Ib Bondebjerg, pp. 19–30. Luton, UK, 2000.

———. "Writing the History of American Film Reception." In *Hollywood Spectatorship: Changing Perceptions of Cinema Audiences*, ed. Melvyn Stokes and Richard Maltby, pp. 19–32. London, 2001.

Stanley, Jo. "Including the Feelings: Personal Political Testimony and Self-Disclosure." *Oral History* 24, no. 1 (1996): pp. 60–67.

Stassinopoulou, Maria A. "Creating Distraction after Destruction: Representations of the Military in the Greek Film." *Journal of Modern Greek Studies* 18, no. 1 (2000): pp. 37–52.

Stearns, Peter N. *Sexuality in World History*. Abingdon, UK, 2009.

Stearns Peter N., and Carol Z. Stearns. "Emotionology: Clarifying the History of Emotions and Emotional Standards." *The American Historical Review* 90, no. 4 (1985): pp. 813–36.

Stefanidis, Ioannis. *Stirring the Greek Nation: Political Culture, Irredentism and Anti-Americanism in Post-War Greece, 1945–1967*. Hampshire, UK, 2007.

Stefatos, Katherine. "*Engendering the Nation*: Women, State Oppression and Political Violence in Post-War Greece (1946–1974)." PhD diss., Goldsmiths College, University of London, 2012.

Stokes, Melvyn. "Introduction: Historical Hollywood Spectatorship." In *Hollywood Spectatorship: Changing Perceptions of Cinema Audiences*, ed. Melvyn Stokes and Richard Maltby, pp. 1–16. London, 2001.

Svolopoulos, Konstantinos. *I elliniki exoteriki politiki, 1945–1981* [The Greek foreign policy, 1945–1981]. Vol.2. Athens, 2001.

Szreter, Simon, and Kate Fisher. *Sex Before the Sexual Revolution: Intimate Life in England 1918–1963.* Cambridge, 2010.

Theodorou, Thanasis C. "Viografikes rixeis kai ithikos panikos: I koinotita ton hippies sta Matala, 1965–1975" [Biographical ruptures and moral panic: The hippy community in Matala, 1965–1975]. MA diss., University of Crete, Rethymno, 2007.

Thomadakis, Stavros B. "The Greek Economy and European Integration: Prospects for Development and Threats of Underdevelopment." In *Greece Prepares for the Twenty-First Century,* ed. Dimitri Constas and Theofanis G. Stavrou, pp. 101–23. Baltimore, MD, 1995.

Thompson, Edward P. *The Poverty of Theory and Other Essays.* 4th impression. London, 1981.

Thompson, Paul. *The Voice of the Past: Oral History.* Oxford, 1978.

Thompson, Paul, and Joanna Bornat. "Myths and Memories of an English Rising: 1968 at Essex." *Oral History* 22, no. 2 (1994): pp. 44–54.

Tosh, John. "Hegemonic Masculinity and the History of Gender." In *Masculinities in Politics and War: Gendering Modern History,* ed. Stefan Dudink, Karen Hagemann, and John Tosh, pp. 41–58. Manchester, 2002.

Tragaki, Dafni. *Rebetiko Worlds.* Newcastle, 2007.

Trentmann, Frank. "Beyond Consumerism: New Historical Perspectives on Consumption." *Journal of Contemporary History* 39, no. 3 (2004): pp. 373–401.

——— , ed., *The Making of the Consumer: Knowledge, Power and Identity in the Modern World.* Oxford, 2006.

Tsartas, Paris. *Koinonikes kai Oikonomikes Epiptoseis tis Touristikis Anaptyxis* [Social and economic consequences of tourist development]. Athens, 1989.

Tsoukalas, Konstantinos. *Kratos, koinonia, ergasia sti metapolemiki Ellada* [State, society and work in postwar Greece]. Athens, 1986.

Tsoulfidis, Levteris. *Oikonomiki Istoria tis Elladas* [Economic history of Greece]. Salonica, 2003.

Tziovas, Dimitris. *The Nationism of the Demoticists and its Impact on Their Literary Theory, 1888–1930.* Amsterdam, 1986.

Tunstall, Jeremy. *The Media are American.* London, 1977.

Vamvakas, Vassilis, and Panayis Panagiotopoulos, eds. *I Ellada sti dekaetia tou '80: Koinoniko, politiko kai politismiko lexiko* [Greece in the 1980s: Social, political, and cultural encyclopedia]. Athens, 2010.

van Boeschoten, Riki. *Anapoda chronia: Syllogiki Mnimi kai Istoria sto Ziaka Grevenon (1900–1950)* [Troubled years: Collective memory and history in Ziakas of Grevena]. Athens, 1997.

———. *From Armatolik to People's Rule: Investigation into the Collective Memory of Rural Greece, 1750–1949.* Amsterdam, 1991.

———. "I adynati epistrofi: Antimetopizontas to chorismo kai tin anasygkrotisi tis mnimis os synepeia tou Emfyliou" [The Impossible return: Coping with separation and the reconstruction of memory as an outcome of the Civil War]. In *Meta ton polemo: I anasygkrotisi tis oikogeneias, tou ethnous kai tou kratous stin Ellada, 1943–1960* [After

the war was over: Reconstructing the family, nation, and state in Greece, 1943–
1960], ed. Mark Mazower, pp. 139–59. Athens, 2000.

Vansina, Jan. *Oral Tradition as History.* Madison, WI, 1985.

van Steen, Gonda. "Joining our Grand Circus." *Journal of Modern Greek Studies* 25, no.
2 (2007): pp. 301–32.

Verbij, Antoine. *Tien rode jaren: Links radicalisme in Nederland, 1970–1980* [Ten red
years: Left radicalism in the Netherlands, 1970–1980]. Amsterdam, 2005.

Veremis, Thanos. *The Military in Greek Politics: From Independence to Democracy.* New
York, 1997.

Vernardakis, Christoforos, and Yiannis Mavris. *Kommata kai koinonikes symmachies stin
prodiktatoriki Ellada: Oi proypotheseis tis Metapolitefsis* [Parties and social alliances in
predictatorship Greece: The preconditions of the Metapolitefsi]. Athens, 1991.

Vernikos, Giorgos A. *Otan thelame na allaxoume tin Ellada: To antidiktatoriko foititiko
kinima; I EKIN kai oi katalipseis tis Nomikis* [When we wanted to change Greece:
The antidictatorship student movement: EKIN and the law school occupations].
Athens, 2003.

Vervenioti, Tasoula. "Left-Wing Women between Politics and Family." In Mazower, *After
the War Was Over*, pp. 105–21.

Vitti, Mario. *I Genia tou Trianta* [The Generation of the 1930s]. Athens, 2000.

Vlachoutsikou, Christina. "I katanalosi: metafora gia to monterno kai rogmi sti gynaike-
iaafaneia" [Consumption: Metaphor of modernity and rupture in women's oblivion].
Synchrona Themata 66, no. 1–3 (1998): pp. 87–103.

Voglis, Polymeris. *Becoming a Subject: Political Prisoners During the Greek Civil War,
1945–1950.* New York, 2002.

———. "'The Junta Came to Power by the Force of Arms, and Will Only Go by Force
of Arms': Political Violence and the Voice of the Opposition to the Military Dictatorship in Greece, 1967–74." *Cultural and Social History* 8, no. 4 (2011): pp. 551–
68.

von der Goltz, Anna. ed. *"Talkin' 'bout my generation": Conflicts of Generation Building
and Europe's "1968."* Göttingen, 2011.

Voulgaris, Giannis. *I Ellada apo ti Metapolitefsi stin Pagkosmiopoiisi* [Greece from the
Metapolitefsi to globalization]. Athens, 2008.

———. *I Ellada tis Metapolitefsis, 1974–1990: Statheri Dimokratia Simademeni apo
ti Metapolemiki Istoria* [Post-dictatorship Greece, 1974–1990: Stable democracy
marked by postwar history]. Athens, 2002.

Wagnleitner, Reinhold. *Coca-Colonization and the Cold War: The Cultural Mission of the
United States in Austria After the Second World War.* Chapel Hill, NC, 1994.

Wemheuer, Felix. "Einleitung. Die vielen Gesichter des Maoismus und die Neue Linke
nach 1968. In *Kulturrevolution als Vorbild? Maoismen im deutschsprachigen Raum,* ed.
Sebastian Gehrig, Barbara Mittler, and Felix Wemheuer, pp. 9–23. Frankfurt, 2008.

Werner, Michael, and Bénédicte Zimmermann. "Beyond Comparison: Histoire *Croisée*
and the Challenge of Reflexivity." *History and Theory* 45 (2006): pp. 30–50.

Wicke, Peter. "Music, Dissidence, Revolution, and Commerce: Youth Culture Between
Mainstream and Subculture." In Schildt and Siegfried, *Between Marx and Coca-Cola,*
pp. 109–26.

Williams, Raymond. "Culture is Ordinary." In *Conviction,* ed. Norman McKenzie, pp. 74–92. London, 1958.

Wittner, Lawrence S. *Toward Nuclear Abolition: A History of the World Nuclear Disarmament Movement, 1971 to the Present.* Stanford, CA, 2003.

Yannakopoulos, Kostas. *Jeux du désir, jeux du pouvoir: corps, émotions et identité sexuelle des hommes au Pirée et à Athènes.* PhD diss., Paris, École des Hautes Études en Sciences Sociales, 1995.

Yfantopoulos, Argyris. "I organotiki anaptyxi tou Riga Feraiou sta prota metadiktatorika chronia: I periptosi ton synoikiakon organoseon ths Athinas" [The expansion of RF in the first post-dictatorship years: The case of the districts in Athens]. In Karamanolakis, Olympitou, and Papathanasiou, *I elliniki neolaia* [Greek youth], pp. 94–99.

Yow, Valerie. "'Do I like them too much?' Effects of the Oral History Interview on the Interviewer and Vice-Versa." In *The Oral History Reader,* ed. Alistair Thomson and Robert Perks, pp. 54–72. New York, 2006.

Yurchak, Alexei. *Everything Was Forever, Until It Was No More: The Last Soviet Generation.* Princeton, NJ, 2006.

Zaimakis, Yiannis. "'Bawdy Songs and Virtuous Politics': Ambivalence and Controversy in the Discourse of the Greek Left on *Rebetiko.*" *History and Anthropology* 20, no. 1 (2009): pp. 15–36.

Zestanakis, Panagiotis. "Ekdoches tou andrismou sta ellinika lifestyle entypa tis dekaetias tou '80: Playboy, Status, Klik (1985–1990)" [Types of masculinity in the Greek lifestyle publications of the 1980s: Playboy, Status, Klik (1985–1990)]. MA diss., University of Crete, Rethymno, 2008.

Zinovieff, Sofka. "Hunters and Hunted: *Kamaki* and the Ambiguities of Sexual Predation in a Greek Town." In Loizos and Papataxiarchis, *Contested Identities,* pp. 203–20.

Zubak, Marko. "The Yugoslav Youth Press (1968-1980): Student Movements, Subcultures and Communist Alternative Media." PhD diss., Central European University, Budapest, 2013.

Index

www.ingramcontent.com/pod-product-compliance
Lightning Source LLC
Chambersburg PA
CBHW070907030426
42336CB00014BA/2318